New Labour, Old Labour

The Wilson and Callaghan
Governments, 1974–79

**Edited by Anthony Seldon
and Kevin Hickson**

Routledge
Taylor & Francis Group

LONDON AND NEW YORK

First published 2004
by Routledge
11 New Fetter Lane, London EC4P 4EE

Simultaneously published in the USA and Canada
by Routledge
29 West 35th Street, New York, NY 10001

Routledge is an imprint of the Taylor & Francis Group

© 2004 Anthony Seldon and Kevin Hickson selection and editorial matter;
individual chapters the contributors

Typeset in Baskerville by
Taylor & Francis Books Ltd

Printed and bound in Great Britain by
MPG Books Ltd, Bodmin

British Library Cataloguing in Publication Data
A catalogue record for this book is available from the British Library

Library of Congress Cataloging in Publication Data
New Labour, old Labour : the Wilson and Callaghan governments,
1974–9 /
edited by Anthony Seldon and Kevin Hickson.
    p. cm.
Includes bibliographical references and index.
  1. Great Britain–Politics and government 1964–1979. 2. Labour Party
(Great Britain) –History–20th century. 3. Wilson, Harold, Sir, 1916
4. Callaghan, James, 1912– I. Seldon, Anthony. II. Hickson, Kevin, 1974–
  DA589.7.N486 2004
  941.085'7–dc22
                                                          2003020388

ISBN 0–415–31281–7 (hbk)
ISBN 0–415–31282–5 (pbk)

Contents

Contributors

Chris Ballinger is completing his doctorate on House of Lords' reform in the twentieth century and lectures at the University of Oxford. He has published several articles and chapters and is associate author on the biography of Tony Blair (author, Anthony Seldon).

Vernon Bogdanor is Professor of Government and Fellow of Brasenose College, University of Oxford. He has written widely on British politics. His recent publications include *Devolution in the United Kingdom* (2001, 3rd edition) and (as editor) *The British Constitution in the Twentieth Century* (2003).

Steven Fielding is Professor of Contemporary Political History at the University of Salford. He is author of *The Labour Party: Continuity and Change in the Making of 'New' Labour* (2003) and *The Labour Governments 1964–70* Vol. 1 *Labour and Cultural Change* (2003).

Ed Gouge is a teaching fellow at the University of Leeds and has written several articles on local government. His other research interests are in regional and EU politics. He is author of the Department of the Environment Research Report 'The Use of Planning Agreements'.

Kevin Hickson obtained his PhD on the 1976 IMF Crisis from the University of Southampton in 2002. He teaches at Liverpool and Manchester Universities. He is joint-editor of *The Struggle for Labour's Soul*, a study of the political thought of the Labour Party, with Raymond Plant (2004).

Dilys M. Hill is Emeritus Professor of Politics at the University of Southampton. She has published widely on British and US politics and is recognised as a major authority on urban politics and regeneration issues and constitutional affairs.

Stuart Holland is Professor of Economics at the University of Coimbra, Portugal, and was MP for Vauxhall 1979–89. His books include *The Socialist Challenge* (1975) and *The European Imperative: Economic and Social Cohesion in the 1990s* (1993), which was the basis of Jacques Delors' 1993 White Paper on Growth, Competitiveness and Employment.

Dennis Kavanagh is Professor of Politics at the University of Liverpool and was previously based at Nottingham University. He is a leading authority on British politics. He has published widely, and is the joint author of recent Nuffield general election studies with David Butler.

Ann Lane is Lecturer in War Studies at King's College London. She is author of several books and articles on British foreign policy since 1945. She is author of *Britain, the Cold War and Yugoslav Unity: 1941–1949* (1996).

Roy Lowe OBE is Professor of Education and Head of Department at the University of Swansea. He is a leading authority on the education policies of post-war British Governments. His publications include *Education in the Post-war Years* (1988) and *Schooling and Social Change, 1964–1990* (1997).

Kenneth O. (Lord) Morgan FBA was Vice-Chancellor of the University of Wales, Aberystwyth, and is Honorary Fellow at Queen's and Oriel Colleges, Oxford. He wrote the official biography of Lord Callaghan, *Callaghan: A Life* (1997) and has written several major studies of Labour Party and twentieth-century British history. He is writing the official biography of Michael Foot.

Philip (Lord) Norton is Professor of Politics at the University of Hull and is a Conservative peer. He is a distinguished authority on constitutional issues, especially Parliament. His works include *Dissension in the House of Commons 1974–1979* (1980).

Brendan O'Leary is Lauder Professor of Political Science and Director of the Solomon Asch Center for the Study of Ethnopolitical Conflict at the University of Pennsylvania and was based for many years at the LSE. His works include *The Politics of Antagonism: Understanding the Politics of Northern Ireland* (1996, 2nd edition, with J. McGarry).

Raymond (Lord) Plant is a Labour peer and Professor of Jurisprudence at King's College London, and has been Master of St Catherine's College, Oxford. He was Chairman of the Labour Party Commission on Electoral Reform ('the Plant report') and of the Fabian Commission on Taxation and Citizenship.

Peter Riddell is a political columnist and commentator of *The Times* and Visiting Professor of Political History at Queen Mary College, University of London. He is author of several books on recent British politics including *Parliament under Blair* (2000) and *Hug Them Close* (2003), a study of Blair's recent relationship with the United States.

Anthony Seldon is Headmaster of Brighton College and was co-founder of the Institute of Contemporary British History. He wrote the biographies of John Major (1997) and Tony Blair (2004) and has edited several books on post-war British politics.

Eric Shaw is Senior Lecturer in Politics at Stirling University. He has written widely on Labour Party history and politics. His books include *Discipline and Discord in the Labour Party* (1988), *The Labour Party since 1979: Crisis and Transformation* (1994) and *The Labour Party since 1945* (1996).

Robert (Lord) Skidelsky is Professor of Political Economy at Warwick University and Chair of the Centre for Global Studies. He sits on the cross-benches in the House of Lords. He is the author of many works on British political economy and history including the major biography of Keynes (three volumes, single volume abridgement published November 2003).

Robert Taylor is Research Associate in the Centre for Economic Performance at the LSE. He has published books including *The Fifth Estate: Britain's Unions in the Modern World* (1978 and 1980), *The Trade Union Question in British Politics: Government and the Unions since 1945* (1993) and *The TUC: From the General Strike to New Unionism* (2000). He is writing a centennial history of the Parliamentary Labour Party to be published in 2006.

Kevin Theakston is Professor of British Government at the University of Leeds. He has written widely on the civil service. He is author of *The Labour Party and Whitehall* (1992) and *Leadership in Whitehall* (1999).

Jim Tomlinson is Professor of Economic History at Brunel University. His major works include *Modernising Britain? The Economic Policies of the Labour Governments 1964–70* (2003) and *Democratic Socialism and Economic Policy: The Attlee Years 1945–51* (1997).

Polly Toynbee writes for the *Guardian*. She is co-author of *Did Things Get Better? An Audit of Labour's Successes and Failures* (2001) with David Walker on New Labour and has recently written an account of her experiences living on the minimum wage, *Hard Work: Life in Low-Pay Britain* (2003).

David Walker writes for the *Guardian* and is co-author of *Did Things Get Better? An Audit of Labour's Successes and Failures* (2001) with Polly Toynbee. He is author of several book chapters and pamphlets.

John W. Young is Professor of International History at the University of Nottingham. He was previously Professor of Contemporary History at Salford (1991–3) and Professor of Politics at Leicester (1993–2000). He is author of several works including *Britain and European Unity, 1945–99* (2000).

Acknowledgements

In a book such as this it is difficult to thank everyone who has been involved in its preparation and who has given advice and made useful suggestions along the way.

We owe special thanks, however, to the following. First and foremost we would like to thank the contributors themselves for the speedy delivery of their chapters and for the high quality of their work.

Secondly, we would like to thank David Butler and the Warden and Fellows of Nuffield College, Oxford for making possible an enjoyable, lively and informative conference in December 2002, and to those who attended this event and contributed to the discussions. At the incomparable Institute of Contemporary British History I would like to thank Harriet Jones, Virginia Preston and Michael Kandiah.

The book itself was wholly the idea of Kevin Hickson. Two years ago, he came to me with the suggestion of a joint book. He has been indefatigable since, both intellectually and organisationally. I wish to record mine and the contributors' gratitude and appreciation to him.

Anthony Seldon
August 2003

A brief chronology

1974

February
7   Heath calls general election. At the election Labour have five more seats than the Conservatives

March
4   Heath resigns after failing to obtain the support of the Liberals
6   Miners' strike ends with 29 per cent pay settlement
7   End of three-day week
26   Healey gives first budget

May
        Northern Ireland Assembly collapses
20   Benn announces industrial strategy to the TUC–Labour Party Liaison Committee

June
        Consultative papers for Welsh and Scottish devolution published
26   TUC accepts the social contract

July
        Plans for Northern Ireland Constitutional Convention published
22   Healey announces increases in public expenditure which adds £340 million to PSBR
25–26   Benn grants money to set up worker co-operatives
31   1971 Industrial Relations Act repealed

August
15   Benn launches White Paper 'The Regeneration of British Industry'

September

18   Wilson calls general election

October

10   General election – Labour wins with majority of three

17   Jack Jones calls for wage restraint

November

12   Budget adds £800 million to PSBR

19   Queen's Speech announces plans to phase out pay beds in NHS hospitals and a land tax

1975

January

22   EEC referendum announced

31   Government publishes Industry Bill

February

19   29 per cent average annual wage increase

March

18   Government recommends vote to stay in EEC after Cabinet votes in favour of continued membership

27   Government publishes report on EEC renegotiations

April

15   First programme of cuts agreed

26   Labour Party special conference calls for withdrawal from EEC

May

9   Crosland makes 'party is over' speech warning local councils of excessive spending

June

5   EEC referendum votes by large majority to stay in

10   Wilson shuffles Cabinet and moves Benn to Energy in what is seen as a demotion and setback for the left

13   Inflation rises to 36.3 per cent

July

1   Cash limits introduced on public spending for the first time

9–11   Government and TUC accept pay restraint

24   Unemployment rises above 1 million

August
1   £6 pay policy introduced
5   Industrial democracy inquiry begins

November
7   First IMF loan applied for

1976

February
12   £220 million package of measures to reduce unemployment announced
19   £1 billion cuts in public expenditure announced

March
        Direct rule in Northern Ireland begins
5   Sterling falls after Bank of England sells sterling
10   Government loses vote on public expenditure cuts after left-wing rebellion
11   Government wins confidence motion
16   Wilson resigns

April
5   Callaghan elected Prime Minister
6   Extension of cash limits to cover most areas of public spending
        Inflation halved in nine months

May
5   Second year of pay restraint agreed
7   Six-month international credit facility agreed

July
22   £1 billion cuts announced following further pressure on the pound.

September
7   Labour NEC calls for further public ownership
28   Callaghan makes conference speech appearing to undermine Keynesian framework of economic policy
29   Healey announces application to the IMF

October
7   Minimum lending rate raised to 15 per cent
18   Callaghan delivers key speech on education reform at Ruskin College

November

2	IMF delegation arrives
4	Labour loses two by-elections and is now in a minority
16	Lever visits United States to try to moderate IMF demands
23	Cabinet starts debate over IMF loan and spending cuts
29	Government withdraws commitment to wealth tax

December

2	Cabinet agrees to cuts and IMF loan
15	Healey reads Letter of Intent to Parliament
21	Twenty-seven MPs vote against public expenditure cuts

1977

January

3	IMF grants $3.9 billion
26	Bullock report on industrial democracy published
28	Callaghan promises legislation on industrial democracy by summer based on Bullock, but backs down on 15 February after pressure from CBI

February

22	First devolution bills defeated, only passed in late 1978

March

	Nationalisation of aircraft and shipbuilding
23	Lib–Lab Pact begins

April–May

	Year 3 wages policy made more flexible after TUC protests

September

16	RPI = 16.5 per cent
20	Unemployment reaches 1.39 million

October

26	Budget, increasing PSBR

November

14	Firefighters' strike. Not supported by the TUC executive on 21 December

1978

January

1	Callaghan states aim of achieving a 5 per cent wages norm
12	End of firefighters' strike
26	Government repays £1 billion to IMF early

February

17	Inflation down to 9.9 per cent

March

15	£300 million unemployment measures introduced
29	Jack Jones retires

April

11	Reflationary budget

May

23	Government announces plans for industrial democracy

June

8	Deflationary budget

July

21	5 per cent pay policy declared

August

24	Ford workers offered pay increase in excess of 5 per cent norm

September

7	Callaghan rules out autumn election

October

	Government repays a further £1 billion to IMF

November

22	Ford workers accept 16.5 per cent after nine-week strike

December

5	Government refuses to join European Monetary System
12	NHS and local government workers vote for strike action

1979

January
3   Lorry-drivers' strike
10   Callaghan makes statement denying there is a crisis in industrial relations
22   Hospital workers' strike

March
1   Devolution referendums held. Defeated outright in Wales and fails to secure sufficient majority vote in Scotland
28   Government loses confidence vote by 311 to 310 votes

April
6   Parliament is dissolved

May
3   General election, Conservatives win with overall majority of forty-three

Introduction

Anthony Seldon and Kevin Hickson

New Labour, Old Labour is published on the 30th anniversary of the Labour Governments of 1974–79 coming to power. Why publish this book? Why now? Why in this form?

This Government has been among the most criticised in the twentieth century. Thatcherite Conservatives as well as the Labour left and New Labour all have had their reasons for denigrating its reputation. For Thatcherite Conservatives it was an important part of their statecraft to undermine the record of the outgoing Government in order to argue that there was no alternative to their radical prescription. For the resurgent Labour left, who initially found a champion in Michael Foot between 1980–83, it was important to show that the right of the Party had failed in government in order to promote its own alternative programme. The Government was regarded as a period of timid leadership and capitulation to the forces of capitalism at home and abroad. New Labour, meanwhile, has also attacked the record of the 1974–79 Government in particular in order to show how it is different from 'Old' Labour. To them, the Government showed finally the folly of trying to rule Labour by balancing the right and left/union interests. Rather, one had to jettison the hard left union bosses, and rebrand as a 'new' party. Of all postwar governments, that of 1974–79 has been the most misrepresented and denigrated.

This Government has been attacked for mishandling of the economy, symbolised by the 1976 IMF Crisis, for its failure to manage relations with the trades unions, culminating in the 'Winter of Discontent', and for its failure to implement major changes in social policy and the constitution. The Government has been further criticised for failing in major areas of foreign policy and for squandering the opportunities that membership of the EEC in 1973 would arguably have brought by reverting back to a more sceptical position. The personal leadership of Wilson has been criticised for being erratic, directionless and indeed being tawdry and that of Callaghan for failing to manage a divided Cabinet and parliamentary party and ultimately for losing the General Election in 1979. Academic and journalistic commentary naturally focused on what was seen as a radical break in British politics with the election of the first Thatcher Government in 1979 with the result that there has been comparatively little serious attempt to reappraise the record of Labour in power from 1974 to 1979.

But are these criticisms justified? Did the Governments achieve so little? The book has been produced to allow us to view the work of the Government afresh, and not through the prism of its critics or of those who have written memoirs and biographies, who have tended to see it through rose-tinted spectacles.

Why publish now, on the eve of the documents becoming available to researchers at the Public Record Office in Kew? Will the documents not render the book rapidly redundant? Publication on the eve of the 30-year rule in fact has its own value, because the book can take account of thirty years of writing, debate and interviewing of participants, and help collate the latest thinking and research for when the documents do become available. Earlier books on the Churchill Government of 1951–55 and the Heath Government of 1970–74 were similarly published, in 1981 and 1996 respectively, shortly before the documents were released. Even when the vast swathes of state documents are released in the Public Record Office from 2005–2010, it is unlikely that they will substantially revise the facts and judgements contained in this volume. As Vernon Bogdanor has written, 'recent releases of papers under the thirty-year rule have done little to change the picture of the Wilson (1964–70) and Heath (1970–74) Governments ... In a democracy, the release of government documents serves generally to confirm rather than overturn what is already known.'[1]

We have decided to publish in this form because an edited collection, in contrast to a single-author volume, allows for a variety of viewpoints, discipline and approaches, as well as the clear benefit of having those writing on specific subjects who are very authorities on those subjects. The questions they address include:

- Did the Government of 1974–79 mark more the end of the 'Old' Labour Party, or was it the harbinger of 'New Labour' which came to office in 1997? Was it a staging post on the road to New Labour from Gaitskell and Crosland to Kinnock and then Blair? Or was it the last gasp of 'Old' Labour?
- Did first Wilson, then Callaghan, 'make a difference' to the direction of governmental policy to that offered by the Heath Government, and if so, why, and in what areas?
- What might this Labour Government have done if it had not been hamstrung by such serious disadvantages, economic, political and social? Should we judge governments which come to power in unfortunate circumstances by the same exacting yardsticks as those which come to power with unprecedented advantages, such as the Blair Government in 1997?
- What were the new ideas and new thinking that came to the fore in 1974–79, and how far did they result in change?

The aim of the book, in short, is not only to bring into clear focus the actions of the Labour Government in 1974–79, but also to provide a perspective on the work of the Blair Government. One should never judge governments in isolation from the period in which they existed. The book reaches no emphatic conclusion, and we do not seek as editors to mould our audience into just one reading. Rather, the different perspectives in the subject chapters and in the six concluding chapters challenge received wisdom and allow the reader to form their own conclusions.

Notes

1. Seldon, A., *Churchill's Indian Summer: The Conservative Government 1951–55* (Hodder and Stoughton, London, 1981); Ball, S. and Seldon, A., (eds) *The Heath Government 1970–74: A Reappraisal* (Longman, London, 1996).
2. *The Times*, 25 August 2003.

Part I

The framework of ideas

1   1974

The crisis of Old Labour

Vernon Bogdanor

I

Socialist hopes in twentieth-century Britain have flourished best in opposition. In office, by contrast, the contradictions both in Labour's ideology and indeed in the very structure of the Labour movement have often become painfully apparent. So it had been with the first Wilson Government of 1964–70. For that Government's most powerful defeats had been inflicted not by its political enemies but by its trade union allies, who had rejected both a statutory incomes policy and the curbs on their legal immunities proposed in the White Paper, 'In Place of Strife'.

Labour found a convenient excuse for the shortcomings of the first Wilson Government by diagnosing the cause of its defeat as the breach between the political and industrial wings of the movement. This meant that there was no need critically to examine the record of the 1964–70 Government. The legend soon became established that all had been well before the squabbles between government and unions. This suited the outlook of Labour's leaders, Wilson and Callaghan, whose views on socialism and how it was to be achieved had always been vague and undefined. Indeed, by 1974, Wilson had little to offer beyond the hope of a quiet life. He sought to become the Stanley Baldwin of the 1970s.

The left, however, which had been growing in strength in constituency parties, as after previous defeats in 1931 and 1951, wanted more than a quiet life. After 1931 and 1951, and also after 1979, the Party went through an internal civil war before it could become electable again. That this did not happen after 1970 was largely due to Wilson and Callaghan who pre-empted the left through the skilful use of ambiguous formulae, a method which was to store up trouble in the future when the ambiguities came to be exposed.

For the struggle between left and right was coming, after 1970, to change its character. Labour was beginning to appear an incompatible coalition between reformists and socialists, the latter buttressed by extra-parliamentary activists, whose commitment to democracy was not always apparent. These extra-parliamentary activists were assisted by the abolition of the proscribed list in 1973, which had excluded those with non-democratic affiliations from member-ship of the Party. Abolition meant that members of the non-democratic left were now to be found within, rather than outside, the Labour Party. In 1973, the Campaign for Labour Party Democracy was formed, to press for greater powers for the Party outside Parliament in the selection of candidates, the writing of the party manifesto and the selection of the party leader. This would shift the battle-ground away from the parliamentary party where, the right had a majority, to the extra-parliamentary party where the chances of the left were much greater. The extra-parliamentary left found a leader in Tony Benn, who, until 1970, had called himself Anthony Wedgwood Benn, but now chose to democratise his name. The Bennite left mounted a determined assault on the Labour leadership after 1970, proposing widespread nationalisation through a new National Enterprise Board, compulsory planning agreements and withdrawal from the European Community, which Britain entered in 1973. To repel this assault, Wilson and Callaghan needed the support of the trade union leaders, and this constituted a further reason to discover formulae which could repair the breach between the parliamentary and industrial wings of the movement.

It was Callaghan who found the formula of 'renegotiation' to accommodate left and right over the European Community; and Callaghan who played a major part in formulating the 'Social Contract'. Both of these formulae were ambiguous. For it was never clear whether renegotiation meant revision of the Treaty of Rome, or renegotiation within the framework of that Treaty. The left took one view, the right another. Nor was it clear whether the Social Contract entailed a voluntary incomes policy, or whether it was compatible with the reten-tion of free collective bargaining. This ambiguity was a positive advantage in uniting a divided party which, by 1974, could be held together only through the tactical skill of a Wilson or Callaghan.

The Labour movement had always been a strange and at times uneasy alliance between the parliamentary and the industrial wings, united by history, sentimental ties and also, seemingly, by common values. Both claimed to stand for socialism, a society in which community values would prevail against private interests. The politicians would seek to achieve this through parliamentary action, the trade unions through using their collective industrial muscle. Each side would respect the interests of the other. 'I told you last year not to tell the unions how to do their job,' declared Frank Cousins, General Secretary of the Transport and General Workers' Union, to the Party Conference in 1956, 'and I am certainly not going to tell the Labour Party how to do its job.'[1]

This demarcation agreement, however, was gradually breaking down. By the late 1950s, strikes, poor industrial relations and malpractices in the unions were affecting support for the Labour Party, while the need to contain inflation in a society committed to full employment meant that a Labour Government would have to intervene in the processes of free collective bargaining. Besides, was it not an anomaly that a socialist government could plan everything except wages? That was the question which the Social Contract sought to evade.

The term 'Social Contract' was first used in a Labour Party context by Tony Benn in his Fabian pamphlet, 'The New Politics: A Socialist Reconnaissance', published in September 1970. Then, at Labour's 1972 Conference, Callaghan declared that 'what Britain needs is a new Social Contract'. The contract would restore relations to what they had been in a bygone era of partnership and co-operation, 1964, or perhaps even 1945. It was, moreover, so James Callaghan told the TUC Conference in 1974, a 'means of achieving nothing less than the social and economic reconstruction' of the country.[2]

The contract was inaugurated when, in April 1971, Callaghan, as Chairman of the NEC's Home Policy Committee, gave the unions an unconditional guarantee that the next Labour Government would repeal Edward Heath's hated Industrial Relations Act, even though its provisions differed only in degree from 'In Place of Strife', which Callaghan had, from within the Cabinet, opposed. The unions responded by calling for a dialogue. In September 1971, Jack Jones, General Secretary of the Transport and General Workers' Union, and the dominant figure in the TUC, told Labour's annual conference:

> there is no reason at all why a joint policy cannot be worked out. But let us have the closest possible liaison. Let us put an end to the stress and strain between the trade unions and intellectual wings of the Party [an odd way to speak of the parliamentary party or the National Executive]. In the past we have not had the dialogue necessary.[3]

A Labour–TUC Liaison Committee was established early in 1972. It agreed to allow the TUC to write the legislation which would replace the Industrial Relations Act. The parliamentary leaders promised that the next Labour Government would introduce price controls, food and housing subsidies, increase expenditure on pensions and social services, and engineer 'large-scale' redistribution of income and wealth. The unions offered little in return for these goodies. Perhaps they had little to offer. For, according to Barbara Castle:

> So bruised and sensitive were the trade unions that any mention even of a voluntary policy was taboo. When at one of the Liaison Committee meetings someone dared to refer to the role of incomes in the management of the economy, Jack Jones jumped in at once to say, 'it would be disastrous if any word went from this meeting that we had been discussing prices and incomes policy'.[4]

Labour, however, needed a credible policy against inflation. Therefore, when, in January 1973, Wilson and TUC General Secretary Vic Feather presented the policy document, 'Economic Policy and the Cost of Living', in which the details of the contract were outlined, they agreed that an incoming Labour Government's 'first task' would be to secure a 'wide-ranging agreement' with the TUC 'on the policies to be pursued in all these aspects of our economic life and to discuss with them the order of priorities for their fulfilment'. This would, so it was suggested, 'further engender the strong feeling of mutual confidence which alone will make it possible to reach the wide-ranging agreement which is necessary to control inflation and achieve sustained growth in the standard of living'.[5]

'This', Harold Wilson declares in the memoirs of his second administration, *Final Term*, 'was widely interpreted as a voluntary agreement to accept restraint in pay demands as part of a wider social agreement.'[6] It is unclear whether the unions shared this interpretation.

By January 1974, with a general election looming, the leadership felt that it needed a more concrete commitment. It was now in the position of a supplicant. 'If the Labour government fulfilled its side of the social compact,' Shadow Chancellor Denis Healey asked the union leaders on the Liaison Committee, then, without pressing for a pay norm or 'rigid commitments', surely, 'the TUC for its part would try to make the economic policy work'. Len Murray, the new TUC General Secretary, poured cold water on even this severely limited aspiration. The greatest disservice the TUC could perform would be 'to pretend it could do more than it could and the disillusion from that would be far more damaging than the refusal to make impossible promises in the first place'. Undeterred, Wilson intervened to suggest that what was needed was 'more the creation of a mood than a compact'. Murray 'nodded vigorously'.[7]

II

Armed with little more than this fig-leaf, Wilson formed his second administration, following the February 1974 general election, an election which most of Labour's leaders did not expect to win. Indeed, Roy Jenkins, leader of the social democratic wing of the Party, not only believed that Labour would lose. He also believed that Labour *deserved* to lose, declaring in his memoirs that

> 1974, according to my strategy, was the year in which temporising Labour Party leadership was due to receive its just reward in the shape of a lost general election.[8]

The Government which unexpectedly won office in 1974 was called upon to combat the most serious economic challenges that Britain had faced since the war, with international monetary disturbance following the breakdown of the Bretton Woods system, the turning of the terms of trade against Britain, and the first oil crisis which, in 1973, had led to a quadrupling of the oil price and world-wide inflation. These challenges were, in Edmund Dell's view, 'preparing the final crisis of British democratic socialism'.[9] Yet, because the Party was so divided, and because of the sensitivities of the trade union leaders, there had been little genuine thinking on how the challenges were to be met. 'If Denis Healey had worked out a plan for a Parliament,' declared Joel Barnett, Chief Secretary of the Treasury, in his memoirs, 'I am bound to say he kept it secret from me. ... The real worry was that we had worked out no short-, medium- or long-term economic and financial policies.'[10]

The crisis was compounded by the lack of a parliamentary majority. In the 1920s, following the first Labour Government, Ernest Bevin had urged Labour never again to take office as a minority on the grounds that it would be in office but not in power, unable to take strong measures yet held responsible for what went wrong.[11] Bevin's advice, however, was rejected by the Labour Party Conference in 1925, and, in the circumstances of 1974, it would almost certainly have been impracticable. For it would have meant an immediate second general election, in the middle of a miners' strike which had to be quickly settled. Moreover, when Labour did come to fight a second general election, seven months later, in October 1974, it won an overall majority of just three. There is no reason to believe that a second general election held in March 1974 would have yielded any more favourable outcome.

A possible alternative might have been to secure an agreement with the Liberals, although this would not have yielded a parliamentary majority. But at the 1973 Labour Party Conference, Harold Wilson had given a pledge against co-operation with other parties in terms which it would have been difficult even for him to evade:

> Let this be clear: as long as I am Leader of the Party, Labour will not enter into any coalition with any other Party, Liberal or Conservative or anyone else. [*Prolonged Applause*]
>
> As long as I am Leader of this Party there will be no electoral treaty, no political alliance, no understanding, no deal, no arrangement, no fix, neither will there be any secret deal or secret discussions.[12]

In 1974, as in 1924, 1929, 1950 and 1964, therefore, there would be no question of seeking an agreement with the Liberals. As in 1924 and 1929, Labour took office as a minority government.

A minority government based on just 37 per cent of the vote, however, would hardly enjoy the democratic authority to deal with the crisis which confronted it. The inevitable outcome was that difficult discussions on economic policy were postponed until after the second general election, due in a few months' time. Bernard Donoughue, Head of the Downing Street Policy Unit, could not 'recall a single sustained discussion in Cabinet or Cabinet Committee of central economic policy – of fiscal or monetary management, or any direct measures to curb public expenditure growth or wage inflation – until December 1974'.[13] Instead, the Government sought to meet the crisis by borrowing to pay for the social benefits to which Labour had committed itself under the Social Contract, a policy characterised by Joel Barnett as 'spending money we did not have'.[14] The Social Contract, therefore, had to be implemented, in desperately unfavourable circumstances, by a minority government and a divided Party which

> due to its divisions, and to different interpretations within it of the experience of the 1960s ... was also unprepared. There is no comparable example of such intellectual and political incoherence in a party coming into office in the twentieth century history of the United Kingdom.[15]

III

'To my mind the only give and take in the contract,' so Joel Barnett declared in his memoirs, *Inside the Treasury*, 'was that the government gave and the unions took.'[16] That is an exaggeration, though perhaps a pardonable one. After the abolition of statutory wage controls in 1974, the TUC urged restraint in wage negotiations and did its best to minimise industrial disruption. From 1975 to 1978, the trade unions agreed to co-operate in a voluntary incomes policy, and this greatly assisted the process of economic recovery. But the price needed to secure this co-operation was high. It included acceptance by the Government of policies, such as food and housing subsidies and an increase in public expenditure, which were hardly likely to assist with economic recovery. Moreover, increases in social expenditure, or what Barbara Castle called 'the social wage', were not regarded by trade unionists as substitutes for increases in money wages. For, in the post-war welfare state, regular improvements in the social services had come to be taken for granted.

The trade union leaders co-operated perhaps as much as they could. Yet their much-vaunted power and influence was primarily negative. They could certainly prevent policies which they disliked from being carried out, not only in the field of industrial relations and incomes policy, but also in the public services. An earlier generation of trade union leaders, the most prominent of whom was Ernest Bevin, had hoped that the unions could also play a more constructive role vis-à-vis government. But this was to misconceive the function of trade unions, which were

> reactive, bargaining organisations, ill-prepared for writing the agenda for government. ... In attempting to placate, for tactical economic reasons, a largely unprepared trade union movement, the government did that movement lasting damage.[17]

Thus, as Joe Gormley, the miners' leader, complained, the Social Contract

> put us in a false position. Our role in society is to look after our members, not run the country. What's more, I think the TUC overstepped its powers in trying to interfere with the authority of the individual unions. In point of fact, the TUC doesn't *have* any powers – it's a federation, and all its members are autonomous.[18]

Jack Jones and Hugh Scanlon, President of the Amalgamated Union of Engineering Workers, did provide genuine leadership for a limited period, partly in reaction to the panic induced by the economic crises of the years 1974–6. But both retired in 1978, just before the 'Winter of Discontent', and their successors did not enjoy equivalent authority either within the movement or over their members. Moreover, industrial bargaining was becoming more fragmented and decentralised, and the shop stewards movement was growing in importance.

Indeed, Harold Wilson had presciently told the House of Commons in December 1970 that 'the growth of shop floor power ... is the central fact of the 1970s'.[19] This development was welcomed and encouraged by Jack Jones, a strong proponent of industrial democracy. 'If the trade unions speak of participation for others,' Jones said, 'then they must be prepared to practise it for themselves. ... We must welcome and provide for local initiative, and recognise the value of the shop steward at grass roots level.'[20] But the consequence, inevitably, was to make it more difficult for union leaders to exercise authority and to deliver the agreements which they had made with the Government.

IV

Labour took the electoral verdict of February 1974 as an endorsement of the Social Contract. Yet the Party had tragically misdiagnosed the social trends which had been responsible for its defeat in 1970, and which were causing a continuing drift away from Labour. For the collapse of incomes policy in the late 1960s had been due less to a new generation of militant trade union leaders than to the inability of the union leaders to control their members. This was itself a result of the collapse of deference and growing scepticism towards authority. The social revolution of the 1960s had been a revolution of individual aspirations. Far from strengthening the collective solidarity on which the Labour Party was based, it was coming seriously to undermine it. The anarchic industrial relations of the 1970s were the consequence of an upsurge, not of collectivism, but of individualism. Labour's programme had presupposed a society in which, as in 1945, the leaders, both in the Government and the trade unions, led and the followers followed. The Party had no answer to a condition in which the leaders still sought to lead, but the followers were no longer willing to follow.

The Labour movement saw the general election of February 1974 as a reversal of the verdict of the General Strike. In 1926, a Tory Government had defeated the miners. In 1974, by contrast, the miners had defeated a Tory Government and installed in its place their own Government. Moreover, Labour had won the election on what seemed a left-wing manifesto, *Let Us Work Together: Labour's Way Out of the Crisis*, described by the authors of the standard work on the February 1974 general election as 'a decidedly radical document'.[21] The manifesto proposed a substantial extension of public ownership, including the nationalisation of mineral rights, shipbuilding, ship repairing, ports and aero engines, with public holding companies for pharmaceuticals, road haulage, construction, machine tools, and North Sea oil and gas. 'We are all Clause IV men now', left-winger Ian Mikardo had told Labour's Party Conference in 1972.[22] The manifesto in addition proposed 'a fundamental and irreversible shift in the balance of *power* and *wealth* in favour of working people and their families', while retaining 'free collective bargaining'. The outcome of the election proved, to many Labour supporters, that a left-wing programme, far from handicapping the Party, could actually assist it to return to office. Indeed, in January 1974, Tony Benn had predicted that if the Labour Party wins the Election on the slogan 'Back to Work with Labour' ... then the balance of power in the Labour Party is absolutely firmly on the Left; because one of the great arguments of the Right is that you can't win an Election with a left-wing programme. If you have a left-wing programme and you win an Election, then the Right will have lost that argument, and that will be a historic moment in the history of the British Labour movement.[23]

The hypothesis that one could win an election on a left-wing programme was to be tested again in 1983, under the leadership of Michael Foot, when it was, as it were, tested almost to destruction.

For what Benn and the left overlooked was that Labour had 'won' the February 1974 general election only in the sense that it had gained more seats (though not more votes) than any other party. It had, however, lost around 6 per cent of its vote since its defeat in 1970, and this was the largest loss of support by a major opposition party since the war. Indeed, Labour's 37 per cent of the vote in February 1974 was its lowest at any general election since 1931 when the Party had been nearly wiped out by the landslide victory of Ramsay MacDonald's National Government. Labour's vote, at around eleven and a half million, was lower than at any general election since 1935, despite the increase in the size of the electorate and lowering of the franchise to eighteen in 1969. Thus the outcome of the February 1974 general election was far from being an endorsement of the Social Contract, or the manifesto, and the vagaries of the electoral system served to mask Labour's declining electoral support. The election marked a low point in the Party's electoral fortunes, rather than an upsurge of support. The general election of February 1974 thus showed the weakness of socialism in Britain, not its strength, a weakness resulting from social changes to which the Party had failed to adapt. Perhaps it was not capable of adapting to them.

Nor were there any grounds for thinking that Labour's close links with the trade unions enjoyed public endorsement. In September 1972, Gallup had first asked whether 'trade unions are becoming too powerful, are not powerful enough or are about right'. It continued to ask this question at regular intervals throughout the 1970s. The responses were as given in Table 1.1.

Table 1.1 Gallup poll results on Trade Union power from 1972–75

	Too powerful	*Not powerful enough*	*About right*	*Don't know*
September 1972	52%	13%	26%	9%
September 1974	63%	8%	21%	8%
September 1975	73%	4%	17%	6%

In October 1972, Gallup asked whether the trade unions, the leader, the National Executive Committee, ordinary Labour MPs or Labour voters 'has the most say in the policies of the Labour Party'. Most – 43 per cent – replied 'the trade unions', with only 23 per cent answering 'the leader'. However, just 4 per cent of respondents thought that the trade unions 'should have the most say in the policies of the Labour Party'. By September 1975, 60 per cent believed that the trade unions had the most influence, as compared with just 15 per cent who thought the leader of the Party had the most influence.[24] By contrast then with 1945 and 1966, Labour took office at a time when its central themes were being repudiated by the electorate.

Some of Labour's leaders themselves shared the public's fear that the unions were becoming too powerful. In January 1974, Callaghan, who had taken the side of the trade unions in 1969 in the controversy over 'In Place of Strife', 'expressed his anxiety' to Tony Benn 'about the power of the trade unions'. 'They are still much too powerful. This is our problem.'[25] In 1975, Anthony Crosland warned that 'some of the commanding heights of the economy are now to be found in union headquarters in Euston Road.'[26] Yet, despite the clear evidence that most people thought the trade unions to be too strong rather than too weak, the new Government proceeded with a raft of measures whose purpose and effect was to make the trade unions even stronger, and to give them an influence over government policy which most voters resented.

Heath had sought to win the February 1974 general election on a cry of 'Who Governs?'. The country, he insisted, was in a state of crisis and had to confront the issue of irresponsible trade union power. Labour's response was that the crisis was primarily one of Tory mismanagement. A Labour Government armed with the Social Contract would yield a quiet life after the tumult of the Heath years. This theme was to be echoed in the October general election when Heath called for a coalition government to meet the crisis, but Wilson, after winning the election, declared that

> What the people want, what every family needs, is a bit of peace and quiet so that they can plan for the future on a basis of real security for the whole family.[27]

In calling for 'peace and quiet', Wilson probably summed up the temper of the British people. But perhaps behind the desire for a quiet life lay the nagging fear that the Government was becoming impotent in the face of organised labour, and that the Wilson Government might prove little more than a holding operation. There was a real fear for the future, a fear that trade union power and accelerating inflation would destroy democracy. This fear was by no means confined to those on the right. In 1974, Samuel Brittan, the respected economic commentator, published an article in *The British Journal of Political Science* entitled 'The Economic Contradictions of Democracy', while Peter Jay wrote in *The Times* on 1 July 1974 on 'How Inflation Threatens British

Democracy with its Last Chance before Extinction'. It was this growing fear, which reached its culmination in the 'Winter of Discontent', which was to make Thatcherism possible.

The post-war settlement had required Governments, through intelligent use of macro-economic policy, and consultation with the forces of organised labour, to preserve full employment, higher living standards and a steadily expanding welfare state. This could only be achieved in a society in which civic cohesion and a sense of social obligation, if not deference, were strong. Citizens would have to accept the decisions made by Governments, while trade unionists would have to accept the decisions of their leaders. The post-war settlement could not work if ordinary trade unionists felt free to untie the packages which had been agreed by their leaders. Respect for authority, there-fore, was the key to the successful operation of the settlement. Leaders could lead only if followers were willing to follow.

The culture of social obligation, however, was being undermined by the consumerism and hedonism generated by the affluent society of the 1950s and 1960s. The left had been profoundly ambivalent about this revolution of rising expectations. 'This so-called affluent society,' Aneurin Bevan had declared in his last speech to a Labour Party Conference in 1959, 'is an ugly society still. It is a vulgar society. It is a meretricious society. It is a society in which priorities have gone all wrong.'[28] In accepting the baubles of consumerism, the working class was, in Bevan's view, betraying the Labour movement. 'History gave them the chance and they didn't take it. Now it is probably too late', he told Geoffrey Goodman in 1959.[29] In 1971, Tony Benn reacted against an Austrian Social Democrat who thought that 'socialism means everybody being allowed to have a Rolls Royce'. This, Benn believed, was 'the individual escape from class into prosperity, which is the cancer eating into the Western European Social Democratic parties; it is what Crosland believes'.[30]

It was indeed what Crosland believed. He, together with others on the right, welcomed affluence rather than repudiating it. Indeed in his revisionist bible, *The Future of Socialism*, first published in 1956, Crosland had railed against the puritanism which had for so long appeared to be part of the Labour ethic. 'Total abstinence and a good filing-system are not now the right sign-posts to the socialist Utopia: or at least, if they are, some of us will fall by the wayside.' Labour, Crosland believed, should welcome, rather than being suspicious of, rising living standards, a greater variety of consumer goods, social fluidity, and a lessening of the restraints on sexual behaviour. In the blood of socialists, Crosland insisted, there should 'always run a trace of the anarchist and the libertarian'.[31]

The trouble was, however, that a society dominated by hedonistic individu-alism would hardly be likely to accept the obligations entailed in the Social Contract. Consumerism was rapidly dissolving traditional community ties: self-assertion, both by individuals and by groups, was coming to replace collective solidarity and class loyalty. By the 1980s, Peter Shore could lament that we were engaging in what I called occupational tribal warfare, as though every separate group in the country had no feeling and no sense of being part of a community, but was simply out to get for itself what it could.[32]

The ethic on which Labour depended was disappearing, while at the same time its social base was fragmenting through economic change and changes in the class structure.

'Think nationally,' Heath had exhorted the unions when trying to persuade them to accept his incomes policy, 'think of the nation as a whole. Think of these proposals as members of a society that can only beat rising prices if it acts together as one nation.'[33] Such an exhortation which, during the time of Churchill or Attlee, would have been received with respect, elicited little more than a belly-laugh in the conditions of 1973–4. Labour believed that its links with the unions and its socialist ethic would yield a more positive response. Under a government which emphasised principles of fairness, the national interest would receive more of a hearing, and trade unionists would become more responsible in their wage claims. In this way, the conditions of 1945 could be recreated. Seen in this light, Labour's victory in February 1974 and the programme on which it won that victory, far from being a triumph for radicalism, was a last desperate attempt to preserve an old order, the moral community of the 1940s. It was an order which Labour sought to preserve, not to subvert, as both Tony Benn and Margaret Thatcher would later seek to do.

The Social Contract, then, can be seen in retrospect as a last attempt to rally support for the preservation of the post-war settlement.[34] Yet the conditions for such a *rassemblement* no longer existed. For the crisis of the 1970s was to destroy not only Edward Heath's One Nation brand of Toryism, with its futile exhortation to 'Think nationally', but also Labour's politics of social obligation. For both of these political philosophies relied on a sense of civic cohesion which was rapidly passing away. The 1970s were to destroy the hopes of believers in the beneficent state in both parties, the hopes of Anthony Crosland as much as the hopes of Edward Heath. The frantic attempts to preserve the post-war settlement by bringing the trade unions into a closer relationship with government were to shatter both parties, the Conservatives in 1973–4, and Labour in 1978–9. The 1970s were to see both the climax and the shattering of attempts to resurrect the post-war settlement, and the disintegration of that settlement ended the aspirations of Old Labour.

The collapse of the 1974–9 Labour Government in the 'Winter of Discontent' had already been foreshadowed in its beginning, the Social Contract. The Labour Party had been formed to give expression to the sentiments of the working class when that class could be said to form a reasonably united socio-economic bloc. With the erosion of Labour's social base and the weakening of collective solidarity, both the sociological and ideological foundations of Labour came to be eroded. So it was that 1974 proved to be not a resurgence but the last rallying cry of Old Labour before the electorate sent it into opposition for eighteen years. The Party would not again be able to achieve electoral success until it had transformed itself from Old Labour to New Labour.

Thus, whereas in the last decade of the nineteenth century, Sir William Harcourt could say, as Liberal Chancellor of the Exchequer, 'we are all socialists now', by the end of the twentieth century, Labour could win power only after it had assured the electorate that 'we are none of us socialists now'.

Notes

1 Quoted in Jenkins, P., *The Battle of Downing Street* (Charles Knight, London, 1970), p. x.
2 Quoted in Taylor, R., *The Trade Union Question in British Politics: Government and Unions since 1945* (Blackwell, Oxford, 1993), p. 230.
3 Quoted in Taylor, ibid., p. 224.
4 Castle, B., *The Castle Diaries 1974–76* (Weidenfeld and Nicolson, London, 1980), Intro., p. 10.
5 Cited in Taylor, *The Trade Union Question in British Politics*, p. 226.
6 Wilson, H., *Final Term: The Labour Government 1974–76* (Weidenfeld and Nicolson, London, 1979), p. 43.
7 Castle, *Diaries 1974–1976*, p. 20. Entry for 4 January 1974.
8 Jenkins, R., *A Life at the Centre* (Macmillan, London, 1991), p. 364.
9 Dell, E., *A Strange and Eventful History: Democratic Socialism in Britain* (HarperCollins, London, paperback edition 2000), p. 433.
10 Barnett, J., *Inside the Treasury 1974–79* (André Deutsch, London, 1982), p. 15.
11 Bullock, A., *The Life and Times of Ernest Bevin*, vol. 1, *Trade Union Leader, 1881–1940* (Heinemann, London, 1960), pp. 258–60.
12 Labour Party Conference Reports (Labour Party, London, 1973), p. 197.
13 Donoughue, B., *Prime Minister: The Conduct of Policy under Harold Wilson and James Callaghan* (Cape, London, 1987), p. 51.
14 Barnett, *Inside the Treasury*, p. 23.
15 Dell, E., *A Hard Pounding: Politics and Economic Crisis 1974–6*, (Oxford University Press, Oxford, 1991), p. 12.
16 Barnett, *Inside the Treasury*, p. 49.
17 Brown, W., *The Changing Contours of British Industrial Relations* (Blackwell, Oxford, 1981), p. 66.
18 Gormley, J., *Battered Cherub: The Autobiography of Joe Gormley* (Hamish Hamilton, London, 1982), p. 193.
19 House of Commons Debates, Hansard, vol. 808, col. 1233, 15 December 1970.
20 Jones, J., 'The Human Face of Labour', Dimbleby Lecture, BBC, 1977, p. 9.
21 Butler, D. and Kavanagh, D., *The British General Election of February 1974* (Macmillan, London, 1974), p. 50.
22 Cited in Panitch, L., *Social Democracy and Industrial Militancy: The Labour Party, the Trade Unions and Incomes Policy, 1945–74* (Cambridge University Press, Cambridge, 1976), p. 228.
23 Benn, T. *Against the Tide: Diaries 1973–76* (Arrow, London, 1989), pp. 93–4. Entry for 17 January 1974.
24 Gallup, G..H. (ed.), *The Gallup International Public Opinion Polls*, vol. 2, *1965–75* (Random House, New York, 1976), pp. 1200, 1353, 1447, 1207, 1443.
25 Benn, *Against the Tide*, p. 96. Entry for 21 January 1974.
26 Crosland, C.A.R., 'Socialism Now', in Leonard, D. (ed.), *Socialism Now and Other Essays* (Cape, London, 1975), p. 29.
27 Butler, D. and Kavanagh, D., *The British General Election of October 1974* (Macmillan, London, 1975), p. 291.

28 Cited in Foot, M., *Aneurin Bevan*, vol. 2, *1945–1960* (Davis-Poynter, London, 1973), p. 645. Foot entitles chapter 16 of his biography dealing with the years 1958–60, 'The Meretricious Society'.
29 Foot, *Bevan, 1945–1960*, p. 626.
30 Benn, T., *Office Without Power: Diaries 1968–72* (Hutchinson, London, 1988), p. 356. Entry for 16 July 1971.
31 Crosland, C.A.R., *The Future of Socialism* (Cape, London, 1956), pp. 524, 522.
32 Taylor, D.J., *After the War: The Novel and English Society since 1945* (Chatto and Windus, London, 1993), p. 197.
33 Campbell, J., *Edward Heath: a Biography* (Cape, London, 1993), pp. 472–3.
34 See Middlemas, K., 'Power, Competition and the State', *Contemporary Record*, 5(3), 1991, p. 521.

2 Political thought

Socialism in a cold climate

Raymond Plant

In February 1977 Anthony Crosland, Foreign Secretary in James Callaghan's Government, died suddenly of a stroke at the early age of 58. He had been successively Secretary of State for Education, President of the Board of Trade, Environment Secretary and finally Foreign Secretary in the Labour Governments of the 1960s and 1970s. However, he was also the pre-eminent Labour political and social theorist of the post-war world and indeed had published a book, *Socialism Now*,[1] on the prospects for socialism under a Labour Government just before Labour came back to power in the 1974 election. He was, however, much better known for his path-breaking book *The Future of Socialism*,[2] which had first been published in 1956. This book defended a revisionist form of social democracy against the Marxist left. It argued that in the post-war world capitalism had fundamentally been changed, that nationalisation or the common ownership of the means of production, distribution and exchange articulated in Clause 4 of the Labour Party's constitution should be seen as a means to socialist goals and not an end in itself. The basic socialist goal was the creation of a more equal society embodying social justice in the distribution of resources, and opportunities. These basic goals could be achieved by means other than nationalisation and planning. They could indeed be achieved by the use of Keynesian demand management and the political will to improve the position of the worst off. He put the point pithily in a Fabian Pamphlet on *Social Democracy in Europe*,[3] where he argues that the fundamental aim of socialism was to improve the relative position of the worst-off members of society while maintaining the absolute position of the better off. Growth was the way to achieve these goals. The absolute position of the better off had to be maintained in order to produce the political coalition necessary to vote the Labour Party into office. It is true, of course, to say that the Labour Party at this time had not had its Bad Godesberg moment as the SPD in Germany had in 1959, which led the SPD to turn its back explicitly on a Marxist analysis of society and to adopt a revisionist stand. Indeed when Hugh Gaitskell as the then leader of the Party had tried to change Clause 4 following the 1959 election defeat he had been unsuccessful. Nevertheless it was the revisionist position that triumphed in practice and the Labour Governments of the 1960s and 1970s more or less until Crosland's death adopted broadly speaking a revisionist approach while at the same time not explicitly repudiating elements in its own ideological formation. So, for example, by 1968 even such a quintessentially figure of the left as Michael Foot accepted what can be called the revisionist/Croslandite position as the way forward for Labour.

So Crosland's death was a significant event in the development of the Labour Party's political thought. However, it was seen as more than this because with considerable irony Crosland died at more or less exactly the same time as the fundamental tenets of his position, which had been repeated without much modification in 1974 in *Socialism Now*, were under attack as never before from both the left and the right, and under the pressure of events and economic changes which culminated in the IMF loan the terms of which requiring as they did significant cuts in public expenditure Crosland had resisted until more or less the last moment before the loan had been agreed. Many thought by 1977 that revisionist social democracy of the Crosland variety was dead as well as its progenitor. The left was in the process of developing an alternative economic strategy associated primarily with Tony Benn and on the left too Stuart Holland had produced a book, *The Socialist Challenge*,[4] which was a severe critique of the Crosland position and which argued for the significance for the future of socialism of some of the features of what have subsequently come to be called 'globalisation'. On the right there was a growing interest in economic liberalism among both politicians such as Maragaret Thatcher, Keith Joseph, Geoffrey Howe and Peter Thorneycroft, who had indeed resigned from the Conservative Cabinet in 1957 on essentially an economic liberal critique of the Macmillan Government, as had his colleague Enoch Powell, and among academics and think tanks, particularly the Institute for Economic Affairs and the Centre for Policy Studies. Both the left and the right believed that Croslandite social democracy had reached a dead end and therefore the main thrust of policy of the Labour Party both in and out of office under Gaitskell, Wilson and Callaghan was mistaken. So in this chapter we need to do three things: to understand more clearly the revisionist case which, as I have said in practice, dominated Labour Party policy particularly in office, even though the Party at large as represented at the Party Conference by the unions and constituency members regularly dissented from this approach; to understand the nature of the economic liberal critique of this approach which I shall argue was profound and which Labour found no way of answering during this period; and finally to understand the alternative strategy of the left, although, of course, it was the economic liberalism of Mrs Thatcher that actually won the day in 1979 against both Croslandite social democracy and the left's alternative strategy.

Social democracy

In *The Future of Socialism* Crosland had two main aims: to provide a critique of Marxism and to defend a conception of socialism defined in terms of equality rather than in terms of the common ownership of the means of production – a view that he still held in 1974. It was the critique of Marxism that made the term revisionist appropriate to this position. In a letter to his Oxford friend, Phillip Williams, written during the war, Crosland says that he wanted to be the 'second Bernstein'. The force of this comment is that in 1899 Eduard Bernstein, a prominent German socialist, had written *Die Voraussetzungen des Sozialismus*, initially translated as *Evolutionary Socialism*, which is a good summation of the theme of the book, but more accurately retranslated recently by Henry Tudor with the exact title *The Preconditions of Socialism*.[5] Bernstein was regarded by Lenin, Kautsky and Luxemburg as a revisionist since a major theme of the book was the attempt to detach a socialist or social democratic project from a reliance on Marx's analysis of capitalist society and its place in the materialist development of history. Croslandite revisionism had the same aim and it was important since Marxism had been a popular element in Labour's pre-war history, particularly in the 1930s, and a rather inexplicit and unsystematised Marxism still had a significant place in the minds of many Labour supporters. In Crosland's view this approach was fundamentally misconceived, for whatever may have been the accuracy of Marx's account of the nature of capitalism in the late nineteenth century, capitalism after the Second World War had fundamentally changed. In short form the reasons Crosland adduces for the change are as follows:

1   Capitalism had changed first of all because the ownership of the means of production which Marx attributed to a class of capitalists was now much more dispersed and this dispersal was a continuing process. Hence a Labour Government pursuing an agenda of social justice would not confront a number of individual owners of the means of production who formed a class with homogeneous interests opposed to such an agenda.

2   In any case the sector of private ownership had been diminished in crucial industries by the 1945 Labour Government's programme of nationalisation of coal, steel, railways, electricity, gas and telephony. It seemed both in 1956 with *The Future of Socialism* and in 1974 with *Socialism Now* that the public ownership of these infrastructural industries would stay and revisionists showed no desire to change that, although they thought that further nationalisations were unnecessary to achieve socialist/social democratic goals.

3   Because of the dispersal of ownership, ownership and control were no longer synonymous. The practical control of business and industry was in the hands of managers. The task was, according to revisionists, to ensure that managers not only managed according to the profitability of the company but also took account of socially desirable objectives.

4   It was argued that the greater democratisation of British life had put severe constraints on the power of private ownership of capital. Not only had the dispersal of ownership undermined the power of privately owned capital but democratic institutions, practices and attitudes were a clear countervailing power against the power of private owners.

5   Alongside this there had been the growth of unionism which diminished the unilateral power of both private owners and managers and compelled them to take into account the interests of the workforce.

6   There was the post-1945 development of the welfare state, which meant that in terms of the basic goods of health, education and welfare citizens were no longer subject to the vagaries of the market or charity but had a stake in society mediated not just by non-capitalist institutions such as the NHS but also by the recognition of the collective responsibility for meeting need which, as we shall see later, is a profoundly anti-capitalist notion.

7   The revisionists also argued that while the sense of class was still strong in Britain and affected life chances there had been neither the growing polarisation of classes nor the immiseration of the working class which Marx had predicted based on his materialist theory of history and his view of capitalist development. This criticism of Marx is a feature which Crosland and the revisionists shared with Bernstein.

8   In many ways, however, the most fundamental change was the acceptance of Keynesian techniques of economic management. Keynesian economic techniques meant that government was able to manage the general macro-economic climate within which firms operated and the idea that capitalists (even assuming that there had been little dispersal of ownership) could pursue an agenda which did not take account of government's management of demand and macro-economic conditions was false. Keynesian economic management meant to a degree the relative autonomy of politics. It did not have to be seen as an arena of class interests. Governments using Keynesian techniques could pursue macro-economic policies that would serve the public interest and which in turn would be shaped by political values. In the view of the revisionists, therefore, Keynesian techniques would allow steady growth to be achieved, the fiscal dividends of which could be invested in the public services and the social security system with the aim of creating a more equal society by – as was said earlier – improving the relative position of the worst off while maintaining the absolute position of the better off. Growth was the solvent of distributional dilemmas in politics and growth could be achieved by Keynesian means.

9   This in turn meant that the common ownership of the means of production and detailed economic planning were no longer necessary to achieve growth, to confront power and to achieve a more socially just society. Nationalisation could therefore be seen as a means to an end – a more socially just society. It did not have to be seen as an end in itself since there were now available better means, namely demand management techniques. Keynes himself made this point exactly when he said in his *General Theory of Employment, Interest and Money*:

> It is not the ownership of the instruments of production which it is important for the state to assume. If the state is able to determine the aggregate amount of resources devoted to augmenting the instruments and the basic rate of reward to those who own them it will have accomplished all that is necessary.[6]

It seems to be absolutely clear that had not the Keynesian revolution taken place then there could never have been social democracy on the post-war model. In his classic study of the relationship between Keynesianism and social democracy, in *Capitalism and Social Democracy*, Adam Przeworski argues as follows:

> The fact is that social democrats everywhere soon discovered in Keynes' ideas, particularly after the appearance of his General Theory, something they urgently needed: a distinct policy for administering capitalist economies. The Keynesian revolution – and this is what it was – provided social democrats with a goal and hence the justification of their governmental role, and simultaneously transformed the significance of distributive politics that favoured the working class. ... Society is not helpless against the whims of the capitalist market, the economy can be controlled and the welfare of citizens can be continually enhanced by the active role of the state: this was the new discovery of social democrats.[7]

By the mid-1970s, however, it was precisely Keynesianism which was under attack, particularly from economic liberals, and therefore because of the closeness of the link between Keynesian ideas and post-war social democracy this economic liberal attack was also an attack on the major tenets of social democracy. Indeed paradoxically by the time of the Labour Party Conference in 1976 the Prime Minister James Callaghan had gone a long way to repudiate one central plank of Keynesian thought but at that time there was no sustained attempt by social democrats to reformulate their approach to politics and economics in the light of the difficulties which Keynesianism was encountering in both theory and practice. However, before moving on to the critique of the social democratic state and economy mounted by economic liberals I want to dwell just briefly on the other side of the social democratic project.

As was argued earlier, social democrats of the post-war generation saw equality as the defining principle of socialism. They understood by equality as Crosland makes clear in *Socialism Now* far more than a meritocratic society of equality of opportunity narrowly conceived since such a society would be likely to mean that the highest rewards in income and status would go to those with fortunate family backgrounds and fortunate genetic inheritance. Both of these were arbitrary from a moral point of view since no one could be said to deserve their more fortunate backgrounds or their genetic inheritance – a point which Crosland argued in *The Future of Socialism* well before John Rawls whose monumental *A Theory of Justice* had been published two years prior to *Socialism Now*.[8] However, in *Socialism Now* Crosland does explicitly link his own conception of equality with Rawls' idea of 'democratic equality'. That is to say, a society of equal basic liberties with inequalities being justified only if they benefit the worst off. That is to say that the social democratic position on equality was not one either of equality of opportunity purely or equality of outcome since in Crosland's view strict equality of outcome was not consistent with economic efficiency. He argues that certain inequalities are functional for the operation of the economy but these are justified in terms of the rent of ability, not on the basis of desert which would be the meritocratic approach. This level of democratic equality was to be produced by the benefit system (as he makes clear in *Socialism Now*); by public expenditure which is to the benefit of the less well-off members of society, and in *Socialism Now* he takes pride in the fact that the percentage of GDP taken up by public expenditure had been very considerably increased during the Wilson Governments of the 1960s, whereas at this time his one-time friend, close colleague and fellow social democrat, Roy Jenkins, was arguing that such high levels of public expenditure could be a threat to personal liberty and a pluralist society; and by sustaining the commitment to comprehensive education which was seen as a central plank in the attempt both to extend opportunities and to create a greater degree of social equality through having children of different abilities and different backgrounds being educated together. Some critics have argued that this form of social democracy concentrated on equality at the expense of both liberty and fraternity or community. This is an unfair criticism. While it would be true to say that Crosland, for example, has little to say about liberty, there are two reasons for this. First of all, as *Socialism Now* makes clear, he does endorse Rawls' approach, and the principle of equal basic liberty is the first of Rawls' lexically ordered principles; second, as he pointed out in *The Future of Socialism*, in his mind there was no dispute between the main parties in British politics about the importance of personal liberty and therefore it seemed to him to be rather redundant to dwell on it. This is a rather poor argument since part of the onslaught of the economic liberals on the social democratic state is in terms of personal freedom. However, while Crosland may have said little about liberty from a philosophical point of view, no one could reasonably read the conclusion of *The Future of Socialism* and not be struck by his commitment to personal freedom – indeed he says that:

> So, in Britain as we approach the socialist goals described above, the reformer will bend his energies more and more to issues which cannot be classified as specifically socialist or non socialist, but which lie in other fields altogether. There are two such fields in which social action is already called for: the freedom of personal and leisure life, and social responsibility for cultural values.[9]

Neo-liberalism

So we need now to move on to the economic liberal critique of the social democratic position which was being developed at this time, particularly in a political context by Margaret Thatcher, Keith Joseph, Geoffrey Howe, Enoch Powell, Nigel Lawson and others; in academia by Friedrich von Hayek, Milton Friedman, James Buchanan, Gordon Tullock, William Niskanen etc.; in the world of think tanks by the Institute for Economic Affairs and its indefatigable founders Ralph Harris and Arthur Seldon, the Centre for Policy Studies set up by Thatcher and Joseph, the Adam Smith Institute, the Karl Menger Society and on the international plane the Mont Pelerin Society. At the beginning of the 1970s economic liberal ideas were adopted to some degree by Edward Heath in the sense that the programme agreed at the Selsdon Park Hotel in Surrey which gave birth to 'Selsdon man' as a rather shorthand term for economic liberal man but with the connotation that this was a kind of reversion to a pre-Keynesian Neanderthal form of economics, did indeed contain quite a strong dose of economic or neo-liberalism. However, by 1972 the Heath Government had been forced onto the defensive and had performed a spectacular economic U-turn in the nationalisation of Rolls-Royce engines after the imminent bankruptcy of the firm as the result of the financial pressures of developing the RB211 engine. At that time most people would have thought that the U-turn had been so spectacular that there could be no return to economic liberalism and that it was safe to continue to regard thinkers like Hayek and Friedman as wholly marginal, which is how they were thought of in the 1950s and 1960s. However, as the Heath Government wore on and as the Labour Government succeeded it in 1974, it soon became clear that there could be no reversion to orthodox Keynesianism. In the international context the Bretton Woods exchange rate agreement collapsed under the impact of decisions made by Richard Nixon when he was President of the United States; the oil price hike made the costs of production much increased as well as flooding the West with petro dollars from oil-rich states; and finally the phenomenon of stagflation – the combination of very low levels of growth with very high levels of inflation which a Keynesian perspective ought to have ruled out. So the world scene and the domestic scene were set for a frontal assault on Keynesian approaches and upon the whole social democratic project which had been erected on the basis of the Keynesian revolution.

In this chapter I shall not consider the detailed issues in economic policy which led to this situation since they have been dealt with elsewhere in this book. I shall rather in this chapter, which is to do with theoretical issues, concentrate on the theoretical critique of what might be called Keynesian social democracy by the economic liberals. This critique is wide ranging and challenging and I think that it is fair to say that in the period covered by this volume it did not receive an adequate answer from social democrats. Indeed, in many respects it was ignored, but ignoring it had rather dire political consequences since economic liberalism proved not to be a throwback or a passing fad but rather what recently Perry Anderson the Marxist historian has called in the *New Left Review* 'the most successful ideology in the history of the world'. So what are the main features of this critique? In the short space available I can only indicate them and not elaborate on them in detail, nor can I evaluate them (a role I have sought to fill elsewhere).[10] I shall divide them up initially between arguments about political economy and arguments about the welfare state, but for the economic liberal there is a very close connection between the two.

Let us look at political economy first of all (which is dealt with in greater detail in Kevin Hickson's chapter). If we emphasise the political in political economy for the moment it leads us to focus on the core functions of the state as understood by economic liberals. This has obvious theoretical importance since economic liberalism incorporates a theory of the state but the emphasis on limited government in economic liberal thought had a political salience too in the mid-1970s. The defeat of the Heath Government after two miners' strikes, the rise of industrial militancy and so forth led to quite a journalistic industry in discussions of whether or not Britain was ungovernable or not. It was thought by many critics of social democracy that the state had become too large and that its reach was exceeding its grasp. One of the aspects of neo-liberalism which appealed to conservative critics of social democracy was that it had a rigorous view about the limits of government vis-à-vis both society and the economy. Keynes himself had argued in *The General Theory* that the changes needed to macro-economic policy will 'involve large changes in the traditional functions of government'.[11] Social democrats clearly followed him in this and it was intrinsic to demand management. In a situation of recession, for example, a Keynesian social democrat would want to use government money to increase investment to break the downward spiral of demand, engage in programmes of public works, lower interest rates, give subsidies and increase spending and do this when necessary by running deficits at least in the short term. Economic liberals disputed this case and the role for the state that it engendered. In their view inflation was, at least in the longer run, the central cause of unemployment and that inflation is essentially a monetary phenomenon which is made worse by Keynesian social democratic assumptions that it was possible to spend one's way out of recession. So in their view the very techniques which government used to secure full employment were inflationary and would act against employment in the long run. Each time demand is expanded by deficit financing, a greater stimulus is required to produce smaller and smaller improvements in the rate of unemployment. This view seemed to be borne out in the mid-1970s when there were occasions when inflation was running at 25 per cent on an annualised rate and unemployment was rising inexorably. So the economic situation provided a backdrop to the claims of neo-liberalism in political economy to have a better way.

One central element of this was monetarism which when combined with conservative doctrines struck at the heart of the social democratic state. Monetarism is itself a rather technical economic position which entails usually the following assumptions:

- A government should seek a neutral supply of money based upon feasible assumptions about the real rate of growth in the economy.
- Inflation which is regarded as the main cause of unemployment should be the major focus of economic policy. Since inflation (on the monetarist view) is caused by excess increases in the money supply both the problem and its solution lie with the government. However, this requires that the government should stick rigidly to its monetary targets and not be seduced into a general reflation of the economy by a panic over a short-term decline in employment and decline in output.
- The government and the monetary authorities should have a measure of money which is clearly definable and which it is within the competence of government to control.

In practice monetarism also became allied with a critique of public expenditure but in a sense technically it is not. It has nothing to say about the appropriate level of public expenditure per se. It is about how public expenditure should be financed, i.e. by not running a deficit rather than a doctrine about the appropriate levels of public expenditure. It is only when it is combined with arguments about the baleful effects of high levels of public expenditure, which are central to social democracy's egalitarian strategy and the baleful effects of high level of taxation to finance that level of public spending, that it turns into an argument about limited government and more restricted public expenditure.

It is the combination of monetarist arguments together with the critique of public expenditure which provides the basic case against social democracy. I shall note these elements as: supply side theories; the crowding out thesis and the fiscal crisis thesis.

The supply side theory has two aspects that are relevant in the present context. The first is concerned with the level of taxation. On this view the free market, free of government interference and domination, is a field of dynamism and wealth generation. It depends on individuals using their own skills and knowledge and in these circumstances the supply of goods and services will increase. This will lead to sustained economic growth which will benefit all including the worst off through the trickle-down mechanism whereby what the better off are able to consume today will come within the reach of the less well off. Crucial to this is taxation. People work best when they have an incentive to do so and that incentive is secured by low levels of taxation. Instead of taxing the rich until the pips squeak as Denis Healey once memorably put it, it will be of the greatest help to the poor to have a more dynamic economy with low levels of tax so that the poor can take advantage of trickle-down mechanisms. This is a fundamental challenge to the social democrat in two related respects. First of all it entails abandoning the idea of the tax system as a means of creating greater social and economic equality since it will certainly mean that if we have low levels of tax, then inequality will increase. Second, it more or less completely inverts Crosland's position mentioned earlier about improving the relative position of the worst off and maintaining the absolute position of the better off. The supply-side-oriented economic liberal is interested rather in improving the relative position of the better off via tax cuts in order to improve the absolute position of the worst off. That is to say, tax cuts will increase economic dynamism and if the poor take advantage of trickle-down effects they will be better off on a year-by-year basis even though the gap between rich and poor will have increased. If tax is to be lowered to the level to generate dynamism then public expenditure will have to be cut and that too was central to the social democratic project. This was a crucial economic liberal challenge to Keynesian social democracy and it remained unanswered in this period.

The second element of the critique of public expenditure is to do with the claim that public expenditure led to a crowding out of private investment and again in this respect impinged on the dynamism of the market. There are two aspects to the crowding out thesis which became popular in the 1970s: physical crowding out and financial crowding out. Physical crowding out is really a consequence of the argument discussed above, i.e. high levels of public expenditure in pursuit of an egalitarian project produce a tax burden for individuals and firms which given the supply side assumptions mentioned above means that such a regime will lead to lower productivity and lower investment. Financial crowding out has to do with the financing of the public sector and the issuing of government bonds. Government will issue bonds which are a gilt-edged security (on the assumption that governments cannot go bankrupt) and given high levels of public expenditure and resistance to higher levels of taxation government will issue more and more bonds and borrow money that would otherwise have been borrowed by the private sector. These ideas run entirely counter to Keynesian social democracy, which assumed that appropriate levels of expenditure could increase the supply of goods and services, increase economic growth and act as a stimulus to the private sector, particularly in periods of recession.

The final element in this supply side critique of social democracy is what has come to be called the fiscal crisis of the state after the title of a book by J. O'Connor published in 1973.[12] Boiled down to its essential insight this is the view that the social democratic state with its pursuit of high levels of public expenditure with its high levels of tax and borrowing to sustain it is killing the goose that lays the golden egg; that is to say, the wealth-creating power of the private sector. On this view social democracy is incoherent: it wants to achieve socialist or social democratic aims on the back of the market economy and to do that it has to rely on growth (as we have seen), but the very level of taxation, borrowing and public expenditure will actually curtail the very growth which is required. It follows from all of this that it is the level of public expenditure which is of central importance to the economic liberal critique of the social democratic project and to reduce public expenditure it is necessary to attack two interrelated features of the social democratic state, namely the pursuit of equality and the welfare state. This involves both a moral critique and a more broadly based political/economic critique of the welfare state. In his book on *Equality* published in 1979 and co-authored with Jonathan Sumption,[13] Keith Joseph argued that it was the object of the book to challenge one of the central beliefs in British politics: 'the belief that it is the proper function of the state to influence the distribution of wealth'.[14] It was of course central to the social democratic project that the state should be a distributive state, pursuing social justice. So we need to get some understanding of what the case against both equality and the welfare state is. This involves a lot of very complex arguments to which justice cannot really be done here but I will outline them very briefly.

First of all a distributive state is obviously concerned with social justice and egalitarians focus upon one conception of social justice, namely greater equality. The economic liberal typically rejects the distributive state for reasons best set out by Hayek in *The Constitution of Liberty* and in *Law Legislation and Liberty* whose three volumes were published in the 1970s.[15] The first reason is that market outcomes are not unjust whatever the degree of inequality. Injustice is the result only of intentional action. Market outcomes are not intended by anyone. Those at the bottom of the heap may be suffering misfortune or bad luck but they do not suffer injustice. The job of the state is to rectify injustice but not to take people off the wheel of fortune as Keith Joseph calls it. Hence, we have no collective moral responsibility to correct the unequal outcomes of the market. In addition one of the points that Hayek makes is that our moral views are irredeemably subjective. We do not agree on merit, on desert, on need, on entitlement or any of the other possible principles on which goods and services might be distributed. In those circumstances, in his view a state will be compelled to act unjustly to some groups in society because it will favour one group's view of social justice and what it requires to another. For these two reasons social justice is an illusion.

Second, it has been a social democratic argument since the late nineteenth century that freedom requires resources and that if the state is to be the guarantor of equal freedom it must secure for individuals at least equal access to basic resources which they may not be able to get in a market. So freedom in this positive sense, of being able to do something as well as the negative sense of not being prevented from doing something, requires the provision of resources by the state and that at least in respect of basic goods such as health and education there should be some rough equality about access and provision. The economic liberal position rejects this. On for example Hayek's view there is a categorical distinction between being free to do something and being able to do something and no amount of rhetoric about 'real freedom' will get around this. They are categorically different because no one is able to do all that he or she is free to do. I am free to do all those things that I am not prevented by the actions of others from doing but this leaves open an infinity of things that I might do and by definition I am able to do only a small number of the infinite number of things that I am free to do.

The welfare state depends upon ideas about needs and economic liberals regard this as an extremely slippery concept. Because we do not have a consensus on what will satisfy needs a commitment to satisfy needs via collective state action will become a bottomless pit of public expenditure with no intellectually clear stopping place. Hence to recognise the principle of need satisfaction as a principle of state action which is central to social democracy is to open up public expenditure to intolerable pressures.

Needs are also related to welfare rights. If we think that needs should be satisfied by collective action then it is a very small step for those with the needs to think that they have a right to their satisfaction. A failure to satisfy such claimed entitlements will cause resentment and perhaps even a decline in legitimacy for government if it is perceived not to be protecting people's rights. T. H. Marshall held in the 1950s that welfare rights were a twentieth-century kind of right unlike civil and political rights and certainly social democracy has put a lot of emphasis on the idea of welfare rights.[16] For the economic liberal this is entirely misplaced both philosophically in that one cannot, it is said, have a right to a scarce resource and socially in that the idea that the state owes one resources can lead to dependency, sap initiative and an unwillingness to provide for oneself and one's family.

A welfare state will require a welfare bureaucracy to administer it. From the economic liberal perspective this causes two problems. The first (which was actually noticed by Crosland in a footnote in the conclusion to *The Future of Socialism*) is that this will entail quite a lot of necessarily arbitrary power being conceded to the welfare bureaucrat. The reason is this: it is impossible to write clear rules of law securing particular resources to individuals since their needs (slippery concept) will differ and there will have to be a great deal of discretion about the use of public resources. It is no good on this view arguing that this discretion should be made accountable since we cannot formulate the rule-governed system within which accountability will make sense. Hence on this view the social democratic state ensconces arbitrary power right at its heart. Second, drawing upon work by public choice theorists such as J. Buchanan, G. Tullock and W. Niskanen which was published in the 1960s and 1970s, economic liberal politicians such as Nigel Lawson and Nicholas Ridley argued that civil servants whether national or local were not the disinterested servants of the public good but rather operated like people in a market, i.e. they sought to maximise their utilities. However, unlike people in markets their behaviour was not subject to bankruptcy constraints and thus they were able to increase the size of their bureaux, increase the scope of their responsibilities, increase their incomes – all of which were forms of utility maximisation in ways that embodied a sense of producer rather than consumer interests in contrast to utility maximisation in the market which is supposed to benefit the customer, otherwise bankruptcy will follow. So for the economic liberal the social democratic state actually protects producer interests because it relies on bureaucratic delivery of services, a good deal of which is discretionary and which it is difficult to make accountable to the public interest.

The final important point about the distributive state in the view of economic liberal critics is that it leads to the growth of interest groups and a destructive form of zero sum politics. The reason for this is that the social democratic state is supposed to be about securing social justice but as we have seen from their point of view social justice is an illusion. What an individual or a group thinks of as its legitimate and just share of the social product will be highly subjective and there is no way of showing that this subjective view is false. Hence there will be clashes between highly subjective views of proper apportionment. However, the problem will go beyond that in that coalitions of groups seeking to extract some benefit from government will be drawn into being and the chances are that these coalitions will be coalitions of the most powerful groups in society and particularly trade unions in a social democratic society. They will be able to hold government to ransom, particularly in the public sector, and those most likely to lose out are the unorganised and the vulnerable. There will be a large premium on organisation and this in the context of relative scarcity of resources means a destructive zero sum form of politics.

So we can see why the economic liberals regarded the Keynesian social democratic state as fundamentally flawed. No effective defence was made during this period against this critique and indeed in his speech to the Labour Party Conference in 1976, Callaghan went some way, if not to endorsing economic liberalism, at least to agreeing with some of the case about government expenditure and how to deal with a recession. This is what he said:

> We used to think that you could spend your way out of a recession and increase employment by cutting taxes and boosting spending. I tell you in all candour that the option no longer exists and that in so far as it ever did exist it only worked by inflicting a bigger dose of inflation into the system.[17]

All of this put the Labour Party's social democrats on the back foot at least until they came to see the force of the critique and to respond to it. Unfortunately this did not happen in the 1970s despite the critique being mounted at the time.

The Labour left

However, what I have argued was that the dominant social democratic project which had been at least implicit in Labour's approach to policy making since the early 1960s was under attack not just from the economic liberals but from other Labour politicians and intellectuals who dissented from this project. Important in this context were Stuart Holland and Tony Benn. I shall treat them separately since the main thrusts of their critiques were rather different.

Holland in his book *The Socialist Challenge* was an explicit critic of the Crosland position and interestingly enough his critique focuses on one of the issues that Crosland neglects, that is to say the capacity of the state to manage the economy according to Keynesian principles in circumstances in which that capacity has been undermined by the growth of multinational companies and what he calls meso power. This critique is interesting in two respects. First of all because it casts doubt on the social democrats' reliance on Keynes and also because in some ways it anticipates the debate about globalisation and social democracy that has been central to Labour's rethinking of its model in 'Third Way' terms under Tony Blair's leadership. For the Keynesian approach to work an economy has to be capable of being subjected to macro-economic management and therefore has to be seen essentially as a national economy and therefore the power and competence of the national state is essential to that. In Holland's view the revisionist social democratic position predicated as it is on this assumption has been radically undermined by the rise of multinational companies. In *The Socialist Challenge* he argued that 'the new giant companies have created a new mode of production, distribution and exchange in the heartland of the British economy'.[18] The rub here for the revisionist is twofold. First of all, as I have said, this undermines the capacity of the state to engage in the management of the economy in the approved Keynesian manner. Second, it is itself a revision of the revisionist's claim that post-war capitalism had changed fundamentally. It certainly had in Holland's view, but thinkers like Crosland and Douglas Jay had not taken into account sufficiently the growth of the multinational company. The rise of the multinationals and the need to attract their investment into Britain meant that governments through subsidy, regional policies, tax breaks and the like were actually encouraging the growth of multinational companies, which in his view created little by way of employment since they were mainly capital rather than labour intensive and these companies were now coming to dominate the centre of production in the British economy with smaller non-multinational firms being pushed to the periphery. Hence, as Crosland says in his rather short and not very satisfactory critique of this position in *Socialism Now* which was published before Holland's authoritative text on these issues against the revisionist position this new approach reinstates the centrality of the role of the means of production, the rejection of which as we saw was central to the revisionist position together with the view that politics was rather powerless in the face of the multinational firms which as Crosland himself said according to the type of thesis represented by Holland 'were able to frustrate the efforts of the last Labour Government to create or induce greater equality, faster growth, higher investment and exports, regional justice, price and profit restraint and industrial democracy'.[19] Because of this in Holland's view it was likely that a social democratic reliance on the private sector to produce the tax levels to sustain the public sector and the benefit system as a means of sustaining public services and increasing equality was misplaced. We were going to face a fiscal crisis of major proportions as we have seen O'Connor argue in *The Fiscal Crisis of the State*. The remedy was to be found in a reversion to pre-revisionist ideas of public ownership and planning. In his view – directly contrary to the revisionist one – revisionist-inspired Labour Governments had failed to grasp that: 'social redistribution depended upon socialist transformation, it was forced to cut back on the very social expenditure supposed to alleviate injustice and inequality'.[20] This goes to the absolute heart of the revisionist case that socialist goals can be achieved by a wide variety of means including what they claimed to be a fundamentally changed form of capitalism and market economy. In Holland's view the nature of capitalism had indeed changed but not in a way that made it any more compatible with the revisionist position.

To respond to this situation and to challenge the growth of what he called meso power two things were needed from a Labour Government: public ownership and state-guided investment via planning agreements with major companies. In Holland's view a National Enterprise Board would be able to act as a stimulus to the private sector through a policy of state intervention and direction. What both Holland and the revisionists really neglected in all of this, and this is a point well made by David Marquand, is that Labour thinkers of both the right and the left lacked a coherent account of the range and capacity of the state and it is this issue which proved subsequently to be such a strong card in the hands of the economic liberal form of conservatism (at least in the economic and welfare spheres) which was ushered in after the 1979 election.

I now want to turn briefly to Tony Benn. Most of Benn's writings on the nature of socialism fall rather outside the period under review with his *Arguments for Socialism* appearing in 1980 and *Arguments for Democracy* in 1981,[21] but nevertheless these books consolidated and articulated a position which he had taken by the mid-1970s. It is completely facile to take the tabloid view and see Benn as some sort of Marxist. Indeed many of his central positions are either contrary to orthodox forms of Marxism or would be regarded by Marxists as utterly utopian forms of socialism. The reason for this is that Benn wants to assert the primacy of democratic politics over economic forces whereas for an orthodox Marxist politics is relatively inert in relation to basic economic interests and structures. Benn is certainly very radical but it is a mistake to see him as a Marxist thinker. In his writings and speeches on democracy he has sought to produce what Marquand argued thinkers of the revisionist left did not have, namely a view of the state and its democratic accountability. Central to this aim was in Benn's view strengthening the role of Parliament over the executive; the abolition of the House of Lords; the reform of the prerogative so that the prime minister would become more accountable to Parliament – and all of this with the aim of extending the capacity of democratic institutions to challenge the power of capital within Britain. He accepted the mixed economy but he did think that there had to be greater countervailing power to that of capital. It was Crosland's view that post-war capitalism did have sufficient countervailing power for the reasons set out earlier. While Benn might have agreed with this up to a point, the degree of countervailing power was not sufficient and he wanted to see more democratic and political power exerted against capitalism. This led him also to advocate workers' control and workers' co-operatives which he had supported as a minister. As he claimed in *Arguments for Socialism*:

> Investors there will always be, but there is no valid reason why the investors' money should give them first claim to control, before those who invest their lives. Political democracy wrested the control of Parliament from those who owned the lands and the factories. Industrial democracy is a logical and necessary development of it.[22]

This kind of argument puts Benn firmly in the Bernsteinian social democratic tradition. The whole point of social democracy as originally conceived was to extend democratic power from the purely political sphere exercised through purely political rights to the civic, social and economic spheres. No doubt Benn is at the radical end of that but it is clearly more social democratic than Marxist. It also means that it is quite difficult to define socialism in terms of specific outcomes such as greater equality

Because while this is the most likely outcome from a radically democratised society, nevertheless the emphasis on democracy does mean that outcomes cannot be prejudged. So whereas someone like Crosland saw equality as the basic end of socialism/social democracy, for Benn it is possibly fair to say the end was actually the democratisation of life from which equality would be the most likely but not assured outcome. It is rather ironic that when Benn left Parliament after the first Blair Government he gave as his reason for leaving that he wanted to leave Parliament to go into politics – this is a commentary on how far his ideals went unrealised within the Labour Party.

Conclusion

So 1974–9 was not perhaps the most glorious period for Labour's political thought. No doubt the pressure of being in government with a very small majority inhibited the opportunities to rethink the position particularly of the revisionists in the light of the impact of economic liberalism and globalisation. In the 1980s, however, the Labour Party paid a very heavy price for either an unwillingness or inability to confront the challenges facing it.

Notes

1 Crosland, C.A.R., 'Socialism Now', in Leonard, D. (ed.), *Socialism Now and Other Essays* (Cape, London, 1975).
2 Crosland, C.A.R., *The Future of Socialism* (Schocken, New York, 2nd edition, 1963).
3 Crosland, C.A.R., *Social Democracy in Europe* (Fabian Society, London, 1975).
4 Holland, S., *The Socialist Challenge* (Quartet, London, 1975).
5 Bernstein, E., *Evolutionary Socialism* (Schocken, New York, 1961, first published 1899); Bernstein, E., *The Preconditions of Socialism* (ed. and trans. Tudor, H., Cambridge University Press, Cambridge, 1993).
6 Keynes, J.M., *The General Theory of Employment, Interest and Money* (Prometheus, New York, 1997), p. 378.
7 Przeworski, A., *Capitalism and Social Democracy* (Cambridge University Press, Cambridge, 1985), p. 36.
8 Rawls, J., *A Theory of Justice* (Harvard University Press, Cambridge, MA, 1971).
9 Crosland, *Future of Socialism*, p. 354.
10 See, for example, Hoover, K. and Plant, R., *Conservative Capitalism in Britain and the United States: A Critical Appraisal* (Routledge, London, 1989).
11 Keynes, *General Theory*, p. 379.
12 O'Connor, J., *The Fiscal Crisis of the State* (St Martin's Press, New York, 1973).
13 Joseph, K. and Sumption, J., *Equality* (Murray, London, 1979).
14 Ibid., p. 22.
15 Hayek, F.A., *The Constitution of Liberty* (Routledge and Kegan Paul, London, 1960) and Hayek, F.A., *Law Legislation and Liberty* (Routledge and Kegan Paul, London, 3 vols, 1982).
16 Marshall, T.H., *Citizenship and Social Class* (Cambridge University Press, Cambridge, 1950).
17 Labour Party Conference Report, 1976 (Labour Party, London, 1976), pp. 188–9.
18 Holland, *The Socialist Challenge*, p. 51.
19 Crosland, 'Socialism Now', p. 27.
20 Holland, *The Socialist Challenge*, p. 34.
21 Benn, T., *Arguments for Socialism* (Penguin, London, 1980) and Benn, T., *Arguments for Democracy* (Cape, London, 1981).
22 Benn, *Arguments for Socialism*, p. 43.

3   Economic thought

Kevin Hickson

The inclusion of two chapters dealing directly with ideas in a book discussing the record of a government noted for its pragmatism may seem perverse. Both Jim Callaghan and Denis Healey were cautious pragmatists, rather than adherents to a particular economic doctrine. Moreover, the absence of a parliamentary majority for most of its existence ensured that the Government had to proceed cautiously, maintaining a working majority. However, the 1970s were a period of economic change in which the post-war Keynesian consensus was replaced by a government committed to New Right ideology in 1979. In his chapter Raymond Plant has noted the degree to which social democracy had been challenged and gradually replaced as the governing ideology by the New Right. The purpose of this chapter is to examine the nature of economic thinking within the Government.

Specifically, the chapter asks to what extent the Labour Government of 1974–9 embraced the economic theories advanced by those sympathetic to the New Right. Non-Keynesian ideas had been developed in the universities in Britain and the United States since at least the late 1950s. However, it was in the 1970s that these ideas were popularised in Britain in the media, in the output of think tanks such as the Institute of Economic Affairs and later the Adam Smith Institute and by Conservative politicians such as Keith Joseph.[1] This chapter outlines first the ideas which constituted collectively 'economic liberalism' and then goes on to discuss the thinking of senior ministers in general and of Healey in particular at the time of the 1976 IMF crisis, which was the episode when the Government's thinking on the economy became most exposed.

The chapter offers two arguments: first, that the Government did not introduce monetarism; second, that Healey in particular was influenced strongly by the crowding out thesis (i.e. that the growth of the public sector undermined national economic performance by taking resources away from the wealth-creating private sector). The first argument is not particularly original – Healey has asserted strongly that he was not convinced of the theoretical arguments outlined by monetarists and other commentators have accepted that Healey used targets for largely cosmetic reasons. The second argument is more original. Although there were passing references to the impact of the crowding out thesis on Healey at the time,[2] the point has been missed in subsequent accounts which have sought to argue that the most significant shift in policy at this time was away from the objective of maintaining full employment to reducing inflation, even at the cost of higher unemployment. The chapter argues in contrast that the most significant consideration in an examination of the economic thought of the Labour Government is the extent to which public expenditure was reduced.

Economic liberalism

The 1970s witnessed the emergence of a broad critique of Keynesian political economy in the form of economic liberalism. Economic liberalism was part of a wider philosophical critique of social democracy: the 'New Right'. The New Right consisted of neo-conservatives and neo-liberals, and sought to restate traditional political values in order to challenge the policies of the post-war consensus.[3] My concern here is with economic liberalism, which was that aspect of the New Right which sought to critique the role of government intervention in the economy. Economic liberalism can be defined as a broad movement against the existing mixed economy and in favour of a free market with minimal state intervention and comprises several distinct theories. I will therefore summarise the main elements of each theory and relate them to liberal economic thinking more generally. The leading figure in the rise of economic liberalism had been Hayek, and so I begin with a brief discussion of his work.

Hayek[4]

Friedrich von Hayek had been a long-standing critic of all forms of government intervention and all but a minimum level of welfare protection. He was a firm advocate of free market policies. However, this was not because he believed that the free market was a perfect model of economic activity, unlike the classical liberals, since he accepted that markets had imperfections, but he did believe them to be the best option available. This was so for two reasons. The first was his rejection of rationalist principles as the basis for public policy. Markets had not been invented by a deliberate act by individuals or by governments, but had in fact emerged spontaneously. This was important since it did not mean that markets were based on rationalist principles. Such principles cannot be based on objective foundations since they ultimately depend on subjectivist moral reasoning. Any measure based on such subjectivist foundations reflects the moral predilections of their originator, and in a morally pluralist society cannot reflect any general interest, only the interests of those who promote such a policy. It is therefore not possible to formulate principles of social or distributive justice. Such an argument has also been presented by Samuel Brittan in his work on public expenditure.[5] Given that it is not possible to establish general principles on which to distribute public expenditure, there will be a competition among particular interests for the distribution of resources. Public expenditure will therefore be directed to those who campaign the most effectively. Similarly, the public choice school argues that since the state does not act in the general interest, it seeks the allocation of resources in order to fulfil its own interests.[6] Only the market is capable of acting in the true public interest since it was created spontaneously and is not based on abstract principles.

The second reason why Hayek favoured free markets is that he was based in the 'Austrian school' of economic thought.[7] The Austrian school accepted the imperfection of the market, since economic activity took place between consumers with imperfect knowledge and companies with differing market shares. However, the Austrian school accepted the imperfect market model as the best that could be achieved, since the interaction of supply and demand was based on the free flow of knowledge, or information. The market allowed for alterations in consumer tastes and information automatically by allowing the level of prices to alter. The price mechanism is a means of demonstrating changing consumer tastes. Such knowledge, or information, for Hayek is largely subjective, or tacit, and is not therefore amenable to objective and explicit ratio-nalisation. This point is explained by Norman Barry:

> in a complex society knowledge (or information) is dispersed among millions of actors, each one of whom can only be acquainted only with that knowl-edge which affects him personally. The idea that social and economic knowledge (of production costs, consumer tastes, prices and so on) can be centralised in the mind of one person, or even in one institution, is an epis-temological absurdity for Hayek.[8]

Only the market therefore can allow the efficient spread of such information for Hayek, which in turn is essential for the preservation of human freedom. This point is echoed in the work of 'new classical' economists such as Lucas who argued that economic agents reach decisions rationally – that is as utility maximisers – and do so after taking account of the likely effects of government policy. This assertion led the new classical school to reject government interven-tion on the basis that changes in policy would have predictable results and would therefore be discounted by economic agents in the market. For example, varia-tions in the rate of public spending would inevitably mean changes in the level of taxation later so that short-term counter-cyclical fiscal policy as advocated by Keynesians would have little or no effect and could even make situations worse. The policy response advocated by the new classical school would be the setting of targets for both fiscal and monetary policy.

The assertion that markets occurred spontaneously and that human knowl-edge is not subject to rationalist principles is a strong argument in favour of free markets, especially when combined with the more overtly political arguments from the neo-liberals concerning the nature of rights and justice, and forms the basis of a wholesale rejection of the mixed economy.[9] Indeed, as Norman Barry makes clear, the operation of the free market is so efficient that, 'for liberal polit-ical economy, it is clear that dislocations and break-downs in the market system can only occur through impediments to the exchange process'.[10] There are specifically two impediments that economic liberals tend to emphasise. The first is the state. State intervention is wrong because it is not possible to plan the economy in a given way due to the nature of human knowledge, as outlined above. Moreover, given the absence of any objective basis for the allocation and distribution of resources, the state will be faced by competing demands from sectional interests. Ultimately, this will destroy the legitimacy of political institutions and the efficiency of the free market. The second impediment concerns the role of the trade unions, which distort the pricing mechanism of the labour market, undermine the free supply of labour and coerce employers into accepting certain rates of pay, conditions of work and under a closed shop arrangement as operated in Britain in the 1970s ensure that the trade union has a monopoly on the representation of a workforce. The drift of post-war policy was towards intervention. The economic liberals therefore demanded nothing less than the rejection of post-war orthodoxy. I now wish to discuss further three particular elements of economic liberalism that have a direct bearing on the following discussion of the IMF crisis: monetarism, crowding out thesis and supply side theory.

Monetarism

The most widely known idea within economic liberalism was that of monetarism. Monetarism developed first in the United States, particularly at the University of Chicago with Milton Friedman and his associates. It became more popular in Britain in the 1970s with the output of the IEA and the journalism of Samuel Brittan in the *Financial Times* and Peter Jay in *The Times* and the academic studies of Laidler and Parkin among others.[11] The central assertion of monetarism was that inflation was caused by excess growth in the money supply. Following the writing of Friedman[12] we can take as our starting point the quantity theory of money and the equation formulated by Irving Fisher nearly 100 years ago:

$$MV = PQ$$

MV represents the stock of money multiplied by its velocity of circulation, which is equal to the nominal national product (*PQ*). This was a simple identity that represented in the form of an equation the circular flow of income. The significance of monetarist theory, and in particular the writings of Friedman, is the connection made between the money supply and inflation. Friedman believed that evidence of US monetary policy showed that the velocity of circulation is either constant or moves in the same direction as the stock of money. A rise in the money supply will therefore result in higher inflation in the long run since output cannot increase. Friedman claimed that he had gathered sufficient evidence to support this thesis, although others disagreed.[13] There was a clear implication to be drawn from this, which was that the use of fiscal deficits to boost economic performance, a policy advocated by Keynesians, only resulted in higher inflation in the long run.

Friedman therefore rejected a central part of post-war economic wisdom, the Phillips curve, which suggested that there was a trade-off between inflation and unemployment. Although not a specifically Keynesian idea, the curve had been used by Keynesians to justify demand management policies. Governments could choose between varying rates of inflation and unemployment. Friedman rejected this logic saying that government intervention in the form of fiscal expansion to finance measures designed to raise aggregate demand and reduce unemployment would only result in a short-term reduction. This was because deficit financing would result in growth in the money supply and raise the rate of inflation. As people adjusted to this rise in inflation unemployment would shift back to the long-term rate but at a higher level of inflation. This was the so-called 'expectations-augmented Phillips curve' and was used to explain the occurrence of 'stagflation' – simultaneously rising levels of unemployment and inflation – in the 1970s.

Monetarism was an integral part of economic liberalism in the 1970s. First, the logic of the expectations-augmented Phillips curve led monetarists to reject the Keynesian notion of the manipulation of demand to promote and maintain full employment. In turn, the monetarist explanation of the underlying cause of inflation had political implications for policy makers. The argument that a rise in the money supply will result in higher inflation rests on the assumption that output will stabilise at a long-term 'natural' rate.[14] If this assumption is dropped then there is no reason why a rise in the money supply will not feed through into higher output, or a combination of higher output and prices. In the 'natural rate' model this assumption is explicit, with monetarists arguing that unemployment can be reduced only through intervention on the supply side of the economy: that is, abolition of wages councils, reduction of trades union power and so forth. The importance of monetarism to economic liberalism was made most clearly by Tim Congdon, who argued that monetarists rightly emphasised the need for stable prices to facilitate the flow of knowledge in the market economy.[15] The argument that free markets were the only mechanism to allow for the spread of knowledge and thereby the maximisation of consumer preferences was the core of Hayek's defence of laissez-faire capitalism.

Crowding out thesis

The second economic theory I wish to discuss is the 'crowding out' thesis, which again became popular in the 1970s. The basic argument was that the growth of the public sector had the effect of undermining British economic performance by taking resources away from the wealth-creating private sector. The crowding out thesis was an attempt to address the relative decline of the British economy in the post-war period, a fact that was becoming readily apparent in the 1970s. In this sense, crowding out arguments can be seen as part of a much wider concern with decline.[16]

Specifically, there were two distinct elements of the crowding out thesis. The first was the notion of 'financial' crowding out. This idea was developed by the monetarists as a further argument against deficit financing. The idea again began to emerge in the United States before being popularised in Britain by journalists, notably Tim Congdon.[17] The argument runs that public sector borrowing crowds out the private sector by taking resources, in the form of speculative and investment capital, away from the wealth-creating private sector of the economy and raises the rate of interest so as to deter the private sector from borrowing. The crowding out argument was a critique of Keynesian notions that public sector expansion added to national output. Instead, the expansion of the public sector undermined private sector growth by taking away resources that could have gone into the wealth-creating private sector. Fiscal expansion could therefore result in lower rates of economic growth. Although this became a key part of the monetarist critique, it should be noted that it was neutral on the issue of public expenditure, at least to the extent that it was primarily concerned with public sector deficits. Far more explicit on the issue of public expenditure was the 'physical' crowding out thesis put forward by Bacon and Eltis.[18] The Bacon and Eltis argument became very popular at this time through the publication of a series of articles in the press. Bacon and Eltis argued that the expansion of the public sector, which had occurred at a dramatic rate in the 1960s and early 1970s, had a damaging impact on the wealth-creating private sector by taking resources, in the form of labour, away from industry. There was a clear policy implication in the physical crowding out thesis: that governments must cut taxes and expenditure in order to reduce the size of the public sector and thereby free resources for the use of the private sector.

It must be stressed clearly at this stage in the argument that the crowding out thesis was an integral part of the economic liberal paradigm. A similar resources argument had been made by early exponents of the Alternative Economic Strategy (AES). Certain left-wing economists, mainly those associated with the Cambridge Economic Policy Group, had argued in the early 1970s that the growth in the public sector had a crowding out effect by undermining the capacity of manufacturers to export, thus causing a deficit in the balance of payments. This was a rather technical argument, seeking to show a statistical relationship between the balance of payments and the PSBR, and was not in any case a core part of the AES with its emphasis on protectionism and was later rejected by the Cambridge economists themselves. At a superficial level the Bacon and Eltis thesis was also similar to traditional Labour concerns with the productivity of the manufacturing sector.[19] The centre–right of the Labour Party had always been concerned with manufacturing output since the Attlee Governments and was keen to ensure that increases in welfare expenditure did not impact on manufacturing. However, the Bacon and Eltis thesis was different in that it sought to establish a causal relationship between the growth of the public sector and the decline of manufacturing. The explicit argument was that the public sector was too large and ought to be reduced. Hence, the monetarist and crowding out theses were both integral parts of the wider economic liberal paradigm, seeking to reduce the role of the state in the economy. Monetarism sought to undermine the rationale for state intervention to reduce unemployment and the crowding out thesis provided a further argument for cutting public expenditure. Given that the chapter goes on to assert that the Bacon and Eltis thesis was influential in the economic thinking of the Labour Government, one further point should be made at this stage. This is that the argument made by Bacon and Eltis was widely criticised, in particular for failing to prove the central causal relationship asserted in the thesis that there was a link between the growth of the public sector and the decline of the British economy. Instead it was pointed out that the growth in the public sector may equally have been the result of the decline in the economy.[20] The Bacon and Eltis thesis thus failed to demonstrate the causal link asserted in the thesis and the argument was rejected at the time by several economists and has not really been taken seriously since.

Supply side theory

Supply side theory, as developed in the 1970s, comprised two elements. The first was a concern with taxation, while the second was concerned with the labour market. Both, however, emphasised the importance of incentives and were concerned explicitly with the reduction of state intervention. The supply side approach to taxation was most clearly elaborated by Arthur Laffer.[21] According to Laffer, there is a strong relationship between direct taxation and incentives. As income tax rates increase there is a disincentive to work, and so total tax yield declines as people work less. Equally, tax yield will increase with rising tax rates up until the point at which people begin to feel that there is a disincentive to further work. There is therefore a 'tax rate structure which maximises government tax receipts'.[22] Although there is a definite point at which tax revenue is maximised, this point will in fact vary with cultural and historical circumstance.[23] Two points follow from this. The first is that tax rates have to be introduced with the consent of taxpayers. Second, it is likely that lower tax rates will increase economic output, so that tax cuts for higher earners will benefit the poor through the 'trickle-down' effect. Similar arguments were advanced by US commentators regarding other forms of taxation, specifically corporate taxes which were seen as having a disincentive effect on business activity.[24]

The second element of supply side theory concerned the labour market. The basic assertion was that British economic performance, which had been lagging behind that of major competitors throughout the post-war period, was largely due to the persistence of supply side problems. In this sense, economic liberalism and the AES, which was being advanced by the Labour left at this time, were in agreement since both regarded Keynesian demand management as ineffective given the inefficiencies present in industry.[25] However, it was over the exact nature of the supply side difficulties, and therefore remedies, where the AES and economic liberalism differed. For advocates of the AES the problem was the alienation of the worker, and the remedy was therefore to be found in a radical extension of public ownership and industrial democracy. In contrast, the economic liberals emphasised the barriers to the operation of the free labour market. It was necessary to restore individual incentives and to remove the collectivist and coercive barriers within the labour market. In terms of policy, this came to mean two things above all others. First, the reduction in the power of trade unions in order to restore a true market price for labour and the reduction in workers' privileges in order to make them more responsive to changes in market rates. Second, the reduction of both the scope and the level of welfare benefits in order to make employment more attractive financially. Increasingly, a moral argument was added to this by neo-conservatives that benefit payments should be reduced as this created a culture of welfare dependency and reduced individual responsibility.

The IMF crisis

Having outlined the major developments in economic thought in the 1970s, the chapter proceeds by analysing the main ideas within the Government and the Treasury during the 1976 IMF crisis. Before going on to look at the thinking of Healey and other senior ministers, it is first necessary to recap on the main developments leading to the 1976 IMF crisis. The chapter, for reasons of space, does not discuss at length the narrative of events, which is covered adequately elsewhere.[26] Two points need to be re-emphasised in the conduct of economic policy in the period 1974–76. The first is that the British economy had been under severe constraint from international developments since the Labour Party came to power in 1974. The second is that many of the reforms often said to have originated with the intervention of the IMF in late 1976 were in fact introduced much earlier

Strictly speaking the IMF crisis refers to the period from October to December 1976, during which time the Government negotiated with the IMF and the Cabinet debated the likely conditions which would be attached to the loan. However, to see these events in isolation from the wider conduct of economic policy since 1974 would be misleading since the crisis was to emerge more gradually. The Labour Government began to cut public expenditure in April 1975, against the manifesto commitments expressed the previous year. In fact, Healey had raised expenditure in 1974 and the first quarter of 1975. The policy reversal came in April 1975 when the first cuts were made. The reason for this reversal of policy can be found in the wider international context. Healey had earlier raised expenditure, and with it the PSBR in line with advice from the IMF. As Mark Harmon has shown, Johannes Witteveen, the Managing Director of the IMF, had urged the major industrialised countries to raise expenditure in response to the OPEC price shocks.[27] He did so in line with Keynesian analysis, since he thought that the main impact of the oil price rises would be in raising the level of unemployment. Deficit financing would avoid a world-wide recession, even at the cost of moderate inflation. However, at meetings of the IMF Executive and elsewhere, Witteveen came under the sustained pressure of US financial authorities, particularly William Simon and Arthur Burns, the Treasury Secretary and Chairman of the Federal Reserve respectively, to argue for the reduction of deficits. The United States argued that the oil price increases were important since they added to inflationary pressures already present in the international economy. Governments should therefore seek to reduce inflationary pressures by reducing public sector deficits, the US argued. Healey's attempts to create new international credit facilities with limited conditionality met with the opposition of the United States and to a lesser extent West Germany. Witteveen himself came round to supporting deficit-reduction strategies in the face of US pressure.

Healey therefore began to cut the PSBR from April 1975 in response to international pressure and to deteriorating economic variables.[28] The process of cutting public expenditure was assisted by the introduction of 'cash limits' in 1975. Previous budgetary allocations had been allocated in real terms so that the Treasury would cover the rising cost of departmental programmes. In contrast, cash limits sought to control the level of expenditure by imposing a nominal figure on public spending allocations, which meant that the Treasury would not fund additional costs.[29] In 1975 cash limits were implemented in building programmes. As well as constricting expenditure directly, it also had the indirect effect of creating under-spending as departments sought to avoid overshooting their allocations, which amounted to cuts greater than those in the actual packages. Both budgetary decisions and cash limits therefore had the effect of cutting public expenditure prior to IMF intervention. An additional measure was announced by Wilson that the Treasury could not be overruled in Cabinet committees on spending decisions. This would mean that ministers who opposed spending plans formulated by the Treasury would have to go to the full Cabinet, with less chance of getting agreement for additional spending. The relative power of the Treasury was further increased by the inclusion of the First Secretary to the Treasury, Joel Barnett, in the Cabinet. These measures were followed by further reductions in public expenditure in the January 1976 Public Expenditure White Paper,[30] implemented after prolonged Cabinet debate in late 1975 and totalling £1 billion in 1977–8 and £2.4 billion in 1978–9. By the end of February, the Treasury felt that the economy had improved significantly since Labour came to power, with public expenditure now under control. In addition, the Government had negotiated incomes policy in the spring of 1975, seen as the main way of reducing inflation.

However, as the head of the public expenditure section of the Treasury, Leo Pliatzky, pointed out, it was at this time that the pound came under sustained pressure on the currency markets.[31] The pound had been rising in value and it appears that the Treasury and the Bank of England agreed to act in order to avoid a further appreciation of sterling, which they felt would damage British manufacturing competitiveness. This was done by selling sterling on 4 March and then reducing the minimum lending rate the following day. Although Healey argued that he had not been consulted, it seems unlikely that these decisions would not have been taken without his consent.[32] What should have been a technical adjustment turned out to be a rout as the markets interpreted the move as a way of achieving depreciation. The pound fell in value over the course of 1976 from $1.91 on 10 March to $1.63 by 28 September.

The conduct of economic policy from March was therefore concerned to stop the slide in the value of sterling. The Government decided that in order to restore international confidence it was necessary to reduce the PSBR and the rate of inflation still further and to correct the balance of payments deficit. This was delayed by the sudden resignation of Wilson on 16 March, precipitating a lengthy leadership contest, which Callaghan eventually won on the third ballot on 5 April. Healey announced the extension of cash limits in the spring to cover nearly 75 per cent of public expenditure (the main area of spending exempted from cash limits was social security). A second year of pay restraint was agreed with the trade unions in May and an international credit facility totalling $5.3 billion was secured in June. However, the pound continued to slide so a further package of public expenditure cuts was announced in July totalling £1 billion with a further £1 billion increase in National Insurance. The measures were opposed by many in the Cabinet including Tony Benn and Tony Crosland. In many ways the debates were similar to those in November–December, so there is no need to say any more here. The measures were seen by the Cabinet, and probably Healey himself, as sufficient to restore the value of sterling. The Government also published monetary targets for the first time. During August the pound stabilised, but downward pressure resumed in September. Healey therefore announced his decision to approach the IMF at the Labour Party Conference. From October to December the Treasury negotiated with the IMF visiting delegation and the Cabinet debated the terms the IMF were likely to demand, notably further cuts in public expenditure.

Before going on to examine Healey's views in greater detail it is necessary to look briefly at the views of other leading members of the Cabinet and at Healey's response to them, which helps us to understand Healey's opinions. First, Tony Benn argued that the Government should oppose cuts and negotiate with the IMF on the basis of the AES, including large-scale import quotas, together with compulsory planning agreements with private companies, the extension of public ownership and so forth.[33] A more moderate proposal came from Peter Shore who argued for selective import restraints in the form of selective import deposits and for the Government to refuse publication of the balance of payments account for two years.[34] However, both failed to convince the Cabinet. Benn's proposals in particular appeared to Cabinet colleagues to lack a sense of realism, with an international climate hostile to any such measures. Moreover, both proposals, resting as they did on import restraint, had, Healey argued, employment implications that offset any benefits they could attain. Healey was to be consistent in the Cabinet in voicing his opposition to the AES, and particularly the protectionist measures that it proposed. He was supportive instead of an open international trading order.

Tony Crosland put forward an alternative proposal outlining the real economic improvements achieved over the course of the preceding 12–18 months, with lower inflation, PSBR and balance of payments deficit.[35] Moreover, Crosland argued that many of the measures agreed had yet to be implemented and the IMF should be made aware of this. He went on to say that further cuts would be counterproductive since they would increase unemployment, thereby adding to the PSBR by cutting tax revenue and raising social security expenditure, and destroying the Social Contract with the trade unions. Against criticism that he did not allow scope for bargaining with the IMF he proposed limited cuts and threats of withdrawing the troops from Cyprus and the Rhine and cutting EEC contributions. By the end of November, Crosland had shifted again to advocate moderate import deposits. Although he argued that this would result in some unemployment, the introduction of selective measures would offset any impact on unemployment figures. In his memoirs, Healey concedes that Crosland's economic analysis was essentially correct, but he had not taken account of the importance of financial confidence. In fact, at the time Healey was to also criticise Crosland's essentially Keynesian analysis by raising the resources argument. Although he had some initial support, Crosland was to be almost completely isolated as his support shifted to Healey. Shirley Williams and Bill Rodgers were opposed to measures which, they believed, threatened Britain's international military role and apparent commitment to the EEC. Williams also voiced concern over the impact of trade restrictions to the Third World and Williams, Rodgers and Harold Lever argued for the principle of free trade.[36] Only Roy Hattersley was left supporting Crosland by the end of November.[37] Meanwhile the left refused to support Crosland's moderate embrace of trade restrictions for largely political reasons. Crosland came under pressure to back down, which he did in Cabinet on 2 December, after the Benn and Shore proposals had been rejected by the Cabinet the previous day and Callaghan had stated his support for Healey.

These were the two proposed alternatives to the strategy of public expenditure cuts. They were clearly related to currents in economic thought at the time. The main fault line in centre–left thinking on the economy in the 1970s concerned the nature of international trade and finance. Keynesian economists close to the Government had supported an open international trading order. Initially, this was the position taken by Crosland, at least until the end of November when he came round to supporting modest import deposits. A new strand of left-Keynesianism had emerged in the 1970s, advocates of which argued, following Stuart Holland,[38] that the development of large-scale multinational corporations had reduced the capacity of national governments to manage the domestic economy along Keynesian lines free from the intervention of private corporations. Added to this was the increased flow of international transactions, which had made exchange rates much less stable. Left-Keynesians therefore came to advocate the AES, a broad economic framework which combined national economic protection with conventional Keynesian techniques. Differing attitudes towards the international trading order therefore became a major point of contention, as seen in the differing responses of Crosland, Benn and Shore to the IMF loan. Given that Healey was strongly critical of Benn it would appear unlikely that Healey gave much credence to the AES. Given that he was also critical of the Shore and Crosland positions, we can say that his own position was a shift away from Keynesian economics.

Callaghan's position is slightly more difficult to define.[39] His concerns were largely political. His first objective, successfully achieved, was to hold together his

Cabinet and ultimately the Labour Government. This was achieved by allowing Cabinet discussions to drag on over several weeks, thus allowing the arguments to run their course and to allow all those who held a particular view the opportunity to express it. His other explicitly political motive was to attempt to build international support for the approach of the British Government, particularly in the United States and West Germany where he hoped that his political friends would exert some pressure on their financial ministers and central banking officials to soften their attitudes. This was of more limited use as both West Germany and the United States continued to demand cuts and refused to accept an agreement on sterling deposits until after an agreement was reached with the IMF on the loan. Given that Callaghan was concerned with the political situation, it seems unlikely that his famous 1976 Labour Party Conference speech was truly an endorsement of monetarist economics. His speech was interpreted as such by many left-wing critics of the 1974–9 Government.[40] Yet it is unlikely that a politician with a pragmatic nature like Callaghan would entertain seriously economic doctrine of any kind. Indeed, Callaghan sees his speech in a different context, saying that he had two aims: to issue a warning to the Labour left who had been pushing through motions in favour of further public ownership and increased spending, apparently unaware of the international situation, and to help to restore international confidence.[41] Whether it was wise to do so in this way is another matter, and Healey, who claims that he did not know about the speech in advance, felt certain that it did not help.

Turning to Healey, it becomes apparent that he was interested in economic theories, but not in the way that is usually understood. According to Adrian Ham, Healey's senior economic adviser, Healey was interested in economic theory as a way of formulating decisive policies. He did not want to be overtaken by events.[42] Healey is often seen, particularly by left-wing critics, as a monetarist Chancellor. Indeed, the first monetarist Chancellor, enacting large parts of the economic framework associated with Thatcher and Howe after 1979. Monetarism is seen to date from 1976, largely as a result of the introduction of monetary targets. However, such an interpretation is misconceived. Monetary targets in themselves do not equate to the introduction of a monetarist framework. Instead, it is best to see the adoption of targets as a cosmetic exercise. It seems unlikely that Healey took the targets seriously, but instead regarded them as necessary to restore international confidence. In contrast, monetarism requires the adoption of clearly stated targets as the central objective of policy, as with the Medium Term Financial Strategy (MTFS) after 1979 and arguably with New Labour. Healey simply did not take the targets seriously, at least in terms of domestic economic policy. A more accurate term was that used by Samuel Brittan at the time: Healey was an 'unbelieving monetarist'.[43]

The use of the term 'unbelieving monetarist' is useful in that it questions the extent to which Healey had endorsed monetarist doctrine. However, it fails to identify one influential strand of economic thought. This is the physical crowding out thesis developed by Bacon and Eltis, which had a major impact on Healey's approach to policy in the IMF crisis. Before going on to examine this point further, it is first necessary to state briefly two other reasons why we can say that Healey was not influenced by monetarism. First, he did not accept the 'natural rate' hypothesis. Although he accepted that unemployment would rise as a result of public expenditure cuts, he did introduce with Albert Booth, the Employment Secretary, a package of measures designed to limit the effect on unemployment levels.[44] Moreover, in 1977 and 1978, Healey raised expenditure in an attempt to reverse some of the damage done in 1975–6, albeit still within targets agreed with the IMF. The argument that the Labour Government abandoned full employment policy is exaggerated. Second, Healey continued with the policy of wage restraint he had negotiated in 1975–6 in an attempt to reduce further inflation. If he had accepted monetarist theory, there would have been no need for this since monetarists reject explicitly the causal relationship between wages and prices. Instead, inflation is caused by excessive growth in the money supply. Thus, far from being a monetarist policy, the Social Contract was neo-Keynesian in origin.[45] For these reasons therefore it is possible to reject the interpretation of Healey as a monetarist.

Let us now turn once again to the crowding out thesis developed by Bacon and Eltis, where it is possible to detect the influence of these ideas on Healey at this time. The crowding out thesis had clear implications for the level of public expenditure as we have seen, differing in crucial ways from the AES and earlier Labour concerns with manufacturing. There are several reasons why we can say that Healey was influenced by the crowding out thesis. First, Healey is quoted as saying that the view expressed by Bacon and Eltis was the 'most stimulating and comprehensive analysis of our economic predicament which I have yet seen in a newspaper'.[46] According to Ham, Healey would set out his objectives and then utilise economic theories in order to support his objectives and to undermine the arguments of his opponents. As Ham contends, the crowding out thesis was used in this way: 'Healey would use every argument that came to hand, and the crowding out thesis was a good one.'[47] Healey therefore used the crowding out thesis as a political weapon. He needed an argument to use against those within the Cabinet who opposed cuts and the crowding out thesis was useful in this context.

Indeed, it is possible to develop this argument by adding that Healey endorsed the crowding out thesis as a guide to policy: that is, that he came to accept the underlying argument of crowding out. Healey asked senior Treasury officials to produce papers on the crowding out thesis, and how it applied to policy.[48] This was done in 1975 in the run-up to the debates over cuts at the end of the year. Healey had argued, as we have seen, consistently for cuts to public expenditure since April 1975. Increasingly over the course of 1976, two arguments were made to support cuts. The first was the need to restore international confidence. The second was the need to free resources for the use of the private sector. In making this argument Healey was raising the crowding out thesis. He was supported within the Treasury by Alan Lord and Derek Mitchell and from within the Cabinet by Edmund Dell. Indeed, Dell was a firm advocate of the crowding out thesis as he makes clear in his own account of the crisis.[49] Dell was to be, with Reg Prentice, a firm supporter of Healey, with the latter arguing that the cuts agreed in December did not go far enough. Dell was an expert economist and Healey appears to have welcomed his support and advice.[50] Dell was to be the leading critic of the essentially Keynesian position put forward by Crosland, as was seen in a meeting at 10 Downing Street on 18 November when Dell put forward the resources argument in full as a critique of Crosland's argument against cuts.

Supply side theory also played a role in Healey's policy stance at this time, although to a lesser extent than the crowding out thesis. Healey argued that there was a need to restore industrial competitiveness and an emphasis was placed on supply side reforms. This did not mark a shift to the right in industrial policy, however, since it has been noted that advocates of the AES also came to emphasise the importance of supply side reform and policy was based on a tripartite model bringing the trade unions, the Government and the private sector together. A more overtly political argument was made by Healey, however, in the Cabinet meetings of 6–15 December when it was being decided where the cuts should fall.[51] Healey argued for the need to reduce, or at least limit, the increases in benefits and also to reduce direct taxation as the working classes were hostile to the material conditions of benefit claimants and that this was having a disincentive effect on the unemployed. The significance of this should not be overstated as it is unclear what impact these arguments had on policy, with the majority of cuts falling on capital projects and social security being protected.

Conclusion

It has been the main argument of this chapter that the 1976 IMF crisis marked a turning point in post-war political economy. It is usually argued that monetarism was incorporated into British economic policy at this time, but this chapter has shown that this argument is misguided and with it the assertion that the Government abandoned the objective of full employment has been exaggerated. Instead it has been asserted that Healey was influenced by the crowding out thesis and to a lesser extent by neo-liberal supply side arguments. First, this was as a means of criticising his Cabinet colleagues who opposed cuts. Second, more controversially it is suggested that Healey accepted the essential causal argument of the crowding out thesis that rising levels of public expenditure undermined wealth creation in the private sector. The publication of the official papers on the IMF crisis in 2007 will help establish this argument by showing the attitudes of key ministers and officials in private negotiations. The objective of reducing public expenditure was met by the Government.[52]

The longer-term implications varied. On the one hand the crowding out thesis was, as has been noted, criticised and has since been rejected. Monetarism was more important in the conduct of policy after 1979, along with other aspects of economic liberalism and neo-conservatism. A long-term significance of this shift, however, has been in the growth of income inequality, which began around

1976 with rising unemployment and reductions in public expenditure. As Roy Hattersley has said, 'the Labour Party lost its faith in public expenditure'.[53] This is a controversial claim, yet like most controversial claims it does contain an element of truth. Certainly the Labour left did not lose their faith in higher public expenditure, and continued to advocate large increases in spending and public ownership, without reference to economic conditions. Yet the right of the Party did begin to move away from a commitment to social equality, or at least the Croslandite commitment to obtaining greater social equality through higher levels of expenditure.[54] Traditional, universalist, spending commitments gave way to more selective measures and a greater emphasis on the voluntary sector. This can be seen in policy post-1976, since the increases in expenditure in 1977–8, were within limits agreed with the IMF.

Moreover, similar commitments can be found in New Labour's approach to public services and to redistribution. One of the major differences between 'old-style' social democracy, represented by the leading figures in the 1974–9 Government, and New Labour is the attitude to the so-called 'third sector', that is the charitable sector of the economy. New Labour sees a much bigger role for charitable provision in core services, as a more localised and consumer responsive set of institutions than state provision. This is a relatively new development within social democracy since the traditional right of the Labour Party regarded equal provision, which in turn meant centrally controlled provision, of welfare as the means of achieving greater social and economic equality. Many on the traditional right of the Labour Party regarded charities with some scepticism – as an alternative to the state. New Labour has redistributed substantially in its first term by a means of complex welfare and fiscal reforms and in the second term by a more conventional means of National Insurance increases. However, this has been sufficient only to maintain levels of inequality at the 1997 level. Indeed, New Labour is ambiguous on the issue of substantive inequalities. Although the crowding out thesis has been rejected by academic economists and has not been a conscious part of economic policy making since, it is still possible therefore to see the effects of the shift in attitudes to economic management and the public sector in the years 1974–9 today.

Notes

1   The development of ideas and the output of think tanks at this time are well covered in Cockett, R., *Thinking the Unthinkable: Think-tanks and the Economic Counter-revolution 1931–1983* (HarperCollins, London, 1994) and Denham, A. and Garnett, M., *British Think-tanks and the Climate of Opinion* (UCL Press, London, 1998).

2   See, for example, Hadjimatheou, G. and Skouras, A., 'Britain's Economic Problem: The Growth of the Non-market Sector', *Economic Journal*, 89, June 1979, pp. 392–401. More recently Robert Skidelsky and Peter Jackson have made passing comments to the significance of the crowding out thesis. See Skidelsky, R., 'The Fall of Keynesianism', in Marquand, D. and Seldon, A. (eds), *The Ideas that Shaped Post-war Britain* (Fontana, London, 1996) and Jackson, P.M., 'Public Expenditure', in Artis, M. and Cobham, D. (eds), *Labour's Economic Policies, 1974–79* (Manchester University Press, Manchester, 1991).

3 I define neo-liberals as those who wanted to restore political and economic freedoms and who defined freedom negatively, that is freedom from external constraint. By neo-conservative I mean those who thought that there had been a decline in moral values in the 1960s in particular. Both groups were part of the New Right although there were clearly major differences between them, particularly over the role of the state. See Gamble, A., *The Free Economy and the Strong State: The Politics of Thatcherism* (Macmillan, London, 1988), ch. 2.

4 My discussion is based on Barry, N., *Hayek's Social and Economic Philosophy* (Macmillan, London, 1979) and Barry, N., *The New Right* (Croom Helm, Beckenham, 1987).

5 Brittan, S., *The Economic Consequences of Democracy* (Temple Smith, London, 1977).

6 For a discussion of the public choice school see Hoover, K. and Plant, R., *Conservative Capitalism in Britain and the United States: A Critical Appraisal* (Routledge, London, 1989), pp. 60–70.

7 Other leading members of the Austrian school included Carl Menger and Ludwig von Mises.

8 Barry, *The New Right*, p. 30.

9 For a discussion and powerful critique of Hayek's political philosophical position see Plant, R., *Modern Political Thought* (Blackwell, Oxford, 1991).

10 Barry, *The New Right*, p. 40.

11 See Britton, A.J.C., *Macroeconomic Policy in Britain 1974–1987* (Cambridge University Press, Cambridge, 1991), pp. 93–104, for a more detailed discussion of these ideas.

12 See, in particular, Friedman, M., 'The Role of Monetary Policy', *The American Economic Review*, LVIII, 1968, pp. 3–15; Friedman, M., 'The Counter-revolution in Monetary Theory', IEA Occasional Paper No. 33, Institute of Economic Affairs, London, 1972; Friedman, M., 'Unemployment Versus Inflation? An Evaluation of the Phillips Curve', IEA Occasional Paper No. 44, Institute of Economic Affairs, London, 1975; Friedman, M., 'Inflation and Unemployment: The New Dimension in Politics', IEA Occasional Paper No. 51, Institute of Economic Affairs, London, 1976.

13 Notably, Hendry, D. and Ericson, N., *Monetary Trends in the UK* (Bank of England Panel of Academic Consultants, London, 1983).

14 The term 'natural rate' was used by Friedman, but has since normally been termed the NAIRU (Non-Accelerated Inflation Rate of Unemployment).

15 Congdon, T., *Monetarism: An Essay in Definition* (Centre for Policy Studies, London, 1978), pp. 75–83.

16 See Gamble, A., *Britain in Decline: Economic Policy, Political Strategy and the British State* (Macmillan, London, 1st edition, 1981) for a discussion of New Right ideas in relation to relative economic decline.

17 See Congdon, T., 'Monetarism and the Budget Deficit' (1976), reprinted in Congdon, T., *Reflections on Monetarism: Britain's Vain Search for a Successful Economic Strategy* (Edward Elgar, Aldershot, 1992).

18 Bacon, R. and Eltis, W., *Britain's Economic Problem: Too Few Producers* (Macmillan, Basingstoke, 2nd edition, 1978). See also Eltis, W., 'The Need to Cut Public Expenditure and Taxation', in Minford, P., Rose, H., Eltis, W., Perlman, P. and Burton, J., *Is Monetarism Enough? Essays in Refining and Reinforcing the Monetary Cure for Inflation* (Institute of Economic Affairs, London, 1980).

19 I am grateful to Jim Tomlinson for this point.

20 See Hadjimatheou and Skouras, 'Britain's Economic Problem: The Growth of the Non-market Sector'; Bosanquet, N., 'Has Manufacturing Been "Crowded Out"?', *Socialist Commentary*, January 1977, pp. 4–5.

21 Canto, V., Joines, D. and Laffer, A., 'Tax Rates, Factor Employment, Market Production and Welfare', in Canto, V., Joines, D. and Laffer, A. (eds), *Foundations of Supply-side Economics: Theory and Evidence* (Academic Press, New York, 1983), pp. 1–24.

22 Ibid., p. 23.

23 Wanniski, J., 'Taxes, Revenues and the "Laffer Curve"', *Public Interest*, 50, 1979, pp. 3–16.

24 See Blyth, M., *Economic Ideas and Institutional Change in the Twentieth Century* (Cambridge University Press, New York, 2002), pp. 152–61, for a detailed discussion of the growth of supply side ideas in the United States.

25 For which see Hodgson, G., *The Democratic Economy* (Penguin, Harmondsworth, 1984).

26 Burk, K. and Cairncross, A., *'Goodbye, Great Britain': The 1976 IMF Crisis* (Yale University Press, New Haven, CT, 1992); Harmon, M.D., *The British Labour Government and the 1976 IMF Crisis* (Macmillan, London, 1997); and Hickson, K., '1976 IMF Crisis and British Politics', (forthcoming 2004, IB Tauris).

27 Harmon, *The British Labour Government and the 1976 IMF Crisis*, pp. 62–78, 121–30.

28 Figures published on 19 February showed that wages had risen on average by 29 per cent in 1974, the rate of inflation was 25.4 per cent in April 1975 and the previous budget of November 1974 had increased the PSBR by a further £800 million.

29 For details see Pliatzky, L., *Getting and Spending: Public Expenditure, Employment and Inflation* (Blackwell, Oxford, 1982), pp. 143–7.

30 Cmnd 6393, 1976.

31 Pliatzky, *Getting and Spending*, p. 148.

32 Private information from former senior Bank of England official.

33 Benn, T., *Against the Tide: Diaries 1973–76* (Arrow, London, 1989), pp. 661–9. Interviews with Tony Benn (28 February 2000, telephone) and Albert Booth (2 May 2001, London).

34 Interview with Peter Shore (30 January 2001, London).

35 Jefferys, K., *Anthony Crosland: A New Biography* (Cohen, London, 1999), pp. 207–16; Crosland, S., *Tony Crosland* (Cape, London, 1982), pp. 374–83.

36 Interviews with Baroness Williams (21 November 2000, London) and Lord Rodgers (19 March 2001, London).

37 Interview with Lord Hattersley (31 October 2000, London).

38 Holland, S., *The Socialist Challenge* (Quartet, London, 1975).

39 The most authoritative account of Callaghan's views at this time is Morgan, K.O., *Callaghan: A Life* (Oxford University Press, Oxford, 1997). I am also grateful for my discussions with Lord Morgan on this issue.

40 See for example the contributions in Coates, K. (ed.), *What Went Wrong: Explaining the Fall of the Labour Government* (Spokesman, Nottingham, 1979).

41 Written information from James Callaghan, 6 June 2000.

42 Interview with Adrian Ham (15 August 2002, London).

43 The term 'unbelieving monetarist' was used frequently by Brittan in his columns in the *Financial Times*. The more recent use of the term 'pragmatic monetarist' by Pepper and Oliver therefore adds nothing new, in what is a rather uninteresting discussion of monetary policy during the 1980s. See Pepper, G..T. and Oliver, M.J., *Monetarism Under Thatcher: Lessons for the Future* (Edward Elgar, Cheltenham, 2001), pp. xxvi–xxviii.

44 Interview with Albert Booth.

45 Monetarists do see a role for the stabilisation of wages, which is that uncontrolled growth in wages reduces company profits. This though does not take away from the argument that the Government's concern with incomes policy was neo-Keynesian since it was seen as the main anti-inflationary weapon.

46 Bosanquet, 'Has Manufacturing Been "Crowded Out"?', p. 4.

47 Interview with Adrian Ham.

48 Private information.

49 Dell, E., *A Hard Pounding: Politics and Economic Crisis 1974–6* (Oxford University Press, Oxford, 1991), pp. 256–8.

50 Healey, D., *The Time of My Life* (Penguin, London, 2nd edition, 1990), p. 431.

51 Benn, *Against the Tide*, makes this point in his diary entries for this period.

52 In this, the Government was largely successful. Public expenditure was cut from 44.9 per cent of GDP in 1974 to 42.8 per cent by 1979.
53 Interview with Lord Hattersley.
54 Neo-revisionists within the Labour Party made this point around the time of the IMF crisis.

Part II

Domestic and foreign policies

4 Economic policy

Jim Tomlinson

The mid-1970s are commonly seen as a watershed in post-war economic policy. The 'golden age' of the 1950s and 1960s came to an end in a period of 'stagflation' and crises over public spending, borrowing and the exchange rate. The 'Keynesian' consensus about how to conduct economic policy was fundamentally challenged by the sharp rise in both inflation and unemployment coupled to a major loss of financial confidence. Subsequently, both Conservative and New Labour politicians and their academic allies have seen ideological advantage in painting the period in the worst possible light. If historical distance is unlikely to lend enchantment to our view of the period, it does at least allow some perspective, and such perspective is what this chapter seeks to offer. In assessing Labour's economic policy in this period, the discussion is divided into four sections. The first deals with Labour's inheritance from the Heath period (1970–4), the second with the Government's policy responses to the problems it faced, the third with the outcomes of those policies, and the final part attempts to set these years in a broader perspective of post-war economic policy evolution. The focus throughout is on macro-economic policy, other issues only being discussed if they bear on this macro aspect.

The inheritance

On coming to power all governments say that they have inherited an economic mess from their predecessors. But few governments have received such a poisoned chalice as awaited the Labour Government in March 1974. Following its 'U-turn' in 1972 the Heath Government had embarked on an unprecedentedly expansionary fiscal and monetary policy and allowed the exchange rate to float – which meant, in practice, to sink. This put the economy on a path of sharply rising public spending, fiscal deficits and money supply. Some minor attempts were made to slow down the rate of growth in November and December 1973, but the impact of these expansionary policies was to be felt for several years into Labour's term of office.

Second, the new Government took office at a time of the worst industrial relations crisis since the 1920s. The dispute with the miners had led to the imposition of a three-day week over most of industry. In addition, as an accompaniment to fiscal expansion and increasing inflation, there was a surge in pay under way, especially in the public sector. The Conservative Government's attempt to counter wage inflation had led to an agreement on threshold payments, which tied permitted wage increases to the inflation rate and consequently institutionalised inflation. This locked the new Government into a wage–price spiral.

Externally, the world-wide economic expansion of 1970–3 had meant a sharp deterioration in both the terms of trade (the price of imports relative to exports) and the balance of payments. These trends were capped by the quadrupling of oil prices agreed by OPEC in December 1973. This imparted both a powerful inflationary impact via its effects on costs and simultaneously a deflationary one by requiring the oil-importing economies (which included Britain in 1973) to redistribute resources towards exports in order to pay for the higher priced oil.

Last but not least was the very rapid increase in import penetration in manufactures. Imports' share of the home market rose from 15 per cent in 1970 to 22 per cent in 1974 (and was to rise to 30 per cent by 1980).[1] The early 1970s' growth was fuelled by the rapid expansion of demand in Britain, the competitive weakness of many domestic suppliers, and the reduction in barriers to trade, especially because of entry into the EEC in January 1973. The rapid rise in imports, not offset by a parallel rise in exports, led not only to a marked deterioration in the current balance of payments, but perhaps even more importantly to the profit squeeze on the private sector which formed a key backdrop to Labour's problems in managing the economy.[2]

In sum, when Labour took office almost every economic indicator was moving adversely: inflation was around 10 per cent, the balance of payments had moved sharply into the red after recording a current surplus in 1971, the exchange rate was falling after floating from June 1972, and the public sector deficit was at a peacetime high. The last of these was perhaps the most intractable of the legacies of the 'Barber boom'. Not only was the deficit itself a key factor in financial confidence in British economic management, but the rise in interest on the debt meant that many of the great battles to cut public spending under Labour did no more than offset higher payments to holders of government paper.[3]

Towards the end of 1973 the Conservatives recognised that the pace of expansion since the spring of 1972 was unsustainable and began to tighten both fiscal and monetary policy. In retrospect it is clear that a cyclical peak had been reached in May 1973, but the downturn was mild before Labour came into office. Thus Labour inherited a condition of 'stagflation' that largely justifies the new Chancellor's assertion that 'my predecessor left me an economy on the brink of catastrophe'.[4]

The government response

The Labour Government was poorly prepared for the scale of the economic problems it faced – as indeed were governments in all countries in the 1970s. In opposition Labour had been crucially concerned with the relationship with the unions, partly because of the unhappy development of that relationship under the previous Labour Government of 1964–70, partly because in the early 1970s it was apparent that industrial relations and wage inflation were the key issues of the time. Labour had agreed a 'social contract' with the unions designed to deal with the problems of the early 1970s rather than the much worse conditions after 1974. In return for policy concessions from the government, the TUC had promised to exercise restraint on the wage front, but without any intention of conceding the case for a formal incomes policy. The social contract was then 'insipid and toothless', a papering over of the cracks between the leadership of the Party and trade union opinion.[5]

Initially this contract had little effect, as unions sought to stay ahead of accelerating price inflation. But in 1975 union leaders 'looked into the abyss' of hyperinflation, and after reaching a peak of almost 30 per cent in the summer of that year, wage inflation slowed down. The Government was able to negotiate an agreement with the TUC on the basis of a flat-rate increase of £6 per week. Although this limit was widely exceeded, it did have a significant impact, especially notable in the public sector where the Government tightened the purse strings, but the process of deceleration was generally aided by the sharp rise in unemployment, which more than doubled between 1974 and 1976, and the squeeze on profits in the private sector. In 1976 a further agreement was reached with the TUC, aided by the novelty of making tax cuts dependent on restraint in wage claims. But the Government's attempt to extend further the life of this beefed-up social contract was met with decreasing enthusiasm and then outright opposition from the trade unions, now that the immediate crisis was seen to be past. Down to 1978 and despite these tensions the policy can be seen as facilitating the reduction of inflation without a rise in unemployment, which stabilised from 1976. But in 1978–9 the Government sought to achieve an unrealistic 5 per cent wage target, which could be made effective only in the public sector, where low-paid workers had already borne much of the brunt of the social contract. The result was the 'Winter of Discontent', as union members sought at least to maintain their real wage at a time when inflation was running at 8–10 per cent per annum. In retrospect, this limit of 5 per cent must be seen as a grievous error, the Government failing to recognise the strength of feeling among rank and file union members, and the inability of union leaders to contain such powerful discontent.

Alongside the social contract Labour had committed itself to a radical departure in industrial policy. In particular it was envisaged that Labour would create a National Enterprise Board to take a controlling share in a large number of large manufacturing firms. Such proposals for 'competitive public enterprise' originated on the right of the Party as an alternative to 'old-fashioned' sectoral nationalisations as far back as the 1940s. They gained support from wide sections of the Party in the early 1970s, but even before Labour came to office it was apparent that many in the leadership of the Party were worried about the hostile reaction to such proposals from the private sector. The radical version of the

NEB proposals was spelt out in *Labour's Programme* of 1973, but even as early as August 1974 with the publication of *The Regeneration of British Industry* the tone had shifted markedly. The stance was no longer one of government attempting to change industry's behaviour by heavy controls, but of co-operation in a joint enterprise of recovery.[6] In a macro-economic context these proposals, even as watered down, were significant for the way they added to the loss of private sector confidence and thus put downward pressure on investment, an issue that was very important in the crisis of the mid-1970s.

Earlier episodes of incomes policy had been based on the economists' argument that if this instrument was used to contain inflation, demand management, especially fiscal policy, could be used to maintain full employment. But such a happy division of labour proved unfeasible in the mid-1970s. The social contract proved insufficient to contain inflation, and so fiscal policy could not be used to pursue full employment. Almost from the beginning, therefore, fiscal policy was downgraded to a supporting role, essentially seeking to aid the effectiveness of the social contract. Despite increasing unemployment the March 1974 budget was mildly deflationary. In contrast, that of November 1974 was slightly expansionary, but with the main aim of easing company finances, which had been hard hit by the fact that they were being taxed on paper profits on stock whose price had only risen because of inflation.

By 1974 Britain was undoubtedly suffering from a serious profits crisis, significantly worse than other OECD countries, and particularly noticeable in manufacturing. This profit squeeze had existed in milder form since the 1960s, but the recession of 1974–5 brought levels to an all-time low, and government action was inescapable. Profits reached their lowest point in 1975, and then recovered, partly because of government action and partly as a normal consequence of the upturn of the cycle. The link between profits and investment is not a straightforward one, but the reversal of the profit squeeze does seem to have facilitated a degree of investment recovery after 1976. However, it has been plausibly argued that the still depressed levels of investment were insufficient to support full employment of the labour force. However difficult the circumstances, Labour's response to the profit problem may reasonably be labelled 'too little, too late'.[7]

Crucial in the evolution of fiscal policy for the whole period of the Labour Government was the budget of April 1975. In it the Chancellor, Denis Healey, argued:

> I fully understand why I have been urged by so many friends both inside and outside the House to treat unemployment as the central problem and to stimulate a further growth in home consumption, public or private, so as to start getting the rate of unemployment down as fast as possible. ... I do not believe it would be wise to follow that advice today. ... I cannot afford to increase demand further when 5p in every pound we spend at home has been provided by our creditors abroad and inflation is running at its current rate.[8]

For a Labour Government to give priority to reducing inflation by cutting public spending when unemployment was so high marked a turning point in post-war economic policy. As Britton notes, 'in the circumstances it was a very un-Keynesian budget'.[9] Also very important to the development of fiscal policy was the cash limits policy announced in July 1975 and embodied in the February 1976 White Paper. Cash limits gave priority to containing the financial consequences of rising public spending, and had the unexpected consequence of underpinning the sharpest ever peacetime fall in public spending, amounting to 6.9 per cent between fiscal 1976–7 and 1977–8.[10] The April 1976 budget was framed explicitly to try and gain support for the social contract, with a stabilisation of public spending allied to conditional tax cuts. Further public expenditure cuts were announced in July and December, the last as part of the deal with the IMF that figures so largely in accounts of this Government (see below for further discussion).

The cuts in public spending planned from 1975 onwards had a differentiated pattern. In the light of the squeeze on private sector profits not only was tax relief to companies greatly extended, but also industrial subsidies shot up. To some extent history was repeating itself; in the 1960s Labour had sought to encourage private investment by large subsidies, and indeed it was the perceived failure of this policy which fuelled the call for more direct government control over that sector as embodied in the idea of the NEB.[11] Now, in much less favourable macro-economic circumstances, the policy was tried again. Coupled with the rising payments on debt, the switch of public spending was away from social programmes, especially where this involved capital as opposed to current spending; most conspicuously 'the party is over' was an accurate summary of the position for local authority housing spending which was never again to reach the heights it reached in the early 1970s. Many of the problems of underinvestment in public infrastructure, which were to plague Britain into the twenty-first century, began in the mid-1970s.[12]

Another very important feature of spending policy in the 1970s was linked to the broader debate about de-industrialisation which gathered pace in this period. Historically Labour had been a party which gave high priority to industrial modernisation.[13] This continued in the 1970s – for many the radical industrial policy was about finding new ways to pursue this agenda, given what was seen as the incorrigible complacency and ineffectiveness of privately owned companies, especially with regard to their willingness to invest. Historically, too, Labour had seen such modernisation as the necessary underpinning for its aim of 'social justice', especially secured by expanding government social programmes. But in the climate of slowing growth in the 1970s there appeared to some to be a direct clash between resources going to higher investment and resources for public spending. Such a view animated the Treasury desire to curb public spending growth and boost company finances. But perhaps most strikingly it affected the outlook of key figures in the TUC, whose views in the context of the social contract were especially important for the Government.

Most interesting in this regard is Hugh Scanlon, leader of the engineering union and a key figure in union discussions with the Government. While he tended to put his weight behind many of the policies of the left in the Labour Party in this period, as the leader of a largely private manufacturing union he was very much concerned with industrial investment, and attracted to the position which argued that public, social spending had to be held back to finance such investment.[14] In public discussions Scanlon and other TUC leaders were willing to face up to the logic of this argument. For example, the 1975 *TUC Economic Review* noted that in the context of the need to 'increase productive investment … there could be little scope for real increases in consumption at the present time'. The following year, in discussing the social contract Scanlon argued that economic recovery would only come 'on the basis of a viable, efficient manufacturing industry with emphasis on those who make and sell and, if necessary, somewhat less emphasis on those who serve'.[15]

As well as sympathising with the Government's fiscal priorities, Scanlon was lukewarm on the radical industrial policy partly because he did not see how it could guarantee the shift in resources he wanted to secure. Yet the kind of strategy he desired was difficult to deliver in this period. In 1974–5 the threshold agreements inherited from the Conservatives protected households against the slump, while the Government was trying to stabilise the public sector deficit: the result was a big financial squeeze on the private sector. As we have seen the Government then came to the rescue with measures of tax relief, but already considerable damage had been done to both investment and employment. From a union point of view, advocacy of squeezing consumption in order to pay for investment was never likely to be a popular policy; to do so when the recession was depressing incomes was perhaps wholly politically implausible. From this perspective, analysis of the social contract which emphasises the strains put on the trade unions by their leaderships' attempts to subordinate the unions' policy to national economic priorities appears all the more crucial to understanding the 1970s.[16] The first serious recession since the war was not an environment in which giving priority to industrial investment was likely to find much ready support.

On 28 September 1976 Callaghan made his famous speech asserting that the option of spending Britain's way out of recession 'no longer exists, and that insofar as it ever did exist it only worked on each occasion since the war by injecting a bigger dose of inflation into the economy'.[17] As a description of post-war policy this seems to be entirely inaccurate, but at the time and subsequently it has been regarded as a hugely important symbol of Labour's renunciation of 'Keynesian' policies. In fact it is difficult to see it in that light. Not only was the speech made during the 'crisis of confidence' period which led up to the IMF visit, and to be seen very much as aimed at trying to restore confidence, but it did not portend a move away from Keynesian policies. On the contrary, not only was policy moving away from 'Keynesianism' well before the speech, but in 1977 and 1978 the direction of fiscal policy was to become *more* expansionary as the economic environment improved.

Down to the autumn of 1976 the fall in the exchange rate, which gathered pace in 1975, was not regarded as a problem, as it aided the balance of payments. In the spring of 1976 the authorities seemed to encourage a further fall, but the decline in the pound's value got out of hand in the summer of 1976. This led to the IMF deal in December 1976, by which Britain was granted further support for the pound in return for a 'Letter of Intent' on future policy which included public spending cuts, only agreed after a major crisis in the Cabinet and the Government. Politically the IMF episode was undoubtedly of major importance, in arousing opposition to what can be regarded, according to taste, as either an illegitimate interference in a national government's policy decisions or a stark demonstration of the incompetence of Labour in managing the economy.[18]

But in economic terms the episode is a puzzle. As we have seen, it is a myth to suggest that Labour reversed its policies sharply only in response to the IMF's demands. The major arguments within the Government about the priority to be accorded to full employment in framing fiscal (and monetary) policy took place in 1974 and 1975, and by 1976 policy was clearly set on according priority to inflation, coupled to trying to encourage support for the social contract. The evidence suggests this stance had already led to the economy starting to recover well before the IMF arrived. Output bottomed out in August 1975, inflation started to fall from the same month and the balance of payments to improve (for the whole of 1976 the current account deficit was less than a third of that of 1974). The public sector finances were improving from early 1976 as cash limits started to have their impact. Yet until the end of the year the pound would not stop falling. Undoubtedly there was a major loss of financial confidence in the mid-1970s, and the issue was not so much Labour's policies as the need for that confidence to be boosted by the granting of the IMF's seal of approval to Labour's 1975 reversal of priorities.[19]

The size of the PSBR and the inflationary splurge of 1975 underpinned financial market views that Labour Governments are prone to extravagance. In the summer of 1976 there was what *The Economist* referred to as a 'gilt strike', which exposed the weakness of any government with a large borrowing requirement.[20] The floating exchange rate meant there was no 'anchor' against inflationary policies as had existed in the 1950s and 1960s. In these circumstances policy credibility could only be restored by an outside agency trusted by financiers; this was the role of the IMF.

If it is inaccurate to see the IMF as the major instigator of Labour's policies, it remains to be asked where these policies did come from. Partly this is a matter of the internal politics of the Labour Party. While never a whole-heartedly Keynesian party, Labour in the 1950s and 1960s was united around a belief that full employment could and should be achieved by active demand management. While there were long-term doubts about the capacity of such demand management to achieve faster growth, the basic idea that fiscal policy could be effectively used to achieve full employment was only just beginning to come under serious critical scrutiny in the 1970s.[21] The stagflation of 1974–6 was a body-blow to such assumptions, and sharply divided Labour economic opinion. On the left an 'Alternative Economic Strategy' emerged which, in macro-economic terms, wanted to expand demand but protect the external account by import controls. But also on the left (though overlapping with elements on the right) were people like Scanlon who, it has been suggested above, wanted to give a higher priority to industrial investment and was willing to sacrifice Labour's traditional social agenda in doing so, unlike advocates of the AES.

On some sections of the right there was a nascent 'monetarism' that believed the central concern should be to reduce inflation and government borrowing to hold back government spending to expand the scope for increases in both take-home pay and investment. But others on the right argued that while financial confidence could not be ignored, the basic social democratic commitment to full employment and high spending was sustainable with a little trimming.[22] These divergent views emerge fairly clearly in the agonised discussions of 1976, both at the time of the July cuts and the IMF visit. Ultimately, however, what mattered in that period was what seemed likely to resolve the crisis quickly. As Thompson suggests:

> one is left, though, with the overwhelming impression that in this period economic ideas and economic philosophies proved influential to the extent that they contributed to political survival. When they did so they were embraced or modified, when they did not they were jettisoned. Economic policy did not so much bear the imprint of ideas as the scars of expediency.[23]

But if this is a period of disarray in Labour's economic doctrine, what of the institutions of policy making? Here, of course, the key role was played by the Treasury. The Treasury in the 1970s sustained its position as the most important department in Whitehall, and possessed an ability to shape the agenda that its opponents found very hard to shake. As the Cabinet diarists of the 1970s make clear, opposition to the Treasury line always lacked intellectual weight because no minister other than the Chancellor had access to sufficient resources to make a well-grounded alternative case.[24] In Cabinet the Chancellor, always in the end receiving support from the Prime Minister, was able to dominate economic discussion and face down opposition. But recognition of this power should not lead us to think of the Chancellor as a mouthpiece of the carefully crafted, consistent and monolithic 'Treasury View' as opponents such as Benn suggest.[25]

First, it is clear that Labour's Chancellor in the 1970s, Denis Healey, was not a simple mouthpiece for an institutional position. He (like the PM, and former Chancellor, Jim Callaghan) was critical of quite a lot of what the Treasury did, especially its forecasting errors and the policy mistakes that such errors could lead to.[26] In this environment he was willing and able to make up his own mind on many important issues.

Second, it seems clear that, like everyone else in this period, the Treasury found it hard to navigate its way through the crisis of the mid-1970s. Not only did much of its forecasting appear error strewn, but it suffered a huge blow when it appeared to have lost control of public expenditure, perhaps its most central function. While the degree of loss of control may have been exaggerated, the fact that such an allegation could plausibly be made by a previous government economic adviser (Wynne Godley) suggests how far the Treasury found itself under pressure in the mid-1970s.[27]

This pressure partly found its expression in a sense of panic, notably over the negotiations over the IMF agreement in late 1976. And, far from being a mono-lith, there is evidence of serious divisions of opinion within the Treasury in this period, some linked to doctrinal disputes, especially concerning the continuing relevance of Keynesian policies, others more pragmatic, such as how to respond to the loss of financial confidence in 1976.[28]

Last but not least, the Treasury seems to have made serious errors of judge-ment in this period. First there was the confusion about the level of public expenditure, which allowed critics to allege erroneously that the share of such spending was reaching the 'dangerously' high level of 60 per cent. Even more important, there was what Healey calls a 'muddle' on exchange rate policy, espe-cially on the extent to which a depreciation was to be welcomed as a means of restoring competitiveness, or feared as a harbinger of future inflation.[29] Such confusion was especially important in the crisis of 1976, because it was initial Treasury (and Bank of England) support for depreciation of the pound which began the process which eventually led to the accelerated decline of the currency, and the battle to restore financial confidence eventually achieved only through the political humiliation of the IMF visit.

If the Treasury was divided and rattled by the problems of economic management in the 1970s, that is hardly surprising. If the Labour leadership was similarly affected, we may feel that this was only to be expected; the Party had always contained an often uneasy combination of economic opinions, and even before coming into office had been sharply divided over the key area of indus-trial policy and able to produce only a highly fragile agreement on wages. To be then faced with a macro-economic crisis, which nothing in earlier experience could be used as a helpful precedent in solving, was bound to lead to deep argu-ments. In the event, and after much division and dispute, the Government managed to agree economic policies which kept it surprisingly intact; for all Benn's invocation of the horrible example of 1931, no such political disaster came close to occurring in the 1970s. Healey's 'eclectic pragmatism' proved to be sufficiently agile to keep the economy, and the Government, on a path which, in retrospect, appears defensible as dealing with some success with a disastrous legacy combined with unprecedented external adverse conditions, and in circumstances where the norms of post-war economic understanding appeared to have disintegrated.

Outcomes

In assessing the outcomes of Labour's period in office, it is important to look in a comparative context because the economic problems facing the British

Table 4.1　Inflation in the West European 'Big Four' 1972–9 (percentage change from previous year in private consumption deflator)

	France	Italy	West Germany	Britain
1972	6.3	6.4	5.7	6.5
1973	7.4	13.8	6.3	8.5
1974	14.8	21.3	7.0	16.9
1975	11.8	16.6	6.2	23.7
1976	9.9	17.7	4.2	15.8
1977	9.4	17.5	3.6	14.8
1978	9.1	13.2	2.7	9.0
1979	10.7	14.5	3.9	13.6

Source: OECD, *Economic Outlook*, 47, 1990, Table R11

Government were far from unique, and similarly the dilemmas and difficulties in responding to the deterioration in the international economic environment were strongly paralleled in other West European countries. In this section comparisons are made with the West European 'Big Three': West Germany, France and Italy.

Inflation rates are shown in Table 4.1. Plainly there was a marked upward trend everywhere in the first part of the 1970s, except in West Germany, with Britain on average not as bad as Italy (or, the OECD figures suggest, Spain). Inflation was an international phenomenon, and though in Britain it threatened to get out of control in 1975, in fact the upward trend was sharply reversed after that year.

Table 4.2 on public expenditure shows the rapid expansion of the 'Barber boom' of the early 1970s reversed after 1975, and the share of public spending in GDP lower in Britain than elsewhere by 1979. Perhaps it is particularly striking that the share of GDP taken by public spending was considerably lower in Britain than in 'virtuous' Germany by the end of the decade.

Table 4.2　Public expenditure in the West European 'Big Four', 1972–9 (total outlays of government as a percentage of GDP)

	France	Italy	West Germany	Britain
1972	38.3	38.6	40.8	39.3
1973	38.3	37.8	41.5	40.4
1974	39.3	37.9	44.6	44.9
1975	43.4	43.2	48.9	46.6
1976	43.9	42.2	47.9	46.3
1977	43.7	42.5	48.0	43.8
1978	44.6	46.1	47.8	43.3
1979	45.0	45.5	47.7	42.7

Source: OECD, *Economic Outlook*, 47, 1990, Table R15

Table 4.3 Government surpluses and deficits in the West European 'Big Four', 1972–9 (general government financial balances as a percentage of GDP)

	France	*Italy*	*West Germany*	*Britain*
1972	+0.8	8.6	0.5	1.3
1973	+0.8	7.9	+1.2	2.7
1974	+0.1	7.8	1.3	3.9
1975	2.2	12.9	5.6	4.6
1976	0.6	9.8	3.4	5.0
1977	0.8	8.6	2.4	3.4
1978	2.1	10.4	2.4	4.4
1979	0.8	10.2	2.6	3.3

Source: OECD, *Economic Outlook*, 47, 1990, Table R 14

Table 4.3 shows the fiscal balance; these are the unadjusted 'headline' figures. They show that France had a much better performance, Italy much worse, Germany surprisingly not much different. These are 'headline' figures, upon which much contemporary attention was focused. But much of the increase was not due to policy decisions, but to the automatic effects of the economic cycle. If the cycle is taken into account, and we adjust the numbers for the impact of the recession, the main increase in the deficit was under the Conservatives in 1970–3, the trend being flat thereafter. There is also the huge issue of inflation adjustment to these raw numbers, with the 'burden' of the debt much reduced by the rise in prices.[30]

In comparative terms one of the curious features of the 1970s is that Britain's relative growth performance improved. This reflected the fact that the golden age of the 1950s and 1960s had seen a process of 'catch-up' by the major continental West European countries, but by the 1970s that process was more or less complete. West European growth rates slowed down sharply, while the British rate decelerated much less from a lower starting point. Britain's performance in the 1970s was helped by the exploitation of North Sea oil, which Crafts suggests added about 0.5 per cent to annual expansion. Labour productivity in manufacturing stands out for its poor performance in the 1970s, though by this date manufacturing was only 30 per cent of total output. The causes of this poor performance are contentious. Some have argued that it reflected the exhaustion of increasing returns from the early 1970s spurt in investment. Others see it as a consequence of labour hoarding as employers anticipated a cyclical revival which never came.[31] In any event, this nadir of manufacturing productivity performance should not obscure that fact that for the economy as a whole this was a period of sharp recession followed by substantial recovery, but with the trend performance understated by the unsustainable peak of 1973.

Conclusions and implications

In the 1980s accounts of this Labour Government suggested that the events surrounding the IMF crisis of 1976 formed a key turning point in post-war British politics. Holmes typified this argument in suggesting that 'the change in attitudes and ideologies after 1976 was possibly the most profound ... since that engendered by the 1945–51 Labour government ... the post-1976 change of approach saw reducing inflation regarded as the prime policy objective ahead of full employment'.[32] This now seems mistaken in two respects. First, the shift towards giving primacy to inflation began well before the IMF visit, 1976, going back to at least Healey's budget of 1975, as noted above. Second, this shift in objectives was much less profound than this quotation posits; as Burk and Cairncross persuasively counter, 'economic policy in the last years of the Labour government differed little from what it had been before the arrival of the IMF'.[33] Once the IMF seal of approval had been given, and the exchange rate strengthened, Labour started to reflate the economy and to limit inflation by continuing with the social contract. Keynesianism was not dead.

This is not to suggest nothing changed in the 1970s. In the broadest terms an important part of the social democratic 'project' did suffer mortal blows in the 1970s, the part which saw expanding public spending – 'tax and spend' – as the centrepiece of social democratic egalitarianism.[34] The year of 1976 saw the end of the upward trend in spending and taxing which had (with interruptions) characterised the previous three-quarters of a century – an upward trend that was not to be restarted until the beginning of the next century.

If at the macro-economic level 1976 was not the historic turning point early commentators suggested, it did mark the beginnings of a notable improvement in economic performance. As Gardener argues: 'the story of the years 1977 and 1978 is one of paradox. The statistics now available suggest success, but attitudes at the time spoke of failure.'[35]

It is not only attitudes of the time that spoke of failure; for many superficial analysts as well as political opponents the whole period of the Labour Government remains one spoken of in absurdly exaggerated terms of breakdown and disaster. How did such views gain so much credence? Part of the answer is to be found in the contemporary panic which surrounded the economic instability of these years. Evidence of this panic can be found in the pages of such respectable journals as *The Economist*, which as early as March 1973 was suggesting inflation was threatening 'Latin American modes of both price inflation and societal decay'. A year later the *Banker* was suggesting that Britain faced the last chance 'for the parliamentary system to cope with Britain's economic problems'. By summer 1975 *The Economist* was suggesting that 'Britannia's dream of apocalypse is horribly close to coming true'.[36]

Such arguments were not the result of sober economic analysis so much as part of a wider 'great fear' on the part of many in Britain. As Johnson suggests, 'in 1974–76 important sections of the middle classes did lose confidence. For the first time parts of the Establishment began seriously to consider the alternatives to our present forms of parliamentary democracy.' Johnson goes on to suggest that 'a future social historian may well experience some difficulty in comprehending the cacophony of the Great Fear'.[37] But the historian also needs to explain why this immediate overreaction to events of the 1970s has been replicated in so many later accounts.

Part of the explanation lies in the exaggerated accounts of long-run economic 'decline', in which the 1970s are represented as a culmination of the disastrous post-war economic trends brought about by Keynesian social democracy. This, of course, was the key historical narrative of Mrs Thatcher, and one she used to great effect in securing her leadership role.[38]

But the highly political use of stories about the 1970s is not of course confined to the Conservatives. For New Labour exaggerated stories about the 1970s provide a useful counterpoint to contemporary 'prudence'; for New Labour the suggestion that the 1970s were a disastrous period serves to emphasise the distance travelled between the 'Old' and the 'New'. But to compare a more realistic account of the 1970s with Labour under Blair/Brown suggests considerable similarity as much as stark difference. The label 'monetarily-constrained Keynesianism'[39] has been applied to the Wilson–Callaghan years, and this is a not inaccurate characterisation of economic policy around the end of the century under New Labour. In the 1970s Labour was faced with a world recession at the beginning of its period in office, and this forced a focus on monetary and fiscal tightening to beat inflation, which was then relaxed after 1976 as inflation seemed to be under control. Under New Labour the sequence has been reversed. Having established its anti-inflationary credentials in the first term, the second brought a recession in which Keynesian policy (the overriding of the automatic stabilisers) was vigorously pursued. Also, in a direct reversal of the mid-1970s, the automatic stabilisers were augmented by a substantial expansion of public capital spending. In the earlier period, because inflation was high financial markets lost confidence in the Government's policies, and this was not to be restored until the IMF gave its seal of approval. Under Gordon Brown there seems to have been no such loss of credibility despite fiscal deficits which are projected to rise to over 3 per cent of GDP, and with debt rising to 43 per cent of GDP (in excess of the limits for each of these figures under the Growth and Stability Pact of the European Union).[40]

It is interesting to compare the fiscal experience of the 1970s with Brown's golden rules for fiscal prudence. First, because of inflation, the debt/GDP ratio fell fast, from 48.8 to 40.6 per cent between 1974 and 1979. Second, the overall fiscal deficit was larger than investment spending only because capital spending fell from 4.8 to 2.6 per cent of GDP. But even this lower figure is significantly *above* public investment under New Labour, even in 2007–8, when it is projected to rise to 2.2 per cent of GDP, from the very low level of 0.9 per cent in 2001–2.[41]

In sum, while the public finances did deteriorate sharply in the early to mid-1970s, this was quickly corrected, in part because Labour accepted the Treasury analysis of the likely consequences in terms of resources for investment and exports, and later because of the loss of financial confidence. Recent work in international political economy has emphasised that financial markets usually employ rather simple judgements on financial credibility.[42] If a government combines high inflation and big fiscal deficits confidence will soon be lost; hence the crisis of 1975–6. But if inflation is under control, which it clearly is in New Labour's second term, the scale of fiscal deficit which will induce a loss of confidence is much less clear, and the scope for 'Keynesian' policies seemingly becomes substantial. To put this point slightly differently; high inflation in the 1970s forced a (temporary) reversal of Labour's priorities towards bringing inflation down. As long as the rate of price increase stays down (and the current threat in 2003–4 seems to lie more with deflation), Keynesianism, in the sense of counteracting recession with budget deficits, appears a realistic option for a government to choose. In this long-term perspective, the crisis of the 1970s appears much more conjunctural, and much less systemic than most discussions of the period allow.

Notes

1   Williams, K., Williams, J. and Thomas, D., *Why are the British Bad at Manufacturing?* (Routledge and Kegan Paul, London, 1983), pp. 18–19.
2   Ormerod, P., 'Incomes Policy', in Artis, M. and Cobham, D. (eds), *Labour's Economic Policies, 1974–79* (Manchester University Press, Manchester, 1991), p. 65. This book provides by far the best account of Labour's economic policies, albeit focused on the macro-economy.
3   Browning, P., *The Treasury and Economic Policy, 1964–1985* (Longman, London, 1986), pp. 71–2.
4   Healey, D., *The Time of My Life* (Penguin, London, 1990).
5   Thompson, N., *Political Economy and the Labour Party* (UCL Press, London, 1996), p. 234.
6   Forester, T., 'How Labour's Industrial Strategy got the Chop', *New Society*, 6 July 1978; Wickham-Jones, M., *Economic Strategy and the Labour Party: Politics and Policy-Making, 1970–1983* (Macmillan, London, 1996), ch. 6.
7   Brown, C. and Sheriff, T., *De-industrialisation in the UK: a Background Paper*, National Institute Discussion Paper 23 (National Institute for Economic and Social Research, London, 1978), pp. 27–31; Sawyer, M., 'Prices Policies', in Artis and Cobham (eds), *Labour's Economic Policies, 1974–79*, pp. 77–9; Ormerod, P., 'Incomes Policy', in ibid., pp. 168–9.
8   Commons, Hansard, 15 April 1975, col. 282; Harmon, M., *The British Labour Government and the 1976 IMF Crisis* (Macmillan, Basingstoke, 1997), p. 95.
9   Britton, A., *Macroeconomic Policy in Britain 1974–1987* (Cambridge University Press/NIESR, Cambridge, 1991), p. 25.
10 Pliatzky, L., *Getting and Spending: Public Expenditure, Employment and Inflation* (Basil Blackwell, Oxford, 1982), Table A.1.
11 Tomlinson, J., *Modernising Britain? The Economic Policies of the Labour Governments 1964–70* (Manchester University Press, Manchester, 2003).
12 Clark, T., Elsby, M. and Love, S., 'Trends in British Public Investment', *Fiscal Studies*, 23, 2003, pp. 305–42.
13 Tomlinson, *Modernising Britain? The Economic Policies of the Labour Governments 1964–70* and Tomlinson, J., *Democratic Socialism and Economic Policy: The Attlee Years 1945–51* (Cambridge University Press, Cambridge, 1997).

14 Minkin, L., *The Contentious Alliance* (Edinburgh University Press, Edinburgh, 1991), pp. 170–3.

15 *TUC Economic Review* (TUC, London, 1975), p. 58; TUC, *The Social Contract 1976/77* (TUC, London, 1976), p. 28.

16 Brown, W., 'Industrial Relations', in Artis and Cobham (eds), *Labour's Economic Policies, 1974–79*, pp. 213–28.

17 Callahan, J., Speech at Labour Party Conference, in *Labour Party: Annual Conference Report* (Labour Party, London, 1976), p. 182; Benn refers to this as a 'most patronising lecture'. *Against the Tide: Diaries 1973–76* (Arrow, London, 1989), p. 615.

18 Ludlam, S., 'The Gnomes of Washington: Four Myths of the 1976 IMF Crisis', *Political Studies*, 40, 1992, pp. 713–27.

19 Allsopp, C., 'Macroeconomic Policy: Design and Performance', in Artis and Cobham (eds), *Labour's Economic Policies 1974–79*, pp. 31–4; Burk, K. and Cairncross, A., *'Goodbye, Great Britain': The 1976 IMF Crisis* (Yale University Press, New Haven, CT, 1992).

20 Keegan, W. and Pennant-Rea, R., *Who Runs the Economy?* (Temple Smith, London, 1979), chs 4, 5.

21 Thompson, *Political Economy and the Labour Party*, chs 14–16.

22 Barnett, J., *Inside the Treasury, 1974–79* (Andre Deutsch, London, 1982), p. 103; Dell, E., *The Chancellors* (HarperCollins, London, 1996), ch.14; Healey, *Time of My Life*, p. 431.

23 Thompson, *Political Economy and the Labour Party*, p. 239.

24 Benn, T., *Against the Tide: Diaries 1973–76* (Arrow, London, 1989); Castle, B. *The Castle Diaries 1974–76* (Weidenfeld and Nicolson, London, 1980).

25 For example, *Against the Tide*, p. 593.

26 Healey, *Time of My Life*, pp. 380–1, 401–2, 433–5, 449–50.

27 Pliatzky, *Getting and Spending*, pp. 130–42.

28 Barnett, *Inside the Treasury, 1974–79*, p. 103; Browning, *The Treasury and Economic Policy, 1964–1985*, ch. 14; Young, H. and Sloman, A., *Yes Minister* (BBC Publications, London, 1982), p. 25.

29 Healey, *Time of My Life*, pp. 433–5; Pliatzky, *Getting and Spending*, pp. 156–63.

30 Allsopp, 'Macroeconomic Policy', pp. 24–8.

31 Middleton, R., *Government versus the Market* (Edward Elgar, Cheltenham, 1996), p. 465; Crafts, N., 'Economic Growth in the 1970s', in Coopey, R. and Woodward, N. (eds), *Britain in the 1970s: the Troubled Economy* (UCL Press, London, 1996), pp. 81–5.

32 Holmes, M., *The Labour Government, 1974–79* (Macmillan, London, 1985), p. 182.

33 Burk and Cairncross, *'Goodbye, Great Britain'*, p. 228.

34 Clark, T., *The Limits of Social Democracy? Tax and Spend under Labour, 1974–1979*, Working Papers in Economic History No. 64/01 (LSE, 2001).

35 Gardener, N., *Decade of Discontent* (Basil Blackwell, Oxford, 1987), p. 214.

36 *The Economist*, 31 March 1973; *Banker*, March 1974; *The Economist*, 17 May 1975.

37 Johnson, R., *The Politics of Recession* (Macmillan, London, 1985), pp. 131, 130.

38 Cannadine, D., 'Apocalypse When? British Politicians and British "Decline" in the Twentieth Century', in Clarke, P. and Trebilcock, C. (eds), *Understanding Decline* (Cambridge University Press, Cambridge, 1997), pp. 261–84.

39 Fforde, J., 'Setting Monetary Objectives', *Bank of England Quarterly Bulletin*, 23, 1983, pp. 200–8.

40 Barrell, R., Kirby, S., Riley, R. and Weale, M., 'The UK Economy', *National Institute Economic Review*, 184, April 2003, pp. 40–1.

41 Allsopp, 'Macroeconomic Policy', p. 26; Jackson, P., 'Public Expenditure', in Artis and Cobham (eds), *Labour's Economic Policies, 1974–79*, p. 79; Barrell *et.al.*, 'The UK Economy', p. 40.

42 Mosley, L., 'Room to Move: International Financial Markets and National Welfare States', *International Organization*, 54, 2000, pp. 737–73.

5   The Rise and Fall of the Social Contract

Robert Taylor[1]

A fundamental and irreversible shift in the balance of power and wealth in favour of working people.

(Labour's Programme 1973)[2]

We shall use the crisis we shall inherit as an occasion for making the fundamental changes and not as an excuse for postponing them.

(Tony Benn at the 1973 Labour Party Conference)[3]

We have more influence now on the Labour Movement than at any time in the life of our Party. The Communist Party can float an idea early in the year. It goes to trade union conferences in the form of a resolution and it can become official Labour Party policy by the autumn. A few years ago we were on our own but not now.

(Bert Ramelson, Communist industrial organiser in December 1973)[4]

The significance of the Social Contract

The Social Contract between the Labour Party and the Trades Union Congress lay at the core of the domestic programme of both the Wilson and Callaghan Governments between March 1974 and May 1979. The ups and downs of the always 'contentious' party–trade union alliance was to mirror the changing fortunes of the Labour movement during those adverse times. The Social Contract has so often been written off by its innumerable critics as a flawed, one-sided arrangement under which it is argued that the trade unions were provided with too much power by the state but in return they refused to shoulder much responsibility in helping to resolve the country's intractable economic problems for no more than a limited period. The Conservatives, who were increasingly convinced that the control of the money supply was the key to effective economic management, used to argue that the Social Contract threatened the market economy and even brought the functioning of parliamentary democracy into serious question. For their part, many on the left denounced the TUC for its alleged collaborative involvement with a Labour Government. They regarded the Social Contract as a form of crony corporate capitalism that sought to frustrate the militancy of a self-confident and aggressive trade union rank and file, intent on the pursuit of radical change.

But even leading figures in the running of the Social Contract cast doubt on its merits, at least with hindsight. 'To my mind the only give and take in the contract was that the government gave and the unions took', recalled Joel Barnett, Chief Secretary at the Treasury during that period.[5] His former Cabinet colleague, first Paymaster General and then Trade Secretary, Edmund Dell, agreed with him in retirement. He believed the Social Contract was 'disastrous' because he said it fuelled inflation, brought a return to mass unemployment and 'put a respectable face on submission to trade union power'.[6] But even Len Murray, the TUC's stoical General Secretary, was not overenthusiastic about the experience of the Social Contract either. He believed it compromised the freedom and independence of autonomous trade unions from the demands of the democratic state and strained the loyalty of trade union members towards their elected leaders when it led to attempts to impose wage restraint under the guise of a national incomes policy. In Murray's considered opinion the Social Contract was asking too much of the trade unions, urging them to accept burdens in the running of the political economy that their structures and desire for freedom made it almost impossible to fulfil with success for more than a limited period of time. Nor was he convinced that the Social Contract advanced trade union purposes: 'I believe the Confederation of British Industry got more out of the Labour governments than we did', he recalled.

> We made very little impact on its economic policy and we achieved no industrial democracy. Most of what we got in labour law was to help non-unionists and not unions. It is true we got union recognition provisions but this was dust and ashes, useless, indeed even dangerous to us.[7]

Jack Jones, the impressive General Secretary of the Transport and General Workers' Union and the Social Contract's founding father, was understandably more sympathetic. But as a fervent champion of shop steward power and workplace bargaining throughout his life as a trade union militant, he turned out to be a late and rather ambivalent convert to the virtues of national understandings or accommodations on economic management. Even the inspirers of the Social Contract were uncertain about its ultimate purposes. For much of the time they saw it as a necessary but only temporary means to save the fragile economy from utter collapse and not as a sensible and long-term way to bring about a more rational and co-operative organisation of industrial life.

But no period of labour history has suffered from more distortion and caricature as the years that are covered by the Social Contract. The myths that surrounded its existence indelibly shaped the making of the New Labour project after John Smith's death in 1994, twenty years later, and the election of the modernising Tony Blair as party leader. It was the Social Contract's ignoble demise in the so-called 'Winter of Discontent' in 1978–9 that convinced many people that the alliance between the Government and TUC that it reflected had turned out to be nothing but a national disaster. The intimidating scenes of flying pickets, garbage piling up in the streets, the unburied dead on Merseyside, hospitals under siege and disrupted food supplies came to characterise popular memories of that time. Mr Blair's later verbal assaults on the culture of old-style trade unionism stemmed to a very large extent from the perceived excesses of those striking militants. It is true that often the realities were somewhat different and more complex than tabloid newspaper hyperbole might suggest. If we examine the evolution of the Social Contract throughout the whole of its mostly troubled life it differs in important ways from the conventional wisdom. Indeed, it is possible to argue that the Social Contract was less a mistaken strategy and more a lost opportunity both for the transformation of the Labour movement and for Britain's renewal into being a successful social market economy comparable with its competitors in mainland Western Europe.

The relations between Labour Governments and the trade unions have never been easy, as Labour's first Prime Minister Ramsay MacDonald found himself in conflict with Ernest Bevin, General Secretary of the Transport and General Workers' Union during his minority Labour administration in 1924. Even the Labour Party's most successful leader and Prime Minister Clement Attlee struggled to establish and maintain a harmonious alliance with the TUC throughout his Governments of 1945–51, especially in the enforcement of a voluntary national wages policy in response to financial crisis. In the post-war period Labour Governments sought direct support from the trade unions in delivering voluntary pay restraint from their members in order to help resolve Britain's intractable economic troubles. In the 1960s Harold Wilson believed that the co-operation of the trade unions was necessary in order to protect a vulnerable currency from the speculators, correct a soaring balance of payments deficit and above all reassure a doubting international financial community about the economic competence of a Labour Government. Between October 1964 and June 1970 no formalised alliance existed between the Labour Government and the trade unions. Ministers were forced instead to rely on the residual loyalty of national union leaders towards the Labour Party to win their support or more often their uneasy acquiescence in holding back the wage expectations of workers. By the end of the 1960s the relationship had degenerated into a bitter, self-destructive conflict, provoked by the Government's futile attempt to reform the trade unions through resort to legislation in early 1969, a move that nearly threatened to split the union–Labour alliance asunder. The humiliating retreat made by the Wilson Government on that famous occasion seemed to confirm the popularly held belief that the trade unions were turning themselves into over-mighty subjects in the land with a virtual veto power over the actions of the democratic state.

The original purpose of the Social Contract when it was first formulated in the early 1970s was to try and establish a much closer and more effective relationship between the Party and the trade unions that would prevent any repetition of the kind of trouble that had occurred with previous Labour Governments. In early 1972 – mainly under the initiative of Jack Jones and

David Lea, head of the TUC's economic department – the Liaison Committee was established that gave institutional expression to the proposed new arrangement. The newly formed body was tripartite and brought together six representatives each from the Party's National Executive Committee, the TUC General Council and Labour's Shadow Cabinet in Parliament. It met each Monday of every month and soon became an integral part of Labour's complex policy-making process. Indeed, it was to last for the whole period, continuing to meet regularly after Labour's return to government in March 1974. Its minutes provide a fascinating glimpse into how decisions were taken with trade union participation. In its early days the Liaison Committee concentrated its attention on the formulation of a precise but limited programme of action that trade unions wanted to see implemented when Labour was re-elected to office. Its main aim was to restore Labour's legal immunities in industrial disputes which it had lost under the 1971 Industrial Relations Act. But it was also concerned to develop a credible set of social and employment policies with special concern for the well-being of pensioners. This jointly agreed approach was to become known as the Social Contract.

The making and unmaking of industrial policy

In parallel with the development of the Liaison Committee, an important shift in political power took place in the early 1970s on Labour's National Executive Committee. It moved decisively leftwards, mainly under the inspiration of an increasingly radicalised Tony Benn, the former Minister of Technology who had become Shadow Industry Secretary. The resulting 1973 Labour Programme that emerged from an intensive network of party subcommittees was the most left-wing document to be accepted by the Party Conference since the early 1930s. It gave the regeneration of British industry the highest priority for action from the next Labour Government. This was to involve a firm commitment to a sweeping agenda of state control of the commanding heights of private industry, the introduction of compulsory planning agreements in the country's largest firms, the imposition of import controls against foreign manufactured goods, a huge expansion in public expenditure to stimulate manufacturing and Britain's withdrawal from membership of the European Common Market. The radical move in policy direction threw doubt over Labour's belief in a market economy and the maintenance of a thriving private sector. But it also reflected a genuine and widespread party disillusionment that stretched much further than the resurgent left. Many across the Party's broad spectrum were disappointed with what they regarded as the limited achievements of Wilson's Governments in the 1960s. Next time that the Labour Party secured political power – they argued – it would have to pursue a much more determined and focused strategy that would challenge the dominant capitalism of powerful multinational companies and speculative financial markets. The Party's economic documents of the period reflected a surprising insularity of thought, an ideology of building socialism in one country as if the rest of the interdependent world was an irrelevance.

However, the heavily dirigiste policies failed to arouse much direct, intellectual counter-challenge from Labour's demoralised revisionist right wing, who found themselves forced onto the defensive and seemingly incapable of renewing their ideas about the future of the political economy. The analysis of the existing economic crisis and the urgent demand for swift state action to deal with it were central to the thinking of the Liaison Committee as well as the National Executive Committee. In fact, no strong voices were raised at the time to question the signing of the Social Contract inside the mainstream Labour movement nor the radical overhaul of industrial policy. Even Roy Jenkins, the Party's Deputy Leader until his abrupt resignation in 1972, recognised the sense of establishing a more amicable understanding between the Party and the trade unions. In fact, strategic public policy alliances between centre–left governments and trade union federations were commonplace across much of democratic Western Europe by the early 1970s. In the Nordic countries, but also in West Germany and Austria, such relationships were an accepted precondition for the development of a successful social democracy in managing market economies through co-operation on demand side management strategies to boost growth rates in combination with progressive social policies that extended the frontiers of the post-war welfare state. Indeed, outwardly genuine agreement seemed to exist over Labour's overall reassessment between June 1970 and March 1974 on what needed to be done to avoid any repetition of the perceived mistakes and failures of the Party's recent term in government. Both the right and the left accepted there could be no return to a statutory prices and incomes policy, although at the same time they recognised the need for a more interventionist approach to economic policy making.

Nor was there any principled division of opinion inside the Party on the formulation of a radical strategy to deal with the widening concern about the country's de-industrialisation due to the persistent failure of the private sector to invest in its own future. The creation of a state-holding company – the National Enterprise Board – with sweeping enabling powers to stimulate new sectors of technology and innovation through the selective provision of taxpayers' money was broadly accepted. It was seen by many in the Party as a logical advance from the mixed experiences of the Industrial Reorganisation Corporation of the late 1960s and based on the supposedly successful model of Italian corporate capitalism's Industrial Reconstruction Institute. Other admired examples of state-holding companies were found in Sweden, France and West Germany. But under Tony Benn's general direction bold, statist plans for an industrial revival went much further than Wilson and his colleagues had really envisaged. Benn wanted to extend direct state intervention into the commercial operations of many successful, leading private sector companies across all sectors through the introduction of compulsory planning agreements. Those instruments of centralised planning would enable the state to become intimately involved in the future development strategies of larger firms. It was not until the autumn of 1973 that Wilson revealed his increasing alarm at what he saw as the menacing thrust of the new industrial programme. His personal and belated intervention was a rearguard action, designed to recover lost ground, and it led to the hurried abandonment of any commitment to nationalise the top twenty-five private sector companies as one of the Party's urgent policy objectives. The leadership may have shared Benn's genuine concern about the future of British manufacturing but it was not going to embrace any policy that seemed to threaten the existence of the mixed economy. And yet it needs to be emphasised that common ground existed across the Party at that time about the active role the state needed to play in industrial regeneration, which transcended traditional divisions. After all, a state-led restoration of the country's manufacturing base was then being attempted by Edward Heath's Conservative Government after the spring of 1972. His resulting Industry Act provided sweeping powers to the state for its intervention in industrial affairs. Benn even thanked Heath for paving the way for the kind of fundamental change that he was seeking.

But the proposed industrial strategy was not envisaged as corporatist by the left. Benn in particular wanted to see a fundamental shift in power in industry away from private capital and oligarchies through the development of industrial democracy and encouragement of worker co-operatives. Worker participation was to go hand in hand with the advance of state control and influence over broad swathes of the private industrial sector. As an April 1973 party document explained: 'a steady enlargement of the public sector on the basis of democratic consent is more urgent today than it has ever been'. The industrial strategy's grand ambition was to preside over 'the transfer of economic wealth and power from a small economic oligarchy to the people'.[8] The full ambitions of the National Enterprise Board would not be realised 'for a fairly long period', it was acknowledged. Nevertheless, the avowed aim was to ensure a third of the annual turnover of the country's largest hundred firms, 40 per cent of their profits and half their employment should be vested in the new state-holding company within five years of its creation. This would have still required the state takeover of twenty to twenty-five successful private companies in leading industrial sectors 'early in the government's period in office'.

What was so conspicuously lacking from most of the analysis was any practical discussion about the levels of management competence required and the internal structure of companies as well as the way they financed their activities. Little detailed policy work had been done on ways of reforming the banking system before March 1974. It was unclear why either senior civil servants or academic economists would turn out to be any better than entrepreneurs and even company shareholders in spearheading a successful industrial revival and picking winners. In fact, surprisingly few people with any practical knowledge of industry or finance took part in Labour industrial policy making before 1974. It was Richard Pryke, a former party researcher in Transport House and then economics lecturer at Liverpool University, and Stuart Holland, one-time member of Wilson's Downing Street team and adviser to Roy Jenkins, who were the main architects of Labour's industrial strategy. Judith Hart, the Labour MP who chaired the Party's Industrial Policy Committee's public sector group, was not known for her business acumen either. Benn's own political advisers – Frances Morell and Francis Cripps – were equally ill-equipped for the challenging task ahead of carrying through an industrial miracle. Employers sympathetic to Labour such as Peter Parker and Fred Catherwood may have attended the occasional committee meeting but they took no full part in the creation of the industrial strategy. But Benn was not averse to dealing with industrialists. He was particularly impressed by Frank Kearton, Chief Executive of Courtaulds, the textile conglomerate.

The 1973 Party Conference revealed a surprising degree of common ground on the need for a more determined strategy for redistribution, high public spending and state ownership of industry. Moreover, the Liaison Committee enabled the trade unions to set out a long wish-list of demands they expected a future Labour Government to meet once it was elected. Despite some outward signs of doubt and anxiety Wilson was able to establish a degree of common agreement across the Party. But his main priority was to solidify a closer alliance with the TUC through the practical development of the Social Contract. As Britain's economy plunged into severe crisis in the winter of 1973–4 with a miners' strike and the threat of hyperinflation in the aftermath of the quadrupling in world oil prices following the Yom Kippur War, Labour promised that if elected back into government it would work amicably with the trade unions in the implementation of a programme of economic and social change.

All the same, the Party's sudden and unexpected return to office in March 1974 surprised many among the Party's leadership who had feared they faced abject defeat in the general election. Wilson may not have taken Labour's general election manifesto seriously enough but now he was compelled to try and put much of it into practice. For the first eight months before the October 1974 general election, the minority government pursued its programme with a close eye on choosing the best moment to dissolve Parliament with the likeliest chance of achieving a second election victory and securing an overall workable parliamentary majority. This was never going to be easy in the face of raging wage-push inflation, a mounting balance of payments deficit and an unrealistic economic growth strategy. The first priority was, however, to put an end to industrial militancy. The trade unions insisted on the immediate repeal of the hated 1971 Industrial Relations Act and acceptance of free collective bargaining combined with an expansion in social spending. Wilson and his colleagues were in too weak a strategic position to impose any kind of wage restraint during 1974 even if they had wanted to. All they could hope for was the delivery of the TUC's public assurance of an orderly return to collective bargaining with an agreed promise that a twelve-month interval should separate pay agreements to prevent an unruly reopening of existing wage arrangements and a resulting wages free-for-all. More disastrously, ministers also accepted the need to maintain the threshold clause of the statutory incomes policy inherited from Heath that continued to ratchet up wage levels month after month until its expiration in July 1974.

In fact, the minority Labour Government honoured most of its promises under the Social Contract. An independent Advisory, Conciliation and Arbitration Service was established. Very much the brain-child of Jack Jones, it still provides an impartial and impressive function in resolving disputes and encouraging good industrial relations practice. A permanent tripartite Health and Safety at Work Commission followed the passage of what Jones called 'the most comprehensive legislation ever drafted covering people at work'.[9] In addition, a Manpower Services Commission was established to develop a more active labour market policy to deal with unemployment and improve job placements. Old-age pensions were raised substantially. A price and rent freeze was imposed and food subsidies were introduced. The Pay Board was abolished and the Price Commission provided with greater powers to control and delay price rises.

It was clear by the autumn of 1974 that the Government was honouring its side of the Social Contract despite severe economic difficulties. But what were the trade unions doing in return? The answer was – not much and never enough. During the winter of 1974–5 inflationary wage settlements did not suggest many trade unions were willing to exercise much self-restraint in their collective demands whatever verbal promises they might make to reassure increasingly anxious ministers. The deterioration in economic conditions did not even lead the Cabinet to initiate at least a discussion about the merits of a national wages policy after Labour's narrow general election victory in October 1974. Ministers were still reluctant to confront the TUC with any such attempt if it threatened the existence of the Social Contract. Wilson's almost single-minded preoccupation with the renegotiation of the terms of Britain's membership of the European Common Market proved to be an added distraction. The Prime Minister needed to settle that vexatious question first of all through a promised referendum before he could turn his attention to any policy designed to deal with the mounting dangers of hyper wage inflation. It was only after the achievement of the majority 'Yes' vote in the June 1975 European Common Market referendum and the forced shift of Tony Benn from the Department of Industry to the Department of Energy that the Prime Minister felt strong enough to contemplate the negotiation of a new deal with the trade unions that involved wage restraint in the shape of the £6 a week flat-rate policy for pay increases over a twelve-month period.

But Wilson did not hold back until the late summer of 1975 in exercising a restraining influence over the direction of the Government's industrial policy. In fact, the Prime Minister lost little time after his return to 10 Downing Street in virtually taking over the making of the industrial strategy from Benn in June 1974. As he admitted on reading a draft of Benn's proposed White Paper: 'it proved to be a sloppy and half-baked document, polemical, indeed menacing in tone, redolent more of a national executive committee home policy committee document than a command paper'.[10] The Prime Minister established a public enterprise cabinet committee with himself as chairman to oversee the plans with his Chancellor of the Exchequer Denis Healey and other senior Cabinet colleagues in attendance. In the event, it was the Number 10 Policy Unit and not the Department of Industry that wrote the resulting White Paper. Wilson insisted that its introduction should explicitly praise the mixed market economy.

As it asserted:

> Britain's prosperity and welfare depend on the wealth generated by its industry and all who work in it. It matters vitally to all of us that British industry should be strong and successful. We need both efficient, publicly owned industries and a vigorous, alert, responsible and profitable private sector working with the government in a framework which brings together the interests of all concerned.[11]

But the White Paper acknowledged the severe crisis facing manufacturing. It pointed out that investment per worker in Britain was only half what it was in France, Japan and the United States and far below the levels being achieved in Italy and West Germany.

However, the document went on to remove most of the threatening proposals that Benn had wanted to include in its pages. Planning agreements between individual companies and the state were to be made voluntary and not compulsory. This move more or less rendered such arrangements non-existent. Only two were actually signed by the time Labour lost office in May 1979. One was with the National Coal Board and the other with Chrysler, which the American company tore up unilaterally only a year after signing it with the sale of its British operations to the French firm Peugeot Citroën. The financial resources of the National Enterprise Board were also to be tightly restricted by a triumphant Treasury. It was promised that neither the machine tool nor the pharmaceutical industries were to be nationalised. Benn did not resign after what was portrayed as his personal humiliation. He even expressed his relief that much of what he had wanted remained in the resulting White Paper. In fact, despite the rhetoric Benn's outlook was much more restrained than often recognised. As he admitted in a paper in May 1974 to the Liaison Committee: 'very few people knew what the programme says or what the argument is all about'. Apparently, there was no hope of winning public support for the industrial strategy without 'a background of understanding of Britain's long-term industrial difficulties'.[12] This meant launching a nationwide public campaign of persuasion and explanation. But Benn's isolation in the Cabinet was painfully apparent with his failure to gain much sympathy for his cause among left-wing colleagues such as Employment Secretary Michael Foot and Barbara Castle, the Social Services Secretary. Benn's political ascendancy appeared to be on the wane, at least for the moment, as the Treasury reasserted its authority. However, the Cabinet did agree on carrying through a substantial programme of public ownership. The shipbuilding and aerospace industries as well as North Sea oil were to be nationalised during Labour's years in government. State assistance was also still to be provided, at least for a short time, for three worker co-operatives – Meriden motor-cycles, the *Scottish Daily Record* and Fisher-Bendix on Merseyside –that Benn had championed. The deepening crisis in the British car industry also brought about the nationalisation of British Leyland. State subsidies were poured into the ailing steel industry despite its chronic overcapacity in production facilities. The

National Coal Board became a special beneficiary of substantial taxpayer largesse in the Government's new energy policy that sought to reduce dependence on oil imports to meet the country's energy needs. Both Rolls-Royce and the engineering firm Alfred Herbert were also saved from collapse through government action. Indeed, it was the 'lame ducks' and not new industries that benefited primarily from Labour's industrial strategy, even after Benn's departure from the Industry Department. Wilson and Benn both agreed, in the face of stiff Treasury resistance, on the need to persevere with the Anglo-French Concorde aerospace project despite its horrendous costs, with £1 billion of its debts being written off and an eventual cost per plane that turned out to be ten times higher than the original estimate. Apparently the manufacture of fourteen subsonic planes to carry business people and civil servants backwards and forwards across the Atlantic at speed was an acceptable use of taxpayers' money despite the mounting constraints on other public spending in both Britain and France.

The nadir of the Government's defensive approach towards industry was apparent in the crisis over Chrysler when the normally shrewd Harold Lever, Chancellor of the Duchy of Lancaster, recommended a lavish rescue operation in 1975 for the American company's UK operations at the taxpayers' expense even if it meant supporting a firm that was in stiff competition with the recently state-owned British Leyland. The National Enterprise Board devoted most of its £777 million allocation from public funds up to March 1979 to the rescue of British Leyland and Rolls-Royce. Under Eric Varley, Benn's successor as Industry Secretary, a tripartite industrial strategy was launched in late 1975 within the auspices of the tripartite National Economic Development Council. In practice, it produced predictably little more than a depressing collection of sector working party reports that merely outlined the malaise that was gripping much of manufacturing and offered timid policy recommendations. In fact, the industrial strategy failed to develop any credible programme to deal with the familiar troubles that it chronicled. However, it must be arguable whether much could have been achieved through direct state action to improve the country's international competitiveness at that time. Britain was going through the early stages of what turned out to be a painful process of industrial restructuring. Inevitably a Labour Government in such circumstances found itself forced pragmatically to pursue reactive rescue operations rather than implement an ambitious plan to stimulate the creation of new industries. A 1978 internal party paper presented to the Industrial Policy Subcommittee was scathing. 'Without real planning and a coherent planning framework, industrial policy will continue to be an uninspired and largely ineffective exercise in ad hockery', it complained. It suggested the policy had reached an 'impasse'.[13] In fact, the Labour left was already preparing more radical moves to state intervention in industry in time for the Party's next general election manifesto.

It must also be questionable whether the British state was really equipped to play successfully either an interventionist or a catalytic role in any industrial regeneration. The country's international competitiveness was brought into serious question by economic events. Inevitably ministers were compelled to respond to the rising troubles of ailing loss-making firms and industries and they could not devote sufficient resources or time to the encouragement of innovation and new technologies. Benn and his supporters had never wanted the National Enterprise Board to turn into a mere 'repository for companies reduced to the status of lame ducks'. Indeed, they had hoped the new body would 'provide new jobs, new investment and new growth opportunities'.[14] A June 1975 Party document had affirmed: 'we have no desire to ossify the structure of UK industry. Market forces must be taken into consideration for there is no point in continuing to produce goods for which there is no demand.' The intention had been to build up 'a portfolio of profitable concerns, capable of carrying out the tasks assigned to it'. As Bernard Donoughue, head of the Prime Minister's Policy Unit at the time, has written:

> looking back, it is striking how most of us in that Labour government, whether on the right through the French dirigiste model or on Labour's left aping Stalinist centralism, still believed state intervention in the markets and the direction of capital would actually improve the performance of the economy over the longer term. Our subsequent experience in government provided a rude awakening and education.[15]

Labour's handling of the nationalised industries was no more successful than its industrial strategy for the private sector. As a chastened Richard Pryke observed in 1981, while under Labour they had been 'subject to many constraints', they had been 'under remarkably little discipline'.[16] The one-time enthusiast for state action had now become an ardent Thatcherite on industrial matters as a result of his bitter, personal experience. Trade union resistance to necessary change had been assisted by the absence of tight cash limits on the spending programmes of the public corporations and the constant belief that in a crisis the state would always come to their financial rescue. The transformation of the public industries into 'instruments of economic and social policy' and their inability to act as 'commercial undertakings' may have started under Heath in 1972 but the Labour Governments of Wilson and Callaghan were even more unwilling to allow them to operate in a business-like way if it meant closures, job losses and contraction.

There were a few, belated signs that the Government realised the urgent need to take a more harshly realistic view of what needed to be done in the transformation of British industry. Wilson's appointment of Don Ryder, Chief Executive of Reed International, as Chairman of the slimmed down National Enterprise Board and the elevation of the abrasive South African industrialist Sir Michael Edwardes to run British Leyland with a free hand suggests mounting official concern to seek out the best in business life to administer what remained of the industrial strategy rather than like-minded Labour sympathisers more susceptible to political influence. But most employers, both in ideology and practice, remained unsympathetic to any state intervention in industry that involved any kind of outside government control over the way they ran their companies. They disliked notions of managed corporatism even if they were ready to accept and even demand state financial assistance when they believed it was necessary for their own survival. However, as so often in the past, they continued to resist any form of industrial reconstruction that involved active and direct participation by the trade unions, let alone their own employees.

However, the trade unions were themselves not entirely free from fault. In the creation of a successful industrial state it was necessary for them to help in the training of a professional cadre of worker activists at national and company level who could become intimately involved in the making of industrial policy. No such group really existed in most of British industry. And when some did emerge, such as the combine of shop stewards at Lucas Aerospace with their alternative plan for production, they were denounced by their own national union for alleged political extremism. It is true that the cause of industrial democracy was taken half-seriously by the Government. A committee of inquiry was established under the chairmanship of the Oxford historian Alan Bullock with both Jack Jones and David Lea from the TUC among its members. Its purpose was to recommend ways of introducing trade union participation in the running of private sector companies based very much on what the TUC favoured. The resulting report, published in February 1976, made ambitious recommendations that if implemented would have ensured the direct participation of shop stewards on the executive boards of many leading firms. Even the employer members of the Bullock Committee recommended the transplant of the West German works council system into British industry, a significant sign of just how much capital had been thrown onto the defensive at the time in the face of assertive trade union ambitions. But the larger trade unions, most notably the Engineering Workers, the Electricians and the General and Municipal Workers, rejected industrial democracy as proposed by the Bullock Committee as overwhelmingly as most employer organisations and the broad left. The whole controversy was dispatched by the Government to a Cabinet committee chaired by the moderate Shirley Williams for further consideration. However, the resulting White Paper, presented by Callaghan to Parliament in May 1978, sketched out the possible framework for future industrial democracy legislation. As it argued:

> we spend a large part of our lives at work and invest our skills and energies in industry. There is growing recognition that those of us who do so should be able to participate in decisions which can vitally affect our working lives and our jobs. This development is no longer a question of 'if' but 'when and how'.[17]

The Government called for 'a positive partnership between management and workers rather than defensive co-existence'.

However, Britain's political economy has always lacked a meritocratic elite of trained functionaries needed to manage a successful modern industrial state on democratic principles. Labour's industrial policies in the 1970s failed to recognise the massive obstacles that blocked the road to modernisation. Perhaps most fatally of all, the Government, and in particular the Treasury, was simply not prepared in practice to reallocate limited financial resources from current to capital expenditure, from public services to private sector manufacturing. Union leaders like Hugh Scanlon, President of the Engineering Workers, wanted the Government to give the development of manufacturing its highest priority with a corresponding restraint on public services expansion. A growing chorus of economists began to criticise what they saw as the adverse consequences of the growth of the service economy, which was crowding out the needs of manufacturing industry. But by the late 1970s the Labour Party was increasingly dominated by the public service sector unions and their members who rejected any suggestion that industry should become the predominant concern of government. The widening gulf between Labour and manufacturing was to separate the Party from much of its core electorate with devastating consequences at the polls.

Contrary to popular myth, Britain had not been turned into a fully fledged corporatist economy. Its tripartite representative institutions of capital and labour remained weak, voluntarist and unprepared to perform a decisive role in any co-ordinated industrial revival. The country's political economy lacked the institutional means or focused attention to implement a successful industrial strategy. The problems of chronic underinvestment, poor labour productivity and limited skills were familiar enough. What was missing was any realistic policy to solve them. In fact, a way forward was found during the next decade. The return of mass unemployment and withdrawal of subsidies and state supports to industries in crisis marked the hardening attitude of the Conservatives under Margaret Thatcher after May 1979. Many of Britain's vulnerable industries were compelled to come to terms with commercial realities, although in doing so they inflicted pain on many communities and damaged social cohesion. It was a course of action that Labour governments had fought unsuccessfully to avoid.

The struggle for wage restraint – the role of the Communist Party

However, even at the height of its apparent hegemony in 1975–6 the Social Contract always looked like a rather flimsy, temporary arrangement. Its declared objective was certainly ambitious enough – in Jim Callaghan's words, the 'means of achieving nothing less than the social and economic reconstruction of our country'.[18] But it was never conceived by the trade unions as a permanent agreement to manage the political economy based on any form of social dialogue. The Confederation of British Industry was absent from most of the Social Contract's deliberations and employers remained very much on the margins of formalised industrial politics even if they exercised considerable influence behind the scenes. The Party–union Liaison Committee continued to meet each month but progress mainly took place on a bilateral basis. Over time the committee became a much more congenial place for ministers to do business than on the

Party's increasingly bitter and left-dominated National Executive Committee. The six union representatives on the National Economic Development Council became the key actors in the Social Contract's development, regularly wined and dined in Downing Street. Known as the Neddy gold-plated six, they came to symbolise the increasing unreality of the union–Government relationship as seen from the workplace.

In fact, the Social Contract represented at least an implicit attempt to impose some responsibilities on organised labour for the management of the national economy in what was becoming an increasingly fragmented and decentralised trade union movement. Trade unions in Britain in the past had always sought to avoid turning themselves into social partners in the running of the political economy by contrast to so many of their continental European counterparts who had practised such arrangements since the so-called social settlement of the immediate post-war years. They valued their autonomy and freedom, not least because their own archaic and competitive structures made it difficult for them to exercise much effective centralising authority or cohesion over disparate and insecure memberships. Inter-union rivalries and the endless competition for members in the labour market hampered their efforts to achieve successful common strategies that were of any lasting permanence. Experience suggested nationally conceived incomes policy could last for only short lengths of time. In addition, the decline in industry-wide national bargaining and the rise of more self-confident and aggressive shop steward organisations in the early 1970s imposed further intolerable strains on trade unions who usually lacked either the will or the institutional means at the centre to ensure the development of long-term co-ordinated bargaining systems. Moreover, workplace culture by the 1970s was no longer conducive to collectivist values of solidarity and equity or traditional appeals to class loyalties. Rising levels of personal taxation and the unending wages struggle in the face of a relentless upsurge in price inflation were stimulating serious worker discontent, especially among skilled manual workers in the more labour-intensive industries such as engineering and auto production. Wage restraint was to hit those aristocrats of manual labour the hardest because it brought about an inevitable narrowing in their pay relativities and differentials compared with other manual workers and staff in the public sector and beyond. White-collar workers were able to escape the full force of any restraint on their pay rises by ensuring their existing annual pay increments were protected under the incomes policy guidelines. This was an important concession that self-interested senior civil servants were successful in achieving. The resulting discontent of the rank and file in many other trade unions was, however, understandable and they were difficult to appease by assurances about the growth of the social wage. Moreover, by the mid-1970s many workers had come to believe that they enjoyed unchallenged bargaining power in a labour market where the maintenance of full employment was still regarded as politically necessary if any party hoped to win and remain in government. The advance in the strength of the shop floor in private manufacturing was combined with a rising self-awareness among organised public sector workers of the strength they could apply to prevent any government pursuing economic policies that weakened their own bargaining position. The industrial relations system had become inherently more unstable and unpredictable in worsening economic circumstances. The Social Contract envisaged an agreed programme to advance the social and industrial aims of trade unions but it failed to develop the kind of tripartite institutions that could have closed the widening gap between shop-floor realities and national imperatives. The crisis called for a degree of centralising discipline and authority but this was becoming impossible to achieve in a trade union movement that had the power to obstruct but lacked either the legitimacy or the power to innovate. As the Oxford sociologist John Goldthorpe explained insightfully in 1974:

> throughout a large part of British industry at the present time no authority prevails at workplace level which is capable of establishing and maintaining coherent normative systems to govern relations between employers and employees. There exists only a proliferation of generally unrelated, small-scale systems of doubtful effectiveness, whose inconsistencies serve often to intensify disorder and conflict.[19]

In fact, the Social Contract was confronted from its beginning by a formidable political force that emerged to take advantage of the underlying weaknesses in the country's increasingly decentralised, workplace unionism. The most effective, organised trade union resistance to the Social Contract throughout the whole of its tempestuous life came from the activities of the industrial wing of the small Communist Party and its trade union allies on Labour's broad left. Politically the communists were heading rapidly towards oblivion with a mass membership which had dropped to less than 30,000 by 1975. But such weakness was not true for their influence over the general direction of Britain's industrial politics. Under the shrewd direction of Bert Ramelson, head of the Party's virtually autonomous Industrial Department and his successor after 1978, the urbane Mick Costello, it came to exercise a remarkable degree of influence, far greater in extent than the small size of its mass membership might suggest, over the making of strategy and tactics across a wide cadre of broad-left activists inside many trade unions. Communist influence was not only increasingly evident among the composition of national union leaderships and full-time staff. It was also apparent inside the ranks of senior convenors and stewards at many of the larger industrial plants such as the Ford Motor Company complex at Dagenham and British Leyland in Birmingham's Longbridge plant. These were to become the pace-setters in the development of an effective shop-floor trade unionism.

It is no exaggeration to suggest that the Communist Party's industrial wing at least brought an ideological if flawed coherence to what was an often chaotic, fragmented and unpredictable scene. Its front organisation – the Liaison Committee for the Defence of Trade Unions under the leadership of Kevin Halpin – had spearheaded the impressive growth of rank and file militancy against the Heath Government's Industrial Relations Act in the early 1970s, particularly in pushing an often reluctant TUC General Council into adopting a more hostile response than it wanted to do. In its capacity to mobilise thousands of workers in protest between 1969 and 1974, Halpin's organisation was an industrial force to be reckoned with. Ramelson came to believe it enjoyed more influence inside the trade unions during those years than the communist-led Minority Movement had done between the wars. It was communist convenors like Jimmy Airlie and Jimmy Reid who led the battle to save all four yards at Upper Clyde Shipbuilders. Again in the 1972 building workers' dispute it was the communists who were a dominant influence on union leaderships. The Party was at the forefront of the effective mass picketing in the 1972 coal strike, especially in the closure of Saltley Coal Depot in Birmingham where 10,000 engineering workers turned up in solidarity with the miners. Comrades like Mick McGahey, Vice-President of the National Union of Mineworkers, were at the forefront of the struggle.

With Labour back in government, the Communists continued to pursue a militant trade union strategy through their considerable influence on Labour's left. Their purpose, from the beginning, was to destroy the Social Contract, even before it developed a voluntary incomes policy with an agreed norm. The Party's rejection was at least consistent. In his seminal tract – *The Social Contract – Cure All or Con Trick?* – published in November 1974, Ramelson set out the ideological argument for a complete repudiation of the Social Contract. He defined the arrangement as 'an undertaking by the TUC to restrain workers from using their bargaining strength to achieve wage and salary increases which they feel necessary, justified and attainable'.[20] As Ramelson explained:

> there can be no argument that the Social Contract is an instrument for exerting pressure on trade unions and groups of workers to frame claims, not in accordance with their freely determined views on what they should be, but restricted to a framework determined by others, which is the very negation of free collective bargaining.

However, Ramelson and his Party admitted they faced a serious difficulty. In the past, the broad left in the trade unions had opposed incomes policies but the position was rather different by 1974–5. As he acknowledged:

> with a few honourable exceptions most of the left trade union leaders who played a key role in convincing Congress to reject unconditionally all forms of incomes policy are amongst the foremost champions of the Social Contract which was undoubtedly the reason the Engineering Workers' challenge to the Social Contract at Brighton's Congress last September failed.

At that stage Ramelson wrote that he did not doubt 'the sincerity and genuineness' of left-wing union leaders in their support for the Social Contract. He believed it was essential to develop a constructive dialogue with them in an effort to convince them they were mistaken, 'that in advocating the Social Contract they were causing incalculable harm to their members, the economy and facilitating the right-wing core in the government to betray the spirit of the manifesto'. 'Only by smashing the Social Contract could the government be forced to take a new direction that involved seizing the economic and political levers of power', he insisted. The planning of wages which would not harm working people could only take place when not only labour but all other resources in the economy were planned.

In 1974–5 it was not merely an issue of pressing for free collective bargaining at all costs. The broad left were also developing what became known as the Alternative Economic Strategy. This involved a number of inter-related policy objectives – Britain's rapid withdrawal from the European Common Market, the repudiation of the country's massive foreign debt, an end to military spending abroad, the introduction of strict import controls on finished goods, essentials and raw materials, the rigid control of the export of capital, and the selling off of shareholdings with compensation in sterling to eliminate the balance of payments deficit. A price freeze of at least six months and a drastic cut in domestic interest rates were also advocated. A state takeover of the country's largest monopolies, as well as banking and financial institutions, was to be coupled with an expansion in demand at home with no restrictions on wage increases and a substantial improvement in social benefits in education and health.

The first real battle over the Social Contract took place at the 1974 Trades Union Congress. It was spearheaded by Ken Gill, General Secretary of the white-collar TASS section of the Engineering Workers' Union. A tough and able communist, he became the most formidable and effective trade union opponent of the Social Contract. On that occasion Gill came under pressure from the Engineering Union's President Hugh Scanlon and agreed to withdraw the hostile composite motion, a move that brought strong criticism from inside the Party and particularly from his ally the *Morning Star* newspaper which suggested it had been wrong of him 'to withdraw the resolution under the erroneous conception of duty'. Gill's 'error' was mitigated to some extent by the TUC's acceptance of the eight 'conditions' demanded in the composite motion which laid down the essentials of the Alternative Economic Strategy. Moreover, overall the Party was still well pleased by the outcome of the 1974 Congress. It claimed that as many as 97 of the 1,032 delegates were openly Communist Party members and 17 of them had spoken out during its debates. Gill secured over 7 million votes in his election to the TUC General Council. He was the first communist ever to be elected to a seat on that august body and he had won it with an impressive vote from trade union delegations.[21] The Party's breakthrough into the inner sanctuary of TUC decision making was followed a year later by the election of the communist Jimmy Milne as General Secretary of the Scottish Trades Union Congress. In a further advance George Guy, a communist and General Secretary of the Sheet Metal Workers' Union, was elected to the TUC General Council in September 1977. Over the next few years Gill took the lead in the development of an influential group of broad-left union leaders on the TUC General Council. They used to meet every month in various union headquarters in London before General Council sessions to go through the TUC agenda and decide what line to take on each item. This ensured a strong discipline and co-ordination in resisting the Social Contract. No minutes were taken of group proceedings and its membership was fluid. But Gill was not in any doubt that it enabled the broad left and through it the Communist Party to take the ideological offensive over a wide range of issues with some success.

By early May 1975 the pressures on the Government for the introduction of a statutory incomes policy were becoming irresistible in the face of soaring inflation. It was then that Jack Jones seized the initiative with his simple but appealing proposal for the introduction for a twelve-month period of a voluntary £6 a week flat-rate increase for anybody earning less than £8,500 a year. For the better off there would be no pay rise at all. Jones was convinced rightly that the Government would collapse if effective action was not taken to ensure pay restraint. He raised the spectre of another 1931 political crisis with prominent Cabinet members deserting Labour to form a national coalition government with the Conservatives. There was no real evidence that such a development was ever likely but its very suggestion was enough to worry Labour supporters who possessed a sense of history. But it was also true that Jones's proposal for a flat-rate pay norm was very much in tune with the needs and aspirations of his lower-paid members in the Transport and General Workers' Union. Not for the first time, here was a fortuitous convergence of national and sectional interests behind a common approach. Within weeks Jones had won round the TUC General Council, at least to agreement on the principle of a voluntary pay policy with a norm. Only Scanlon seemed to reject the idea on the grounds that the trade unions would be unable to deliver any form of wage restraint. He was concerned understandably that such a proposal would have an adverse impact on skilled engineering workers whose pay was still often linked to individual performance. In fact, the introduction of the £6 policy with the TUC's approval was by no means a certainty until the very last moment. Ideally, the Treasury would have much preferred a statutory approach to dealing with pay, complete with legal sanctions against those workers who defied the incomes policy's norms. It was understandably sceptical that the TUC would ever be able to deliver enough restraint from all of its affiliate members. Moreover, the £6 flat-rate pay policy was only carried narrowly by nineteen votes to thirteen on the General Council. If all its members had turned up on that occasion it is conceivable that the policy might have been rejected.

At the 1975 Trades Union Congress Gill moved a composite motion that denounced the new £6 voluntary pay policy outright. The motion argued that the policy treated 'the symptoms of inflation instead of tackling the underlying causes of instability in the UK economy'.[22] The motion also spelt out the need for the implementation of the Alternative Economic Strategy to deal with rising unemployment: 'There have been crises before, indeed every year there has been a Labour government. The reality is this – that in 1931, in 1958 and in 1964 and again in 1974 there has been financial manipulation on national and international levels,' Gill argued. 'It will always happen when a Labour government takes office. If we do not face it this time we shall have to face it next time.' His motion was lost on a show of hands and it was not put to a card vote. However, support at the Congress for the £6 policy was passed by 6,945,000 to 3,375,000 voting against it. The forces of resistance inside the TUC turned out to be stronger than might have been expected. Ramelson observed that 'the left trend which was a feature of the past decade, far from being reversed, has been consolidated and even advanced'.[23] The removal of the right-wing Roy Grantham, leader of APEX, the clerical union, from the TUC General Council was a particular event for congratulation inside the Communist Party.

A second year of 'voluntary' pay restraint was also supported at the 1976 Congress but it was becoming apparent that the ability or willingness of the trade unions to continue their support for voluntary wage restraint was growing severely limited. Indeed, Jack Jones had not really abandoned his instinctive belief in the virtues of free collective bargaining. But he was a realist and a party loyalist and recognised that any trade union confrontation with the Labour Government over pay would hasten its early collapse. In such circumstances, the alternative would not bring about a strategic shift to the policies of the broad left but the return of Margaret Thatcher's Conservative Party at the next general election. But this did not mean that either Jones or Len Murray were willing to agree to the formation of a permanent or long-term arrangement on pay determination as both Jim Callaghan and Chancellor Denis Healey hankered for. No machinery was even actually established to monitor wage movements under the Social Contract. There was to be no resurrection of a National Prices and Incomes Board on the model of the 1960s. Moreover, the TUC found it hard to negotiate on the tax cut/wage restraint package offered by the Chancellor in the spring of 1976. In fact, with a few exceptions, union leaders were all agreed on the temporary character of voluntary wage restraint. The Prime Minister may have looked for inspiration to Helmut Schmidt's Social Democratic West Germany on how co-ordinated national pay bargaining might work in practice. But as early as June 1976 Jones warned Callaghan and Healey there would have to be 'an orderly return to free collective bargaining' by the following summer. He also told them that no further twelve-month understanding deal on pay was possible with the Government even if it chose not to believe him. But Jones did not mean a return to free collective bargaining should signal a resurgence of the kind of chaotic pay free-for-all that would precipitate an inevitable upsurge in wage-push inflation. Jones was well aware of the perilous condition of the economy, beholden by the end of 1976 to the International Monetary Fund for financial assistance and at the mercy of foreign money markets. What he wanted to see was at least the exercise of what he liked to call 'responsible' negotiations. Unfortunately even this modest aspiration was to prove an over-ambitious objective.

In fact, the Communist Party seemed to articulate a growing discontent among many trade union activists. In early 1977 Ramelson wrote an uncompromising attack on the Social Contract. Its main call was for a return to the traditional trade union objective – 'unfettered' collective bargaining. 'Free collective bargaining is not a free for all with the sky the limit', he reassured:

> Trade unions always have been and are responsible bodies with their membership having the power, if they use it, to decide policy. In deciding what its wage claims should be a trade union takes into consideration a number of factors, including the changes in the cost of living and the economic capacity of the employer to pay. If the government pursues policies which bring down prices, increase the social wage and reduce the gap between the workers and the rich, all this will be taken into account as it always has been by the unions.[24]

Ramelson appealed to a strong emotional feeling inside the unions:

> The British trade union movement's distinctive characteristic is the sovereignty and independence of each union. It is a decentralised movement. A Social Contract implies a highly centralised movement with a handful of bodies deciding for all the unions. It undermines the independence and democratic right of each union and reduces collective bargaining to a meaningless pre-ordained exercise.

But Ramelson and Gill faced serious criticism from within the Communist Party for their single-minded commitment to free collective bargaining and their emphasis on the primacy of the wages struggle. The party veteran George Mathews, head of its Press and Publicity Department, believed they were guilty of the unpardonable sin of 'economism'. It was also conceded by many communists that a substantial number of rank and file trade unionists were still prepared to back the Government's restrictive line on wage increases. An internal report from the north-west region of the Communist Party in August 1976 spoke of 'a sense of frustration' in many workplaces. 'There is a widespread acceptance of Social Democratic ideology and policies that has permeated a wide section of the grass roots', it complained.[25] It also criticised what it saw as the lack of any cohesion and clarity among workers. There was special concern expressed about rank and file attitudes in the engineering industry around Manchester in what had been Hugh Scanlon's broad-left power base during the 1960s and early 1970s. His own move away from his former supporters at that time reflected a clear shift in the political balance towards the right wing in the Engineering Workers' Union. This trend was also apparent on its normally balanced fifty-two-strong policy-making National Committee. The decisive election of the right-wing West Midlander Terry Duffy to succeed Scanlon as union president in 1978 was a clear defeat for the communists in a union where they had managed to exercise substantial influence for more than a decade, mainly through Gill's control of the TASS section of the Engineering Union and a strong broad-left presence on the Executive Council and in many districts. However, the clear move to the right did not mean the union's members were willing to tolerate further bouts of pay restraint.

They did believe that free collective bargaining was a left-wing cause. Calls for an end to any wage restraint won a sympathetic following among workers who were hostile both to communism as well as the Alternative Economic Strategy. The growing pressure among British Leyland toolmakers to form a breakaway union in 1977–9 was indicative of the upsurge of serious unrest that was spreading among the skilled manual working class. They believed their own wage differentials were being squeezed whereas the real pre-tax pay of production workers employed in the same company continued to rise. But workplace frustrations over pay restraint did not point to any noticeable growth in left-wing feeling among workers. On the contrary it suggested an increasing momentum towards non-socialist politics. The populist attraction of Margaret Thatcher's Conservative Party was already becoming apparent across many of the country's industrial heartlands.

The Communist leadership acknowledged in September 1976 that 'the commitment of TUC leaders to the government's economic strategy, including some who had previously earned the respect and trust of militants' had helped to win considerable rank and file acceptance of wage restraint.[26] 'The theoretical basis of the Social Contract is that the government will carry out a political programme encompassing the important social and economic demands of the movement in return for wage restraint', noted a policy paper presented to the Party's Executive Committee.

> The TUC negotiators were blackmailed. As the mood grows in the factories and unions to struggle against government policy, this form of blackmail will be intensified. It will not be the responsibility of the left if Thatcher ever gets into Number 10. Any possibility of a Tory return is a result of what the right wing is doing. It is they who are betraying Labour policy and creating cynicism, disillusionment and anger with the Labour Movement amongst working people and not the left.

By February 1977 the industrial wing of the Communist Party was ready to launch an all-out offensive through the trade unions centred on both the struggle over the wages question and the Alternative Economic Strategy. As a draft report by Chris Myant prepared for the Party's Executive Committee argued:

> the sense of purpose and power in the movement's involvement in the key area of class conflict, the central form of trade union activity at the point of production, the wages has been cut off, its life blood drained away through the Social Contract. The movement is inhibited from thinking politically about the main political issue of Britain today – wages – because that issue has been deftly removed from the battleground. In the wake of the Social Contract straitjacket immobilising and demobilising the movement the right can launch its witch-hunts seeking further to silence the left into silence and timidity.

Myant added:

> the basis for any future Labour government programme must be a return to free collective bargaining. Nothing would help the British economy more than a wages offensive on the part of the Labour Movement to restore living standards, fuel economic expansion, and build the movement capable of imposing the alternative policy advocated by the left as the prime joint first stage in a counter-attack.[27]

Ramelson and his allies on the Party's industrial wing believed the moment had come to confront what they saw as the dangers of turning the Social Contract into 'a semi-permanent feature of life' with the emergence of a new consensus between capital, labour and the state. Now the Party would have to work inside the trade unions to prevent any move for an agreement on further pay guidelines before the onset of the unions' conference season in the spring and early summer. As the strategy document explained:

> attack the move to have the deal wrapped up quickly before the conferences. The movement should not allow such a coup against it. In place of wage restraint it should raise the banner of a wage offensive but to succeed it must be a clear headed and united offensive.

A fuller political report in March 1977 for the Party executive reinforced the belligerent message for a wages offensive. It pointed out that

> in important factories the workforce has taken the decision not to accept another Social Contract round of pay curbs. Several significant unions and union bodies have joined them. Some have still not freed themselves of the illusion that the pay policy helps the low paid but already the rising tide of anger within the movement has frustrated the attempt by the government to have the next round swept up.[28]

The communist call was for days of action, demonstrations of protest, the creation of local workplace committees, factory occupations and plant sit-ins in order to 'release the people from all the constraints dictated by monopoly capital'.

Only three months later the Social Contract suffered what turned out to be a fatal blow when Jack Jones was overturned by the majority of delegates at his union's biennial conference on the pay policy issue. Contrary to myth, Jones had not proposed any further round of wage restraint but he told his conference that he was determined to ensure an 'orderly return to free collective bargaining' and not a resort to 'unfettered chaos'. Above all, he was concerned to ensure no moves should be taken by the trade unions that would threaten the maintenance of the Labour Government. Jones believed that if the unions did not exercise 'some collective responsibility', there would be a descent into industrial chaos and conflict within the movement. His wise words went unheeded by the angry delegates who insisted there should be an unequivocal return to free collective bargaining. Many of them were shop stewards from the docks, the car industry and engineering, who had been the main beneficiaries of Jones's radical philosophy of strong workplace unionism. They had suffered from a loss of power and authority as a result of the national pay restraint policy and many were under pressure from the members to reassert themselves. Jones was convinced that the communists played an important role in the change of mood within the Transport and General Workers' Union. He once warned Ramelson publicly to stop interfering in the affairs of his union. But the Party's wages offensive went with the current of growing frustrations and genuine discontent among rank and file workers at the perceived consequences of two years of voluntary wage restraint.

In fact, the 1977 Trades Union Congress did not turn out to be a complete triumph for the broad left. It was agreed to operate a twelve-month rule between wage settlements to prevent a rush into a pay free-for-all as Jones had wanted. Ramelson complained that 'we have a long way to go to eradicate the confusion that exists particularly on the relationship of the economic to the political aspects of pay as the lynchpin of the Alternative Economic Strategy'.[29] Indeed, the 1977 version of the Party's *British Road to Socialism* programme emphasised the need to combat the dangers of economism. It seemed that the wages struggle was not nearly enough. What had to be done was to link this 'with a political perspective if it is to produce lasting gains for the working class'.[30] Moreover, the policy needed to involve a campaign of persuasion in workplaces and not just among full-time trade union national leaderships. But the communists complained that the Labour left 'still lacked a clear political perspective' and could not 'bring about the necessary transformation in the outlook and activity of the Labour Movement'. This could only come from a vanguard role that was to be played by the Communist Party inside the unions and through a diversity of extra-parliamentary struggles and the build-up of new factory branches.

The primacy of the wages struggle through an aggressive strategy of trade union advance failed to convince more thoughtful communists. Professor Eric Hobsbawm expressed a prophetic disquiet at what was happening in his seminal Marx Memorial Lecture that was delivered in the spring of 1978. Entitled 'The forward march of Labour halted?' it drew attention to what Hobsbawm saw as a critical moment in the evolution of the Labour movement. Out of the proletarianism and class consciousness of the early twentieth century, under the influence of structural and occupational changes, a new sectionalism had emerged. 'We now see a growing division of workers into sections and groups, each pursuing its own economic interest irrespective of the rest', he explained.[31] What was novel, he contended, was the ability of each group or section to mobilise its bargaining strength not so much by placing pressure on their employer but on the general public: 'In the nature of things such sectional forms of struggle not only create potential friction between groups of workers but risk weakening the hold of the labour movement as a whole.' The resulting 'economist militancy' brought a corresponding decline in social solidarity among workers. Hobsbawm provided an ideological explanation for what was a widely recognised phenomenon. The anomie of workplace life, however, had failed to stimulate a heightened awareness of the need to channel worker discontent beyond demands for high wages. Inner Party opponents like Gill and Kevin Halpin were critical of the Hobsbawm analysis. They continued to insist that campaigns to boost pay through the use or threat of strikes in defiance of government policy would not only defeat social democratic tendencies in the Labour movement but radicalise workers in struggle and extend their political perspectives to accept the Alternative Economic Strategy. But this analysis was based on little more than a bout of wishful thinking and not a hard-headed appreciation of the existing grim realities. Events were soon to vindicate Hobsbawm's perceptive analysis. Communist enthusiasm for an uncompromising wages struggle may have been an acknowledgement of the unstable and chaotic character of the industrial relations system by 1978 but it failed to appreciate the underlying dynamics of the moment.

Even the Party's industrial department was by no means optimistic about prospects. As it was explained in May 1978 to the Political Committee: 'the danger is that whether or not there will be formal trade union consent, the aggressive noises being made by some trade union leaders will hide their readiness to accept continued wage restraint in real life'.[32] Despite advances there was an underlying concern:

> The problem facing the militant forces in the trade union movement has been demonstrated at both the Shopworkers' and AEU union conferences. The Shopworkers' conference adopted a resolution calling for the restoration of free collective bargaining and a substantial increase in the minimum wage but their general secretary Lord Allen spoke in support of wage restraint. Scanlon defended wage restraint and while speaking of youth unemployment with all its dangers gave no lead in the fight for an Alternative Economic Strategy. Duffy's election as president with a substantial majority and the other victories gained by right-wing candidates in the AEU undoubtedly strengthens the position of the right wing within this union. The majority of divisional committees have put down resolutions demanding the return to free collective bargaining but the broad left faces a hard battle both to win progressive decisions and secure their implementation when won.

Such worries seem to have been misplaced. Jim Callaghan's determination to tighten the Government's pay policy by insisting on a 5 per cent overall wage rise norm for the 1978–9 wage round confounded his own supporters in the trade unions. They refused to believe he was serious in his insistence on such a low pay rise figure for the next wage round but on the other hand they were anxious not to cause him any trouble on the assumption that he was planning to call an autumn general election. In fact, Callaghan underestimated his mounting troubles and miscalculated in his assumption that the Government could achieve a further period of wage restraint, even tougher than it had been before. The Prime Minister was further weakened by the retirement of both Jones and Scanlon during the early months of 1978. Moss Evans, the new General Secretary of the Transport and General Workers' Union, turned out to be a weak and ineffective leader with neither the authority nor influence of his predecessor but then it is very doubtful whether Jones himself could have made much difference to the outcome if he had remained in office. His defeat in 1977 at the hands of his own union's conference had revealed just how much his authority had been diminished. Terry Duffy was a staunch anti-communist loyalist but he was in no position to offer Callaghan much support as many of his own members in the Engineering Workers' Union were now in open revolt against any further wage restraint. Its General Secretary, the right-wing Gavin Laird, might have been personally sympathetic to Callaghan but it was signifi-cant that he spoke out so strongly against any more Government-directed pay policy at the tempestuous 1978 Labour Party Conference. On the wages issue both right and left in the trade unions were now of common mind.

Mick Costello, the communists' newly appointed industrial organiser, was well pleased with the events at the Trades Union Congress in September 1978. As he told his Party's executive, its decisions were 'a vindication of the struggle by Communists' against the Social Contract.[33] Arguing that workers would now want to see a massive offensive on wages, jobs, working hours and the social services, Costello believed there were good grounds for the broad left to be opti-mistic. After all, the anti-Government resolutions passed at the TUC had not come out of thin air. They represented the pressure from below of tens of thou-sands of the rank and file through their trade union branches and upwards. Costello estimated that, just as at the 1977 Congress, about 100 or one in eleven of the delegates were Communist Party members, although he estimated the Party's real representative strength in those unions who were affiliated to the TUC to be only about one in every 600 members. Despite substantial mass membership losses and the desperate financial plight of the *Morning Star* news-paper, the Communist Party was still able to play a crucial role in policy making at the highest level of the trade union movement out of all proportion to its numerical strength. Costello admitted yet again that many of the tens of thou-sands of ordinary union members were being represented at important trade union activities by communists and other extremists who benefited 'from the low attendances at branch meetings'. And no doubt the bountiful supply of financial assistance from the Soviet Union continued to fund the Party's industrial activi-ties and the well-being of its cadre of full-time staff.

However, the TUC's decisive rejection of wage restraint and the Government's 5 per cent wage norm did not mean many union members were willing to swallow the broad left's Alternative Economic Strategy. As Costello explained: only if there is a greater understanding of the need for the Alternative Economic Strategy as a complete challenge to the government's policies will it be possible to speak of lasting gains being won from the battles now unfolding. Yet clearly of the items contained in the AES, the struggle around wages is being fought the hardest and its potential is therefore the greatest.[34]

Costello envisaged a twofold task lay ahead – to pursue the wages battle and drive home the lessons about it through solidarity actions, meetings and petitions. 'In generating mass struggle around wages, the arguments about inflation, balance of payments, imports and the rest must be tackled', he warned. Otherwise the potential for mass struggle and the battle to deepen understanding about the importance of a new course for Britain would not be realised.

George Matthews's handwritten notes of the passionate debate inside the Party's Executive Committee meeting on 13 January 1979 provides a fascinating insight into the divisions within the Party about its response to the unfolding industrial events.[35] Ken Gill is reported to have said that 'in 1974 the working class made an absolute advance. Healey's options were a left policy (Labour Party Manifesto), Social Contract, tighter fiscal and monetary policies'. During 1977–8 the Chancellor went for a combination of the first and second options while the movement went for the first option. Gill insisted that the 'wages struggle did raise political consciousness'. George Guy, General Secretary of the Sheet Metal Workers' Union, suggested realistically:

> people take the money rather than fight on unemployment. Underestimate working people if don't understand that they do realise politics implies wages struggle. TUC not a substitute for political party – problem is our party is too small. Strikes won't take place on alternative strategy. Only way to get there is to inject politics in. Don't get so frustrated that divide ourselves. May have to go through a Tory government. But don't write off wages struggle.

Ramelson accused some of his comrades of 'slandering' the trade union movement for their attack on the wages free-for-all, or 'grab what you can' mentality. He was especially incensed by the growing doubts expressed inside the Party's Executive Committee about the virtues of the Alternative Economic Strategy.

Tony Chater, Editor of the *Morning Star*, wrote in his seminal paper to the Party's Political Committee that it was necessary for the Communists to combat the widely held opinion that wage rises caused inflation. He was well pleased by the massive wage settlements being achieved through strikes or threats of industrial action and the campaign for a thirty-five-hour working week without loss of pay.[36] Chater believed the events testified 'to the advances made by the left both policy-wise and in positions of leadership under the stimulus of the militant struggles on wages and trade union rights in the late sixties and early seventies'.

He argued that

> the acceptance of wage restraint under the Social Contract demobilised the developing mass movement and took off the pressure for the implementation of the policies in the alternative strategy. The situation has now changed. We must seize the opportunities which it provides. Our fight for the alternative strategy – in practical action and in the battle of ideas – is of top importance in assisting the further advance of the left in the labour movement and the defeat of the Tories in the general election.

There can be little doubt that Callaghan's decision not to hold an autumn general election and his determination to stick to his 5 per cent pay policy guidelines brought about the rapid disintegration of the Social Contract. Many trade union leaders felt angry and some humiliated and even betrayed by what they saw as his charade about whether to call an election or not. The first serious victory in the wages offensive came at the Ford Motor Company after a seven-week official dispute ended with a 17 per cent pay rise for its employees, more than three times the Government's proposed norm. A final effort was made by the TUC General Council to reach some kind of understanding on pay with the Government which suggested union negotiators would try and keep wage deals to less than 10 per cent if the Chancellor controlled prices. But the proposed document from the TUC Economic Committee advocating this approach led to a 14 to 14 tied vote on the General Council and its right-wing Chairman Tom Jackson used his casting vote to declare that the policy recommendation was lost. The Government was then defeated in December in the House of Commons by 285 votes to 279 against when it tried to reassert its right to apply financial sanctions against errant private companies that defied the pay policy. Now ministers stood defenceless against the waves of uncoordinated assaults that followed from a widening range of groups – lorry drivers, television technicians, water and sewage workers, and bakers – in search of wage rises that led to agreements of up to 30 and even 40 per cent. The official lorry drivers' strike brought a shortage of food as ports and depots were blockaded by flying pickets. On 22 January 1979 the public service unions launched a co-ordinated local government workers' offensive in pursuit of a new £60 a week minimum wage.

The collapse of the Social Contract seemed to be turning into a Hobbesian struggle of all against all. The real victims of the growing disruptions were not employers but some of the most vulnerable in society – the poor, the sick, children, the bereaved and the disabled. The moral damage done to the Labour movement by such behaviour proved to be incalculable. By the end of January Callaghan seemed paralysed about how he should respond and he was to regret later that he failed to call a state of national emergency. The Government was gripped for a few days by an alarming inaction. It seemed ministers were suffering from a collective breakdown of will. Belatedly efforts were made to try and retrieve at least something from the wreckage by early February. The Cabinet agreed to establish an independent pay comparability commission under the chairmanship of Professor Hugh Clegg from Warwick University. Its purpose was to try and resolve public sector pay disparities through the recommendation of wage awards that would seek to bring public service workers' pay more into line broadly with private sector comparators. The resulting commission was not abolished immediately by Margaret Thatcher when she formed her Government in May 1979 and she agreed to honour its first awards. But it was to be terminated within twelve months. Frantic negotiations also took place between the Government and the TUC to hammer out a so-called Concordat which sketched out an agreed programme for the next three years including a more structured approach to wage bargaining. But no common ground could be found on what to do about pay in the meantime. For its part, the TUC issued some sensible, voluntary codes of conduct that dealt with closed shops and how pickets ought to behave. This was a belated move to discourage the more anti-social forms of industrial protest that had done so much to alienate and antagonise public opinion. But all of this turned out to be too little, too late.

The collapse of the Social Contract brought no obvious political dividends to the Communist Party. Its individual membership dropped dramatically from 25,293 to 20,599 between July 1977 and early 1979. 'This represents a severe setback to the party and the progressive movement,' admitted the Party's executive. 'The principal reason is that we have not succeeded in convincing, by our actions as well as our words, large numbers of people in the labour and democratic movement of the crucial need for a stronger Communist party.'[37] In fact, the so-called 'Winter of Discontent' had done little to suggest workers were ready to keep on voting for the Labour Party. In the 1979 general election 'the heaviest desertions' from Labour came from among young, skilled, male manual workers in the new towns of south-east England, on the Lancashire and Yorkshire coalfields and car worker districts such as those in Dagenham, Birmingham, Coventry and Oxford. The ultimate beneficiary of the industrial conflicts was not to be Labour's broad left or the trade unions in general but Margaret Thatcher and the Conservative Party. Her fierce determination to confront and defeat trade union power appeared vindicated by the often reckless behaviour of the pickets. The Tory's populist appeal to free collective bargaining and cuts in marginal tax rates found many enthusiastic supporters among the manual working classes, some of whom voted Conservative for the first time in their lives. Indeed, in May 1979 more working-class voters identified themselves with views on issues like trade union power, social welfare recipients and public ownership that were much closer to the Conservatives than to the Labour Party. In a devastating post-election analysis, Professor Ivor Crewe concluded that there was no 'historically predestined rendez-vous between Socialism and an industrial working class, least of all in Britain'. The data suggested that the Labour Party as a whole and not just the broad left had failed during the 1970s to come to terms with the social and occupational changes that had taken place in working-class interests over the previous twenty years.[38] The huge wages bonanza had done nothing to make workers feel more grateful but merely added to inflationary pressures and a climate of sour discontent. Nor did the inflationary pay agreements convert workers into enthusiasts for the broad left's Alternative Economic Strategy. Some union leaders might have deluded themselves into believing that they would be able to do to Mrs Thatcher what they had done to Edward Heath between June 1970 and March 1974. Instead, the trade unions and the Labour Party were to find themselves cast out into the political wilderness for more than a generation.

The Social Contract and the trade unions: an assessment

The Social Contract may have turned out to be limited and tentative in practice but despite this it helped to enflame destructive workplace attitudes. The better way may have pointed to the introduction of a permanent statutory incomes policy, substantial measures of social redistribution, a reform of wage bargaining structures, picking winners in technology and science and thereby making Britain a more productive and prosperous economy. But the Social Contract foundered in the anomie and decentralisation of workplace unionism. It seemed that the appeal of a broad-left socialism through the creation of a national autarchy failed to convince or win electoral approval. Margaret Thatcher was soon to declare that in fact there was really 'no alternative' to her own unyielding conviction that the stern application of monetarism through a tight control of the money supply was the method to cure the British disease. If the country was to regain its national self-confidence and achieve future economic success it would have to endure a painful but necessary course of treatment that it had postponed for far too long.

The lessons of the Wilson–Callaghan Governments suggested that any hopes of a transformation through the creation of a voluntary national consensus were a delusion. The Labour movement itself repudiated forms of long-term wage co-ordination although it favoured a degree of centralised economic planning not seen outside the command economies of the Soviet bloc. Instead, the country was to be tested in extremis in what was to become a bold experiment in economic management under Margaret Thatcher. The failure of the Social Contract suggested Labour's forward march had not merely ground to a halt but been forced into a humiliating and disorderly retreat. The events of 1974–9 were to cast a long shadow over the industrial events of the next two decades. They led inexorably to the formation of the New Labour project, Mrs Thatcher's greatest achievement. More poignantly, they also ushered in a remorseless decline in trade union power and influence in Britain and years of falling membership. Unlike most other West European countries Britain failed to establish and develop a social partnership during the last quarter of the twentieth century. But it would be wrong to suggest that the communists alone were responsible for what happened. Labour's broad left of which they were an important part cannot so easily escape from criticism either. Moreover, Wilson, Callaghan and Healey were often exhausted by the endless economic difficulties and unsure of how the Government could build on the uncertain foundations of the Social Contract. The revisionist right seemed as bankrupt of fresh ideas as the rest of the left. The changing public policy climate suggested the emergence of a neo-liberal view of the political economy, reflected in the trenchant speeches of Conservative intellectual Sir Keith Joseph and right-wing think tanks such as the Centre for Policy Studies, the National Association for Freedom and the less politically partisan Institute for Economic Affairs.

In the end, however, profounder underlying economic and social forces were at work in both British society and politics that helped to drive the Labour movement from the centres of political and industrial power for more than a generation. As Callaghan confessed to his Chief Policy Adviser Bernard Donoughue on the eve of polling day in May 1979: 'I am worried that there has been one of those deep sea changes in public opinion. If people have really decided they want a change of government then there is nothing you can do about it.'[39] At a mournful farewell lunch in 10 Downing Street after his decisive defeat a few days later Callaghan added: 'the trade unions did it. People could not forget and would not forgive what they had to suffer from them last winter.'[40] It was a fitting epitaph for the burial of the Social Contract.

The painful years of its short life were in fact some of the most turbulent in post-war British political history. Indeed, many of the Social Contract's innumerable critics both at the time and ever since have expressed the opinion that during the period the country became almost ungovernable. Briefly there was even some feverish talk about the dangers of a military putsch. Maverick agents in the intelligence services seemed absurdly to bring the patriotism of Harold Wilson as Prime Minister into serious question. On the Labour left irrational fears grew that Britain could well go the way of Salvador Allende's Chile, whose democratically elected government had been violently overturned by a military junta under General Augusto Pinochet in 1973. It was suggested that the trade unions had become the new rulers, over-mighty subjects whose power and hubris were destroying the British economy and threatening a democratic state. Even a normally balanced and sympathetic economic historian like Professor Sidney Pollard suggested that on its present course, Britain would become the most impoverished country in Europe with the possible exception of Albania within twenty years – mainly because of trade union attitudes.[41]

With the benefit of hindsight it is easy to dismiss such sweeping and febrile comments. But even in the 1970s much of the contemporary commentary and analysis often sounded extreme and unreal. However, the archives of the Trades Union Congress do not indicate during those years that an omnipotent and all-conquering trade union leadership wanted to rule Britain from Congress House. Too often the men – and they were always men – look uncertain, rather frightened, reactive and muddled. Their real problem was not that they were enjoying the exercise of too much power and authority over the state or any other institution but that they had very little control at all over what was happening. At many moments of crisis union leaders seemed to be little more than helpless bystanders to turbulent events that they could neither influence nor guide into constructive channels of co-operation and restraint. However, it would be quite mistaken to leap to the instant conclusion that Britain's trade union leaders therefore were found to be wanting because they simply failed to live up to responsibilities that they were being asked to shoulder by a Labour Government under almost perpetual strain and without the comfort of an overall parliamentary majority on which to rely for support. Their troubles derived not from some personal inadequacy of character but from much more fundamental weaknesses that lay at the core of the country's political economy in the 1970s. The slow but inexorable disintegration of the so-called post-war social and economic settlement established thirty years earlier was applying intolerable pressures on the authority and structures of British trade unionism.

The fear of inflation and anxieties over the threat to real living standards coupled with rising expectations of a better material life fuelled the upward pressure on a wages system, which in the private sector was becoming more decentralised and fragmented. The continuing post-war commitment to the maintenance of full employment may have grown less convincing as the numbers out of work and on benefit rose to over a million at the end of 1975. But most labour markets remained tight and skill shortages persisted in key areas. In the highly unionised public services sector increasingly large numbers of lower-paid manual workers began to believe they were falling behind comparable workers in private sector jobs although this turned out to be an exaggerated perception and in many cases mistaken. Any attempt by the Government in alliance with the trade unions to develop a form of co-ordinated pay bargaining on the lines of the much admired social democratic approach operating in Helmut Schmidt's West Germany stood little chance of success in the face of such volatile feelings.

But it was not envy of the super-rich or a revival of class warfare that explained the depths of anger and bitterness that boiled over among some sections of the working class at the end of the 1970s. On the contrary, workers sought to hold their own and protect their pay relative to workers in other workplaces and industries.[42] Indeed, the statistics do not support the view that the overwhelming majority of workers suffered from real cuts in their pay packets during the years of the Social Contract, not least because their earnings increases turned out to be much larger than the agreed national wage norms might have suggested. It is true that in 1975–6 the level of pay rises was halved. But over the next two wage rounds average earnings grew at a faster rate than the retail price index. In other words, despite trade union rhetoric, the living standards of most people at work did not suffer any dramatic fall during the period of the Social Contract. Unfortunately, many workers refused to believe this was true at the time.

Again, contrary to trade union beliefs, the majority of people actually favoured the Callaghan–Healey 5 per cent wage policy, at least at the beginning. A Gallup poll conducted in October 1978 discovered that as many as two-thirds of the general public agreed with that figure for pay increases and a huge 69 per cent of trade union members said they did so. The private worries of leading communists over the ambivalent mood of many workers towards government pay restraint were substantiated by such evidence. Such findings suggest it was becoming highly questionable whether trade union activists – either full-time officers or shop stewards – really mirrored accurately the attitudes of the members they claimed to represent. The gap between those who ran the unions and those who belonged to them was to produce a crisis of representation during the early 1980s. The rank and file groundswell of popular support among as many as a third of trade union members for Margaret Thatcher and the Conservatives in 1979 should not be overlooked.

It is true that historically most British workers did not see themselves as a unified and class-conscious proletariat, a new assertive and self-confident class whose time had come to challenge the existing economic and social order. Post-war studies by sociologists like Ferdinand Zweig and Michael Young and evidence from Mass Observation and other independent polling organisations failed to reveal the kind of militant and homogeneous working class, beloved of the Labour left and the Communist Party, ready to build the new Jerusalem. On the contrary, relative deprivation, rivalries and competition over wage differentials and relativities, the increasing attraction of affluent life styles built around consumer durables like motor cars, television sets and washing machines, pointed to the emergence of far more variegated and nuanced social and status differences although a deep sense of class consciousness retained its tenacious hold over British society. The Social Contract as envisaged by union leaders like Jack Jones and politicians such as Jim Callaghan may have laid out a practical and sensible programme of modest social reform and industrial advance. But the collectivist values that lay behind what it stood for came under increasing attack during the 1970s. Many of the leading figures in the Labour movement during that decade had grown up and been strongly influenced in their formative years by the miseries of the Great Depression and the evils of fascism. They had come to believe that the ideology of democratic socialism was the best, indeed the only alternative to the barbarism of right and left. But new social forces with new concepts were at work in society by the 1970s – acquisitive individualism, a decline in notions of solidarity and collectivism, a single-minded desire to pursue consumer and not producer interests, a dislike of paying high marginal rates of taxation and a growing doubt over the virtues of public expenditure. These feelings were growing as widespread among trade union members as they were among the rest of the population.

The scope for the development of any social democratic project was therefore limited and uncertain at that time. However, the difficulties were made much more insoluble because of the attitude of many trade unions. They were unwilling and unprepared to turn themselves into permanent social partners in the development of a political economy that was rooted in centre–left collectivist values. They continued to believe and wanted to go on practising so-called free collective bargaining in a world of paid work with narrow negotiating horizons, jealously protected labour practices and deep insecurity and low status for millions of workers. Union leaders continued to insist that their primary concern had to be to protect their members and negotiate higher wages and better conditions for them, but they could not agree together on a rational system of pay determination that took the wider needs of the political economy and the direct longer-term material interests of workers into account. The endless through-the-year wage round with its competitive pressures and so-called annual rate came to dominate trade union attitudes. The resulting high unit labour costs, relatively low levels of productivity, the inadequate provision of training and skills, above all the deep resistance to fundamental change, were the inevitable consequences stemming from the primacy of the wages struggle that the broad left supported with misguided enthusiasm. The 'self-defeating pay bonanza' of unfettered collective bargaining in 1978–9 revealed the magnitude of the problem with which few in the Labour movement were prepared to grapple at that time, let alone solve. The familiar sectionalism and competitive unionism continued to weaken a positive response to intractable economic difficulties.

The overall conclusion is therefore a bleak one. It was only when a government was elected to power that was prepared to abandon deliberately the conventional wisdom of post-war British politics that the so-called trade union 'question' was settled, at least to the satisfaction of the political class but at an incalculable social cost. This meant, first of all, a willingness to create and tolerate mass unemployment on a scale not experienced in the country since the 1930s. Under Margaret Thatcher the official number of people who claimed benefit for being without paid work soared to more than 3 million by 1985. It is true that official labour market statistics do not suggest wage rates were squeezed automatically as a result of the overall rise in the jobless totals. On the contrary, for the vast majority of people who remained in paid work, real earnings continued to rise significantly during the decade of Thatcherism in the 1980s. But the existence of so much worklessness undoubtedly weakened some union bargaining power.

Margaret Thatcher's Government also abandoned the post-war consensus that the state should provide financial support when necessary for the rescue of ailing industries. The industrial restructuring and de-industrialisation of the 1980s hit the trade unions hard as their areas of dominance contracted. Moreover, the set-piece national strikes from steel in 1980 to the epic struggle in the coal industry during 1984–5 indicated the Government was no longer prepared to seek accommodations and compromise in the practice of its industrial politics. The plethora of labour legislation designed to weaken the trade unions between 1980 and 1993 also played its part in diminishing their fragile power and influence. All of these developments flowed inexorably from the fall of the Social Contract.

The most lasting damage was inflicted, above all, on the powerful mythology of a united and progressive Labour movement that linked a political party together with a disparate trade unionism under the banner of democratic socialism. Professor Eric Hobsbawm's insightful warnings in his Marx Memorial Lecture were confirmed by the unhappy series of events that followed. Back in 1972 the Social Contract had looked to many observers like a far-sighted and practical arrangement to guarantee the democratic advance of the centre–left. By the end of the decade its demise amidst the wreckage of the 'Winter of Discontent' suggested that no future Social Contract was really possible without a fundamental and often painful transformation in the labour market institutions and industrial culture of post-war Britain. However, it seemed sadly that only a determined and ruthless centre–right government could carry through such radical and unpopular change and not a Labour movement under the strong influence of the trade union interest.

Notes

1 I am grateful to the Labour History Archive and Study Centre in Manchester, now part of the John Rylands Library, for access to the papers of both the Labour Party and the Communist Party in the writing of this chapter. I should like to thank Stephen Bird at Manchester, the most helpful and enthusiastic of archivists.

   A more detailed narrative of the national politics of the Social Contract can be found in the author's earlier publications. These include *The Fifth Estate: Britain's Unions in the Modern World* (Pan, London, 1978 and 1980); *The Trade Union Question in British Politics: Government and the Unions since 1945* (Blackwell, Oxford, 1993); *The TUC: From the General Strike to New Unionism* (Palgrave, London, 2000); and *Labour and the Social Contract* (Fabian Society, London, 1978). The most reliable general accounts of the Governments' industrial policy can be found in Artis, M. and Cobham, D. (eds), *Labour's Economic Policies, 1974–79* (Manchester University Press, Manchester, 1991) and Coopey, R. and Woodward, N. (eds), *Britain in the 1970s: The Troubled Decade* (St Martin's Press, London, 1996). The making and unmaking of the Labour left's influence on industrial policy can be found in Hatfield, M., *The House the Left Built: Inside Labour Policy-making 1970–75* (Gollancz, London, 1978) and Wickham-Jones, M., *Economic Strategy and the Labour Party: Politics and Policy-making 1970–1983* (Macmillan, London, 1996). One of the most perceptive accounts of the Social Contract period remains Professor Samuel Beer's *Britain Against Itself: The Political Contradictions of Collectivism* (Norton, London, 1982).
2 Labour's Programme 1973, p. 7.
3 Labour Party Conference 1973 Report, p. 187.
4 Taylor, R., *The Fifth Estate: Britain's Trade Unions in the Modern World*, p. 11.
5 Barnett, J., *Inside the Treasury, 1974–79* (Andre Deutsch, London, 1982), p. 49.
6 Dell, E., *A Strange and Eventful History: Democratic Socialism in Britain* (HarperCollins, London, 2000), p. 401.
7 Taylor, R., *The TUC: From the General Strike to New Unionism*, pp. 231–2.
8 Green Paper draft on The State Holding Company. Rd 742/national executive committee minutes, April 1973, Labour Party archives.
9 Jones, J., *Union Man: The Autobiography of Jack Jones* (Collins, London, 1986), p. 285.
10 Wilson, H., *Final Term: The Labour Government 1974–76* (Weidenfeld and Nicolson/Michael Joseph, London, 1979), p. 33.
11 Regeneration of British Industry, White Paper, July 1974, p. 1.
12 The Current Work Programme of the Department of Industry, Note by Tony Benn, res. 47, May 1974, Labour Party archives.
13 'A New Industry Act', Labour research department paper to the industrial policy sub-committee, May 1978, Labour Party archives.
14 'Planning and New Public Enterprise', Labour research department paper to the industrial policy sub-committee, res. 200, June 1975, Labour party archives.
15 Donoughue, B., *The Heat of the Kitchen: An Autobiography* (Politico's, London, 2003), pp. 140–1.

16 Pryke, R., *The Nationalised Industries: Policies and Performance since 1968* (Robertson, Oxford, 1981), pp. 262–5.
17 Industrial Democracy White Paper, May 1978, p. 1.
18 Trades Union Congress Report 1974, p. 396.
19 Goldthorpe, J., 'Industrial Relations in Great Britain: A Critique of Reformism', reprinted in Clarke, T. and Clements, L. (eds), *Trade Unions under Capitalism* (Fontana, London, 1977), p. 188.
20 Ramelson, B., *The Social Contract – Cure All or Con Trick?*, November 1974, p. 6.
21 Saunders, J., 'The 1974 TUC and a Future Labour Government', *Comment*, 12(19), 21 September 1974.
22 Trades Union Congress Report 1975, p. 462.
23 Ramelson, B., 'What Next for the Labour Movement?', *Comment*, 13(19), 20 September 1975.
24 Ramelson, B., 'Bury the Social Contract', Communist Party publication, 1977, p. 34.
25 Report from the north west region, August 1976, cp/cent/pc/14/01 Communist Party archives.
26 Report to the executive committee, September 1976, cp/cent/pc/14/03, Communist Party archives.
27 Outline of report to the executive committee, February 1977, cp/cent/pc/14/08, Communist Party archives.
28 Draft political report for the executive committee, March 1977, cp/cent/pc/14/09, Communist Party archives.
29 Ramelson, B., 'The TUC Assessed', *Comment*, 17 September 1977.
30 *The British Road to Socialism*, 1977 edition, pp. 23–5.
31 Hobsbawm, E., *The Forward March of Labour Halted?* (NLB, London, 1981), p. 14.
32 Report to the executive committee, May 1978, cp/exec/pc/14/23, Communist Party archives.
33 Mick Costello report to the executive committee, September 1978, cp/exec/pc/14/25, Communist Party archives.
34 Mick Costello, 'Cut the Dole Q's', *Comment*, 25 November 1978.
35 Minutes of executive committee discussion, 13 January 1979, cp/cent/ec/17/01, Communist Party archives.
36 Report to the executive committee by Tony Chater, January 1979, cp/cent/ec/17/01, Communist Party archives.
37 Report to the executive committee on the 1979 general election result, cp/cent/ec/17/04, Communist Party archives.
38 Crewe, I., 'The Labour Party and the Electorate', in Kavanagh, D. (ed.), *The Politics of the Labour Party* (Allen and Unwin, London, 1982).
39 Donoughue, B., *Prime Minister: The Conduct of Policy under Harold Wilson and James Callaghan* (Cape, London, 1987), p. 191.
40 Donoughue, B., *The Heat of the Kitchen*, p. 279.
41 Pollard, S., *The Wasting of the British Economy* (Croom Helm, London, 1982).
42 Beer, S., *Britain against Itself*, pp. 56–60.

6 Social policy and inequality

Polly Toynbee and David Walker

Introduction

As the 1997 Labour Government's tenure matures, so common problems of governing post-war Britain show up – exigencies of holding power independent of election or ideology. For example, governing, let alone governing as Labour, entails living in a world largely made by US economic and security policies. Just as the world economy erupted into British domestic politics in the 1970s and coloured what it was possible for Wilson–Callaghan to do, so the fall-out from the attacks on New York and Washington on 11 September 2001 dominated Blair's second term, inescapably. For Labour in 1974 there was no relief from oil shock just as Blair had to respond to whatever the US administration chose to do. So, from 1974 to 1976 and beyond, Labour had to adapt to international market forces, personified eventually by the arrival of the IMF at Heathrow. Social policies, especially across the dramatic landscapes of income and wealth inequalities, are usually made on Wall Street.

But travel too far down this road and you obliterate political intention, ideology and any capacity to 'make a difference' in office. And the record forbids such a conclusion. True, over the past six decades, it is not easy to spot specific consequences of electoral change.[1] For Julian Le Grand continuity trumps discontinuity: 'Over the 13 years 1974–1987, welfare policy successfully weathered an economic hurricane in the mid-1970s and an ideological blizzard in the 1980s.'[2] Take the relative income of poorer households – it is hard to map the arrival or departure of Labour Governments. On this score, on the interim evidence of the relative income of the poorest tenth of households 1997–2001, it could well be that New Labour turns out the most successfully egalitarian Labour administration since 1945.

Numbers matter, but so do moods, and here political intentionality plays its part. Between 1974 and 1997 the landscape changed as confidence in 'the state' was evacuated, top down as well as bottom up. By the state we mean collective purpose accomplished by government through policy and bureaucracy; Tony Blair's every utterance about 'public sector reform' speaks of this collapse. If there was a 'golden age' for the state, from say 1960 to the early 1970s, expressed by expanding state employment and investment in public infrastructure (albeit most often in the form of roads for private motorists), it featured the following beliefs.[3] Policy makers wanted to promote social welfare; the public sector was controllable from a central point (such as a Cabinet); decisions were reversible; policy makers had control over policy instruments and could rely on honest and efficient public sector employees; policy makers had a good and correct understanding of how economies operated.

It was more or less these nostrums which died while Labour was in power in the 1970s. Did the Wilson–Callaghan Governments demonstrate impotence in the face of international economic pressures (Wilson) and domestic insurgency (Callaghan) and so do lasting – even fatal – damage to belief in the potency of social democracy? If yes, that is not to heap causality on a few months (the 'Winter of Discontent') or to say public sentiment could not recover from, say, the first ever strike by hospital doctors, provoked by Barbara Castle in 1975. It is to say the consequences of action, aided by (in Callaghan's case) loose rhetoric, may swell and come together into lasting change in beliefs about political (and economic) agency.

What politicians think they are doing is not the same as what they say they are doing and neither is the same as what they actually did, as measured in statistical series we assume to be reliable, with the confidence of the rear-view mirror. One question about the 1974–9 Governments is whether they were self-conscious, whether for example in cutting income tax after 1976 Denis Healey had an inkling that inequality would grow as a result. Biography rarely asks questions about effect, autobiography even more seldom.[4] If Wilson and Callaghan give the impression of floundering, intellectually as well as in terms of practical governance, that may be because they were contending with new circumstances, for comprehending which the conceptual tools were just not available. John Dunn talks of the 'formidable power of capitalist economic organisation to impose its conveniences on the huge variety of institutional expedients which human beings have devised in order to bring their sense of form, decency and justice to bear on its outcomes'.[5] Put in those terms, however, you might have thought Harold Wilson, after his first-term experiences, would have been better equipped to understand what he *could do* in 1974, maybe even do it better, second time around. Having failed with *In Place of Strife*, why no revision of thinking, at least to equip 1974's new ministers with some apparatus to understand the limits to rule imposed by the semi-contract with the unions? For another occasion, the story of Labour in the 1970s would address in detail the post-prandial exhaustion/indifference of former ministers between 1970 and 1974.

A similar point could be made about the Labour left. Judging Wilson–Callaghan boils down, time and again, to the laziness and policy innocence of self-advertised alternatives within the Labour Party, qualities the cult of Benn (assiduously attended by its chief priest) has covered up. It is extraordinary, in retrospect, how thin the left's offering was, and in social policy especially. There was, notionally, an alternative economic strategy, worked out by the son-in-law of distinguished official Sir Eric Roll, Professor Stuart

Holland.[6] With the benefit of hindsight this prescription of control and economic isolation was not just flaky (the pathetic spectacle of Fidel Castro perorating in Havana thirty years on shows its mettle) but politically unsaleable to the one 'historical force' within Labour, the trade unions. The alternative social policy was either give 'em the money or, for example, a sketchy few pages in Townsend,[7] not much of a guide to what really existing politicians facing real electorates should do.

Our question

Social policy was once the antithesis of socialism. Ritt Bjerregaard, Danish Minister of Social Affairs, put it neatly at one of many events in the early 1980s diagnosing the welfare state's crisis:[8] 'Social policy is historically the very opposite of socialism.' Citing Bismarck she said it arose 'as a way to combat socialism by mitigating some of the most conspicuous excesses of capitalism and thus removing the mobilisation basis of the Social Democrats'. That is too Continental. In Britain social policy arose, with David Lloyd George, from a no particular desire to defend the capitalist order but equally from no affinity with socialism; its origins are a more heterogeneous individualist–Christian meliorism. In the history of the Labour Party, moreover, social policy for most of the twentieth century had an oddly marginal role, exhibited by half-convinced borrowing from a Liberal, William Beveridge, in the 1940s. The principal flaw of the major post-war welfare scheme, its neglect of the low-waged and workless poor, reflected deficiencies in Labour's economic thinking as much as Beveridge's Edwardian myopia.

Social policy came loosely to mean making people's lives more comfortable by providing public services delivered by professionals, schools, hospitals, housing, community development, and intervening in domestic lives to change relationships (especially children's). A key note of the 1970s, outside government at least, was dawning awareness that the providers of such services had distinct group or private interests. What if the lives being made more comfortable were those of professional people of means rather than the poor? Part of the collapse of faith in collective action for social betterment stemming from the Callaghan period had to do with this sense of capture. Julian Le Grand developed an ingenious theory of substitution.[9] Public spending on social services pretended to serve poorer people. It did not. Worse, it allowed would-be progressives (Labour ministers) 'to avoid the nettle of income redistribution. Through convincing people wrongly that a measure of redistribution was taking place, [they] may even have confused the basic aim.' But Le Grand's position comes close to fomenting distrust of all public spending. Intellectually, the new right was on the march from *circa* 1975 onwards, labelling public spending as wasteful and indeed selfish. If, by accident or design (Callaghan's celebrated conference put-down of spending in 1976), public spending became the villain of the piece, then the Callaghan Government did – as a number of commentators have since argued – anticipate the neo-liberal onslaught to come.[10]

By contrast, social policy is for some socialism. Its prime concern is equality, or at least resistance to the inegalitarian essential of capitalism. In Labour history, a ready synonym for equality has been poverty. Raymond Plant[11] sees (still) 'a fundamental division between neo-liberalism and social democracy' in whether policy should 'seek to improve the relative position of the poor or improve their absolute standard of life'. Capitalism tends to take care of the latter; incomes rise all round, in time. *Relative* difference is the key to social policy. Thus a straightforward test of Labour performance in the 1970s was (and is still): were low-income households better off, relatively speaking, thanks to Labour measures?

The immediate answer is no, for two reasons to do with the labour market. Labour 'measures' included growing joblessness, which ministers accepted was a corollary of participation in the international economy. Social policy is always subordinate to economic policy: 'Labour's failure to solve the problem of relative poverty was in large measure a consequence of the failure of economic policy to solve the problems of inflation and unemployment.'[12]

Also, for a party that talked equality a lot, Labour was strikingly preoccupied by pay 'differentials', which are hard in practice as in semantics to distinguish from 'inequalities'. As Callaghan's Government expired, social policy expert and activist Peter Townsend concluded that if poverty were to be reduced, two conditions applied: 'There must be less differentiation hierarchically of the employed population and a smaller proportionate share of total national resources by higher groups.'[13] On the latter, Callaghan (and his economic ministers and son-in-law) believed that the limits of progressive taxation of income had been reached, if not surpassed. On the former 'less differentiation' struck at the very purpose of British trade unions and so at the heart of Labour. The strength of the unions, both as the arbiters of Labour policy on tax and (as representatives of public service workers) as antagonists of the social democratic state, is not just a characteristic of the era; it helps explain why belief in the benign potential of progressive government died during these years. Trade unionism in public employment speared faith in the benignity of the state and damaged belief in public control, state efficiency and the reversibility of politicians' decisions.

Harvard professor Samuel Beer, writing after a visit to Britain in spring 1979, captures a paradox:

> to hear someone with the incontestable integrity of Len Murray, general secretary of the TUC, affirm his commitment to equality with a fervor reminiscent of William Morris or Tawney, while at the same time fully recognizing the fierce combat over differentials within the movement to which he has dedicated his life is to confront a moral and psychological snarl that is not easily untangled.[14]

Liberal democracy could yet be saved, wrote Samuel Brittan with the near-apocalyptic agitation characteristic of the times, 'if contemporary egalitarianism were to lose its hold over the intelligentsia'.[15] Salvation turned out to be nearer to hand, in what a page earlier he had called the 'present preoccupation with differentials'. Unionism, in its British semi-anarchic, anti-corporatist form, led directly to Labour's adopting tax policies which helped to increase income inequality, certainly from 1977 onwards; it also led to the humiliation and rout of a government, Callaghan's, with progressive intent, if less intensely felt than Wilson's. The dreadful thing was, much of this was predictable. In 1972 Wilfred Beckerman had observed that one of the problems of the Labour Party is 'that of being a pro-equality party relying heavily on support from an organised pro-differential element'.[16] Here was a subject on which Labour's left agonised itself into nullity.

Golden years?

The word climacteric recurs in accounts of the 1974–9 Government, though not all who use it pause to consider whether the trends in social spending and employment interrupted by those critical – and courageous – Cabinets between 1975 and 1977 were sustainable. Public servants implementing social policy increased from 2.1 million to 3.3 million in the ten years to 1976,[17] a rate which long before it 'crowded out' other employment, begged questions about control, quality and productivity in teaching, social services, community development – and medicine.

Conventional wisdom says Wilson and Healey let spending run wild for eighteen months, before first Wilson then Callaghan mounted a (remarkably successful) cut-and-restrain operation. In fact, in volume terms public spending was constant from mid-1974 to mid-1976 before falling significantly to mid-1978, then rising equally dramatically, with spending volume in 1979–80 above 1974–5's level, albeit only by a small amount; 1975–7 is the only recent period to have witnessed substantial reductions in real spending rather than spending as a proportion of GDP,[18] which is a tribute to the effectiveness of Labour Cabinet decision making.

Yet spending consumed a higher proportion of available resources. Measured against GDP, the picture does indeed show a spike. Spending peaked as a proportion of GDP in 1975 at 49.3 per cent, falling by a full 6 per cent of GDP before rising slightly to 44 per cent in Labour's last year. For comparison, spending was 35.3 per cent in the heyday of Harold Wilson's first term; Thatcherite policy pushed it to 47.8 per cent in 1984; it is currently just over 41 per cent.

In terms of what the money was spent on, social security benefited (partly because rising unemployment pushed spending up automatically), along with health, partly in response to burgeoning pay claims. Housing and education fell in volume terms and capital investment was hard hit; over the five years from 1975, public investment was cut from nearly 5 to under 2 per cent of GDP. When David Owen complained of touring the country looking at holes in the ground where hospitals had been due to be built, he was predicting there would (in the 1980s and 1990s) be less health, as those unbuilt buildings would not need clinicians and other staff.

Social spending as a proportion of GDP fell from 25.4 per cent in 1975–6 to 22.9 per cent in 1979–80, though that masks (a) the pick-up in the macro-economy from 1978 and (b) the sharpness of the spending cut between mid-1976 and mid-1978. These were, however, good, maybe unsurpassable, years for social policy makers and commentators. Social administration burgeoned as a discipline. Routledge and Kegan Paul published, from 1971 on, fat yearbooks of social policy; they ceased in 1982. Contacts between civil servants, ministers, journalists, academics and the commentariat at large were denser than they had ever been before or have been since. It was the heyday of the magazine *New Society* – which carried Frank Field's famous leak of Cabinet discussions about deferring the implementation of the Child Benefit Act 1975.[19] Bertorelli's restaurant in Charlotte Street rang with specialist luncheon and dining clubs. Barbara Castle's appointment of Professor David Donnison to chair the Supplementary Benefits Commission and the arrival with her at the Department of Health and Social Security of Professor Brian Abel-Smith personified the close connexion between the social policy community and policy itself. An unnamed senior civil servant at the DHSS declared that resources real-location 'showed a clear political initiative, whose ideas had been stimulated by the social sciences'.[20] Here was a British version of the conjunction of 'faith, intelligence and good works' described for the era of the Great Society programmes in the United States by Henry J. Aaron.[21]

Rationality did not dawn everywhere. These were years when civility within the Labour Party took grievous blows and conference rhetoric flamed. Policy mechanics were much debated, disastrous changes in the make-up of the Labour Party – some of them caused by social policy! – much less so. (If Denis Healey had spent less time on policy and more on brute politics – what was happening to constituencies and local government – he would have had a better chance of succeeding Callaghan.) Though it accomplished little the attempt to 'join up' social policies pushed by the Central Policy Review Staff lodged in the policy community's collective memory. The joint approach to social policy (Jasp) was invented by the Heath Government but under Labour took documentary form in the Joint Framework for Social Policies. It was, according to a book co-authored by some of its progenitors, very much a thing of its time:[22] 'at the end of a decade in which the search for rationality in policy making had been pursued with persistence by successive governments' there was a concentration on improving the techniques of government – Heath's programme analysis reviews could be cited here. For a moment it appeared 'a hesitant, uneven movement towards the creation of a British version of corporatism, with the creation of new machinery for engaging trade unions, employers and government in the process of policy making'. By the time Jasp arrived the moment was ending.

Social policy in action

Labour's manifesto for February 1974 promised, vaguely, to increase social equality by giving far greater importance to full employment, housing, education and social benefits. For two years, social policy was Barbara Castle. Until she was sacked by James Callaghan in a settling of old Labour Party scores, she enjoyed two (hyperactive) years. Wilson set up two giant if futile royal commissions, Diamond on the distribution of wealth and income, Merrison on health. The Callaghan years, 1976–9, were less frenetic though Peter Shore, Environment Secretary, added mightily to the tally of Green and White Papers. Some such as the Layfield inquiry into council finance are still worth reading.[23] Layfield wanted some decision of principle on the balance between central and discretionary local government; the plea fell on deaf ears then, as now.

Social security

Frank Field, then Director of the Child Poverty Action Group, commented sourly that 'the low esteem in which most welfare reform is held by leading Labour politicians can be seen from the way the leading members of the Labour Cabinet tried to veto the introduction of the child benefit scheme'.[24] Perhaps after his own failure in office he might be more charitable. The Callaghan Cabinet sought to defer the implementation of child benefit because of worries about the impact on take-home pay of the loss of child tax allowance, which was being abolished along with the cash family allowance. Child benefit being payable to mothers, this was an issue within the household economy and Field might have observed that Callaghan, typically, sided with male breadwinners who were history's losers.

That was after Castle. Her marvellous years, which linked most social security benefits to earnings rather than prices and saw pensions as well as child benefit reformed, introduced a non-contributory invalidity pension for disabled people who had not qualified for invalidity pension. Invalid care allowance was introduced in July 1976 for single women and others who give up their jobs to care for severely disabled relatives and mobility allowance created. Even Townsend acknowledged 'these allowances have probably reduced the numbers of disabled people living in poverty, but the government has been criticised strongly for a "piecemeal" and by reference to needs "inadequate" programme'.[25] David Piachaud, another close-in observer–participant, was warmer, noting relative improvement for certain groups of the poor continued through the Callaghan years, with real increases in long-term benefit rates and a diminution in numbers requiring Supplementary Benefits.[26]

The Castle era's pensions reform, which came into effect in April 1978, aimed to end pensioners' reliance on income supplements. The plan was that by 2020 enough pensioners would be benefiting from the State Earnings Related Pension Scheme (SERPs) to end pensioner poverty. This, said Castle, was the greatest breakthrough on pensions since Beveridge.[27] There you have Barbara Castle, hyperbolic, wrong and sympathetically reported. Beveridge had failed to see the limits of the contributory principle in the provision of income security in old age; Castle's scheme lasted only a decade. Poverty in old age remains a current policy preoccupation.

It's hard to discern a Castle legacy. For all his work at the Supplementary Benefits Commission, David Donnison established no consensus; the Commission was abolished by the Conservatives. Child benefit, too, needs re-examination as a universal benefit when social democratic progress depends on selectivity. Tax credits, Gordon Brown's favoured method of helping poor children, descend from the child tax allowance it replaced. Castle never confronted the question of whether targeting scarce money was more progressive than the universal benefit she created. As for SERPs, the Conservatives revised and narrowed the scheme only for New Labour to reinvent the 'second state pension'. If its principles have stood the test of time and electoral variance, its arithmetic did not.

Health

In health, Castle had an able junior minister in David Owen, but their tenure lacked strategy. The fight with the consultants over pay beds resulted in distracting noise and only partial victory. The whole period is remembered for strikes and disruption, which is one reason her successor David Ennals gets a bad press: 'Ennals hardly put a foot right during his term of office and appropriately left the health service in a state of seemingly terminal crisis' was Webster's sour verdict.[28]

A 'strategy' for health might have encompassed the continuing growth of acute care relative to the primary sector. Hospital medical staff had been approximately equal to GPs in number in 1964 but were twice as numerous in 1979. That is not to say there were enough of them. By 1979, some 35 per cent of the NHS medical workforce came from overseas. And hospital doctors were becoming measurably more productive in terms of the length of time patients spend in hospital. During these years, hip replacements became a common procedure, giving older people a literal new lease on life; coronary bypass operations became standard procedure.

But governments as concerned with equality as Wilson's and Callaghan's might have sought to focus on the primary sector where much more can be done to reduce the social imbalance in sickness and death. One of Labour's legacies to the incoming Tories was the report on health inequalities by Sir Douglas Black.[29] Surveying the evidence in the early 1980s, Julian Le Grand concluded any aim of narrowing the gap in health standards between different social classes had 'not been realised'.[30]

Labour came to power pledged to reinstate commitments made earlier in the Heath Government to growth in spending. Wilson obliged: 1974–6 saw the biggest step-like increase in the history of the NHS until Gordon Brown's expansion. Health spending was then sharply cut in the 1976–7 crisis of economic management. Taking 1974–9 as a whole, real increases in health spending averaged 5 per cent a year, compared with about 4.5 per cent during Wilson's first period in office, and 5.5 per cent under Heath.

Barbara Castle did try to plan. 'Priorities for the Health and Personal Social Services' published in March 1976 was the first comprehensive statement of norms and targets for service provision since the beginning of the NHS. But, partly because of macro pressures on budgets, historical patterns largely held. Much NHS time was spent on implementing the reorganisation devised by Sir Keith Joseph. Castle tweaked it, increasing local authority membership of health authorities, but otherwise delivered his hierarchical scheme of regions and areas. Between 1968 and 1979 the number of administrative and clerical staff in the NHS increased almost threefold. Structure, like strategy, was something about which Labour had few thoughts. Instead, a royal commission was appointed in 1976, chaired by Sir Alec Merrison, Vice-Chancellor of Bristol University, to look at the 'best use and management of the financial and manpower resources of the NHS'. It is a case study in nugatory inquiry. Sitting while Rome burned, it did not report till after Labour left office and its, as it turned out, oddly tentative conclusions were promptly buried by the Conservatives.

The period of 1974–9 qualifies as the worst phase of industrial unrest in the history of the NHS with action by nurses, junior doctors, ancillary workers and, over pay beds, by consultants. Recollections by Castle and Owen[31] of fraught negotiations with the consultants and the British Medical Association in Arnold Goodman's flat make exciting reading but no settlement was made for the boundary between public and private health or the managerial status of consultants. Webster makes a naïve point when he says the fight left a damaging legacy and many consultants never again gave the NHS the long hours of extra unpaid effort which they had willingly given before;[32] the point was that Labour ministers, even the indefatigable Barbara Castle, did not have the time, energy or sense of strategy to seek to refashion on some permanent basis just what these precious creatures, the consultants, were – agents of state purpose or entrepreneurs.

David Owen claims responsibility for 'the single most important act of redistribution in the history of the Health Service'.[33] In fact both the genesis and the continuing effects of the Resources Allocation Working Party (RAWP) he is referring to indicate just how much policy continuity there was. It had become obvious during the 1960s that the distribution of health resources within the NHS was skewed. A new scheme for allocating hospital revenue appeared in a 1970 Green Paper by Richard Crossman and was partially incorporated in distributions to hospitals from 1971 to 1972. In 1974, Brian Abel-Smith, Barbara Castle's adviser, urged the issue be taken up again amid concern that Labour regions were losing out to more affluent areas. The RAWP, which reported in 1976, recommended the use of death rates, a proxy for illness, as the basis for money flows; since poorer people die sooner this produced an 'egalitarian' or class-compensatory bias.

RAWP has since been mythologised, rather like the Barnett formula, another allocative device invented by the 1970s' Labour Governments. Money went to NHS regions; allocations within them did not reflect class differences. This was hospital money, too; one of its effects was to make consulting and surgery in Manchester and Newcastle more attractive, cementing the provincial middle class in terms of both hospital demand and supply. 'The more affluent regions and acute specialities were efficient at obstructing any rapid shift of resources according to the criteria of spatial equality or in the interests of the groups dependent on community care' according to Glennerster *et al.*[34] The odd thing about RAWP, however, was that it survived: 'It seems paradoxical that successive Conservative Governments during the 1980s, dedicated to reining in spending on the social wage, implemented and administered formulae that were unprecedented in their equity-driven redistribution of resources.'

Social policy and the cities

Like RAWP urban policy wrestled with spatial inequalities. Like RAWP, there was also surprising continuity in policy before and after the Wilson–Callaghan years. That said, the Callaghan years saw official acceptance of the contention that focusing on poorer areas was mistaken.[35] Inner city problems were 'structural', or to do with the general fate of the capitalist economy. So much neo-Marxist-influenced analysis is audible in Peter Shore's own Inner Cities White Paper.[36] The consequential policy was to try to bribe employers to locate in them. Higgins notes how these incentives predated the application of 'New Right' economic theory to the inner cities from 1979.[37] Together Labour and the Tories created a network of paid community development activists, one result of which was to feed the radicalisation of the Labour Party.

Unlike in health, where most of the action occurred in the Wilson years, the climacteric of urban policy under Labour was Peter Shore's 1977 White Paper. When Callaghan took over from Wilson he made urban policy a focus. He went on to preside over the eclipse of his own original community development approach, but not before its activists organised rent strikes and welfare campaigns and seeded the neo-Marxist takeover of parts of his own Party. The new emphasis, he announced in September 1976, was to understand the reasons for the economic decline of the cities, then 'bend' programmes to help them. When he replaced Anthony Crosland, Peter Shore made speeches and wrote papers; it was one of those policy-intense periods later fondly remembered by civil servants, academics and commentators. 'Taking the post-war period as a whole, the most striking thing has been – until three or four years ago – the failure of public policy to recognise the central fact of the economic decline of the inner city', said Shore in a lecture in 1980.[38] But self-congratulation was premature. Where was the plan for national economic decline from which an urban policy might be deduced? Where were the institutional links with industrial policy let alone the 'manpower planning' being talked about in other departments or some tie-in with the efforts of the Manpower Services Commission to address youth joblessness?[39]

Shore's predecessor, Crosland, had told local authorities in May 1975 that the party was over. In fact in political terms it was just beginning as, on Shore's watch, in Lambeth and elsewhere radical leaders took over, anticipating the New Left's incursion into municipal politics, against which the Tories were to react with so much legislative energy. Shore never quite decided whether in the face of economic decline government should go with the flow and accept decentralisation or fight against the evacuation of jobs and people from cities. He never came to terms with the burgeoning critique of Labour urban policy: concentrating on a select number of towns created the impression that poverty was just an isolated occurrence; similarly race. Take the outbreaks of 1981 as a benchmark. Unless you blame them entirely on policies pursued by the Tories during barely two years in power, their causes are to be found earlier. One reason[40] was Labour's refusal directly to confront race. The policy-rich years of Wilson's last Government did, however, see a revised Race Relations Act (in 1976), establishing the Commission on Racial Equality.

Equality

The reputation of the Wilson and Callaghan Governments suffered because 'failure literature' abounded in the early 1980s. The Black report[41] showed how close an association there remained between social class, housing tenure and other measures of prosperity and sickness and death. The year before its publication Peter Townsend had fired his charge:

> poverty is more extensive than is generally or officially believed and has to be understood not only as an inevitable feature of severe social inequality but also as a particular consequence of actions by the rich to preserve and enhance their wealth and so deny it to others.[42]

Labour, it seemed, had made very little difference to fundamental inequality. And if then and now practical egalitarianism is a hallmark of the left or social democratic presence in politics, that is failure indeed.

That is not the whole story. Despite his slim majority, Wilson created space for substantial 'equalities' legislation on gender and race. The Sex Discrimination Act 1975 gave women a right of equal access to employment and equal treatment in jobs; another major statute in a busy year (the Employment Protection Act) established a right to paid maternity leave. Their significance in the lives of working women was limited: 'Though these formal rights were an important breakthrough many women found the lack of affordable child care a barrier to their practical return to work.'[43] Two further comments might be made. Such social legislation might offer a Diceyan case study: does change in the law anticipate or follow changing social mores? Women were entering the labour market in growing numbers during the 1970s and it is not clear what difference, if any, either the law or the absence of a Scandinavian childcare strategy made to their decisions. Employment protection was squarely part of the Social Contract agreed between the Government and the unions, symbolised by the presence on the front bench of Michael Foot. The assistance it offered women at work could thus be attributed to the unions, exculpating them (to some extent) of male chauvinism.

The main event was not gender difference but material inequality. So two questions: did Labour have identifiable ambitions for the reduction of inequalities of income and wealth, and (anticipating the punch line) if they were not realised, why? To the first question, the answer is not really. The Diamond Royal Commission was a curious interlude. It reported – in 1979 – that by the time Labour came to power in 1974 there had not been much change in relative income shares since Attlee left office.[44] During its sittings, it did not give Labour any explicit policies for income distribution; wealth (see below) was different.

It is now accepted there had been a slow overall trend towards greater equality in the distribution of income during the 1960s, especially after 1972. Income inequality reached its lowest point around 1977[45] or 1978.[46] It ticked upwards from 1978 to 1979 (and continued increasing until the 1990s when it seems to have reached a plateau). That suggests 1977–8 was a watershed: 'It should be noted that the large increase in income inequality at the end of the 1970s occurred before Mrs Thatcher came to power.'[47]

There was no single cause. Income inequality declined on Heath's and Wilson's watch because of economic recession, which tends to cut the share of better-off households – though recession also seems to increase the number of people living in 'absolute' poverty. Callaghan's intellectual framework certainly accommodated elements of newly fashionable neo-liberalism and its concern with incentives and markets. Inequality fell under Wilson partly, paradoxically, because of both big pay awards and incomes restraint. It rose under Callaghan because of Healey's tax cuts, the rising gap between the incomes of households in work and not in work – though this was more dramatic after the Tories broke the link between benefits and earnings. After 1977 'there was a marked rise in the gap between high and middle earnings and also a marked increase in the gap between low and middle earnings'.[48] Healey's tax cuts were more than matched by spending cuts, which shows his effectiveness as Chancellor but also makes a mockery of the 'social wage'. Growing unemployment in the later 1970s mattered even if 'there is only partial evidence of consistency between unemployment and inequality trends'.[49] The number of people in social circumstances where they were likely to become and stay poor was growing on the back of longer-run trends, in single-parent households, and pensioners with varying degrees of disability.

Social policy is made by the taxman. Whereas in 1964 income tax revenue exceeded taxes on spending by 5 per cent, by 1975 it raised two-thirds more. Wilson's Chancellor Healey Mark 1 (1974–6) pushed what Clark[50] calls this social democratic trend. Callaghan's Chancellor shifted it into reverse. Taxes on income contributed 45.8 per cent of total revenue in 1975 but only 38.9 per cent in 1980. Jack Jones, the union leader, said the workers were prepared to pay their share to do right by the elderly: 'Given the hostility of wage earners to income tax, it was most unlikely that this would turn out to be the case.'[51] It was not: Healey palliated male, trade unionist wage earners, and was repaid with dismissal.

Fairer taxation of wealth had been 'in the air' even while Heath was in office. The Tories considered reform of taxation of inheritance while Healey had chaired a capital working party. In opposition, however, Labour was curiously idle on an issue which raised so much heat at party and trade union meetings: 'Analysis of Labour Party speeches and documentation reveals how far they failed to develop a clear, coherent philosophy of what they sought in advocating a reduction in the inequality of wealth.'[52] Labour came to power in 1974 poorly equipped to reduce inequality, in the technical sense that little serious thought had been given to the tax system; tax experts were few and social policy experts failed to cross over to help. Having had six years in the practice of power, Labour leaders might, with hindsight, have returned to office forearmed, imbued with the tricks of the trade, especially in handling money, especially in tailoring ideological ambition to possibility.

The first Healey budget in March 1974 delivered, within months, a lifetime gifts tax (capital transfer tax, CTT) and the promise of a wealth tax. This was even before the Royal Commission was set up; CTT was enacted and a House of Commons wealth tax select committee completed its evidence before its first report. But Healey's CTT was full of holes; the exemption made for gifts between husband and wife, during lifetime or at death, made it a sieve. Death and gift taxes formed 1.26 per cent of government revenue from taxation in 1974 but 0.58 per cent in 1979, a fall from 0.51 to 0.23 per cent of GDP. So here was a tax which was barely redistributive that did not yield much revenue either. Healey was the man who was going to squeeze the rich until the pips squeaked. But his November 1974 budget turned out to be the last in the decade to see the introduction of new mainstream taxes. After the Wealth Tax Select Committee – badly assisted, under-informed, amateur – reported in November 1975, the idea was buried for the duration. True, 'the circumstances of high unemployment, low business confidence and high inflation could hardly have offered a less propitious moment for such a tax'.[53] There were reasons for the absence of a wealth tax, to do with the very identity of a social democratic party as working people acquired assets. Was the property of everyone who supported Labour worth less than £99,999? No thanks to policy, there was a decline in share of wealth held by the top 1 per cent and top 5 per cent of the distribution in the Wilson years, probably caused by a sharp fall in share values in the mid-1970s. It was reversed in 1977–8.

Social opinion

'They sensed public opinion moving to the right and tried to back and fill accordingly',[54] but how far was Wilson–Callaghan performance a cause of such movement in opinion? Clark[55] gives polling data in 1959–60, 1978–9 and 1993–5. before concluding that in the late 1970s opinion was 'unusually' anti-statist. One question is whether, by accident or design, Wilson–Callaghan pushed the public in a proto-Thatcherite direction, for example by demonstrating the inadequacies of social democracy or the incompetence of social democratic minders of a capitalist economy. There certainly seems to be some evidence that public appetite for active welfare policy diminished.

We know from the early 1980s there was little or no movement in responses on state provision of welfare. A consistent theme of British Social Attitudes was the disjunction between hardline Thatcherite rhetoric on the social state and public aspirations.[56] So perhaps the people did not really want less welfare, but different –delivered in ways which were less wasteful and more sensitive to the requirements of the final consumer.[57] If opinion was moving in that direction in the 1970s, Labour ministers missed most of it.

Yet a key manifestation of attitude, along with the purchase of right-wing newspapers, is voting. With 37 per cent of the popular vote in February 1974, were Wilson's, and Callaghan's after him, Governments ruling 'against opinion', especially in their social policies? These years saw a dawning realisation that public attitudes towards poverty and certain classes of the poor were distinctly punitive. And trade unionists constituted a section of this public; the proportion of trade union members voting Conservative rose from 25 per cent in 1974 to 33 per cent in 1979.[58] It might have been a perverse result of faltering aggregate growth and dismayed expectation but the weight of this 'restrictive mood'[59] posed this issue. Did Labour efforts to extend and improve the income rights of such minorities as retirement pensioners, disabled people and one-parent families, deeply inadequate though Townsend may have judged them, increase resentment and criticism of welfare provision at large?

> The public continued to assert its confidence in aspects of the welfare state during the Thatcher years. But that is not the same as saying the public (or at least the psephologically demonstrative bit of it) had any enthusiasm for the extension of tax, public spending or redistribution of income.[60]

Did Wilson–Callaghan contribute to that indifference?

Conclusions

The answer has to be affirmative. Conventional wisdom says that the economic crisis (or rather public perception of how it was being managed) penetrated some deep layer of consciousness and did for confidence in Labour for years to come. In social policy, it feels like a caesura: 1974–9 was of 'pivotal importance for the health service'.[61] Until then, Webster argues, there had been a comfortable assumption that growing expectations of provision would be met by an expanding service. Economic crisis killed that. The system

> relapsed into a state of siege. In the last phase of the old Labour Government, the combined effects of cuts in public expenditure, bitter industrial relations, the incubus of the Joseph reorganisation, the tide of resentment from vulnerable groups about failure to improve their services, and the evident bankruptcy of leadership on the part of health ministers precipitated the NHS into a state of crisis and demoralisation worse than ever before or since.

That may be too harsh a judgement. Wilson–Callaghan may also have given the NHS a corporate self-identity based on strength in vicissitude, which was to serve it well during the Tory years to come. Wilson–Callaghan were years, too, when perceptions of professional and public interest were shifting but by no means just in Britain. Meeting in Paris at the beginning of the 1980s, social policy specialists discussed the crisis in the welfare state. Was there such a thing? In Britain health, income support, urban policy all proved remarkably impervious (as systems, as financial blocks) to a strong-minded Prime Minister with a distinct mix of petty bourgeois and neo-liberal proclivities.

But those OECD experts captured a point which is the conclusion of this chapter. Wilson–Callaghan dealt a severe, perhaps even mortal, blow to generic confidence in the capacity of the British state at a time when there was intense questioning of public sector professionalism. Chelly Halsey, the Oxford sociologist, was rapporteur for one session: 'Whether participants favoured accountability through the market or through democratic politics, they tended to question both the justice and the efficiency of professional and bureaucratic power in state systems of welfare.'[62] During the 1970s it was as if social democracy turned on itself. Social policy academics 'were more likely to question the prevailing social democratic assumption that the state was an instrument for good, perhaps because they had given some attention to the way the poor actually came into contact [with it]'.[63] Here you have the origins of that puzzling Blairite rhetoric about public sector reform, apparently so destructive of the trust it is meant to be refurbishing. We earlier listed beliefs about the state allegedly killed or damaged by the advent of neo-liberals to power in Britain and other countries.[64] The question was whether, in social policy, such destruction had been anticipated. The beliefs concerned the benignity of policy makers, central control, reversibility of decisions, effectiveness of policy instruments and the goodwill of implementers in the public sector. Some, but not all, were undoubtedly hurt by Wilson–Callaghan.

What is remarkable about the Wilson–Callaghan years, after the event, is the absence of self-consciousness about the long-term damage Labour ministers, their advisers and state employees might have been inflicting on a certain idea of the state. At an elevated level, Roy Jenkins may have been anticipating party realignment when he had wondered in the early 1970s if high levels of public spending pushed over 'the frontiers of social democracy'.[65] Harold Wilson, too, was aware enough to commission the CPRS to review future outlays on social services. About Labour at large Whiting[66] is more generous, saying 1974–9 was a (painful) learning experience though 'not one in which all sections of the movements shared and the process was incomplete by 1979'. It was, he argues, a specific failing of the left to refuse to understand the exigencies, compromises and opportunities of holding power in a pluralist capitalist democracy.

Our verdict, then, is negative. By the end of the 1970s Labour's capacity to make change in perceptions of public–private balance was exhausted.[67] That was not because of some failure of socialist will or absence of dialogue with social partners – there was no socialist alternative worth attending, for all Tony

Benn's noise, and the problem with the unions was that they had become a force for reaction. Labour's capacity to change perceptions diminished further as the 1980s wore on. Little wonder, then, that stealth and ambiguity on tax and spend, public and private, became the stock in trade of the next set of Labour politicians to win a national election.

Notes

1 Rose, R., *Do Parties Make a Difference?* (Macmillan, London, 1984).
2 Le Grand, J., 'The State of Welfare', in Hills, J. (ed.), *The State of Welfare* (Clarendon, Oxford, 1990).
3 Tanzi, V. and Schuknecht, L., *Public Spending in the 20th Century* (Cambridge University Press, Cambridge, 2000), pp. 16–18.
4 Healey, D., *The Time of My Life* (Michael Joseph, London, 1989).
5 Dunn, J., *The Cunning of Unreason: Making Sense of Politics* (HarperCollins, London, 2000), p. 332.
6 Holland, S., *The Socialist Challenge* (Quartet, London, 1975).
7 Townsend, P., *Poverty in the United Kingdom* (Penguin, London, 1975), pp. 922–6.
8 Organization for Economic Cooperation and Development, *The Welfare State in Crisis* (OECD, Paris, 1982), p. 15.
9 Le Grand, J., *The Strategy of Equality* (George Allen and Unwin, London, 1982), p. 142.
10 Mullard, M., *The Politics of Public Expenditure* (Croom Helm, London, 1987), p. 149.
11 Plant, R., 'Crosland, Equality and New Labour', in Leonard, D. (ed.), *Crosland and New Labour* (Macmillan, London, 1999), p. 17.
12 Peden, G.C., *British Economic and Social Policy* (Philip Allan, Oxford, 1985), p. 21.
13 Townsend, *Poverty in the United Kingdom*, p. 919.
14 Beer, S., *Britain against Itself* (Faber, London, 1982), p. 95.
15 Brittan, S., 'The Economic Tensions of British Democracy', in Emmett Tyrrell, R. (ed.), *The Future That Doesn't Work* (Doubleday, New York, 1977), p.143.
16 Beckerman, W., 'Objectives and Performance: an Overall View', in Beckerman, W. (ed.), *The Labour Government's Economic Record 1964–1970* (Duckworth, London, 1972), p. 41.
17 Lowe, R., *The Welfare State in Britain since 1945* (Macmillan, London, 1993), p. 302.
18 Clark, T., 'The Limits of Social Democracy? Tax and Spend under Labour 1974–79', Institute for Fiscal Studies WP 01/04 (www.ifs.org.uk), 2001, p. 6.
19 Field, F., *Poverty and Politics: The Inside Story of the CPAG Campaigns in the 1970s* (Heinemann, London, 1982), pp. 108–13.
20 Glennerster, H., Hills, J., Travers, T. and Hendry, R., *Paying for Health, Education and Housing* (Oxford University Press, Oxford, 2000), p. 135.
21 Aaron, H.J., *Politics and the Professors: The Great Society in Perspective* (The Brookings Institution, Washington, DC, 1978), p. 146.
22 Challis, L. *et al.*, *Joint Approaches to Social Policy* (Cambridge University Press, Cambridge, 1988), p. 3.
23 Layfield, F., *Local Government Finance: Report of the Committee of Inquiry*, Cmnd 6453 (HMSO, London, 1976).
24 Field, F., *Inequality in Britain* (Fontana, London, 1981), p. 222.
25 Townsend, *Poverty in the United Kingdom*, p. 907.
26 Piachaud, D., 'Social Security', in Bosanquet, N. and Townsend, P. (eds), *Labour and Equality: A Fabian Study of Labour in Power, 1974–79* (Fabian Society, London, 1980).
27 Perkins, A., *Red Queen: The Authorised Biography of Barbara Castle* (Macmillan, London, 2003), p. 377.

28 Webster, C., *The National Health Service: A Political History* (Oxford University Press, Oxford, 1998), p. 67.

29 Department of Health and Social Security, 'Report of the Working Group on Inequalities in Health', Chairman, Sir Douglas Black (DHSS, London, 1980). See also Townsend, P., Whitehead, M. and Davidson, P. (eds), *Inequalities in Health* (Penguin, London, 1980).

30 Le Grand, *The Strategy of Equality*, p. 46.

31 Owen, D., *Time to Declare* (Michael Joseph, London, 1991), p. 237.

32 Webster, *The National Health Service: A Political History*, p. 233.

33 Owen, D., *Personally Speaking* (to Kenneth Harris) (Weidenfeld and Nicolson, London, 1987), p. 64.

34 Glennerster *et al.*, *Paying for Health, Education and Housing*, p. 87.

35 Lawless, P., *Urban Deprivation and Government Initiative* (Faber, London, 1979).

36 Cmnd 6845 (HMSO, London, 1977).

37 Higgins, J., Deakin, N., Edwards, J. and Wicks, M., *Government and Urban Poverty: Inside the Policy-making Process* (Blackwell, Oxford, 1983), p. 78.

38 Higgins *et al.*, ibid., p. 117.

39 Reed, N., 'The Development of Special Programmes for the Unemployed', in Brown, M. and Baldwin, S. (eds), *The Year Book of Social Policy in Britain 1978* (Routledge and Kegan Paul, London, 1980), pp. 81–101.

40 Higgins *et al.*, *Government and Urban Poverty: Inside the Policy-making Process*, pp. 190–3.

41 'Report of the Working Group on Inequalities in Health'.

42 Townsend, *Poverty in the United Kingdom*, p. 893.

43 Glennerster, H., *British Social Policy since 1945* (Blackwell, Oxford, 1995), p. 151.

44 Royal Commission on the Distribution of Wealth and Income Report No. 7, July 1979, Cmnd. 7595 (HMSO, London, 1979), p. 17.

45 Martin, R., 'Income and Poverty Inequalities Across Regional Britain', in Philo, C. (ed.), *Off the Map: The Social Geography of Poverty in the UK* (CPAG, London, 1995), p. 26.

46 Jenkins, S., 'Trends in the UK Income Distribution', Institute for Social and Economic Research, University of Essex (www.iser.essex.ac.uk), 1989, p. 4.

47 Ibid., p. 10.

48 Ibid., p. 13.

49 Ibid., p. 14.

50 Clark, T., 'The Limits of Social Democracy? Tax and Spend under Labour 1974–79', p. 10.

51 Whiting, R., *The Labour Party and Taxation* (Cambridge University Press, Cambridge, 2000), p. 231.

52 Robinson, A. and Sandford, C., *Tax Policy-Making in the United Kingdom* (Heinemann, London, 1983), p. 221.

53 Ibid., p. 106.

54 Whitehead, P., 'The Labour Governments 1974–79', in Hennessy, P. and Seldon, A. (eds), *Ruling Performance* (Basil Blackwell, Oxford, 1987), p. 242.

55 Clark, 'The Limits of Social Democracy? Tax and Spend under Labour 1974–79', pp. 26–7.

56 Taylor, B. and Thomson, K., *Understanding Change in Social Attitudes* (Dartmouth, Aldershot, 1996), p. 25.

57 Pierson, C., 'Social Policy', in Marquand, D. and Seldon, A. (eds), *The Ideas that Shaped Post-war Britain* (Fontana, London, 1996), p. 157.

58 Worcester, R., 'How the Tories Lost the Campaign and Won the Election', *British Public Opinion*, Autumn, 1979.

59 Townsend, *Poverty in the United Kingdom*, p. 881.

60 Dunn, *The Cunning of Unreason: Making Sense of Politics*, p. 157.

61 Webster, *The National Health Service: A Political History*, pp. 138–9.

62　Organization for Economic Cooperation and Development, *The Welfare State in Crisis*, p. 26.

63　Whiting, *The Labour Party and Taxation*, p. 177.

64　Tanzi and Schuknecht, *Public Spending in the 20th Century*, pp. 16–18.

65　Mullard, *The Politics of Public Expenditure*, p. 6.

66　Whiting, *The Labour Party and Taxation*, pp. 272–3.

67　Ibid., p. 257.

7 Education policy

Roy Lowe

It was Margaret Thatcher who said, after the 1987 general election, that she planned to go further in educational policy making than ever before and she necessarily casts a long shadow over any analysis of the governance of education during the period immediately before she came to office as Prime Minister. She went on to enact the 1988 Education Reform Act, which many commentators have seen as being a benchmark, transforming irredeemably the educational landscape in Britain. But the deeper reality of this period was that the years 1974–9 witnessed transformations in attitude, in public rhetoric and to a lesser degree in the day-by-day detail of policy making sufficient for us to conclude that this, and not the 1980s, was the era which saw the real anticipation of Blairite and New Labour educational policy making. This chapter will seek to identify and analyse the key developments in educational policy making during the period which saw Reg Prentice, Fred Mulley and finally Shirley Williams hold office at the Department of Education and which culminated in the initiative by Jim Callaghan to establish unprecedentedly direct Prime Ministerial involvement in the making and direction of educational policy.

A mixed inheritance

At the moment that Labour returned to office in March 1974 the main lines of debate and the focus of activity in this area seemed clear and appeared likely to remain at the heart of political controversy. The period since the Second World War had seen a massive transformation of the education system. Universal secondary education had, belatedly, been realised (although it had not been until the mid-1960s that the last 'all age' schools disappeared). The incremental nature of this change, together with the fact that it had taken place in straightened financial circumstances, had precipitated the debate on the structure of secondary education to the very heart of politics. Comprehensivisation meant that the secondary sector was that which was most controversial and it loomed as large as any educational issue since the late nineteenth-century debate on the funding of church schools. Superficially the two major parties appeared diametrically opposed on the issue of selection versus comprehensivisation, and it had certainly suited Harold Wilson during his first tenure of Number 10 to give the impression that this was the case. But, in reality, what had emerged was a kind of 'educational Butskellism' with figures such as Edward Boyle and Roy Jenkins appearing to be singing from much the same hymn sheet whenever they pronounced on education policy. Gradualism and a readiness by government to acquiesce in a growing number of 'experiments' in comprehensive schooling were the marks of this shared policy.

But by the early 1970s this 'Butskellism' was, to a degree at least, breaking down and this was in no small part due to the fact that the local authorities seemed to be involved in a rush to go comprehensive which no minister could check. Having been encouraged by a groundswell of professional opinion as well as government during the late 1960s, the LEAs continued after Thatcher's appointment as Minister in 1970 to put forward an unprecedented number of reorganisation schemes. The outcome was that, much as she might have wished otherwise, Margaret Thatcher became the Minister of Education who closed the greatest number of grammar schools in modern Britain. This undoubtedly left her with a determination to return to this issue if she ever had the chance, and thus explains much of the tone and content of the 1988 Act. But, equally significant in our context, it gave the impression to observers during the early 1970s that the local authorities were in some senses out of control and that the long-established balance of power between central and local government, which allowed commentators to reflect that education policy making in modern Britain was attuned to both national and local needs, was breaking down.[1]

The other key agent in educational policy making and practice during the early 1970s was the teaching profession itself. Universal secondary schooling, together with a more protracted education for a growing number of young people, meant an unprecedented number of teachers in post-war Britain. The teacher shortage had been met, first by the post-war emergency training scheme, and second by a sudden and vast expansion of teacher education during the late 1960s. The result was that, during the early 1970s, there existed a pool of young teachers keen to involve themselves in the debate on the curriculum and, in many cases, keen to move beyond the regimented and repetitive teacher-centred classroom methods which they had experienced as pupils. This is not to suggest that schoolteachers were of a single mind on how best to educate children. There were many in the profession at this time who held to the view that one of the key functions of schooling was to induct pupils, particularly the most able, to all that was best in European culture and scientific achievement so that they could sustain and develop this heritage. This view of schooling was, necessarily, more predisposed towards the maintenance of selection and of elite institutions.

In this ferment of ideas and attitudes, local authorities sought to develop in-service work, targeted particularly, but not exclusively, at the younger teacher, through the establishment of teachers' centres. By 1974 there was hardly an LEA in England and Wales which did not have some designated meeting point for its teachers and an established programme of in-service training, much of it provided by local authority advisers. In this situation the Schools Council, established in 1964 as 'a hopeful act of reconciliation between central and local government and teachers',[2] had quickly become a major agency for the dissemination of new ideas on teaching method. It gave a major voice to teachers, enabling them to be perceived as the key arbiters of what went on in the 'secret garden of the curriculum' and appeared to be at the heart of a revolution in teaching. Its very success appeared, by the early 1970s, to be raising a question over the ability of government to control or direct what went on in schools.

Yet one further factor promoted this issue of the 'governability' of education as a major political issue at this time. Many parents were witnessing their children going through a system which, in many respects, appeared to have moved well beyond the one they themselves had experienced. Classroom organisation, the content of the curriculum, methods of teaching and the whole nature of teacher–pupil relations appeared to many to be going through a transformation which they did not understand and about which they felt unsure. This uncertainty enabled the popular press to highlight and focus on educational issues in ways it had never done before and to foment an unease about what was going on in schools which politicians ignored at their peril. The Black Papers, the first of which appeared in 1969, gave voice to these fears and seemed to legitimate parental anxiety. Inexorably, education was making its way to the centre of politics, although few at the time realised that this was happening. Whereas, for much of the century, the education office had been little more than a convenient dumping ground for marginalised political figures, from the 1970s onwards it was to become an increasingly central and significant ministerial appointment.

It is worth pointing out too at the outset that, although the issue of comprehensivisation had come to be seen by many as the main focus of educational policy making, there was in fact a wide range of concerns demanding attention by the early 1970s. At primary level there were worries about the curriculum and not least about attempts to reform it radically through devices such as the briefly fashionable Initial Teaching Alphabet. Already some were pressing the case for a greater focus on 'the core curriculum'. Many secondary schools were involved in attempts to 'destream' to a greater or lesser degree, and a wide variety of curricular initiatives were under way, many of them sponsored by the Schools Council. Some of these involved the abandonment or blurring of long-established subject boundaries, another issue which played on parental concerns. A further challenge was the form and extent which the post-Robbins expansion of higher education would take as planners and administrators tried to come to terms with the financial implications of an unprecedented and ongoing expansion of full-time post-18 education. The old chestnut of the private sector offered another challenge as the implementation of at least some of the proposals of the 1968 Newsom report and its 1970 sequel was seen as urgent by many backbench Labour MPs. The integration of the swiftly growing visible ethnic minorities into the education system was another pressing concern. The policies of dispersal and assimilation advocated by both Edward Boyle and Roy Jenkins a decade earlier seemed already to have run into the sand. During what was to become seen as the decade of multiculturalism there were growing pressures on government to come up with policy initiatives that squared the circle of placating white middle- and working-class fears whilst meeting the proper and understandable aspirations of the immigrant communities. Gender imbalances, in both provision and performance, were also becoming increasingly evident as wider legislation during these years came to focus on sex discrimination and equal rights. The identification and integration of special needs pupils was yet another growing concern at this time.

Finally, the whole issue of local government reorganisation had major ramifications for education. The implementation of the Redcliffe-Maud proposals on local government had involved a reduction in the number of LEAs (from 146 to 104). This change, together with the fact that, following the Baines report, many LEAs introduced corporate management, meant a permanent transformation of the landscape of educational politics. It may well have been that the weakening of the LEAs had already been set in train by these changes before the political rhetoric of the mid-1970s appeared to set the process in motion. Any account of the performance of Labour in power from 1974 to 1979 must take account of its impact in each of these policy areas and this growing complexity of educational politics was in itself part of the explanation of why education appeared to be moving steadily and inexorably towards the centre of political debate. Education seemed never to be out of the news and these wide-ranging challenges ensured that it continued to soak up a growing proportion of GNP. By the mid-1970s, education expenditure was an unprecedented 14.5 per cent of the overall public purse.

The return to power

In this chapter I will argue that Labour returned to power in March 1974 largely absorbed in attempts to pursue and round off the educational policy initiatives of the 1960s and to restore those elements of policy which had been derailed under Thatcher as Minister of Education, but that, by 1976, partly because of a growing awareness of this wide range of problems confronting policy makers, and partly as a result of changed economic circumstances, the Government was driven towards approaches to education which were proactive and unprecedented. The Party was led, largely by Callaghan himself and those immediately around him, to expropriate much Conservative thinking on education and, in the process, transformed for ever power relations within English education. Both the teachers and the local authorities were left, by 1979, in a far more vulnerable position than had been the case, and thus, in retrospect, the work of Thatcher as Prime Minister, and later of Major and Blair, was made much easier in respect of education policy making. In brief, these years of Labour Government mark the real sea change in educational politics in Britain which many commentators have attributed to subsequent administrations. Further, the Ruskin speech and all that flowed from it may best be seen in retrospect as a response to circumstances which was largely predictable by the autumn of 1976. The policy initiatives to which it led had probably become inevitable by the mid-1970s. Callaghan was reacting to events as much as making them.

As Labour came to power in the spring of 1974, it looked, at first glance, very much like a return to educational 'business as normal'. The Party was elected on a familiar pledge to end selection and to expand nursery education. Reg Prentice received a sympathetic welcome from the press and seemed to hold familiar Labour views on the role of education in transforming society. In July, in an address at the North London Polytechnic, he told his audience that

> although the education service cannot itself create a more just society, I am convinced that it has a more powerful role than some sociologists are prepared to admit. This conviction will guide me in every decision I make as Secretary of State.[3]

Accordingly, policy initiatives had a familiar ring. It was made clear as soon as the Party came to power that there would be no legislation to enforce secondary reorganisation 'at present', although in April it was announced that ninety-one local authorities were to be asked to submit plans for comprehensivisation by the year's end. Circular 4/74 requested all LEAs to commit to reorganisation. At Westminster a blacklist of recalcitrant local authorities was drawn up although there were no plans to move directly against them. At the same time the Ministry was using the press to prepare the public for a round of expenditure cuts in the 1975–6 budget, with education as one of the big spending ministries which would be a soft target. Commentators such as Anne Corbett in the *Times Educational Supplement* (*TES*) were urging the Government to return to a resuscitation of the educational priority areas which had been one of the key developments of the late 1960s. Only the establishment of the Assessment of Performance Unit in the autumn of 1974 seemed to presage a different future.

But already the storm clouds were gathering. Whilst on the one hand it was easy to criticise Prentice, as Anne Corbett did as early as July 1974, for 'several useful initiatives that hardly add up to a policy', on the other there were several portents of deeper discontents with educational policy at governmental level. In the same critique, Corbett put her finger on what was to emerge as the key issue during the next few years: the inability of the DES to control and direct what was going on in the education system at large. She commented:

> the money ... may present less of a challenge for an education minister than does initiating and monitoring policy which would give the DES more active responsibilities. ... Education is a service locally administered. That does not diminish the Secretary of State's responsibility to see that education is provided. There are certain minimum standards that the government should adhere to.[4]

At the same time, others were beginning to critique the efforts of those local authorities which were seen to be involved in a headlong rush towards comprehensivisation. Ronald Butt, writing in *The Times* in July 1974, identified the Inner London Education Authority as a particular culprit. This was one of the first of a succession of attacks which was to culminate in the closure of this authority as part of the 1988 Education Reform Act. Butt, under the headline 'A sorry tale of conflicting cultures in the country's classrooms', wrote of an educational establishment working towards a situation in which all schools conformed to a particular type, a type from which many parents were trying to escape. He painted a picture of anarchy in London's comprehensive schools. For him, the particular cause of a situation in which 'the abler children and even the willing children were placed at a disadvantage by their minority position' was those local authorities such as ILEA which were pursuing proactive policies regardless of the needs of children and in pursuit of their own ideological goals.[5]

In similar vein Tom Howarth, a retired Birmingham head teacher, reacted to Circular 4/74 on comprehensive reorganisation with a swingeing attack in the *TES* on what he described as 'Reg Prentice's statement that there should be no selection at any age'. He attacked Prentice for failing to offer 'clear and quite unmyopic answers about certain aspects of total reorganisation'. He claimed that his new unit on 'educational underachievement' (the APU) 'will have its work cut out, commending rote learning in early childhood as the necessary basis for sustained educational growth'.[6]

Whilst these may be seen as portents of the right-wing backlash on educational policy which were to make increasingly untenable the position adopted by the Labour Government at the moment it returned to power, there were other indicators at the time of misreadings of the contemporary situation. One of these was the publication in the autumn of 1974 by the NUT of *Teachers talking*, a pamphlet issued to identify and stress how demanding the teacher's job had become in recent years. This attempt by the biggest teachers' union to influence, not without success, the Houghton Committee which was currently deliberating on teachers' pay, chronicled a succession of classroom developments: new mathematics, integrated studies, team teaching and a shift from whole-class teaching. It enabled Tim Devlin, a *TES* correspondent, to observe that ' "chalk and talk" lessons have almost gone. So has homework of the old variety.'[7] In this the NUT were shooting themselves in the foot. The more they publicised the changed and increasingly difficult nature of the teacher's job, the more they laid themselves and the profession open to right-wing critiques that too much was changing too fast. The argument that only the most able teachers could hope to survive and prosper in the modern classroom was to become part of the rhetoric around the Ruskin speech. Thus, Labour's first year back in office might best be summarised as one of changing perceptions and public debate about education met by tried and increasingly tired responses from the new Government. It was a dysfunctionality which meant that, sooner or later, something had to give.

Throughout 1975 the pressure increased, as a succession of commentators identified the control of the local authorities and in particular some reorganisation of the funding of education as the key issue for policy makers. An article in *The Times* on 1 August demonstrated that for some time the local authorities had been fighting a rearguard action against the erosion of their control of post-18 educational provision. More directly, Roland Freeman, who had until recently been Financial Director of the GLC, told the annual conference of the Rating and Valuation Association in Brighton that 'education should be paid for out of the Exchequer and not by the LEAs ... the transfer of education is the "cardinal feature" of ... proposals on reform of local taxation'.[8] Further pressure came from some of the witnesses to the Layfield Committee which was currently investigating patterns of public expenditure. In October written evidence from three Heriot-Watt academics called for independent auditing of local authority expenditure, which was currently out of control. The right-wing think tank, *Aims for Freedom and Enterprise*, put out a pamphlet in October calling for the responsibility for educational expenditure to be taken away from local government.

There were even influential voices within the local authorities who were prepared to press the argument that it was time for the national government to step in and take more direct control of the education service. In November, Dudley Fiske, one of the most prominent Chief Education Officers, told a Manchester audience in the Simon Memorial Lecture, which was widely reported in the press, that since the Baines report appeared in 1972 there had been a strong case for curbs to be placed on the growing bureaucratisation of local government. That report, Fiske argued, had offered a swingeing attack on the performance of LEAs in particular. His most radical suggestion was 'the transfer of control of the education service to national level. ... It is unfortunate that unexpectedly soon after the 1974 reorganisation, it is local government itself which is on trial.'[9] Even the Prime Minister joined in the chorus, telling the 1975 Local Government Annual Conference at Eastbourne in November that 'the responsibility for education could ultimately be taken away from the LEAs'. Although he was prepared to float the idea, Wilson quickly added typically cautionary notes, pointing out that 'at the moment no-one could sensibly conceive of the education service being run by anyone other than the LEAs' and 'no-one sees a further major change in local government in the years ahead'.[10] The very fact that it was thought necessary to say this so soon after the implementation of the Redcliffe-Maud reforms reflects the disquiet which many commentators were feeling about the performance of the local authorities.

1975: set in the old ways?

But, despite this growing sense that there was a need for radical reform, educational policy making remained set in the old ways throughout 1975, despite the fact that Fred Mulley replaced Reg Prentice in the June Cabinet reshuffle. The three icons remained secondary reorganisation, the reduction of class size and the attack on the private sector, all issues close to the hearts of old Labourites. For much of the year the threat of legislation to coerce recalcitrant LEAs to go comprehensive was brandished, with regular forays into the press by ministers to demonstrate a determination to push ahead on this issue. But direct confrontation was avoided, as had been the case under Wilson during the 1960s. At the October Party Conference, Mulley made it clear to delegates that the 'old' targets, the abolition of private education and the limitation of class size to twenty-five, remained the key priorities. The one initiative which could have been seen as radical, although it was very much within these policy parameters, was the abolition of the Direct Grant schools announced in March. This partial response to the two Royal Commissions of the late 1960s avoided a head-on collision with the major public schools, and sought instead to bring the day grammar schools under closer LEA control in order to enforce their involvement in schemes of comprehensive reorganisation. The example of Bradford, which during the 1960s had become the first city to go completely comprehensive, but whose Direct Grant grammar school remained obstinately untouched, rankled in Labour circles and this was the attempt to put the issue to rest. The legislation could hardly have been more badly calcu-lated. Within days the *Sunday Times* was predicting, accurately, that more than a half of these schools would re-emerge as private schools.[11] What was achieved by this initiative was a strengthening of the private sector which was to prove pregnant with significance for educational policy makers for the following thirty years. On the one hand it demonstrated that attacks on the public schools were likely to be counter-productive, and on the other it engendered a stronger private sector which future policy makers would ignore at their peril. It may not be too strong to argue that, in this, Labour in power was the inad-vertent catalyst of Margaret Thatcher's Assisted Places Scheme. The stubborn refusal to contemplate a new politics of education was underlined in November by Fred Mulley, responding to questions in the Commons. When one of his own backbenchers, Edmund Marshall, pointed out that the transfer of financial provision to central government was 'widely advocated', Mulley stressed that 'we have no plans to change the division of responsibility between local authorities and the DES'.[12]

Towards Ruskin: calls for a new approach

Surveying the scene at the start of 1976, a prescient leading article in the *TES* observed that 'this looks likely to be a year in which the curriculum comes to the fore and, perhaps, a year in which the teachers' grip on the curriculum is chal-lenged'. Pleading for a much stronger input of policy from the DES, the article went on to argue that 'the final decisions will lie with the Secretary of State who must wonder why strategic decisions … should be prepared only by the profes-sional group … there is a need to re-establish the public nature of the curricular debate'.[13]

Within a fortnight the attack had been extended to include Mulley himself, who was portrayed as a minister out of touch with the real needs of the educa-tion system. His address to the North of England Conference at Lancaster was lambasted by the *TES* as

a classic example of genteel ministerial hand-wringing in public. … Educational institutions would soon respond to the change of atmosphere engendered by a government which really put 'the brutal necessity of earning the nation's living' first, in terms of policy priorities, fiscal policy, government spending, the containment of bureaucracy and so on. Mr Mulley's cautious foray ... cannot be said in all conscience to go very far.[14]

In fact, although Mulley had conceded that he had no 'magic remedies', he did hint at the changing educational agenda in this speech with his comment that 'we must instil a deeper respect for careers in wealth generating industries and in commerce'.[15] There were then good reasons why on his assumption of the Prime Ministership in early April Callaghan took it upon himself to take a direct interest in educational policy almost immediately. Not only was the press presenting the image of a department out of touch with the real issues, but several industrialists were weighing in with judgements such as that of Arnold Weinstock who described the teaching profession as 'feather-bedded and ineffi-cient' in one public pronouncement at the start of the year. The Chief Executive of GEC went on to say that 'educationists should recognise that they do no service to our children if they prepare them for a world which does not exist'.[16]

Further, despite the resort to the IMF the previous autumn, there was no immediate sign of the economic crisis coming to an end. Education, as the largest item in the budget of the recondite local authorities, needed a tighter rein. There were votes to be lost over education too, if not to be won. During the previous year the Bullock report on standards of literacy, the Bennett report on teaching styles as well as the William Tyndale dispute had enabled the right-wing press to depict a system in disarray and out of control, fuelling a popular belief that standards were falling.[17]

The publication of the Layfield report in May only added to the pressure, since it emphasised the point that education was by far the biggest item in local authority expenditure, even though the monies were put to widely different ends in differing locations, depending on the policies of particular LEAs. It reported a succession of witnesses who had called for greater control of the education service by central government and suggested that 'the cost of meeting national minimum standards' should be centrally financed.[18]

There were two further developments which worked to make the situation pressing for any administration claiming to be in touch. First, following the appointment of Sheilah Browne as Chief HMI in 1974, the Inspectorate had carried out a major survey of primary schooling and were beginning to canvass the need for a more clearly defined core curriculum. Second, not only was the educational establishment beginning to express concern about levels of achieve-ment but so was the Labour Party itself. In a policy document published in *Labour Weekly* in May, there was a call for the Government to intervene to ensure 'minimum standards' in schools. In this context, the events of the autumn of 1976 begin to appear increasingly as a predictable and even belated reaction to events which seemed to be running beyond the control of the DES.

At the moment he took office, Callaghan's Senior Policy Adviser Bernard Donoughue suggested that educational standards might be made one central concern. In doing so, Donoughue was not only setting in motion a process which led direct to the Ruskin speech but also anticipating a new and lasting power structure which was to hold long after Callaghan left office. Whilst the office of the Prime Minister was to be brought directly into the policy-making process, the resort to the DES and the Inspectorate as key agents for the determination and delivery of policy appeared, both to contemporaries and subsequent commentators, to ensure that their roles would be pivotal in any new educational settlement. But, in reality, what was happening was that, not only was the power of the teaching profession and of the LEAs being placed under threat, but by using both the Inspectorate and DES administrators as the 'enforcers' in an unprecedented way, their role was being subtly shifted from policy making to that of administering the new educational settlement.

Mulley was summoned to Number 10 on 21 May, was asked to report on four major questions and 'was surprised' to be told that the Prime Minister's Policy Unit was working on a major speech to be given later in the year.[19] Thus it was Callaghan, as Prime Minister, who identified the primary curriculum, the later years of compulsory education, the reform of examinations and the education of 16–19 year olds as the key battlefields of the summer of 1976. The outcome was a lengthy and confidential briefing paper, which came to be known universally as the Yellow Book, authored within the DES and leaked to the press only a few days before the Ruskin speech, probably in order to soften up the public and to test the waters.

There is no doubt that many within the DES as well as Sheilah Browne (the Chief HMI) saw this as the golden opportunity for which they had been waiting. Browne had been encouraged by William Pile, during his period as Permanent Secretary at the DES, to use her survey of primary education to pave the way for more direct DES intervention in what went on in schools. Pile's replacement during the summer of 1976 by James Hamilton, a known centraliser, only strengthened the feeling that something was afoot.

Certainly the press thought all this to be a cue for the strengthening of the role of the Inspectorate. Shortly before the Ruskin speech the *TES* commented that

> large hints have been dropped by Sir William Pile to the Commons Select Committee and by his successor Mr James Hamilton to the Association of Education Committees that the privacy of the secret garden should no longer be sacrosanct. The obvious instrument for any such intervention is the Inspectorate – hence the part played by HMIs in preparing a memorandum for the Prime Minister.[20]

During the course of the summer suggestions on the content of the planned speech were invited from numerous sources, although control of it remained firmly within the Prime Minister's Policy Unit. Both Donoughue and his assistant Elizabeth Arnott are known to have been closely involved in the drafting, and the speech itself was kept away from the DES and the Minister right up to the moment it was given.

Meanwhile, pressure continued to build for a shift in educational policy. At the start of September the *TES* highlighted the newly released birth rate statistics, which showed an ongoing fall. It reflected that the improved staffing ratios which inevitably followed would also further weaken the position of the teachers themselves.[21] In mid-September Shirley Williams' appointment to the DES as part of a Cabinet reshuffle seemed to presage a new start in education. Within two weeks of her appointment she was telling the Labour Party Conference at Blackpool that she wanted to end the secrecy of the DES and expressed concern that the existing block grant arrangements for LEAs had 'gone too far'. In this she was echoing the Commons Select Committee which, only a week earlier, had called for greater openness in educational planning, still piqued that the planning documents for Thatcher's *Education: a framework for expansion* had not been made available, even to them.[22] By mid-October that Select Committee was demanding a separate educational funding body for specific issues, a permanent Standing Education Commission. Within a few years the separate funding flow from the Manpower Services Commission was to enfeeble semi-permanently DES attempts to retain complete control of policy making.

In his Prime Ministerial Address to the Party Conference on 28 September, Callaghan took the opportunity to rehearse one of the key themes of his Ruskin speech, telling delegates that 'we need to close the gap between education and industry' through far closer co-operation between employers and schools. It certainly seems that one of Callaghan's motives was the expropriation of emergent Conservative education policy. In its document *The Right Approach* and at the Conservative Autumn Conference, the Tory Party had made it clear that it saw political capital to be made out of education, latching on to public anxieties about both standards in schools and the behaviour of young people. As the *TES* put it:

> Much of the language in which this issue is pursued betrays the small 'c' conservatism which is perennially convinced that things aren't what they were, and that young people are going to the dogs. But underneath it all too there are perfectly respectable arguments about the levels of achievement expected from pupils. At different ages and stages, and the methods and styles of teaching appropriate to these expectations.[23]

Against this backdrop, the leaking of the Yellow Book in mid-October set the scene for the Ruskin speech. It is hard to underestimate the significance of this document, since it anticipated several of the key trends which although they appeared radical in the autumn of 1976 were soon to be at the heart of educational policy making in modern Britain.

First, the Yellow Book took the argument advanced earlier in the year by the NUT concerning the increasing difficulty of the teacher's task and turned it against the profession: outlining the revolution in method promoted by the Plowden report, the Yellow Book commented:

in the right hands this approach is capable of producing admirable results. ... Unfortunately, these newer and freer methods could prove a trap to the less able and experienced teachers who failed to recognise that they required a careful and systematic monitoring of the progress of individual children ... as well as careful planning. ... As a result, while primary teachers in general still recognise the importance of formal skills, some have allowed performance in them to suffer as a result of the uncritical application of informal methods ... the time is almost certainly ripe for a corrective shift of emphasis. Similarly, on secondary education, the Yellow Book highlighted 'the feeling that schools have become too easygoing ... the time has probably come to establish generally accepted principles for the composition of the secondary school curriculum.' It called too for a greater emphasis on the basics to enhance the job prospects of school leavers, concluding gloomily that 'employers complain that school leavers cannot express themselves clearly.' Finally, it called on the Prime Minister to make 'an authoritative pronouncement' to refute the view that only the teachers should have a say on what went on in schools.

The signals could hardly have been clearer and the press wasted no time in underlining the historical significance of the moment. On 13 October the *Guardian* devoted much of its front page to the call that 'the State must step into schools', adding in a leader article that 'just as the clinical independence of doctors is eventually going to have to be reduced ... so too is the far more recent professional independence of teachers'.[24] In similar vein the *TES* argued two days later that

> it now remains to be seen how far Mr Callaghan is prepared to go in his speech at Ruskin College. ... If he acts on the DES advice we have reached a turning point in English educational history – the reversal of the long-term trend which since the early 1920s has steadily diminished the curricular influence of the administrators and the public's representatives. The myth of the teacher-controlled curriculum is strong, so strong, perhaps, that the DES have concluded that it needs an initiative from No.10 Downing Street to begin to dispel it.

This journal went on to spell out the key needs as it perceived them; for HMI to spell out proposals for a core curriculum, for a resolution of the strained relationship between the DES and the Schools Council which reflected the Department's low opinion of the Council, and for the development of direct DES funding streams which could put it more firmly and more directly in control:

> Both parties now believe there is a time-bomb ticking away in the schools. The Conservatives think public anxiety must favour them. They strike attitudes in defence of basic standards in the belief that this is the way to

exploit the anxiety. Mrs Callaghan and Mrs Williams may well have reached a not dissimilar political assessment, and believe they must defuse the time-bomb. ... This they hope to do by bringing these curricular issues into the open.[25]

Given the extent to which the speech had been advertised in advance its greatest significance probably lay in the fact that it was made at all. But Callaghan did use the opportunity to underline several of the key themes which the press had already brought into public discussion. Perhaps most notably he stressed the extent to which the education system must work within the £6 billion per annum which it currently claimed. The need to provide an education which fitted children to enter employment and the demands of a core curriculum were restated and a plea was made for a public debate on education involving all interested parties.

A landscape transformed?

The best and most detailed analysis of the circumstances and significance of the speech so far available is that of Clyde Chitty, who concluded that 'it marked at the very highest political level the end of the phase of educational expansion which had been largely promoted by the Labour Party and at the same time it signalled a public redefinition of educational objectives'.[26] On the right of the political spectrum, as Clyde Chitty has shown, figures such as Rhodes Boyson and Norman St John Stevas were quick to welcome what they presented as the adoption by Labour of long-held Conservative views. There can be no doubt that one major significance of the Ruskin speech was a semi-permanent shift to the right in the grounds of educational debate in modern Britain. The post-war drive for the promotion of a fairer society through education and for the making of citizens gave way to a quest for employability, the inculcation of basic competences and efficiency and effectiveness in the running of schools.

The Great Debate, which took place during the months that followed, was of less significance than the flurry which the speech caused in educational circles in its immediate aftermath. First, Shirley Williams threw herself into a frenzy of public pronouncements which offered at least the image, if not the reality, of a Department which was reining in the local authorities and the schools. At the start of November, clearly trying to appease critics who were worrying that the Government might go too far, she told the Commons she would 'seek basic standards in schools but this would not involve any immediate attempts to control the curriculum'.[27] A week later she announced that she would be consulting LEAs on the school curriculum[28] and a week later again she was threatening greater direct control of educational expenditure by the DES.[29] In the middle of November she used a *TES* interview to make clear that she intended to push through legislation prepared under Mulley to make comprehensive reorganisation mandatory.[30] Then, at the start of

December, in a major Commons speech, she depicted a proactive Government which was planning to involve parents more closely than in the past by encouraging them to comment on their children's progress through school.[31] She also spoke of the establishment of scholarships to encourage pupils towards careers in industry. Amidst all this she was not averse to a bit of teacher-bashing. She told the North of England Conference in January 1977 that the problem lay with 'poor teachers, weak headmasters and head-mistresses and modern teaching methods'.[32] Before the end of January it was the Schools Council which came under attack as she spelt out plans for 'drastic changes' to reduce the influence of the teacher unions and to ensure DES supervision of the Council.[33]

Amidst all this it is difficult to discern any effective action from the DES during this period apart from the drawing up of a draft questionnaire for LEAs enquiring as to how they monitored and controlled the curriculum of the schools under their charge. Certainly by the spring of 1978 Shirley Williams was being lauded by the right as a Secretary of State who had put her finger on the issue of falling standards in schools. Noel Annan congratulated her publicly on being 'the first Secretary of State for years to say in public that educational standards were too low'.[34] Brian Simon observed pertinently of this period: 'procrastination, indecision, delay at all costs – endless consultations became the order of the day … these marked Shirley Williams' term of office'.[35] Simon argues that the net political effect of this was to prepare the soil for the 'radical right' initiatives of the 1980s. Equally, her dependence on rhetoric not only anticipated more recent patterns of governance but may well have had the effect of weakening the DES vis-à-vis the Prime Minister's office.

Also permanently weakened by the Great Debate was the Schools Council. Papers already open at the PRO show clearly that by the end of 1976 and for some time afterwards, there was a major debate within the Council on its role, the part it might play in pushing through a single examination at 16+ and how it could dovetail with the growing number of educational quangos. In May 1978, its Secretary, John Mann, drew up a list of 'other agencies at work in the same fields'. It included the Education Policy Unit of the Policy Studies Institute, the NFER, the SSRC, the DES, HMI, the Health Education Council, the CBI as well as the examination boards. He concluded:

> the Schools Council is a victim of its times. It was called into being in the golden sixties … a period of heady expansion in education. It was acclaimed internationally as an ideal way of promoting educational development on all fronts. In the 1970s the Council has been criticised by both its financial backers, the DES and the local Authorities.[36]

Weakened by the events of 1976, the Schools Council struggled on for several years before being wound up under Margaret Thatcher. Its demise stands as a potent symbol of the diminution of the power and influence of the teaching profession at this time.

Conclusions

How, then, can we summarise the changes in the governance of education in Britain which took place at this time? In essence they are twofold. First, there was a perceptible shift in aspiration, in the ends towards which policy makers were directing the education system. The call for economy and efficiency brought with it a renewed quest for employability, for competence in the core subjects and for the assurance of standards. Out of the window went the explorations of curriculum change, the development of pupil interests and the drive towards a fairer society and an open democracy through education. These, together with the quest for citizenship, had been the rallying cries of post-war educators. Now their voices were overwhelmed by demands for value for money. All of this stopped well short of the target setting and league tables which came to dominate the educational landscape during the 1990s, but it was, nonetheless, a once and for all tilt to the right.

Linked to this, and clearly part of the explanation of why this sea change occurred, was a shift in the balance of power in policy making. This too was to become semi-permanent. Callaghan's initiative, which was nothing more than predictable to those in touch with contemporary debate, moved 'the education issue' closer to the heart of politics and made it more susceptible to direct Prime Ministerial influence. Earlier commentators, such as Clyde Chitty and Brian Simon, have stressed the significance of Callaghan's personal involvement, and that is not to be understated. But the reading of the contemporary media on which this chapter is based suggests too that much that was said in October 1976 on the subject of educational policy making was already to some degree foreseen and even preordained. It was, by October 1976, in many ways inevitable that power would be exercised more directly by central government.

Many observers saw in this a strengthening of the role of the DES and the Inspectorate. My own conclusion is that, whether by accident or design, they became far more the enforcers of the policies of others as a result of the developments of the late 1960s. The real losers in this were the local authorities and the teachers. The Association of Education Committees was wound up at this time. It had been one of the major players in the politics of education, particularly since the Second World War. Almost symbolically in December 1978, its best known Secretary, W. P. Alexander (by now raised to a peerage), resigned from the DES Consultative Committee which was overseeing the work of the Assessment of Performance Unit on the grounds that 'I believe the work now being started by the Unit could be used by a future Secretary of State to control the curriculum.' He was right.

Perhaps the greatest casualty of the late 1970s was the teaching profession itself, which emerged from these events permanently enfeebled. The ill-judged industrial action of the mid-1980s was to be the nail in the coffin of its ability to dominate the debate on the future of the schools and on what went on inside them. Although much of reality of the late 1970s was one of rhetoric rather than of performance, the transformation in power structures which was generated has persisted and has shaped the politics of education down to the present time. There can be little doubt that Labour in office from 1974 to 1979 determined the politics of education to the end of the century and beyond. The achievements of the Blair Governments in the field of education are only comprehensible with reference to what went before. They built on Callaghan's legacy. But the edifice was set up during the 1970s.

Notes

1 Lowe, R., *Education in the Post-war Years* (Routledge, London, 1988); Lowe, R., *Schooling and Social Change, 1964–1990* (Routledge, London, 1997).
2 Plaskow, M. (ed.), *The Life and Death of the Schools Council* (Falmer, London, 1985), p. 1.
3 *Times Educational Supplement* (*TES*), 26 July 1974.
4 Ibid.
5 *The Times*, 18 July 1974.
6 *TES*, 10 May 1974.
7 *The Times*, 18 July 1974.
8 *TES*, 10 October 1975.
9 *TES*, 21 November 1975.
10 *TES*, 28 November 1975.
11 *Sunday Times*, 16 March 1975.
12 *TES*, 14 November 1975.
13 *TES*, 2 January 1976.
14 *TES*, 16 January 1976.
15 Ibid.
16 *TES*, 23 January 1976.
17 Centre for Contemporary Cultural Studies, *Unpopular Education* (Hutchinson, London, 1981), pp. 210–15.
18 *TES*, 21 May 1976.
19 Chitty, C., *Towards a New Education System: The Victory of the New Right?* (Falmer, London, 1989), p. 73.
20 *TES*, 15 October 1976.
21 *TES*, 3 September 1976.
22 *TES*, 24 September 1976.
23 *TES*, 8 October 1976.
24 *Guardian*, 13 October 1976.
25 *TES*, 15 October 1976.
26 Chitty, *Towards a New Education System: The Victory of the New Right?*, p. 95.
27 *TES*, 5 November 1976.
28 *TES*, 12 November 1976.
29 *TES*, 19 November 1976.
30 *TES*, 19 November 1976
31 *TES*, 3 December 1976.
32 *TES*, 14 January 1977.
33 *TES*, 21 January 1977.
34 *TES*, 19 May 1978.
35 Simon, B., *Education and the Social Order, 1940–1990* (Lawrence and Wishart, London, 1991), p. 454.
36 Public Record Office, files number EJ 1/62; EJ 3/22; EJ 3/12.

8 Europe

John W. Young

Relations with the European Community (EC), which later became the European Union, have been a consistent challenge for British Governments since the late 1950s, when the Europe of 'the Six' emerged as a political and economic bloc that questioned Britain's own position on the world stage. Whether outside or inside the Community, Labour and Conservative administrations have found it difficult to shape the main developments in the process of European integration and European issues have provoked deep divisions within both the main British political parties. Aside from the premiership of Edward Heath in the early 1970s, when the country actually entered the EC, governments have widely been seen as reluctant Europeans, first dithering about the principle of entry then generally adopting a sceptical approach to new developments. The negative image is not entirely justified and sometimes British Governments could be found at the forefront of efforts to make Europe pull together. The post-war Attlee administration had taken a lead in welcoming the Marshall Plan and four decades later even Margaret Thatcher, for all her supposed 'Euro-scepticism', was a driving force behind the creation of the single market.[1] Yet even Heath found it difficult to march in step with his continental partners in his paltry thirteen months as an EC premier, as the October 1973 Middle East War, the oil price rises that accompanied it and differences of view on the way forward for the Community ruined bold schemes for a fuller union.[2]

The Labour Governments of Harold Wilson and James Callaghan in 1974–9 came at an important juncture in British relations with Europe, taking power very soon after entry to the Community with the opportunity to set the trend for Britain's future European policy. But they immediately fitted into the post-war pattern: Wilson insisted on renegotiating Heath's terms of entry while, under Callaghan, Britain was responsible for delaying the introduction of direct elections to the European Parliament and refusing to take part in the Exchange Rate Mechanism. Nonetheless, the most significant development on the European front in these years was a positive one, the June 1975 referendum that approved membership by a clear two-thirds majority. For ease of analysis the years 1974–9 fall easily into three periods of unequal length: the renegotiation of the entry terms down to March 1975; the referendum campaign over the following few months; and developments subsequent to the referendum. However, in order to understand why the renegotiation and referendum took place, it is first necessary to discuss the impact of European questions on Labour's years in opposition between 1970 and 1974.[3]

Opposition years

The decisions to renegotiate Heath's terms of entry and hold a referendum were deeply wrapped up in the internal wranglings that had blighted the Labour Party in opposition. It is often forgotten that the membership application that carried Britain into the 'Common Market', as the EC was then popularly known, had actually been launched under the last Labour Government, in May 1967. True, it had been vetoed by de Gaulle that November just as the first application, under the Conservatives in 1961–3, had been vetoed by him. But in 1967 the Labour Government insisted in keeping its application 'on the table' and, with the resignation of de Gaulle two years later, interest in it was revived. In June 1970 negotiations were about to begin and there were indications that Wilson wanted them to succeed. He had even offered the Foreign and Commonwealth Office to the leading 'pro-marketeer' Roy Jenkins.[4] But defeat in the general election of that month was followed by deep divisions in the Labour Party on numerous issues, not least European integration.

Jenkins and others, mainly of a social democratic persuasion, remained committed to a European future as the best way to secure British markets and political influence. But there had always been Labour members, and not exclusively on the left, who saw the EC as a capitalist club, undemocratic in its decision making, membership of which would destroy the Commonwealth and undermine Britain's ability to pursue socialist policies at home or 'open' trade policies abroad. Between these principled positions of support for, and opposition to, EC membership most of the Party was more pragmatic. But there was concern in the early 1970s that, in order to make Britain competitive in the EC, it would be necessary to adopt deflationary measures that would worsen the growing problem of unemployment; just as the EC's Common Agricultural Policy, designed to protect farmers' incomes, would add to the menace of inflation by reducing Britain's ability to buy food at the cheapest price on world markets. In the wider Labour movement, trade unionists were deeply concerned over jobs and inflation and tended to be 'anti-European'. Many MPs were primarily concerned with party political battles rather than the pros and cons of EC entry; they simply wished to attack Heath's policy on Community membership, which was central to his whole premiership.

Such disagreements created difficult problems of party management for Harold Wilson whose primary aim was to keep his Party united and whose solution to the dilemma was to focus criticisms on Heath's terms of entry, thus pleasing the anti-market wing, while never ruling out continued membership if Britain entered the Community, thus avoiding a breach with the pro-marketeers. But this balancing act was far from easy. In the decisive Commons vote on Heath's entry terms in October 1971, sixty-nine Labour MPs defied the party whip and walked into the 'yes' lobby and Jenkins resigned from the Shadow Cabinet in March 1972 because of moves to approve a referendum on continued membership. The idea of a referendum had first seriously been pressed by a leading right-wing Labour anti-marketeer, Douglas Jay, in August 1970 and was soon firmly backed by a leading left-winger, Tony Benn. The idea generated its own divisive arguments within the Party.

At that time referendums were quite foreign to British constitutional practice and it was argued against them that they undermined Parliament's sovereign right to make law. But on such an important decision as EC membership, in which the country's sovereignty and independence were at stake, it was logical that the electorate should be consulted. Apart from a referendum, the only other means of settling the decision at a popular level was to call a general election. However, not only would the election have to be called on the single issue of EC membership, it would also, in order to be meaningful, require Labour and the Conservatives to be on opposite sides; and, since the Conservatives with a few exceptions were pro-market (Enoch Powell being the only noteworthy opponent), that implied that Labour must adopt an 'anti' position, something that might have led the Jenkinsites to quit the Party. The message was not lost on Wilson that, however controversial in itself, a referendum could be the way to keep Labour united by throwing the onus for a decision about membership onto the people as a whole. The fact that Jenkins was opposed in principle to a referendum rather undermined such logic but not all pro-marketeers felt as strongly as he did and Wilson cannot have been too disappointed with Jenkins's March 1972 resignation, since this damaged the latter's chances of becoming party leader in future.

In May 1971 another of Wilson's rivals for the party leadership, James Callaghan, came out in support of both a referendum and a renegotiation of Heath's terms. This latter idea evidently came from Douglas Jay's son, Peter, who also happened to be Callaghan's son-in-law. Renegotiation, along with the referendum proposal, soon became the means by which pragmatists like Wilson and Callaghan could keep Labour united on the EC. The idea of renegotiating Heath's terms allowed Labour to continue its attack on those terms even when they were approved by Parliament in 1972, but without necessarily implying that Britain must leave the Community. Wilson could focus his attack on the Conservatives, not by questioning the principle of entry, which was such a dangerous issue for his own Party, but by criticising the particular terms of entry that Heath had obtained.

A strategy emerged by 1974 based on emphasising the need to renegotiate the terms, largely in order to meet political difficulties at home and with little concern for the poor reaction such second thoughts were likely to create among other member countries of the EC. Talk of a referendum was, in the wake of Jenkins's resignation and in light of the constitutional controversy, played down. But Heath was nonetheless attacked for having failed to let the British people decide such a significant decision as EC entry and it was always evident that some kind of popular vote must take place if renegotiation were successful.

Wilson, as subtle – some might say devious – as ever, was also careful to neutralise his rivals in this process. Jenkins had effectively neutralised himself by his hasty resignation. Callaghan would be neutralised by being given the post of Foreign Secretary, which Jenkins had been meant to have back in 1970, and in which position he would have to carry out the renegotiation with the EC, a difficult task in itself and one that would probably commit him to support whatever terms were secured.[5]

Renegotiation

The February 1974 Labour election manifesto was, on the face of it, toughly expressed concerning the EC. It was designed to appeal to an electorate that opinion polls suggested was determinedly anti-membership. Heath, it said, had made 'a profound political mistake ... to accept the terms of entry to the Common Market, and to take us in without the consent of the British people'. The tone was especially negative when the manifesto criticised 'the imposition of food taxes on top of rising world food prices, crippling fresh burdens on our balance of payments, and a draconian curtailment of the power of the British parliament to settle questions affecting vital British interests'. The last statement in particular could be read as a statement against membership *in principle*. The general line, however, was more pragmatic, opposing 'the terms negotiated by the Conservative government' and promising to renegotiate these in five areas with: changes to the Common Agricultural Policy (CAP) 'so that it ceases to be a threat to world trade in food products, and so that low-cost producers outside Europe can continue to have access to the British food market'; budgetary arrangements that were fairer to Britain; the resolution of monetary problems in a global framework rather than through an EC Economic and Monetary Union (EMU); the retention by Britain of the ability to pursue 'effective regional, industrial and fiscal policies' (so as to minimise unemployment), as well as acceptable arrangements on capital movements and proper safeguards for trade with the Commonwealth and other developing countries; and an agreement that Value-Added Tax (VAT), part of which was paid directly to the EC, need not be harmonised across the Community. If renegotiation were successful the deal would be put to the British people 'through a General Election or a Consultative Referendum' and if this resulted in continued membership, then Britain would be prepared to play a full part in the EC.[6]

The last commitment reflected the fact that, whatever the tone of the manifesto, the Party was not actually against EC membership in principle and, on close inspection, the manifesto was less formidable than it appeared on the actual terms of entry that had to be changed. Some of the points raised were simply insignificant. The EC had little hope of pursuing EMU in the uncertain monetary conditions of the mid-1970s, it had no desire to interfere with capital movements and it had, as yet, no aims to harmonise VAT rates. In the unusual international economic circumstances of the time, it was even the case that world food prices were generally above those in the EC so that even this issue –

potentially an explosive one given Britain's tradition of a 'cheap food' policy – did not present much of a problem. Furthermore, the manifesto did not require any amendments to the actual EC treaties, a demand that could have presented real problems for the other member countries and could have led them to rule out renegotiation.

While the new Cabinet included several anti-marketeers such as Tony Benn, Barbara Castle and Michael Foot, many key decisions on tactics were shunted off into a smaller Europe Committee and Callaghan was determined to preserve day-to-day control of the issue. Castle in particular feared that Callaghan was shifting to a pro-EC policy without full reference to the Cabinet.[7] Then again, Callaghan made it clear from the start to his Foreign and Commonwealth Office officials that he was 'an agnostic' on Europe and that the renegotiation might result in failure; and in his first formal talks with EC colleagues on 1 April his tone was quite demanding.[8] Not that the renegotiation proceeded at all rapidly in its early stages. Delays were caused by the political uncertainties in Europe owing to the death of President Georges Pompidou of France in April 1974 and the resignation of Willy Brandt, the German Chancellor, in May. They were succeeded, respectively, by Valery Giscard d'Estaing and Helmut Schmidt. By the time the renegotiation began in earnest in June, the summer holidays were looming. In any case, of course, Wilson was currently the leader of a minority administration, everyone expected another general election in the near future and it probably suited the leadership to keep the EC away from any major decisions that might rekindle intra-party controversy.

In the October 1974 election, the Labour manifesto had much less to say on Europe than it had in February and emphasised that, of the three main parties, only Labour was ready to let the British people decide on their future in the Community through a popular vote. The word 'referendum' was not used in the manifesto but, since a vote on continued membership was promised 'within twelve months of this election', it was doubtful that any other means of decision was possible.[9] No one would welcome a third general election in the space of twenty months. The October election passed off with surprisingly little controversy on the EC just as Wilson wanted, although Shirley Williams, a pro-market minister, did say she would resign if there were a popular vote against continued EC membership.[10] Then again, when the counting was over Labour only had a slender overall majority of four seats, hardly a secure foundation for building a clear policy on Europe given the strong views on EC membership.

With the election over and a twelve-month deadline for a popular vote, the renegotiation process had to quicken and there were now clear signs that Wilson and Callaghan wanted the process to succeed. In November, Helmut Schmidt, a Social Democrat, was invited to the (delayed) Annual Party Conference to plead for Britain to remain an EC member. In December, Wilson held a summit with Giscard d'Estaing in Paris, where it was evident that a compromise was possible on one of the most difficult points, the financial deal that Heath had secured and which left Britain as the second largest net contributor to the EC budget. The French were adamant that payments into the budget, via earnings from external tariffs and a proportion of VAT, were the Community's 'own resources' and as such inalienable; but this precondition still left it open for Callaghan to press for a refund once the payments were made (as opposed to a reduction of payments in the first place). Almost immediately there was a summit conference of all EC leaders in Paris, where it was agreed in principle to create a 'correcting mechanism', to provide a refund to those in budget difficulties. The mechanism would apply to all members and the details had still to be worked out, but everyone understood that Britain would gain most. Britain also stood to gain from the creation of a European Regional Development Fund that was agreed at Paris.

At the same time Wilson became more open in public about his readiness to accept the 'right' terms, backed Giscard's proposal for regular EC summits in future and even accepted that a study should be set up under Belgium's Prime Minister, Leo Tindemanns, to look at the creation of a 'European Union'. It was quite evident therefore that, if Britain remained a member, it could expect the EC to continue evolving in a more integrated way. EMU, though delayed, was not ruled out as a future development and France now backed the idea of direct elections to the European Parliament, whose members were currently nominated from member parliaments. Also, despite signs that it might get a better financial deal, there was no sign that Labour would get the fundamental reform of the CAP that the February 1974 manifesto had promised. But in Cabinet the anti-marketeers, while as vocal as ever, were still a minority and, significantly, opinion polls were moving in favour of continued membership.[11]

Given the favourable signs for remaining inside the EC, it is not surprising that, on 21 January 1975, Wilson formally proposed to the Cabinet that a referendum be held in June, well ahead of the twelve-month deadline set at the last election. Not only was this remarkable constitutional departure agreed upon but, in another move clearly aimed at preventing a schism in the Party, ministers would be allowed to speak on opposite sides in the public debate. According to Barbara Castle the convention of 'collective responsibility' among ministers was cast aside by the Prime Minister, 'as casually as if he had been offering us a cup of tea'. The Prime Minister was careful to argue that this was an issue of such fundamental constitutional importance that the departure from convention was justified.[12] The referendum was announced on 23 January and both the pro-market and anti-market camps lost no time in organising themselves.

Meanwhile the renegotiation had to be completed and, from Wilson's perspective, appear as a victory. In February the British won some vague promises on reform of the CAP and the pursuit of a liberal trade policy, while a more concrete agreement was reached on access to the common market for former colonial territories, through the Lomé convention, thus answering left-wing calls for a better deal for less developed countries. The key meeting, however, was the first regular summit meeting of European leaders at Dublin on 10–11 March, which was dominated by debate over British demands. Wilson, who now posed as the tough defender of national interests, won an improved deal on access for New Zealand butter to EC markets, a satisfactory statement on Britain's ability to follow its own regional and industrial policies and, most important, a detailed arrangement whereby members would receive a 'refund' on payments into the Community budget if their Gross Domestic Product (GDP) fell below a certain percentage of the average GDP of member states.[13]

Referendum

With the renegotiation at an end a special two-day Cabinet was held on 17–18 March. Here Wilson and Callaghan defended the new terms as being superior to Heath's and the Prime Minister, who was always careful to ensure he had a group of pragmatic loyalists in his Cabinet, secured a clear 16 to 7 vote majority in favour of a 'yes' vote in the referendum, which now began in earnest. This was a remarkable coup given that most Labour members and even most of the parliamentary Party were opposed to EC membership. It was achieved in part by Wilson's own low-key approach and his line that he had only come down narrowly in favour of continued membership himself.[14]

But Labour members could question whether the renegotiated terms were much better than Heath's. There was, after all, no firm promise of CAP reform, the Lomé convention (which mainly applied to Africa) would probably have been negotiated regardless of British demands and many Commonwealth countries had still lost their old access to British markets. As seen above, several of the demands in the February 1974 memorandum had been meaningless and EMU had failed to progress, not because of British opposition, but because of the unfavourable economic environment. True, there was an improvement of sorts on the financial side, but one that still left Britain as the second largest net contributor, with a sum amounting to nearly £800 million by 1979. Even for pro-marketeers, the renegotiation was an unnecessary exercise, which antagonised the rest of the EC and whose 'concessions' might just as well have been won by patient negotiation as a committed Community member.[15] The depths of Wilson's problems in keeping his Party together were highlighted in a Commons vote on continued EC membership on 9 April, when more Labour MPs voted against the Government than for it (by 145 to 137) and a clear majority was only achieved thanks to the votes of Conservatives and Liberals.

After the April parliamentary debate all political energies became focused on the referendum. Despite negative opinion polls on the EC during 1974, by the time the campaign got under way, it always looked likely to result in a 'yes' vote. Opinion polls were safely in favour and even Jenkins had now come round to accepting the referendum. There was a certain irony in this of course: it was the anti-marketeers who had pressed most for a referendum in earlier years, believing the British people would always vote 'no', and they even called themselves the 'National Referendum Campaign' as opposed to the pro-EC 'Britain in Europe' group. Furthermore, the campaign itself was always one-sided in favour of continued membership. True, on the surface there was an attempt to create a balance between the National Referendum Campaign and Britain in Europe in presenting their case to the electorate. They received equal numbers of television broadcasts, they were both provided with public finance and they were each allowed to produce a leaflet that set out their case to voters, and which was distributed free to homes. These leaflets frequently talked past each other, with the 'pros' arguing that continued EC membership would mean job security, stable food prices and security for British institutions while the 'antis' insisted it would bring greater unemployment, higher inflation and a threat to parliamentary sovereignty.

However, many factors worked in favour of the Britain in Europe campaign. There might be equality of television coverage, but all the main daily newspapers, including those of the Express Group (usually known for its anti-Europeanism), were in favour of continued membership; the only daily that took an 'anti' line was the *Morning Star*. Britain in Europe was also able to draw on considerable amounts of private funding, including contributions from big business, which was generally in favour of membership. There was even a third leaflet that voters received, setting out the official Government line which of course, thanks to Wilson's majority in the Cabinet, recommended a 'yes' vote. Even without the resources stacked against it, the National Referendum Campaign – itself an odd title when it came to fighting on the issue of EC membership – was a shambles. Ranging from left-wingers like Barbara Castle and Tony Benn to the extremely right-wing Enoch Powell, it found it difficult to present a coherent line in public and could never properly answer the 'pros' insistence that there was no alternative to membership if Britain wished to remain an effective player in world affairs. When Benn did try to take a lead he only provoked resentment among his allies. The Britain in Europe campaign, in contrast, was fronted by political moderates from all three main parties, including Jenkins and the former Conservative leader, Heath, whose Party, now under Margaret Thatcher, said it would not respect a 'no' vote anyway.

However attractive to Wilson it seemed as a way of pasting over Labour's internal differences, the referendum was not necessarily guaranteed to settle Britain's future relationship with Europe smoothly. Had the vote been a narrow one, the defeated side could have continued to fight its corner and those who took a principled position on the question might never be reconciled to the decision. The most dangerous outcome would have been a 'no' vote that Parliament was then expected to put into practice. For a majority of MPs in October 1974 Parliament was pro-market and many considered themselves elected to take decisions on behalf of their constituents. Had the Commons refused to pass an Act of withdrawal from the EC there would have been a major constitutional crisis with the supposed sovereign rights of Parliament pitted against the novel idea that the electorate could decide particular issues. Fortunately for Wilson this crisis never arose. The referendum of 5 June resulted in a vote that was closely in line with opinion poll predictions: 67 per cent voted in favour and the only region to vote 'no' was the Western Isles of Scotland, although there was a reduction of the 'yes' majority the further one was from London and the South East (the region most likely to benefit from the dynamic economic effects of membership).[16]

One biographer has described the result as Wilson's 'finest political hour'.[17] He had managed to keep his Party united and put an end to the debate over EC membership while retaining his low profile. He quickly moved to demote Benn to the post of Energy Minister and insisted that Cabinet differences on Europe must now end. But the process of renegotiating Heath's terms and then putting them to a referendum, while it did indeed keep Labour united, did little good to its standing in the country. Effective government, relations with EC partners and long-standing constitutional practices had, it seemed, been compromised for the sake of keeping a fractious Party together. Within the Government, differences in enthusiasm for Europe still remained and the social democratic wing of the Party was as alienated as ever from the left. Towards the end of the campaign ministers had even been allowed to appear on platforms opposing each other directly on the question of membership.

The Callaghan Government

In March 1976 Wilson resigned as Prime Minister and was succeeded by Callaghan, who shared his pragmatic approach to European issues and was never likely to embrace deeper EC integration even if he did support continued membership. Like Wilson, Callaghan had been counted 'a Commonwealth man' in the 1950s and 1960s and, of course, the two had worked closely together on the renegotiation and referendum. Tony Crosland, another moderate on Europe, became Foreign Secretary but died suddenly in February 1977 and was succeeded by a mildly pro-EC social democrat, David Owen. Given the controversies and intra-party wrangling that had surrounded the referendum it is perhaps not surprising that Callaghan wished to keep the focus away from European questions once he became leader. But other factors reinforced this tendency. The country was in a deep economic crisis and within months the Government reluctantly accepted a rescue package from the International Monetary Fund that included large-scale spending cuts. The problems of inflation, unemployment and currency instability inevitably absorbed most ministerial energy and EC membership worked no economic miracle. Indeed, with world food prices falling back below CAP levels in 1977, a negative trade balance with Europe and a rising financial contribution to the EC budget (despite the deal on a refund), membership arguably made Britain's economic position worse. In November 1978 Callaghan again began to complain about the scale of Britain's net contribution, thus calling into doubt the principal supposed 'success' of the 1974–5 renegotiation. Meanwhile, Labour's majority in the Commons evaporated, forcing Callaghan to rely in 1977–8 on a voting pact with the Liberals, whose enthusiasm for the EC caused further complications.

Callaghan's way of dealing with these challenges was very much in a Wilsonian mould, striking a compromise between those who wanted to play a full part in the EC and those who remained unhappy about membership. A Cabinet review of EC policy in June 1976 showed a desire to expand the

Community further, to Greece, Spain and Portugal, as a way of weakening further moves towards supranationalism. There was continuing criticism of the EC budget and CAP, but a willingness to accept certain limited reforms such as a common passport.[18] In July 1977 Owen circulated a memorandum advocating an enlarged community, 'open' to world trade and with minimal central powers, and three months later Callaghan issued a policy statement to the Party Conference advocating enlargement, decentralisation and CAP reform.[19] There were clear consistent themes here that were in line with traditional British interests in maximising world trade, preserving Britain's own independence and keeping food prices low. They appeared again in a short section on Europe in the Party's 1979 election manifesto. Here Labour stated its desire for a 'fundamental' reform of the EC, in which Britain must be 'able to realise its own economic and social objectives, under the sovereignty of its own parliament and people'. Enlargement of the Community to Greece, Spain and Portugal was backed but moves towards a federation would be opposed in favour of 'a wider and looser grouping of European states, thus reducing the dangers of an over-centralised and over-bureaucratic EEC'.[20]

The Cabinet's differences on Europe were eased slightly by Callaghan's sacking of Barbara Castle when he became premier and by Jenkins's transfer to become President of the EC Commission in Brussels in January 1977. But while Callaghan could try to ease problems of party management at home, he could not prevent pressures arising across the Channel, where two important proposals arose at this time: direct elections to the European Parliament and renewed pressure on monetary co-operation. Direct elections had long been favoured by Italy, Belgium, the Netherlands and Luxembourg as a way of countering the power of France and West Germany in the Community and, when he became French President, Giscard's support of the idea had led to it being agreed in principle at the December 1974 Paris summit. This was confirmed in December 1975 and, in September 1976, a target date of June 1978 was set for the first elections. But Britain's internal divisions came into play. Remaining Cabinet 'anti-Europeans' like Benn and the Leader of the House of Commons, Michael Foot, argued that a directly elected parliament would be a further threat to the sovereignty of Westminster, even though the actual powers of the European Parliament were few.[21] At the other extreme stood the Liberals, on whose support Callaghan relied upon in the Commons. They not only favoured direct elections, but also wanted them to be held under a system of proportional representation (PR): if successfully used at a European level, PR might more easily be accepted in British elections, boosting the number of Liberal seats. But some Labour ministers were also open to the idea of using PR in European elections, partly because it looked as though the Conservatives would win a landslide in any early election under a 'first-past-the-post' system.[22]

Callaghan not only agreed to hold a Commons vote on PR in November 1977 but actually voted in favour himself. There were shades of the referendum campaign in that, to stop the Government tearing itself apart, Callaghan allowed ministers a free vote on the issue. But with the Conservatives opposed to

PR there was never much chance of the measure being carried in this form. Sure enough the Commons approved direct elections but on a 'first-past-the-post' basis. But this meant that the bill on European elections had to be reintroduced, making it impossible to hold the elections in 1978. Ironically, the pro-market Liberals had simply created a situation where the first direct elections to a European Parliament had to be put back a year, an event that further damaged Britain's standing in the EC.[23]

By the mid-1970s monetary union was well established as a proposal for boosting European growth and trade, boosting employment and further binding the Community together. But the Werner report of 1970 had come to nothing thanks to the currency instability that accompanied the move from 'fixed' to 'floating' exchange rates after 1971. Even 'the snake', an attempt to keep European currencies from drifting widely apart, had only mixed success. In 1974–6 of course EMU did not seem a problem for Wilson and Callaghan as they worked towards a referendum. The first sign that this situation might change came in October 1977 when Roy Jenkins, seeking to galvanise his Presidency of the Commission, advocated renewed efforts at a currency union in a speech in Florence. Even continental leaders doubted that such a bold scheme was possible but in 1978 the more formidable Helmut Schmidt took up the theme with ideas – more modest than Jenkins's – for a system that would stabilise European currency values. Schmidt was concerned about the rising value of the Deutschmark against the dollar, leading to a corresponding fall in German exports, and he hoped to find some protection in a broader European group.

The Chancellor proceeded carefully. He won over the key figure of Giscard, then surprised Callaghan with proposals for a currency zone at a European Council meeting in Copenhagen in April; but Schmidt also proposed that Britain should join a study group alongside Germany and France, to look at the proposal. Fearing to be isolated, Callaghan had little choice but to agree.[24] Callaghan's official biographer has argued that the Prime Minister saw the sense of Schmidt's initiative but that most of the Cabinet disliked it.[25] The Treasury, under Denis Healey, believed it would restrict its own ability to manage the pound and there were also fears that European currency co-operation would upset the Americans, with whom Callaghan wanted friendly relations.[26] The British allowed the Germans and French to dominate the study group, whose proposals came to the European Council at Bremen in July. Here it was agreed to begin work on drafting a European Monetary System (EMS) but, in September, Healey revealed that Britain would not join as a full member. It was all very reminiscent of Britain's failure to join in the negotiation of the Treaty of Rome in the mid-1950s, despite initially taking part in studies of a customs union. But politically the decision was quite understandable. A general election had to be held in the near future and Callaghan could not afford to offend Labour anti-marketeers. As a result Britain did agree in December 1978 to use the so-called European Currency Unit (based on a basket of currencies) as an internal measure for Community finances in future. But the Government did not join the more significant Exchange Rate Mechanism that was established in March 1979 and which 'pegged' member currencies within certain flexible bands of one another.[27]

Conclusion

So poor was Britain's standing in the EC by the time Labour lost office in May 1979 that Roy Jenkins welcomed the victory of Margaret Thatcher.[28] It would not take long for their hopes to be dashed as Thatcher, unencumbered by any pact with the Liberals, tried to tap popular suspicions of European integration. While it would be easy to dismiss the Labour Governments of the 1970s as poor partners in the EC, obsessed with domestic considerations and unwilling to enter into the 'Community spirit', a rush to judgement must be resisted. True, Labour's record was hardly impressive. A largely cosmetic process of renegotiation absorbed Community energies, suggested that Britain was, from the first, a reluctant member, and seemed designed to meet Labour's internal difficulties. Then, once inside the EC, the Government continued to look after its own interests, to decide European policy on the basis of political exigencies in London and either delayed, or distanced itself from, major EC initiatives. It is difficult, then, to deny that domestic considerations had a prominent role in shaping Britain's European policy at this time. Of course, these included deep divisions within the Labour movement. It should be remembered that, once in opposition again, the Party would become divided over European issues once more, with the supporters of Jenkins being at the heart of the breakaway Social Democratic Party, while those who remained loyal to Labour promised a 'negotiated withdrawal' in the 1983 election.

However, the 1970s were hard times for the EC as a whole. Britain alone could not be blamed for the failure to progress towards EMU and the ideal of a 'European Union'. The Western world was in the economic doldrums, making an early monetary union unthinkable, and all EC members had their own views on political reform that made agreement difficult. Only in the mid-1980s would an economic upturn bring a real revival of efforts at deeper integration, creating a challenge for the Thatcher administration. At times, Labour leaders did show an ability to play the Community game of multilateral compromises quite effectively. A case in point was the Paris summit of December 1974 when Wilson conceded the possibility of future political reforms and regular leaders' meetings, in return for concessions on the Regional Development Fund and Britain's financial arrangements. In other words, he was quite capable of courting the EC audience when it mattered, even if he courted the domestic audience at the next summit, in Dublin. But it also needs to be borne in mind that Wilson's tactics at Dublin were designed to achieve a very 'European' end: a 'yes' vote in the upcoming referendum. In other words, it may be that, contrary to appearances, external policy needs ultimately had priority over domestic ones.

Indeed, while Wilson may often be dismissed as a short-sighted pragmatist and tactician, the most convincing reading of his tortuous shifts on policy towards the EC as Labour leader, going right back to the mid-1960s, is that he was looking to achieve two long-term, not always easily compatible, goals: to achieve membership of the EC while keeping his Party united. Talk about entering only on 'the right terms' was a means of keeping the Party united by keeping all options open, as well as a justification for attacks on Heath. For all his negative tone at times, Wilson never ruled membership out, he was willing to dilute the original aims of the renegotiation (especially on CAP reform) and, when it came to the referendum, he put his own political reputation on the line to achieve a positive result. Bernard Donoughue, the Senior Policy Adviser in Downing Street in 1974–9, later wrote that the Prime Minister 'was never very sympathetic to the EEC. ... However he viewed it as a wider issue. To have pulled out of Europe would have put Britain in the hands of Little Englander isolationists.' Thus, while no enthusiast for the EC, Wilson can nonetheless be counted among those determined to remain inside.[29]

Exactly why Wilson and his successor, Callaghan, worked for Britain to remain a member of the EC may be explained by discussions in 1974 when the Cabinet considered Britain's shrinking role in the world as part of the case for entry. The country had experienced a steep decline in influence in recent decades, its economy was weakening relative to its major competitors (not least West Germany) and the future would not be easy whether inside the EC or without. But Callaghan was convinced that it was only from inside that Britain could rebuild its power.[30] There was no alternative grouping, now that the Empire was gone and the Commonwealth ineffective. The only other way forward that offered itself was the isolated, socialist state imagined by some on the left. Once again, then, EC membership seemed a 'must' for the country and a price was paid for achieving it in the time and effort devoted to the referendum campaign, when there were many other problems that beset the Government. Again, Bernard Donoughue commented that the referendum was the most important factor that diverted ministers from pressing economic issues in 1974–5.[31] Just as policy towards the EC suffered from the need to placate domestic audiences, so domestic policies suffered from the need to secure continued EC membership. With the referendum won, a return to minority government and continued differences within the Party, it is perhaps unsurprising that further risks on the European front were avoided.

The overall record on Europe is in fact typical of the Government's performance in other areas: inglorious, apparently lacking in direction, crippled by parliamentary arithmetic, economic difficulties and ideological divisions, but not without success given the circumstances. Then again, even if it would be wrong to castigate Labour for its European policy, it would be ridiculous to repaint the period in too optimistic a light. A final example of the limits to Labour's European commitment, but a significant indication of the way other governments would act in future, was the tendency for Wilson and Callaghan, in contrast to Heath, to place good relations with the United States on a par with those with the EC and to act as a kind of mediator between the two. Callaghan, for example, 'consciously sought common US and continental European ground on issues of détente'. Thatcher would adopt a more determinedly pro-American line, but it has been said that John Major's 'understanding of US–UK relations was not unlike that of James Callaghan and other upholders of the "Atlantic intermediary" role'. The desire to play such a role was also evident under Tony Blair, the Prime Minister when Labour finally returned to power in 1997 with a rather more united appearance on Europe, yet who still found it difficult to commit the country to the central new development in European integration, the single currency.[32]

Notes

1　For contrasting approaches see: Denman, R., *Missed Chances: Britain and Europe in the Twentieth Century* (Macmillan, Basingstoke, 1996), a very critical account; and Greenwood, S., *Britain and European Cooperation since 1945* (Blackwell, London, 1992), which sees positive elements in British policy.

2　For a brief review see Young, J.W., 'The Heath Government and British Entry into the European Community', in Ball, S. and Seldon, A. (eds), *The Heath Government, 1970–74* (Longman, London, 1996), pp. 259–84. For a fuller account: Lord, C., *British Entry to the European Community under the Heath Government* (Dartmouth, Aldershot, 1993).

3　For discussions of the 1974–9 Governments and their European policies see: George, S., *An Awkward Partner: Britain in the European Community* (Oxford University Press, Oxford, 3rd edition, 1998), chs 3 and 4; Greenwood, *Britain and European Cooperation since 1945*, pp. 99–108; Young, J.W., *Britain and European Unity, 1945–99* (Macmillan, Basingstoke, 2nd edition, 2000), pp. 111–25.

4　Owen, D., *Time to Declare* (Michael Joseph, London, 1991), pp. 161–2. On the 1964–70 Government see especially: Young, J.W., *The Labour Government's International Policy, 1964–70* (Manchester University Press, Manchester, 2003), ch. 6; Daddow, O. (ed.), *Harold Wilson and European Integration* (Cass, London, 2002).

5　This section is based on Young, *Britain and European Unity*, pp. 100–11.

6　February 1974 Labour Party manifesto, 'Labour's Way out of the Crisis', at www.labour-party.org.uk.

7　Castle, B., *The Castle Diaries, 1974–76* (Weidenfeld and Nicolson, London, 1980), pp. 111–13 and see pp. 125–6, 128 and 143–4.

8　Morgan, K.O., *Callaghan: A Life* (Oxford University Press, Oxford, 1997), pp. 413–17.

9　October 1974 Labour Party manifesto, 'Britain will win with Labour', at www.labour-party.org.uk.

10　Butler, D. and Kavanagh, D., *The British General Election of October 1974* (Macmillan, London, 1975), pp. 30–1, 58, 76–7 and 119–21.

11　On the negotiations in late 1974 see especially: Callaghan, J., *Time and Chance* (Collins, London, 1987), pp. 310–18; Morgan, *Callaghan: A Life*, pp. 420–2; Wilson, H., *Final Term: the Labour Government 1974–76* (Weidenfeld and Nicolson/Michael Joseph, London, 1979), pp. 87–98.

12　Castle, *Diaries*, pp. 287–8. See also Benn, T., *Against the Tide: Diaries 1973–76* (Arrow, London, 1989), p. 305.

13　Callaghan, *Time and Chance*, pp. 320–4; Wilson, *Final Term*, pp. 101–2.

14　Benn, *Against the Tide*, pp. 341–9; Castle, *Diaries*, pp. 340–1; Morgan, *Callaghan: A Life*, pp. 424–5; Wilson, *Final Term*, p. 103.

15　See Pinder, J., 'Renegotiation: Britain's Costly Lesson', *International Affairs*, 51(2), April 1975, pp. 153–65.

16　This account of the campaign is based on Butler, D. and Kitzinger, U., *The 1975 Referendum* (Macmillan, Basingstoke, 1976).

17　Morgan, A., *Harold Wilson* (Pluto Press, London, 1992), p. 469.

18 Benn, *Against the Tide*, pp. 578–9.
19 Owen, *Time to Declare*, pp. 329–31 and 333–4.
20 May 1979 Labour Party manifesto at www.labour-party.org.uk.
21 Benn, *Against the Tide*, pp. 462–3 and 516–17; Benn, T., *Conflicts of Interest: Diaries 1977–80* (Arrow, London, 1990), p. 49.
22 See Owen, *Time to Declare*, pp. 274–6.
23 George, *Awkward Partner*, pp. 119–21.
24 On the origins of the ERM see especially: Ludlow, P., *The Making of the European Monetary System* (Butterworth, London, 1982), pp. 37–55, 63–80 and 88–94; also Jenkins, R., *A Life at the Centre* (Macmillan, London, 1991), ch. 25.
25 Morgan, *Callaghan: A Life*, pp. 614–15; and see Callaghan, *Time and Chance*, pp. 492–3.
26 Healey, D., *The Time of My Life* (Michael Joseph, London, 1989), pp. 438–9.
27 Ludlow, *Monetary System*, pp. 104–6, 112–32, 185–7, 217–25 and 244–6.
28 Jenkins, R., *European Diary, 1977–81* (Macmillan, London, 1989), pp. 374 and 400.
29 Donoughue, B., *Prime Minister: The Conduct of Policy under Harold Wilson and James Callaghan* (Jonathan Cape, London, 1987), p. 59.
30 It is not clear if there was one or two meetings on this: Benn, *Against the Tide*, pp. 142–3; Callaghan, *Time and Chance*, p. 326.
31 Donoughue, *Prime Minister*, p. 57.
32 Quotes from Dumbrell, J., *A Special Relationship: Anglo-American Relations in the Cold War and After* (Macmillan, Basingstoke, 2001), pp. 87 and 110.

9 Foreign and defence policy

Ann Lane

The latter half of the 1970s is most frequently portrayed in the literature as the moment when British decline reached its nadir, marked by further retreat from existing commitments under the pressure of intractable domestic political and economic difficulties. Britain's defining characteristic in this period was a profound lack of confidence as a major power, dependent on its nuclear deterrent for residual status and influence. However, an examination of the policies and events of the second half of the 1970s reveals that this image owes more to the back-projection of Conservative Party hagiography than it does to the policies of the Wilson and Callaghan Governments.[1] Although the predominant impression is that Labour was necessarily preoccupied with domestic issues during this period, the avowal of Britain's diminished power and status provided them with the opportunity for the first time to impose a fresh vision of British interaction with the outside world which was rooted in the principles of socialist internationalism tempered by pragmatic recognition of the realities of world affairs. That they were able to do so was due, it is argued here, to the experimentation with the Cold War system in which the superpowers had been engaged during this transitory decade. Far from being the end of an era in British decline, this period marked the first hesitant beginnings of a renewed British engagement with the rest of the world, albeit defined within more modern parameters. As such, Labour under Wilson and Callaghan was in many respects ahead of its time.

Britain and the world

In 1964, Harold Wilson declared that 'Britain is a world power, or we are nothing.' There is little evidence that he had changed his view significantly in the ten years that elapsed between this statement in the House of Commons and his third term as Prime Minister which commenced in March 1974. Despite the pretensions of the 'Little Englanders' and would-be isolationists within the Labour Party, even the most cursory examination of the history of British foreign and defence policies reveals the underlying assumption to have been that Britain should remain a fully engaged member of the international community. The real debate was about how best this could be accomplished.

From the outset, foreign policy was dominated by the figure of James Callaghan, both in the office of Foreign Secretary which he held during the two Wilson administrations, and then as Prime Minister. This appointment, which disappointed the aspirations of the arguably better qualified Denis Healey and the talented but less favoured Tony Crosland, was central to the political strategy underlying Wilson's management of a potentially difficult and divided Cabinet with only the slimmest of parliamentary majorities. Callaghan represented the conservative wing of the Labour Party, being widely perceived as ideologically to the right of Wilson himself. His appointment signalled to the Party, the country and to Britain's allies and enemies alike that far from retreating into isolation, as a proportion of the electioneering rhetoric had suggested Labour might, the Wilson Government was seeking to sustain British presence on the world stage as a player of influence. At the heart of this was Callaghan's innate atlanticism, his belief in the immutability of the Anglo-American alliance as an article of faith, coupled with his pragmatic if resigned acceptance of the necessity of engaging constructively with the European community. It was in order to manage the dangerous business of renegotiation of British entry into the EEC that Wilson chose Callaghan as Foreign Secretary. Callaghan's overt atlanticism was regarded as an asset which would help dispel the fears both of the anti-Europeanists, whose criticism of the project had been sharpened as a result of the Heath administration's disdain for the Anglo-American alliance, and the anti-isolationists who saw in Europe confirmation of the abdication from global responsibility.

Renewed emphasis on the Anglo-American relationship was embedded in a broader strategy founded in Callaghan's determination that British foreign policy should be informed by the principles of socialist internationalism. Simultaneously, he wanted to sustain and even enhance British influence, but through development of political and economic strength rather than military force. In keeping with the new sense of international interdependence, awareness of which had been promoted as a consequence of the oil crisis and the spectre of world economic depression, Callaghan believed that the best opportunity for Britain to stem and even reverse its declining credibility as a major power lay in its membership of international organisations. This view was confined not just to the influence Britain gained as a consequence of its participation in NATO and now the EEC. Callaghan also wanted a re-engagement with the Commonwealth as a network of connections and a forum for debate, coupled with a parallel improvement in the British standing in the United Nations.[2]

Since the late 1950s, and the emergence of the developing world as a significant voting bloc at the UN, Britain had been treated as the 'whipping boy' whenever issues of human rights and self-determination were raised. This had become particularly wearisome in the context of developments in southern Africa. Recognising that the UN was an ideal forum through which British influence could be exercised in its post-colonial circumstances on a range of subjects involving the promotion of the principles of peace and justice and human rights,

Callaghan directed that the British delegation at the UN actively cultivate their connections with the Commonwealth delegations in order to provide greater co-ordination of Commonwealth policy in that arena. The appointment of Ivor Richard as British Minister to replace the career diplomat, Sir Douglas Maitland, was a gesture designed specifically to symbolise this change in emphasis. This new approach also cleared the way for Wilson to propose initiatives to meet growing trade and financial problems of the developing world at the Commonwealth Conference which was held in Jamaica during 1975.[3]

Balanced against this was his understanding that it was precisely the contributions Britain made to its allies through its military capability, as well as its possession of the nuclear deterrent, that Britain gained some influence over the development of Western military strategy in the Cold War. Inherently this meant that Britain retained a vestige of influence with the United States. It was Callaghan's view, which ran directly contrary to the left wing of the Labour Party, that only when the need for these capabilities had been negotiated away, could Britain afford to consider a reduction in its military capabilities or abandonment of its deterrent force. Consequently the maintenance of a credible and effective defence force was a sine qua non of his assumptions throughout this period.

This view of the world, which was internationalist and pragmatist, and which sought solutions to the world's problems through global rather than regional solutions, was shared in all matters of substance by Harold Wilson whose failing energies and generally more relaxed approach to leadership than in earlier times led him to permit Callaghan a largely free hand at the Foreign and Commonwealth Office (FCO). Wilson was less pro-American than Callaghan but for tactical reasons perceived the value of his Foreign Secretary's prejudices. Healey also shared many of Callaghan's assumptions and despite disagreements over the detail of policy decisions he was a source of reinforcement for Labour's foreign policy approach. For one thing, he had long realised that the stability of sterling depended in large measure on American goodwill. Even more fundamentally, Healey's six years at the Ministry of Defence during the 1960s (a period to which he subsequently referred as the most rewarding of his career) had convinced him of the value and importance of British military strength in the context of relative decline amid the ongoing Cold War.[4] Similarly, while on budgetary grounds Healey was a relentless advocate of significant reductions in the levels of defence spending as an item in government expenditure, he nonetheless recognised the necessity of proper maintenance of the armed forces in terms of both strength and technology in order that the loftier aims of British foreign policy might be pursued.[5]

The result of all this was that Labour came to office with a much bigger view of the world and of Britain's potential for a role in it in the future than had been the case during the Heath administration. Shortly after the second round of the 1974 elections, evidence that the Ford administration had recognised and appreciated this shift can be found in a briefing paper prepared on the occasion of Wilson's visit to Washington in January 1975 which described relations as 'particularly warm and cordial' due largely to the Labour Government's 'determination to ease the strain and tension that developed between us' during the latter months of the Heath government.[6] Among the early successes of this new warmth was a degree of co-ordination between the United States and Western Europe in formulation of a response to the oil crisis which marked a significant step towards recognition of the consequences of growing global interdependence which began to gather momentum as a result of technological developments in this period.[7]

The other area in which there was a marked shift in interpretation and policy development was with regard to the Soviet Union. The 1970s was a period of international crisis and transition in which the assumptions which had underpinned the Cold War framework for international relations were increasingly being questioned. In part this was a consequence of the exposure of American vulnerability both through the Vietnam imbroglio and as a consequence of the unsatisfactory nature of the Nixon presidency in its second term. During the 1970s the United States attempted to deal with its problems by shifting away from the internationalism of Kennedy and Johnson and focused much more on US national interests as a factor in foreign policy decision making, managing its international role by maintenance of the superpower strategic balance on the one hand, while simultaneously curtailing its international commitments on the other.[8]

The détente process and the Strategic Arms Limitations Talks (SALT), which dominated superpower relations in this period, were manifestations of this process in action. This made things difficult for Britain whenever American support was required in order to achieve effective action. The Cyprus Emergency in the summer of 1974 was one such example when American preoccupations with the domestic political crisis occasioned by the Watergate cover-up took American attention from an event in which joint Anglo-American action was required. The resort to partition, which gave the impression of rewarding Turkish aggression, a solution which for historic reasons the British found difficult to accept, was blamed by Callaghan on the failure of the United States to assist the diplomatic process by threatening the Turks with the use of force.[9] More generally it generated an atmosphere, particularly within Western Europe, in which the motivations of the United States became an object of suspicion because, under the Carter administration, the perception developed that the United States was pursuing détente and arms limitations in accordance with its own interests with little regard for the concerns of the European powers on whose territory nuclear weapons were sited. While British foreign policy was necessarily constrained by American diffidence, the divergence of US–European relations provided Britain with an opportunity to bring a new measure of understanding and co-ordination, informed as it was by an essentially revisionist interpretation of Soviet motivations and strategy.

Both Wilson and Callaghan were ideologically resistant to the traditionalist Cold War notion that the Soviet Union was a constant ideological as well as a military threat. Both had long personal experience of dealing with the Russians which stretched back to the early years of the Cold War and each had formed the opinion that far from nurturing intentions to invade Western Europe, the Soviet Union was by the 1970s so preoccupied with the weaknesses of its own economy that it was compelled by necessity, if not by choice, to seek constructive engagement with the West. The Soviet economy required access to Western markets for its raw materials and energy exports as well as acquisition of American technology in order that much needed modernisation could take place. Thus, it seemed that the opportunity had finally arrived for the West to exploit trade and commercial contacts as a means of developing in the Soviet leadership a vested interest in continued co-operation and peaceful existence by the creation of greater interdependence between East and West.[10] During a visit to Moscow in February 1975, Callaghan drew from Brezhnev a definition of the Soviet leader's contemporary understanding of peaceful co-existence which he equated, for the first time, with co-operation alone and applied it to relations between states irrespective of their social systems.[11] Soviet strategy, as the Labour Government now understood it, was focused on détente, the relaxation of trade, expansion of trade credit and a move away from competition in favour of promotion of international contacts.

This interpretation fitted more closely the foreign policy assumptions then held by both the French and West German Governments than the continued preoccupations with the threat of the spread of communism which remained a constant of American containment strategy. However, while both Paris and Bonn had begun actively courting their Eastern bloc neighbours, developing a specifically European strand to the détente process which sought reconciliation with the East, the Heath administration had permitted Anglo-Soviet contacts to fall into abeyance. On coming to office, Callaghan instructed his officials to seek a re-establishment of these contacts and a greater knowledge of contemporary Soviet thinking, beginning with signature of an Anglo-Soviet trade agreement in May 1974 which was intended primarily, from the British perspective, to restart British exports to Russia.

Defence policy

Decisions about defence spending said much about the Labour Government's approach to British interests and responsibilities overseas. Unlike the parallel debates being conducted by some of Britain's European partners, there was never any serious challenge to the assumption that NATO was the framework within which such decisions should be made. There was, however, intense debate both within the Cabinet and throughout the Party about the appropriate scale and purpose of that commitment. For some time the trend in defence spending had been progressively downwards, which was reflected as a percentage of total expenditure in GNP which in 1974 was running at 4.9 per cent. The problem which confronted Labour, as it contemplated the mismatch between overseas commitments and the demands of the security crisis emanating from Northern Ireland on the one hand, and Britain's failing economy on the other, was that rapid technological advances were making a nonsense of the conventional approach to defence spending which focused on the size of the total budget. Advances in technology periodically required a major increase in spending so that British forces could be supplied with up-to-date equipment, but they also demanded an increasingly sophisticated and well-educated military force. To achieve that in armed services recruited on a voluntary basis, salaries, wages and career opportunities had to be attractive to high-calibre personnel. Put simply, for Britain to sustain credible armed forces, a budget which was raised by a factor commensurate with inflation would be inadequate. Far from defence expenditure being frozen at current levels, or declining still further, there was need for a sharp increase just to maintain the status quo.[12]

The Mason review, which was published in December 1974, and the Defence White Paper of March 1975, were reflections of the tensions between these assumptions and British financial weakness and the politics of managing a party deeply divided internally on the question of defence spending. Since NATO had to take priority, Mason sought to address both the budgetary difficulties and the task of conciliating the left of the Party by sheering off some of Britain's remaining far-flung commitments.[13] This process focused on Britain's non-NATO forces, and Britain withdrew from the Five Power Agreement and CENTO and duly disbanded the forces deployed for those roles. Callaghan even considered abandoning British bases in Cyprus when he found his freedom to respond to the Emergency there in 1974 was constrained by the presence of British service personnel and families living outside the military compounds on the island. In the event he was talked out of acting on this idea by the United States.[14] The first round of cuts did not prove adequate, however, and a further review was undertaken during 1976–7 when commitments were streamlined further through termination of the Simonstown Agreement to supply arms to South Africa, by withdrawal from ANZUK and closure of the Goa air staging base. Henceforth overseas responsibilities were to be limited to the Falklands, Gibraltar, Cyprus, Hong Kong and Belize.

The Defence Reviews of 1974 and 1975 were conducted against a background of intense and well-informed debate in the serious press about the balance between budgetary priorities and the hazards to British well-being generally if its security was imperilled.[15] The Chiefs of Staff in both Britain and the United States were acutely concerned during this period that British financial stringency was jeopardising the effectiveness of its fighting forces by undermining both morale and competency through scant provision of ammunition and fuel which militated against the fulfilment of necessary training exercises. American concern was generated as much by self-interest as by wider concerns for NATO's military effectiveness, since Britain's value as a military ally was rising as Soviet strength appeared to increase. These pressures were added to by British dependence on American and German financial support. Both states had been consulted before presentation of the 1974 Defence Review and paradoxically the IMF crisis of October 1976 increased the significance to Britain of German and American concerns about British fighting effectiveness because it was on their financial support that the rescue package assembled to meet British difficulties depended. Britain was under pressure to meet the NATO target of a 3 per cent budget increase per annum. This was achieved, despite considerable opposition within the Cabinet both from the Treasury as well as the left wing of the Party, by linking British participation in NATO with the desire to further détente as well as to the requirements of defence.[16]

The arguments surrounding the maintenance of conventional forces were paralleled in the debate about Britain's ageing nuclear deterrent. In 1966, Labour had pledged not to renew the Polaris system once it became obsolescent. However, the Labour Governments of the 1970s do not appear ever to have seriously considered the idea that Britain should not retain its own deterrent capability. Underlying this was a latent distrust of the United States which inclined Labour to see a necessity to retain the deterrent in order to retain influence over American nuclear strategy.[17] But in general, and despite the presence in Cabinet of three ministers who were to varying degrees vocal critics both of maintaining Britain's commitment to NATO at current levels, and of replacement of the deterrent, the defining assumption was that Britain's role as a major power would be sustained and that replacement of the deterrent was an integral and non-negotiable part of this strategy. The secrecy surrounding these discussions was imposed for reasons of avoiding dissent as much as for security. Both Wilson and Callaghan continued the tradition of confining discussion of nuclear strategy policy to the barest minimum number of Cabinet colleagues, supported by the Permanent Secretaries at the FCO and MOD, and did not put the conclusions of these meetings to either the Defence and Overseas Policy Committee (DOP), the full Cabinet, or far less the House of Commons, for debate.

By 1977, as the major question of replacement was pending, the Cabinet's attention was focused on the issue by the rapidly escalating costs of the Chevaline project to upgrade the existing Polaris system. Chevaline owed its origins to an initiative by David Owen, then Navy Secretary, in 1969 and reflected the underlying reluctance of Labour to fulfil its pledge to end Britain's possession of the nuclear deterrent. The Heath Government had adopted the project and it was re-endorsed by the Wilson administration precisely because it had been perceived as necessary when it was commissioned, which rather suggested that the deterrent effect of Polaris would be discredited if the project was not completed.[18] For this reason, the Nuclear Defence Policy Group set up by Callaghan to handle this aspect of policy concluded in 1977 that despite the quadrupling of costs since the project was first authorised, it should be completed.[19]

The discussion about replacement proceeded in an atmosphere of increasing tension in international relations. While the SALT II negotiations showed progress, the European states generally had become disillusioned with the process, suspecting the United States of perfidiously negotiating to control strategic arms which could affect the American continent, while overlooking the issues surrounding intermediate- and short-range weapons which were sited on

European soil and targeted for use there. Worse, evidence began to accrue that the Soviet Union was taking advantage of these negotiations to improve its own nuclear weaponry; Soviet deployment of the intermediate-range SS-20 missiles in 1976 not only underlined European vulnerability to superpower conflict, but provided a focal point for these concerns. This combined with the instability on NATO's southern flank in Cyprus and the Spanish peninsula, and multiplication of proxy conflicts especially in Africa, to generate a renewal of the very tensions which the détente process had been designed to offset.

From a British perspective, the pressures which beset the European leaders in this period impacted on the decision-making process rather more indirectly. As a nuclear power already, much of the controversy did not arise. Certainly, the Campaign for Nuclear Disarmament was more vociferous in the late 1970s than it had been at any time since the Cuban missile crisis, but Callaghan never felt as vulnerable to that source of pressure as did many of his counterparts in continental Europe.[20]

Discussions about the options for replacement of Polaris were conducted in the Nuclear Defence Policy Group during 1977 and 1978.[21] The choice was between Trident, the best and by far the most expensive system then available, or the cheaper, less sophisticated, but more flexible submarine-launched cruise missiles which would provide Britain with a modern but minimum deterrent capability. For reasons of prestige and influence, as well as of the pressures generated by inter-service rivalry, the MOD favoured Trident, as did the Prime Minister. They were opposed by a small but determined group, centred on the Foreign Secretary, David Owen, who believed that Britain was attempting to play 'out of our league' in financial terms and developed a case for purchase of the 'cut-cost' option.[22] Retrospectively, he claimed that his arguments for sea-launched cruise missiles, over the air- or land-based variety, were determined by the fact that they were less vulnerable to being overrun by the enemy in the event of a real conflict, and were also less controversial in the eyes of the public because they were not sited on land. Overwhelmingly, the Group was in favour of Trident and Callaghan raised the matter with President Carter at the Guadeloupe summit in January 1979 to establish whether the Americans would sell Trident to Britain on the same basis as Polaris and was reassured that Carter had no difficulty with transferring the technology to Britain if that was their decision.[23] In the event Labour was out of office before the final decision was taken, but the working papers were passed to Margaret Thatcher and formed the basis of the decision made at the end of 1979.[24]

Détente, SALT and the Cold War

The debate about the renewal of the British deterrent was necessarily framed within the wider question of superpower détente and SALT which dominated much of the defence and security policy debate of the 1970s. Throughout this period, Callaghan sought to establish the perception world-wide that Britain was a committed and important contributor to shaping the Western view of the détente process. This fitted both with the agenda to retain an internationalist approach to British foreign relations but also suited Britain's membership of the EEC which required some demonstration from Britain of a sympathy for and degree of co-ordination with European preoccupations with the potential consequences of superpower conflict in Europe. Callaghan had an excellent understanding with the West German Chancellor, Helmut Schmidt, who shared his atlanticist focus, and also with Jimmy Carter; these connections enabled him to act as a useful interlocutor when relations between Washington and Bonn became strained over the question of US nuclear weapons in Europe during 1977 and 1978.

Wilson and Callaghan visited Moscow in February 1975, seeking to find out more about current Soviet thinking and to elevate the perception of Britain's role in détente. Neither Wilson nor Callaghan believed that the Soviet Union had any special interest in Britain for itself, but they suspected that it was regarded as useful by the Kremlin for the influence it could exercise with its friends and allies through membership of the EEC and NATO. With European security issues particularly in mind, not least as a consequence of the Portuguese coup which had brought a Marxist-inspired military leadership to power in Lisbon, Callaghan proposed a linkage between stability in continental Europe and Soviet withdrawal from subversion. Both Wilson and Callaghan believed that the Russians were balancing the attraction of a communist bridgehead in Western Europe against the achievement of détente and hoped to pressure them to retreat in Portugal. Brezhnev was characteristically ambiguous in his response, but Callaghan was more successful in gaining some assurance that the Kremlin was moving away from the prism of class struggle as a means of understanding relations between states. Following the Moscow talks, which were widely perceived both domestically and abroad as constructive, Callaghan pressed for practical measures to embed the notion of Anglo-Soviet contacts. This manifested itself in creation of the Anglo-Soviet Round Table, composed of specialists from all walks of life, to exchange ideas on topics of mutual interest, and was paralleled at the political level by a series of ministerial visits and at the military level by defence exchanges.[25]

From the outset, the Labour Governments viewed the relationship between détente and deterrence as inextricable. While US troops were in Europe and were adequately supplied with stocks of nuclear missiles, the prospect that the Soviet Union would attack Western Europe, or provoke a situation in which these terrible weapons might be used, was virtually unthinkable. Inevitably, this approach created a tension: on the one hand there was a fear that the build-up of nuclear weapons in Europe would act as a provocation to the Soviet Union and increase the likelihood that they would be used in anger; on the other hand this was balanced by the recognition that these weapons were needed in order to encourage the Soviet Union to seek disarmament rather than confrontation. As a nuclear power itself and given its geographical location on the periphery of Europe, Britain had less difficulty living with this tension than some of its continental neighbours. The German Government in particular felt especially vulnerable and became increasingly suspicious of American intentions, when, following Soviet deployment of the SS-20s in 1976, the Carter administration vacillated about deployment of the next generation of nuclear weapons. Callaghan admitted to being puzzled by much of the ensuing vitriol, driven as it was by fear and paranoia rather than more rational judgement, but he saw it as his duty, following the European Council meeting held at Downing Street on 30 June 1977, to write to Carter to inform him of Franco-German concern. 'The atmosphere and language was worse than I have ever known', he observed, and while he considered that 'd'Estaing would always go his own way' it was necessary in his view for the United States to win the confidence of Schmidt.[26] This marked the starting point of a series of bridge-building attempts on the part of Callaghan as he recognised that it was vital for Western interests that misunderstandings between the Americans and Europeans on the twin issues of détente and disarmament should not be permitted to develop.

The issue at the heart of the debate was that of modernisation of the nuclear forces in Europe. Several ideas were discussed during this period, one of which was the enhanced radiation weapon (ERW) or neutron bomb which was the subject of highly emotive debate because of its destructive power over people, but not buildings. The issue caused a deep division within the Labour Party and it was a relief to Callaghan when Carter backtracked. The latter recorded that he had made the decision as a consequence of the equivocal responses he had drawn from both the British and German Governments, but eyewitness accounts indicate that Callaghan, like Schmidt, would have risked the political unpopularity of accepting ERW had the Americans pressed ahead. It is likely that the decisive factor in Carter's decision was concern lest adoption of the ERW offer up to the Russians a propaganda coup which, in the light of the adverse publicity the spectre of this weapon had generated, would be difficult to counter.[27]

Following signature of the Helsinki final Act in August 1975, British foreign policy sought to play up the significance of the human rights clauses, partly as a weapon with which to beat the Soviet Union and also as a means of emphasising the influence of socialist principles on British policy under Labour. Such convictions were tested, however, by mounting concerns about Soviet intentions. David Owen was well known for his resistance to the liberal interpretation of current Soviet thinking advanced by the mainstream of the Labour Party. Owen 'despised and distrusted' the Soviet Union and increasingly focused on the arms build-up, and in particular on the dangers of proliferation particularly in South Africa and Pakistan, rather than infringements of human rights as the key issue between Britain and Russia.[28] Britain's principal contribution to arms control negotiations in this period was through work done on closer definition of the so-called 'Grey Areas' which covered all sorts of intermediate- and short-range weapons which might be covered in prospective SALT III negotiations. Meanwhile, some measure of resolution of US–European difficulties was achieved at the Guadeloupe summit which was called primarily to discuss Bonn's concerns regarding the SALT negotiations and the Soviet deployment of mobile SS-20s, targeted on Western Europe. The result was the twin-track approach, with deployment of American cruise missiles in Western Europe, which confirmed the enmeshing of the US nuclear forces in the defence of Western Europe, and negotiations with Moscow to eliminate all intermediate-range missiles.[29]

Although China was not a major issue in British foreign policy during this period, the fact that Beijing had begun to show an interest in developing closer relations with the British armed services was not without interest to the Labour Government and a series of high-level diplomatic and military exchanges took place to encourage such overtures. The British were aware that the Chinese wanted to buy from Britain sophisticated military equipment which was not being made available to the Soviet Union and that this was motivated in large measure by Beijing's wider concerns about the progress of détente, a development which the Chinese clearly feared. But the British interest in relations with China was informed essentially by awareness of the need to establish friendly connections with China in view of developments in policy towards Hong Kong which, while they were not an issue at the end of the 1970s, were expected to become so in the near future.[30]

Conflict resolution

Another new departure under Labour was the fresh emphasis given to Commonwealth affairs. The principal architect of this was Callaghan who viewed the Commonwealth as of great importance and whose long career had enabled him to establish good working relations with many of its leaders. Callaghan believed that Heath's concentration on the EEC had given the impression at home and abroad of a further diminution of the Commonwealth in the British international role and he set out in 1974 to reverse this process. This approach demanded, however, that a fresh effort be made to resolve Britain's biggest failure in the Commonwealth, the transfer of power in Rhodesia.[31]

Since 1965, Britain had sought to deal with the rebel regime of Ian Smith in Rhodesia through a twin approach combining diplomatic isolation and economic sanctions with the tactic of playing Rhodesia off against neighbouring South Africa from which the Salisbury regime drew its principal support. In every direction, this approach had failed. The sanctions ring had been easily circumvented, a process in which British firms had connived, while the failure to act decisively to drive the Rhodesian regime towards acceptance of black majority rule had earned Britain the reputation in the region and beyond as a paper tiger, long on words but lacking any longer the power or will to enforce a solution in the face of Smith's obduracy.[32]

For a series of reasons, conditions became more favourable in the mid-1970s for a renewed attempt at settlement. First, the collapse of the Portuguese Empire following the coup in Lisbon in 1974 changed the strategic balance in the region such that South Africa began to look afresh at its own circumstances. It was clear that the forces demanding black majority rule in Rhodesia were too numerous to be resisted much longer, but in South Africa the existence of what amounted to a white tribe which was well armed and well placed to negotiate, meant that Pretoria at last began to see a settlement in Rhodesia as vital to the chances of the white South Africans to negotiate their way with their own black majority.[33] Shrewdly, Smith recognised that the moment to negotiate had arrived and in February 1976 he secretly let it be known through an intermediary that he was interested in British arbitration.[34] Second, in 1976, the involvement of the Cubans, among others, in the Angolan Civil War focused American attention on the region for the first time, provoking Henry Kissinger, by now Gerald Ford's Secretary of State, to attempt to bully Smith into negotiations leading to an interim agreement. Kissinger's motivation emerges strongly in his correspondence with the British Foreign Secretary, Anthony Crosland, in which he observed that 'the whole enterprise after all only makes sense as a firebreak to African radicalism and Soviet interventionism'.[35] British motivations for seeking an early resolution were probably grounded more in trading interests and the desire for political reasons to be rid of the problem which had been as an open wound in the Commonwealth for over a decade. Nevertheless, Callaghan demonstrated that he was at least partially persuaded of Kissinger's argument when he raised the issue with Andrei Gromyko during the latter's visit to London in March 1976. Détente, Callaghan explained, was not viewed in the West as divisible and the British public would not accept détente in Europe if the same principles were not respected elsewhere.[36] The dangers of the communists gaining a viable foothold in the region were probably exaggerated, but the knowledge that they had links with the South African nationalists and were supplying them with arms was sufficient to bring conviction to such concerns.

The Kissinger approach was deeply flawed in the British view for several reasons. First, and most fundamentally, he was attempting to deal with Ian Smith. Experience inclined the British Government to the view that there was no hope unless Smith could be removed. Second, Kissinger's determination to create a power-sharing arrangement was seen as focusing too much on the means of getting to independence rather than on the end of independence itself. Since the collapse of the Sunningdale Agreement in 1974, the British Government remained deeply suspicious of such arrangements, preferring to seek agreement through consensus. Third, Britain was concerned that any attempt at co-operation with the Smith regime, albeit to support an interim settlement, would lead to HMG being tarred with the same brush as South Africa, an unthinkable outcome in the light of the prospective Commonwealth Conference due to be convened in 1977.

Consequently, the Callaghan Government was visibly reluctant to take on the supporting role in the Geneva negotiations which it had been allotted by Kissinger. The result was that Smith went to Geneva fully aware that Britain possessed neither the will nor the conviction to coerce the parties into a settlement, allowing him simply to pretend to negotiate while simultaneously directing his propaganda machine to encourage the whites to hold out for a more favourable settlement.

The British Government was much more closely engaged in the second attempt at a settlement which was conceived as a joint Anglo-American effort and brought together the negotiating team of David Owen and Cyrus Vance. Owen's approach focused much more on the end state, the black majority regime, and sought to reduce the opportunities for a power struggle that the interim solution offered. At the time his insistence that Britain and the United States be joint partners was a well-judged recognition of the fact that the process was vulnerable to Smith's skills at the game of divide and rule, as well as militating against a repeat of the mistakes made by Kissinger. Owen also adopted the carrot and stick approach: to encourage the warring parties to move towards an agreement he held out the prospect of the establishment of an international development fund for Rhodesia–Zimbabwe, to which the United States would be the principal contributor. The potential for coercion appeared in the form of the proposal for American presence at the conference, despite the resistance to this on the part of certain of the nationalists.[37] The whole diplomatic process was then reinforced by the re-imposition of sanctions, which was becoming increasingly controversial in the Cabinet as a powerful group of ministers, backed by the FCO and a Cabinet subcommittee, resisted this action on economic grounds. Publication of the Bingham report on the breaking of sanctions against Rhodesia did much to help Owen circumvent this resistance.[38]

In 1978, as the crisis deepened, both Britain and the United States made concerted efforts to involve the UN also, particularly in the sphere of sanctions, and Owen himself sought Cabinet endorsement for his suggestion that a Commonwealth force be sent to stop the endemic guerrilla warfare. However, he recognised that until this conflict reached deadlock, and the Smith–Muzorewa interim regime had been seen to fail, there was little point in attempting to hold a conference to get acceptance of the new constitution. By the autumn of 1978, it was clear that the authority of the Callaghan Government itself was increasingly being questioned in the country, and Owen reluctantly accepted advice that Britain hold off on Rhodesia until a general election could be held and a government returned which was strong enough to override Ian Smith. For these reasons, the work done towards the Rhodesian settlement, which by 1978–9 was totally dominating the Foreign Secretary's time, was left uncompleted when Labour was voted out of office.[39]

Throughout this period, Britain played a minor, but useful, role in the Middle East. Both Ford and Carter recognised Callaghan's superior knowledge of some of the key players, particularly on the Egyptian side. Both the Israeli and Egyptian leaderships discussed their plans for the first steps towards a resolution of their conflict with the British leadership allowing Callaghan to interject quiet advice and encouragement as the proposals which formed the Camp David Accord were tentatively being worked out. Less fortunate, perhaps, was British handling of Iran during the final years of the Shah's rule. Overly associated internationally with the Persian royal family, British policy wavered over how far the Shah should be supported with military supplies once the regime began to crumble. Hesitation during the summer of 1978, which was paralleled by a similar lack of policy clarity in the United States, was crucial in losing for Britain any possibility of influencing the outcome of the political crisis which paved the way for the fundamentalist regime of Ayatollah Khomeini.

On issues of more parochial interest, where the British Government had a predominant influence in shaping policy, Labour demonstrated both pragmatism and principle in the handling of foreign affairs. Regarding the spat with Iceland over North Sea cod, Anthony Crosland, whose constituency included the great east coast fishing town of Grimsby, recognised very soon after taking up office in 1976 that British credibility was being undermined as the dispute dragged on, and quickly brokered a deal with Iceland through the good offices of the EEC.[40] Meanwhile, one of the successes of this period was Callaghan's policy of 'watchful defence' in managing the early evidence of a challenge from Argentina to continued British sovereignty over the Falkland Islands. In essence he autho-rised the FCO to negotiate while asserting British rights through deployment of HMS *Endurance* which remained in Falklands waters with the aid of a special defence estimate achieved, ironically, in the face of vigorous opposition from the MOD which considered there were more pressing demands on military spending.[41] While intelligence estimates advised that there was unlikely to be any attempt to use force directly so long as Britain showed an inclination to negotiate seriously, Callaghan did not hesitate to reinforce this indirect and symbolic deter-rence by covert means at moments of tension.[42] Certainly, this approach was successful in achieving its deterrent purpose during this period, but the tensions within Argentina which led the junta to attack the islands directly in 1982 had not yet reached the point of crisis.

Conclusion

During this period the impact of the British Government in world affairs was constrained by the legacy of constant withdrawal and retreat which had charac-terised the period since Suez, by the intractable crisis in southern Africa and by a plethora of domestic political and economic crises on which its attention was necessarily focused during the latter half of the 1970s. The most interesting feature to emerge from a study of this period, however, was the extent to which this Government laid the foundations for the foreign policy successes of the 1980s. It was Callaghan who reinvigorated Anglo-American relations, just as it was Callaghan who demonstrated the art of exploiting the British occupation of the middle ground in the Cold War. Unlike Heath or Thatcher, Callaghan managed to establish a position of trust and respect, from which flowed influ-ence on both sides of the Atlantic simultaneously. At the same time he developed British relations with the Soviet Union with imagination and fore-sight. In placing a new emphasis on the role of the supranational and multinational organisation, the Labour Governments of the 1970s began the process of transition from foreign policy defined along national lines to one which drew on interests defined as a result of the interactions of the community of states. That this was only the beginning of a process, Callaghan himself was clearly aware. Retrospectively he argued that

> foreign policy is a mixture of the old and new. We may initiate but we also inherit; we may vote at the ballot box for changes in policy and personalities, but on acquiring office governments inherit an international situation on which the footprints of the past are heavily marked.[43]

Notes

1 For example, Harris, K., *Thatcher* (Weidenfeld and Nicolson, London, 1988); Cooke, A.B., Introduction to *Margaret Thatcher: The Revival of Britain: speeches on Home and European Affairs 1975–1988* (Aurum Press, London, 1989).
2 Callaghan, J., *Time and Chance* (Collins, London, 1987), pp. 296f.; Howe, S., 'Labour and International Affairs', in Tanner, D., Thane, P. and Tiratsoo, N. (eds), *Labour's First Century* (Cambridge University Press, Cambridge, 2000), pp. 119–20.
3 Callaghan, *Time and Chance*, p. 296.
4 Croft, S., 'Britain's Nuclear Weapons Discourse', in Croft, S., Dorman, A., Rees, W. and Uttley, M., *Britain and Defence 1945–2000* (Longman, London, 2001), pp. 74–9.
5 Howe, 'Labour and International Affairs', p. 123.
6 See Dobson, A., *Anglo-American Relations in the Twentieth Century* (London, Routledge, 1995), p. 143, n. 33.
7 'The Lonely Darkness', *The Economist*, 8 September 1974.
8 Verrier, A., *Through the Looking Glass: British Foreign Policy in an Age of Illusion* (Cape, London, 1983), pp. 323–6.
9 Morgan, K.O., *Callaghan: A Life* (Oxford University Press, Oxford, 1997), p. 449.
10 Bennett, G. and Hamilton, K.A., *Documents on British Policy Overseas (DBPO)*, ser. III, vol. 3 (Frank Cass in association with Whitehall Historical Publications, London, 2001), no. 72.
11 Ibid.
12 Freedman, L., 'Britain's Foreign Policy to 1985: Britain's Contribution to NATO', *International Affairs*, 54(1), January 1978, pp. 30–47. See also *The Economist*, 6 April 1974, p. 24.
13 Hansard, *Parliamentary Debates (House of Commons)*, 1974–5, vol. 882, 5th ser., 25 November–6 December 1974, Mason, R., Statement to the House of Commons, 3 December 1974, col. 1352; *Statement on Defence Estimates 1975*, Cmnd 5976 (HMSO, London, 1975).
14 Carver, M., *Tightrope Walking: British Defence Policy since 1945* (Hutchinson, London, 1992), p. 107.
15 In March 1975 the projected cuts amounted to the loss of some 38,000 personnel, the loss of half the Navy's combat ships, a similar reduction in the RAF's transport fleet and the loss of one-quarter of its anti-submarine patrol planes. For example, 'A Tin Soldier Country', *The Economist*, 18 May 1974, 'When is a Cut Not a Cut?', 15 March 1975, and 'Manpower Cuts', 22 March 1975. See further Baylis, J., *British Defence Policy: Striking the Right Balance* (London, Macmillan, 1989), p. 76.
16 Ovendale, R. (ed.), *British Defence Policy since 1945* (Manchester University Press, Manchester, 1994), p. 154.
17 Healey, D., *The Time of My Life* (Michael Joseph, London 1989), p. 307.
18 Castle, B., *The Castle Diaries 1964–1976* (Macmillan, London 1990), entry for 20 November 1974, pp. 522–3.

19 This was the secret committee which Callaghan formed to discuss nuclear strategy. It consisted of the Chancellor of the Exchequer, the Defence Secretary, the Foreign Secretary and it met under the Prime Minister's chairmanship.

20 Callaghan, *Time and Chance*, p. 604.

21 McIntosh, M. *Managing Britain's Defence* (Macmillan, London, 1980), p. 29.

22 Owen, D., *Time to Declare* (Michael Joseph, London, 1991), pp. 381–2, 409.

23 Callaghan, *Time and Chance*, p. 556.

24 George, B. *et al.*, *The British Labour Party and Defence* (Centre for Strategic Studies, Washington, DC, 1991), p. 37.

25 Morgan, *Callaghan: A Life*, p. 549; Callaghan, *Time and Chance*, p. 365.

26 Callaghan to Carter, 30 June 1977, material in the Callaghan papers which remain closed, but quoted by Callaghan's official biographer. See Morgan, *Callaghan*, pp. 602–3.

27 Carter, J., *Keeping Faith: Memoirs of a President* (Bantam, New York, 1982), pp. 225–6; Owen, *Time to Declare*, pp. 379–89.

28 Owen, *Time to Declare*, pp. 336–7.

29 Healey, *The Time of My Life*, pp. 454–5; Ovendale, *British Defence Policy since 1945*; Carter, *Keeping Faith*, pp. 235–6.

30 Owen, *Time to Declare*, p. 341.

31 Callaghan, *Time and Chance*, pp. 295–6.

32 Owen, *Time to Declare*, p. 271.

33 Darwin, J., *Britain and Decolonisation: The Retreat from Empire in the Postwar World* (Macmillan, London, 1988), pp. 319–20; *The Economist*, 27 March 1976.

34 Morgan, *Callaghan: A Life*, p. 460.

35 Crosland Papers (British Library of Political and Economic Science) CRO 5/14 Kissinger to Crosland (undated).

36 Bennett and Hamilton, *DBPO*, ser. III, vol. 3, no. 88.

37 'The Owen Short Cut', *The Economist*, 23 April 1977.

38 Owen, *Time to Declare*, p. 291.

39 Ibid., pp. 314–15.

40 Crosland, S., *Tony Crosland* (Cape, London, 1982), pp. 324, 329.

41 Callaghan, *Time and Chance*, p. 375.

42 Owen, *Time to Declare*, p. 355.

43 Callaghan, *Time and Chance*, p. 296.

Part III

Government and politics

10 Prime Ministers and Cabinet

Chris Ballinger and Anthony Seldon

Coming to power

Harold Wilson's return to Number 10 in 1974 could not have differed more from the circumstances surrounding the next time that Labour would make the transition from opposition to office, in 1997. Wilson was nearing the end of his political career: had he won the 1970 general election, he intended to retire mid-term;[1] having lost the 1970 election, he determined that he would not serve for long once he returned to Downing Street. It was not an easy time to resume office: Ted Heath, Wilson believed, had made the country ungovernable and the economy and unions were out of control. And in Parliament Labour was in a minority; the October 1974 election, by which a thirty-four deficit was turned into a majority of three, delayed the added problems of minority government for just two years. In contrast, the Labour inheritance in 1997 was golden.

Whether Wilson had expected to win the general election in February 1974 remains disputed,[2] but if he had been pleasantly surprised by the result of this election, his surprise that October was of the unpleasant kind: he had hoped and expected that the October election would have given him a governing majority.[3] Moreover, the Labour Party had moved markedly to the left whilst in opposition between 1970 and 1974.[4] Harold Wilson hoped that, when he returned to power, he would be able to ditch this left-wing baggage but, despite his best efforts, 'the Labour Government in 1974–9 was far more obviously at odds with the party machine than it had been in 1964–70'.[5] Wilson's final term was a markedly tired and lacklustre administration, beset by problems – internal and external – from the very start, and as far from the dynamism and optimism of New Labour as any post-war administration. Wilson had no clear aims, no purpose, in 1974; nor did he bring any fresh ideas to Britain's highest office.

Two years into his final term, and after several procrastinations, Harold Wilson made way for an older man.[6] Jim Callaghan was four years Wilson's senior and, like Wilson, he had been an MP since Attlee's landslide victory of 1945. He was the most experienced Prime Minister: during his career, he held all four 'great offices of State' (Home Secretary, Chancellor of the Exchequer, Foreign Secretary and Prime Minister). Callaghan was constrained by the absence of a parliamentary majority – lost on 7 April 1976, Callaghan's first full day as Prime Minister – which only added to the economic and political troubles that he had inherited.

This chapter assesses the contribution to the conduct of government during the period 1974–9 made by the Prime Ministers and their Cabinets, with three particular areas of focus: the operation of the Prime Ministers' offices and of the Cabinet; the effect of these operations on the process of governance; and the practices of Wilson and Callaghan in the 1970s will be contrasted with the Labour Government that came into power in 1997.

The Prime Ministers at Number 10

Harold Wilson was the first peacetime Prime Minister since Lord Salisbury in 1902 not to make Downing Street his home. After the 1970 election defeat, Harold and Mary Wilson had moved house from the Hampstead Garden Suburb to a Westminster townhouse at nearby 5, Lord North Street. Neither of the Wilsons were keen to live in Downing Street again, and, whilst Mary Wilson felt no great affection for Lord North Street, she 'felt incomparably happier' there 'than in the Downing Street goldfish bowl', with its lack of privacy and the unwanted role of hostess.[7] And so Lord North Street remained their home throughout the 1974–6 premiership. Wilson was driven to the 'office block' in Downing Street each morning, arriving by 9 a.m. (slightly later on Mondays), whereupon he commenced his day by meeting with his Private Office. He returned to Lord North Street in the evening – often late – after his work had been concluded and after he had finished chatting with colleagues over a drink in his study. Mary Wilson spent most weekends at their home in Great Missenden, Buckinghamshire, six miles (10 km) from Chequers, at which they spent much less time together than they had done between 1964 and 1970.[8]

Jim Callaghan was much happier living 'above the shop' than Harold Wilson had become. Indeed, he preferred the convenience of living close to his place of work as Prime Minister to the commuting that he endured during his time as Foreign Secretary (1974–6). Jim and Audrey Callaghan spent most of the time in London staying in Downing Street, although they occasionally stayed over at their flat in Kennington, south of the River Thames, which they kept throughout the three years. Weekends were spent relaxing at their beloved Sussex farmhouse, near Lewes, or at Chequers, which they used for family reunions and pure relaxation, and, sparingly, for work meetings such as his 'seminar' on economic policy, spearheaded by Harold Lever and chaired by the Prime Minister.

Callaghan would start his day at Number 10 with an 8 a.m. meeting with his Principal Private Secretary, Ken Stowe, to discuss the overnight boxes. He then discussed the press digest with Tom McCaffrey, his Press Secretary. In the afternoon, he would go over to the House. He was a regular in the Members' Tea Room – he thought it important to talk with 'the troops' – and would work in the Commons, returning to Downing Street after the 10 p.m. vote.

The pace of life at Number 10 differed markedly under the two Labour Prime Ministers. Harold Wilson enjoyed discussions that could continue into the early hours; under Jim Callaghan, receptions did not last beyond 10.30 p.m., the hour at which he retired for bed. For three years, there were no late-night corrals at Number 10. Moreover, whereas Wilson had increasingly taken solace in brandy – before, as well as after, Prime Minister's Questions – Callaghan forsook alcohol, and so there was no heavy drinking at Number 10 between 1976 and 1979. Despite – or, perhaps, because of – these things, Jim and Audrey Callaghan were regarded by some in Number 10 as being more reliable hosts at official functions in 1976–9, and much better at looking after guests, than Wilson had been in 1974–6.[9]

Style of personal operation

Wilson's modus operandi was to juggle several topics at once; Callaghan preferred to concentrate on a single policy area, sometimes for weeks at a time. He took a more measured pace and had a more formal style than his predecessor, and he preferred briefings to be written. One Cabinet colleague remarked of their styles:

> Wilson could reverse policy overnight if he thought it would make sense. He was an intellectual. Callaghan was not an intellectual at all, but he had a great deal of common sense, and I found it very, very much easier to get on with him than with Wilson.[10]

Wilson's last two years in office were a time of progressive inactivity. There is some evidence of the early onset of Alzheimer's disease that was to afflict him more severely in retirement, often to the embarrassment of those close to him. The occasions on which Wilson could apply his mind were diminishing in frequency. Although his earlier obsession with plots was diminished, which Denis Healey put down to his surprise at winning in 1974 and his forthcoming departure, nevertheless his workload and effectiveness were less than those of any premier since 1945, and was matched only by Churchill from the time of his severe stroke in 1953 until he finally gave up in April 1955. Wilson said to several intimates that he would retire in 1976: Haines knew as early as the previous summer; his deputy in the Press Office, Janet Hewlett-Davies, and Kenneth Stowe both knew by October 1975; within the Cabinet, Callaghan and Healey had prior warning. Nevertheless, there was widespread surprise when the announcement came on 16 March 1976.

Callaghan had been Wilson's *de facto* deputy since before the February 1974 election, but this closeness of operation did not detract from Callaghan's initial advantage when he assumed the premiership in 1976: that he was not Harold Wilson.

Callaghan classified himself as a 'consensus' leader.[11] This was a different form of consensus to that valued by his predecessor. Wilson sought agreement and the holding together of the Party as an end in itself, to be achieved at all costs, even if a temporary split proved necessary. He had to undertake a careful balancing act in Cabinet to ensure an equilibrium between left and right factions. Callaghan's consensus style did not prevent Callaghan taking a principled stance: he 'stressed the reciprocal relationship between the leader and the led, he felt it essential for a political leader to seize the initiative and provide an active and engaged sense of direction'.[12] Whilst Labour remained in power for the whole period 1974–9, 'comparatively speaking,' as Kenneth O. Morgan wrote, 'a new era of open government seemed to begin on 6th April 1976 and so it was to remain.'[13] But government was not different because it was more open: the whole quality and ethos changed from top to bottom.

The Political Office

The Political Office and the Press Office lie at the nerve centre of a prime minister's communications network, keeping a prime minister in touch, respectively, with colleagues in the parliamentary party and with the wider world.

Marcia Williams had become the first Political Secretary to a British Prime Minister when she was appointed by the newly elected Wilson in 1964, and had continued to assist him through six years in government and three and a half years of opposition. She continued in her role (renamed 'Personal and Political Secretary') throughout the final two years of Wilson's premiership, but her influence was much diminished. Yet, despite this diminution in power, Bernard Donoughue (Head of the Prime Minister's Policy Unit, 1974–9) recalled that he and Joe Haines (Prime Minister's Press Secretary, 1969–70 and 1974–6) were made very aware by Williams 'that she was the closest and longest [serving] adviser to Harold Wilson. He clearly deferred to her'.[14]

After the land deals affair, in which Marcia Williams's brother, Tony Field, was accused of profiteering through the development of a slagheap in Lancashire, she worked mostly from her flat in Marylebone, north-west Westminster, although she was in fairly frequent touch with Number 10 and would see Wilson at the weekends. She came to resent the influence that other prime ministerial aides – notably Joe Haines, Bernard Donoughue, Ken Stowe and Robin Butler – had over Wilson. Donoughue recalls that Williams wanted to have his Policy Unit moved from Number 10 to the Cabinet Office next door, to make the Policy Unit geographically further from the Prime Minister and less able to influence him. Having failed in her attempt to evict Haines and Donoughue, she offered to leave Number 10 herself.[15] She also failed to oust Robin Butler.[16] Yet some of her influence remained. As Ben Pimlott, Wilson's biographer, put it, 'though her practical involvement declined, her psychic power over Wilson often seemed as strong as ever, precipitating some furious clashes in the office'.[17] She was a shadowy and sad figure in 1974–6, a ghost of the capable and forceful aide who had shaped Wilson's career at the top.

With Williams distancing herself after 1974, so too went some of Wilson's control over the Labour Party machine. The NEC reduced barriers to the participation of the far left by abolishing the 'proscribed' list, which had excluded the extreme left from the Party: 'Rarely had the gulf between a Labour Prime Minister and his party been wider than it was in 1974.'[18] Clement Attlee (1945–51) had some mechanisms for keeping him in close touch with the Labour Party in Parliament and beyond. From the moment of its creation in 1964, the Political Office had established itself as the vital buckle that linked the Prime Minister and his Party. In Wilson's last two years, the buckle was not operating.

Tom McNally, Callaghan's Political Secretary, headed the Political Office from 1976 to 1979. McNally had worked closely with Callaghan as the International Secretary of the Labour Party when Callaghan was Shadow Foreign Secretary during Heath's Government, and he subsequently became Callaghan's Political Adviser at the Foreign and Commonwealth Office in 1974 during an age in which special advisers were comparatively rare. He had travelled extensively with Callaghan and was part of the small team that had worked on his party leadership campaign in 1976. For two years, McNally became the second most influential party-political figure in Number 10, impressing Callaghan with his knowledge both of policy and of the workings of the Labour Party, and the Political Office's stature re-grew under Callaghan to reach its former status and influence.[19]

McNally pointedly did not take a briefing from Marcia Williams, as was normal handover practice, wanting to create a clean break with the clouds that hung over Wilson's Political Office, which had included questions concerning Marcia Williams's influence over Wilson's resignation honours list (the so-called 'lavender list'). McNally quickly learned by doing. But when he received the parliamentary nomination for Stockport, ten months before the fall of the Government, his attentions were deflected from Downing Street to Cheshire, and his influence over the Prime Minister waned, to Callaghan's loss. Callaghan was of the Labour Party, and always strove to work closely with it as Prime Minister. Blair wasn't, and didn't, which was one reason why the Political Office swelled under him after 1997.

The Press Office

Harold Wilson had broken new ground in media relations in the 1960s, making himself far more accessible to lobby correspondents, collectively and individually, than any of his predecessors and attempting to 'meet the media on their own ground'.[20] Under him, relations between Number 10 and the media were brought into the modern age. But there were no further advances in press relations in 1974–6. Indeed, Wilson became very disillusioned with the lobby after he returned to Downing Street,[21] a symptom of his loss of touch in personal relations, and in June 1975 he agreed to Joe Haines's wish to suspend lobby briefings, in which Haines had given twice-daily briefings to journalists on an off-the-record basis. The suspension of the lobby system, however, had little practical effect on the dissemination of information to the press, according to Janet Hewlett-Davies,[22] and the lobby system remained suspended until Callaghan reinstated the briefings a year later.

Joe Haines, the former lobby journalist who was Harold Wilson's Press Secretary throughout 1974–6, was very much Wilson's man. Haines had fulfilled the role of Prime Minister's Press Secretary in the eighteen months before the 1970 general election, and had remained a close adviser in opposition. For the last two years of Wilson's premiership he became, in effect, Wilson's principal political adviser.[23] Haines had, in the words of Ben Pimlott, 'an anti-Establishment chip, an acute, non-intellectual brain, and an excellent Labour Party feel',[24] and Wilson appreciated these character traits. Haines's first action on re-entering Government in 1974 was to dismiss five members of the Number 10 Press Office. He would have sought to sack more civil servants, had not the Principal Private Secretary, Robert Armstrong, intervened saying that further dismissals would undermine the morale of the Number 10 civil servants. New Labour was to be even more Draconian after 1997. Like Campbell, Haines found he had to cast his attention wider than the organisation of the Number 10 press corps, as he was one of Wilson's foremost policy advisers and speechwriters.

Tom McCaffrey, Callaghan's Press Secretary, was devoted to his Prime Minister and to the Government. A career government press officer, he had previously worked closely with Callaghan: he was Chief Information Officer at the Home Office (1966–71) and Head of the News Department at the Foreign and Commonwealth Office (1974–6). But he was, and remained – in both occupation and mindset – a career civil servant.

McCaffrey was in the tradition of Donald Maitland, who was Heath's Chief Press Secretary (1970–3). He played his role straight, providing the media with information free of a party-political slant ('spin', as it came to be dubbed) – which is exactly what Callaghan desired of him. He kept a lower profile than Haines had, unlike Haines eschewing opportunities to give policy advice, and focused on cultivating relations with journalists in the lobby.[25] Callaghan, when he took over, took a conscious decision not to have in Downing Street the cronies that had populated it since 1974, such as Sir Eric Millar or Lord Kagan, who had been honoured in Wilson's final honours list. Tom McCaffrey, along with Merlyn Rees, Gregor Mackenzie and Jack Cunningham (who was his leadership campaign manager), together formed a Praetorian Guard around him.[26]

Management of the press was not as calculated or as obsessive as it had been for the previous two years, and not nearly so obsessive as it was to become under the next Labour Prime Minister's Press Secretary, Alastair Campbell. There was no large-scale effort to court newspaper editors. On his first day at Number 10, in April 1976, Callaghan reversed Haines's decision to suspend lobby briefings, although he did not see the point in the existence of the lobby. The New Labour media strategy was to control briefings rather than to suspend them; to bring hostile media outlets on side rather than continuing to alienate them. Alastair Campbell and Tony Blair worked extremely closely together. Campbell worked to ensure 'joined-up' media management across departments, although this was much more difficult to achieve in government than it had been in opposition. Control of communications became central to the Government's task, but sometimes came to obscure the message.

The Private Office

The Private Office, led by the Principal Private Secretary (PPS), is the channel for advice to the Prime Minister from Number 10 and Whitehall departments, conveys the Prime Minister's views, and handles the Prime Minister's appointments and correspondence. Wilson retained Armstrong as his PPS. Armstrong had been appointed to this role by Ted Heath upon becoming Prime Minister in 1970, developing a very close working relationship; it was unusual for the PPS to survive for more than a few weeks after a change of party in Number 10. Indeed, during the February 1974 election, Marcia Williams had made it clear that she expected Armstrong to be moved on, and Armstrong himself had been told to prepare himself to go, so identified had he become with the personality and policies of Heath.[27] But Armstrong fulfilled Wilson's requirements exactly, providing him with 'the perfect vehicle of osmosis between the Prime Minister and the official machine',[28] something appreciated not only by Wilson but also by Joe Haines,[29] and it was useful for Wilson to have an experienced PPS, versed not only in the workings of Whitehall but also in the policies of the Heath Government. Bernard Donoughue, the head of the newly formed Policy Unit, regarded Armstrong as a 'man of formidable intellect', and Donoughue and Armstrong quickly developed a very good working relationship.[30] Wilson was therefore happy to have such a formidable figure as his closest civil servant, even if this did vex Marcia Williams.

Kenneth Stowe succeeded Armstrong as PPS to the Prime Minister in 1975, holding the post until after the 1979 general election. Stowe was, wrote Donoughue, 'an easier and simpler man [than Armstrong], entirely without side'.[31] However, even with Stowe's talents the Private Office found it increasingly difficult to focus Wilson's attention on necessary business. In the last months of his premiership, the Private Office was both a supportive crutch and a protective screen for Wilson from the pressures of prime ministerial business. Without the skill and capacity of Armstrong and Stowe, which covered up for Wilson, his infirmities and incapacity for the job would have become far more readily apparent.

Stowe was the most influential voice in Callaghan's ear for the first two years of his administration.[32] He had 'by 1976 become exceptionally self-confident, co-ordinating and annotating advice to Callaghan via his red boxes, liaising with the rest of the machine ... and guiding Callaghan on tactics'.[33] He was closer to Callaghan than were either the CPRS or the Policy Unit, both physically and operationally, and Stowe became so indispensable to Callaghan that he extended Stowe's term of office beyond the usual three years (which would have expired in 1978) until after the general election, whatever the result.[34] Mrs Thatcher after 1979, indeed, soon came to share in the same evaluation of Stowe's qualities.

The Cabinet Secretary

The Prime Minister's relationship with the Cabinet Secretary should lie at the heart of the execution of governmental decision making. Wilson's relationship with his Cabinet Secretary after 1974, Sir John Hunt, was generally good; but it was neither as easy nor as close as had been his relationship with Hunt's predecessor, Sir Burke Trend, with whom Wilson had worked in 1964–70.[35] Wilson preferred the rarefied thoughts on policy that characterised Trend's donnish style to the executive civil service management skills of Hunt. However, Wilson's relations with officials remained better than relations with ministers,[36] and, because the official machine was running Wilson for much of the period, rather than Wilson running the machine, it was relatively easy for Hunt to ensure the smooth passage of business. One suspects that Hunt had qualms about Wilson's *modus operandi* from 1974, which could not have added to the success of the relationship. Prime Ministers and Cabinet Secretaries need to respect and admire each other. Where this is lacking, the quality of government can suffer.

The relationship between Callaghan and Hunt, who remained as Cabinet Secretary throughout Callaghan's premiership, soon established itself on a sound footing based upon just such mutual respect: Callaghan saw Hunt as extremely proficient; Hunt regarded Callaghan as a consummate manager of government business.[37] Hunt also regarded Ken Stowe, in the Private Office, in the highest terms, and relations between Number 10 and the Cabinet Office through the fabled green baize door worked well. But despite the continual improvement in the relationship between Callaghan and Hunt, and for all its pivotal nature, Hunt never grew as close or as influential to Callaghan personally as did Stowe.

Hunt was not, like his successors as Cabinet Secretary from 1981 onwards, Head of the Home Civil Service as well as being Cabinet Secretary. That job was held, successively, by Douglas Allen (1974–7), who combined it with his job as Permanent Secretary of the Treasury, and then by Ian Bancroft who was, concurrently, Permanent Secretary of the Civil Service Department, and who was peremptorily dismissed by Mrs Thatcher in 1981. Hunt regretted not having at his disposal the extra levers of power which the headship of the civil service would have given him. Nevertheless, whereas the earlier Head of the Home Civil Service, William Armstrong, had been dominant over the Cabinet Secretary in the Heath Government,[38] it was Hunt who proved to be the central civil service operator on policy and the management of business in 1974–9, and his main passion remained his restless desire to execute business for the Prime Minister and other Cabinet ministers efficiently and effectively. Callaghan, still less Wilson, did not want to be very activist Prime Ministers. Blair did. This may be one reason why Blair's relations with his Cabinet Secretaries were less happy than those of the previous two Labour Prime Ministers. Robin Butler (1988–98) Blair found overly formal, whilst he thought Richard Wilson (1998–2002) failed to be sufficiently zealous in making the civil service deliver on the Government's ambitious programme. Wilson, it was true, was keen to preserve the political independence and separation of the civil service, as Butler had been before him. But an even more important constraint on Blair driving the governmental machine was the realisation that the manual gearbox and the road ahead were more difficult to negotiate than it had appeared from the opposition seats.

The Policy Unit and the Central Policy Review Staff

The Policy Unit, Peter Hennessy says, was the 'prime ministerial Cabinet in all but name' for Harold Wilson.[39] The Policy Unit was created by Wilson in 1974, to be his 'eyes and ears'. The Unit's first Head, Bernard Donoughue, took two years' leave from his post as Reader in Politics at the London School of Economics in order to take charge of the Unit, but stayed for the full five years of Labour Government. Prior to his earlier appointment as Election Strategy Adviser in 1974, he later recalled, he had met Harold Wilson only once, when interviewing Wilson for his biography of one of the great Labour ministers from the mid-century, Herbert Morrison.[40] Wilson, Donoughue later recalled, 'struck me as a very small man with little to say of political interest about his former colleague'.[41] But from that inauspicious start, their relationship improved once Donoughue joined Wilson's circle of advisers. The Policy Unit, Donoughue wrote, 'must ensure that the Prime Minister is aware of what is coming from the departments to cabinet'.[42] The Unit was the only innovation that Wilson made to the machinery of Cabinet government during the final two years of his premiership,[43] and, given that Wilson had precious few policy ideas he wanted to see implemented in 1974 or thereafter, one might infer a certain irony in his creation of the Policy Unit.

But the importance of the creation of the Policy Unit was considerable. The Unit increased the capacity of the Prime Minister effectively to intervene in the policy-making process. It was especially important in tackling the industrial relations problems of 1975, the IMF crisis of 1976, and the 'Winter of Discontent' of 1978–9. Its influence persisted, through subsequent administrations, for over two decades until Blair merged it with the Private Office after 2001.

The civil service is notoriously suspicious of innovations, especially at the very heart of government. The keeper of the civil service flame, Cabinet Secretary, John Hunt, was less orthodox than some Cabinet Secretaries, but the setting up of the Policy Unit resulted in important discussions between Donoughue and Hunt. They agreed a written 'Concordat', by which Donoughue had access to the Prime Minister's confidential letters on all matters except security and defence, and that he could go to Cabinet Committees which were chaired by the Prime Minister (many of the most important such committees). In return, Hunt was reassured that the Policy Unit would not seek to short-circuit the traditional channels of communication between departmental civil servants and Number 10.[44]

The personnel of the Policy Unit shifted. In addition to Donoughue, the bedrock of the early Policy Unit was Andrew Graham, whose appointment had been specifically requested by Wilson himself.[45] When Graham returned to his teaching duties at Balliol College, Oxford, in 1976, he was replaced by Gavyn Davies, his young researcher and later Chairman of the BBC.[46] David Lipsey came into the Unit and played a decisive role, especially on the environment and on election strategy, until he moved into the Political Office, where he took over from Tom McNally when the latter got a seat.

The Policy Unit submitted 174 papers to Wilson in the last eighteen months of his premiership.[47] Its advice covered a wide range of topics, but the main areas of operation were: the preparation for the inevitable early general election (which took place in October 1974); the renegotiation of the terms of Britain's membership of the European Economic Community; the development of a voluntary incomes policy; and the impending bankruptcies in British industry. The Treasury had proposed that there should be a statutory incomes policy, but Donoughue lobbied hard for a voluntary policy, citing as his reasons that the Treasury's policy was too close to the failed incomes policy under the Heath Government, and that the unions would oppose a statutory initiative. Donoughue claims the voluntary incomes policy as the greatest success of the Unit under Wilson, and the unsuccessful proposals for the right to buy council houses, as promoted by Haines, as the greatest missed opportunity.[48] With such a laid-back Prime Minister, the opportunity for activism was, in a different way, as high as under a high-energy, activist Prime Minister.

Bernard Donoughue had been prepared to leave the Policy Unit upon Harold Wilson's departure from office. Indeed, he was sent a dismissal notice – a standard notice sent to all temporary civil servants on the resignation of a prime minister. But he was then told to continue working in the Unit: Callaghan was aware of the need for him to have a strong alternative source of advice.

The work of the Unit in 1976–9 was more regular, organised and sedate, reflecting the systematic approach that Jim Callaghan took to policy issues. In these three years the Unit sent over 500 memoranda to Callaghan.[49] He used the expertise of the Policy Unit in four key areas: education (Donoughue had significant input into the controversial 1976 Ruskin speech on education); the IMF loan, again in 1976; child benefit (the Unit helped to persuade a sceptical Callaghan of the need for a universal benefit paid to mothers); and addressing the problem of the financing of government debt caused by the drying-up of interest in gilt-edged stocks.

During the 'Winter of Discontent' in 1978–9, the Policy Unit suffered from the general paralysis of the Government. Donoughue's verdict of this period is that

> In the Policy Unit, too much of our time was spent on damage limitation and too little on exploratory new policy horizons (which had no chance anyway of pursuit by the Government). It felt like being locked in a political cage.[50]

Callaghan utilised his considerable political experience in discriminating between his sources of advice. The Policy Unit had a political role, highlighting for Callaghan the political consequences of his policy choices, whilst the Central Policy Review Staff (CPRS), which had been created by Heath in 1971, was used for issues of organisation and administration: longer-term complex projects, including defence procurement and foreign representation (on which its recommendations were blocked by the Foreign and Commonwealth Office). Callaghan used the CPRS more than Wilson, although its position remained peripheral to the operation of Number 10, and it had trouble finding the right time to catch the ear of the Prime Minister.

The Policy Unit complemented, but partially superseded, the CPRS. The Unit had the advantages over the CPRS in its physical and political proximity to the Prime Minister. The Policy Unit was located in the Prime Minister's Office in Number 10; the CPRS inhabited the Cabinet Office, adjacent to Number 10, but cut off by the green baize door. That baize door was permeable; but in the non-hierarchical atmosphere of Number 10 the Unit's location meant that its head, Bernard Donoughue, could catch the Prime Minister's ear at almost any time.[51] Despite the best efforts of Victor Rothschild, the head of the CPRS for a few months after the election, and Kenneth Berrill, who succeeded him for the remainder of the Parliament, the CPRS remained marginal. Its minor resurgence under Callaghan merely stayed its final demise until 1983. Blair did not seek to resurrect it after 1997; but, through an expansion of the Policy Unit, and a plethora of new units within the Number 10–Cabinet Office nexus, he sought to ensure that policy could be driven hard and monitored closely from the centre.

Speechwriting

Joe Haines was Harold Wilson's speechwriter in his final years as party leader. Wilson, for a time, tried dictating sections of his speech on the morning of delivery, but this was increasingly unsuccessful, and during the February 1974 general election campaign Marcia Williams would place Haines's draft of the next day's speech on Wilson's pillow in Lord North Street, for him to read before morning.[52] In government, Wilson showed little enthusiasm for speech-making, such as over the campaign on the Europe referendum, and for much of the campaign he made no public speeches.[53] Harold Wilson claimed in retirement that he wrote all of his speeches, but it is clear that Haines wrote most of Wilson's public speeches in his declining years.[54]

Most of Callaghan's speeches were drafted by Tom McNally or, later, David Lipsey. But the oft-quoted phrase of Callaghan's on monetary policy ('the option of spending yourself out of a recession no longer exists') was dictated by his son-in-law, the economist Peter Jay, who was married to Margaret, who later, as Lady Jay, became Leader of the House of Lords under Blair. And the Policy Unit wrote much of the Ruskin speech on education.

Cabinet

The Labour Cabinet in 1974 was the most experienced incoming Labour Cabinet in history – fourteen members had served in the Cabinet prior to the 1970 general election – and it was the first Cabinet ever to include two women (Barbara Castle and Shirley Williams). Michael Foot joined the Cabinet for the first time: he was appointed Employment Secretary. 'Foot was brought in,' wrote Pimlott, 'both to please the unions and to provide left-wing ballast in what remained, despite everything, a dominantly right-wing Cabinet.'[55] In making these appointments, however, Wilson was following convention (later broken by Blair) and translating his Shadow Cabinet into office.

Wilson had a much more troubled time in Cabinet discussions than Callaghan. Wilson said of himself that he 'used to be a striker, but now I am more of a Jack Charlton – dominating the centre of the park. I regard myself as a deep-lying centre-half.'[56] And whilst he didn't dominate even the centre of the park during his final term, some Cabinet members still lamented the death of Cabinet government and the rise of a so-called 'presidential' style of government.[57]

Barbara Castle's comment on the death of Cabinet government seems to be at odds with the statistics: Wilson, in the two years, chaired over 100 full Cabinets, almost 150 meetings of Cabinet standing committees, and over sixty ad hoc committees (although 'chairing' was thought by some to be a misleading description).[58] But her lament was, specifically, prompted by the Cabinet discussions on the renegotiation of the terms of membership of the EEC. This was one area in which Wilson could not manage to hold the collective line. But his suspension of collective Cabinet responsibility through his 'agreement to differ' in the Europe referendum was a political masterstroke by the once-brilliant wheeler-dealer: it held the Cabinet together after the referendum whilst allowing the left to expose themselves to attack during the referendum campaign. Instead of sacrificing unity, Wilson had ensured it.

Callaghan (Foreign Secretary) and Denis Healey (Chancellor of the Exchequer) were the most important members of the Cabinet, ex officio. Michael Foot (Employment Secretary) carried weight because of his influence with the political left, as did Harold Lever (Chancellor of the Duchy of Lancaster) by virtue of his position as economic counsellor to Wilson. Wilson respected Roy Jenkins and Tony Crosland, but he could be jealous when they were praised as intellectuals.[59] Even a Cabinet of such stature could not, however, overcome the chronic difficulties that faced it, namely the economic problems, the dire weakness of so much industry, and societal divisions provided by the tackling of industrial relations.[60]

Callaghan benefited from the absence in his Cabinet of two of Wilson's stars, Roy Jenkins (whose strong pro-European views caused particular difficulty in the Cabinet) and Barbara Castle,[61] both of them forces who had served to polarise Cabinet discussions. Pimlott, as noted above, characterised Wilson's Cabinet as 'markedly right-wing', but Callaghan's was even more so, and with the later entry to the Cabinet of Edmund Dell, who was on the far right of the Party, the rightward lean of the Cabinet was assured.[62] Callaghan's Cabinet was not as balanced between left and right factions, but divisions remained, as highlighted by the leadership contest.

Callaghan took time to get to know his ministers and their departmental priorities, holding a series of bilateral meetings soon after he became Prime Minister; but, unlike Wilson, he didn't try to fix matters before they came to the Cabinet table. He worked to achieve a consensus view amongst Cabinet members, through open discussions on subjects including public expenditure cuts and the International Monetary Fund negotiations. His strong alliances with Michael Foot on the left and Denis Healey, his Chancellor of the Exchequer, on the centre–right, helped him in Cabinet.

For the final three months of 1976, the Cabinet's energies were wholly absorbed by the battles which followed the Chancellor of the Exchequer's formal authorisation to apply for a large loan from the International Monetary Fund (IMF). The question that faced the Cabinet was the size of the cuts which would be necessary to secure the loan and rescue sterling. Four major Cabinets at the beginning of December 1976 decided the IMF issue.[63] Whereas Denis Healey and Shirley Williams have subsequently praised Callaghan's mastery of the economics and the politics of the IMF decision, Edmund Dell is highly critical of the drawn-out nature of the Cabinet discussions, believing that Callaghan could have closed debate much earlier with the same conclusions being reached.[64] Indeed, colleagues suspected that Callaghan was far more keen on enforcing spending cuts than he let on during their discussions.[65] It is almost inconceivable that a future Labour Prime Minister could allow such protracted negotiations around the Cabinet table, and, as Hennessy notes, certain that the markets would not tolerate such delay.

Healey would have loved to have been Foreign Secretary, had Labour won the 1979 general election, and Callaghan would have appointed him. Indeed, Healey wanted to be Foreign Secretary from 1976,[66] but Callaghan had to leave Healey at the Treasury until the IMF issue and the inflation crisis were solved, and the latter seemed almost to be out of control.[67]

A major change in the frequency of Cabinet meetings occurred in 1977, when the Cabinet began to meet just once each week. The average annual number of meetings each year fell from sixty to forty. This change persisted throughout subsequent administrations.[68] But this headline figure does paint an accurate picture of proceedings.

Even these forty meetings a year did not guarantee the ability of the Cabinet to face down the problems that beset the Government in its final year. David Ennals (Health and Social Security) and Peter Shore (Environment) were less successful in dealing with the trade unions and suppressing wage inflation than their colleagues hoped: 'The reality,' recalled Donoughue, 'was that there were far too many marshmallows and too few vertebrae in Jim's Cabinet.'[69]

The flow of Cabinet documents dried up. Departments proved unwilling to confront the non-governmental groups with which they dealt. 'It is just like it was in February 1979,' Kenneth Stowe told Donoughue. 'Whitehall is waiting to see which way the cat will jump politically.'[70] The period 1976–9 saw the high watermark, and the beginning of the decline, of conventional Cabinet government which was to be accelerated by Margaret Thatcher's spurning of the Cabinet Committee system from 1979 to 1980 and even more from 1983. Tony Blair adopted a more personal, less formal style of conducting Cabinet business. Like Callaghan, he utilised bilateral meetings, but he used them far more extensively than his predecessor, and would even reach major decisions through correspondence. The Cabinet remained important as a collegiate association, but not as a collective decision-making body, reflecting the changed needs of politics and government, and the differing requirements of the Prime Minister's personal skills.

Conclusion: Labour, Old and New

'The 1970s,' wrote Hennessy, 'were a decade that ate prime ministers.' But one should not regard each course of the feast as uniform. The circumstances and the abilities of the three prime ministers of the period 1970–9 differed greatly in appearance and in effect.

Wilson was easy fodder upon which the 1970s could feast. He was a prime minister who had lost interest in the exercise of power. Whilst he could periodically be energised for the game of politics, especially internal Labour Party politics, he had little lust for the wider task of being Prime Minister. In July 1975 Wilson, with great candour, told Joe Haines: 'when old problems recur, I reach for the old solutions. I have nothing to offer any more.' Haines lamented: 'perhaps a line should be drawn under his career some time, but not long, after his first election victory in 1974'.[71] However, had Wilson chosen to retire in mid-1974, there is no guarantee that he would not have clouded his departure with a questionable honours list, or some other lapse of judgement, as he did two years later.

Had a line been drawn under Wilson's career in mid-1974 – as Haines hoped – he would, however, have had an incomplete view of Wilson-the-tactician. The February 1974 general election was an inconclusive point upon which to retire, and this lack of a majority needed to be rectified, although this success was tempered by the temporary nature of the majority with which it furnished Labour, and the opportunity cost of focusing all efforts onto winning the October election. However, by remaining in office for two further years, Wilson did ensure that his Policy Unit became embedded in the system as a legacy of his final term.

Callaghan did not produce great innovations, but he had neither the time nor the inclination for reforming the institutions and structure of government. His calm, measured approach helped to restore faith in the ability of the Government. His great experience had taught him how best to arrange the levers of power. He possessed the right style for the right time.

The situation that faced Tony Blair in 1997 was a world away from that which his two immediate Labour predecessors found upon entering Downing Street. New Labour came into office after a long period of reflection and policy development, hungry for power, united against the Conservatives, resolved not to squander its position through in-fighting. It found an economy that was healthy. The trade unions, which had caused so much trouble for governments of both complexions in the 1970s, were cowed: within the Labour movement, their power having been dispersed by the introduction of one-member, one-vote; in the country, legal and industrial change had combined to emasculate their power of disruption. The majority of 179 was the largest that ever Labour had enjoyed.

'The past,' as L.P. Hartley said in 1953, 'is a foreign country. They do things differently there.'[72]

Despite the very different experience of Tony Blair to that of Wilson and Callaghan, there are still comparisons to be made. Wilson in the 1970s was tired and had lost the enthusiasm to create a 'New Britain', which he had in 1964 and which Blair so conspicuously embodied in 1997. Wilson's capital within his Party had withered: as Labour MP-turned-commentator Phillip Whitehead notes, 'much of the left distrusted him [Wilson] for his record in government'.[73] And, to a considerable extent, Callaghan's Government was defeated from within the Labour movement. These experiences helped to forge the New Labour passion for control over the government machine and the realisation that trying to govern by holding the party together, was arid. The left had to be defeated, and those remaining in the party tightly controlled. For the first few years the strong line held and the election cash register continues to tick over positively. But electorates change their minds. Economies can shrink as well as grow. Incentives for backbench insurgency grow over time. The decades, whose appetite was sated by eating Prime Ministers in the 1970s, may grow hungry once more. New Labour strategists may yet find themselves seeking inspiration in the experiences of their predecessors in the 1970s, about whom it has been easy to be dismissive.

Notes

Chris Ballinger deserves the principal credit for this chapter.

1 He told this to Roy Jenkins. See Jenkins, R., *A Life at the Centre* (Macmillan, London, 1991), pp. 297–8.
2 Dennis Kavanagh and Anthony Seldon in *The Powers behind the Prime Minister* (HarperCollins, London, 1999) state that Wilson had not expected to win the February 1974 general election. This is backed up by Peter Hennessy in *Prime Minister: The Office and Its Holders since 1945* (Allen Lane, London, 2001), and by Alan Watkins in *The Road to Number 10 from Bonar Law to Tony Blair* (Duckworth, London, 1998). However, Joe Haines wrote to one of the present authors that 'it is not true that Wilson did not expect to win; I still have a letter from Marcia [Williams] in which it is quite clear that we expected a victory and Wilson shared our view' (Letter from Joe Haines to Anthony Seldon, 24 September 1998).
3 Private information.
4 See, for example, Hatfield, M., *The House the Left Built: Inside Labour policy-making, 1970–75* (Gollancz, London, 1978).
5 Butler, D. and Kavanagh, D., *The British General Election of 1979* (Macmillan, London, 1980), p. 47.
6 On Wilson's plans for resignation, see, inter alia, Watkins, *The Road to Number 10*, pp. 203–6.
7 Pimlott, B., *Harold Wilson* (HarperCollins, London, 1992), p. 616.
8 Falkender, M., *Downing Street in Perspective* (Weidenfeld and Nicolson, London, 1983), p. 115.
9 Kavanagh and Seldon, *Powers behind the Prime Minister*, p. 110.
10 Private information.
11 Morgan, K.O., *Callaghan: A Life* (Oxford University Press, Oxford, 1997), p. 485.
12 Ibid., p. 485.

13 Ibid., p. 488.
14 Donoughue, B., *The Heat of the Kitchen: An autobiography* (Politico's, London, 2003), pp. 104–5.
15 See ibid., pp. 147–50.
16 Kavanagh and Seldon, *Powers behind the Prime Minister*, pp. 115–16.
17 Pimlott, *Harold Wilson*, p. 621.
18 Kavanagh and Seldon, *Powers behind the Prime Minister*, p. 117.
19 Ibid., p. 135.
20 Seymour-Ure, C., 'Prime Ministers and the Public: Managing Media Relations', in Shell, D. and Hodder-Williams, R., *Churchill to Major: The British Prime Ministership since 1945* (Hurst, London, 1995).
21 Seymour-Ure, C., The British Press and Broadcasting since 1945 (Blackwell, Oxford, 1991), p. 192.
22 Private information.
23 Donoughue, B., *Prime Minister: The Conduct of Policy under Harold Wilson and James Callaghan* (Cape, London, 1987), p. 25.
24 Pimlott, *Harold Wilson*, p. 621.
25 Morgan, *Callaghan: A Life*, p. 497; Donoughue, *Prime Minister*, p. 25.
26 Private information.
27 Kavanagh and Seldon, *Powers behind the Prime Minister*, pp. 112–13.
28 A former official, quoted by Pimlott, *Harold Wilson*, p. 622.
29 Kavanagh and Seldon, *Powers behind the Prime Minister*, p. 112.
30 Donoughue, *Prime Minister*, p. 18.
31 Ibid., p. 18.
32 Kavanagh and Seldon, *Powers behind the Prime Minister*, p. 135.
33 Ibid., p. 139.
34 Ibid., p. 140.
35 Sir John Hunt was appointed Cabinet Secretary in 1973 upon the retirement of Sir Burke (later Lord) Trend, who was Cabinet Secretary 1963–73.
36 Pimlott, *Harold Wilson*, p. 623.
37 Kavanagh and Seldon, *Powers behind the Prime Minister*, p. 141.
38 Baston, L. and Seldon, A., 'Number 10 under Edward Heath', in Ball, S. and Seldon, A. (eds), *The Heath Government 1970–1974: A Reappraisal* (Longman, London, 1996), p. 65.
39 Hennessy, P., *Cabinet* (Basil Blackwell, Oxford, 1986), p. 82.
40 Donoughue, B. and Jones, G.W., *Herbert Morrison: Portrait of a Politician* (Weidenfeld and Nicolson, London, 1973).
41 Donoughue, *The Heat of the Kitchen*, p. 101.
42 Ibid., p. 129.
43 Hennessy, *Prime Minister*, p. 359.
44 Donoughue, *The Heat of the Kitchen*, p. 132.
45 Kavanagh and Seldon, *Powers behind the Prime Minister*, p.119.
46 See, for example, Donoughue, *The Heat of the Kitchen*, p. 130.
47 Ibid., p. 150.
48 Donoughue, *The Heat of the Kitchen*, pp. 161–74. The Policy Unit proposed allowing council house tenants the right to buy their homes, citing political and social advantages of this scheme, 'although most of its [the Policy Unit's] members were clearly worried about this breach of sacred Labour dogma' (p. 174).
49 Ibid., p. 240.
50 Ibid., p. 281.
51 Interview with Bernard Donoughue, cited in Pimlott, *Harold Wilson*, p. 620.
52 Haines, J., *Glimmers of Twilight* (Politico's, London, 2003), p. 75.
53 Donoughue, *The Heat of the Kitchen*, p. 155; Kavanagh and Seldon, *Powers behind the Prime Minister*, p. 118.

54 Private information.

55 Pimlott, *Harold Wilson*, p. 618.

56 Private information. Wilson recalls having likened himself to a pre-war footballer, Roberts of Arsenal, 'moving up-field only for set-piece occasions': Wilson, H., *Final Term: The Labour Government 1974–76* (Weidenfeld and Nicolson/Michael Joseph, London, 1979), p. 17.

57 See, for example, Castle, B., *The Castle Diaries 1974–76* (Weidenfeld and Nicolson, London, 1980), p. 227.

58 Kavanagh and Seldon, *Powers behind the Prime Minister*, p. 108.

59 Private information.

60 Donoughue, *The Heat of the Kitchen*, p. 128.

61 Anne Perkins, in her authorised biography of Barbara Castle, says that Callaghan 'told Benn that he "had to end her career"'; see Perkins, A., *Red Queen: The Authorised Biography of Barbara Castle* (Macmillan, London, 2003), p. 418.

62 Morgan, *Callaghan: A Life*, p. 479.

63 Donoughue, *The Heat of the Kitchen*, pp. 244–7.

64 Dell, cited in Hennessy, *Prime Minister*, p. 388.

65 Private information.

66 Private information.

67 Donoughue, *The Heat of the Kitchen*, p. 239.

68 See Seldon, A., 'The Cabinet System', in Bogdanor, V. (ed.), *The British Constitution in the Twentieth Century* (British Academy/Oxford University Press, Oxford, 2003).

69 Donoughue, *The Heat of the Kitchen*, p. 268.

70 Ibid., p. 267.

71 Haines, *Glimmers of Twilight*, p. 202.

72 Hartly, L. P., *The Go-Between*, (Hamish Hamilton, London, 1953) p. 1.

73 Whitehead, P., 'The Labour Governments, 1974–79', in Hennessy, P. and Seldon, A. (eds), *Ruling Performance: British Governments from Attlee to Thatcher* (Blackwell, Oxford, 1987), p. 245.

11 Parliament

Philip Norton

The period from 1974 to 1979, encompassing two Parliaments, was unique in twentieth-century parliamentary history. It was unique because of the juxtaposition of two not obviously compatible features. The first was the vulnerability of the Government. It was vulnerable to defeat in the division lobbies. It could be, and was, defeated as a result of (i) opposition parties combining against it during the periods when it was a minority government and (ii) its own backbenchers entering the opposition lobby. It suffered more defeats than any government in modern British history. The second feature, peculiar to the 1974–9 Parliament, was the longevity of the Parliament. Despite the fact that the Government was returned in October 1974 with a minuscule parliamentary majority, and lost that majority in April 1976, it survived into a fifth session. It was thus, remarkably, one of the longer Parliaments of the post-war era.

The Government was able to govern during this period but throughout it both Houses of Parliament served as significant constraints on government. Though Parliament was never able to achieve the status of an active, or policy-making, legislature, it was during this period a notably reactive, or policy-influencing, legislature.[1] It was the high point of parliamentary impact on public policy during the twentieth century.

This chapter thus explores the two features of government in relation to Parliament: those of vulnerability and survival. It challenges what may be seen as the received wisdom in respect of both.

Vulnerability

The February 1974 election saw the return of 301 Labour MPs in a 635-member House of Commons. After Edward Heath resigned on 4 March, after failing to reach agreement with the Liberal Parliamentary Party, Harold Wilson formed a government, but one that, like the first two Labour Governments of 1924 and 1929, was in a minority in both Houses of Parliament. Though the Cabinet proceeded with a Queen's Speech predicated on a programme for a full Parliament, there was – as Wilson and other ministers recognised – little likelihood of it being anything other than a short-lived Parliament.[2] Initially, the Opposition was reluctant to try to defeat the Government in the division lobbies:

Mr Heath has let his rank and file know that Opposition tactics will be to win the argument but not to win divisions and thus give Mr Wilson the excuse of saying he is prevented from governing and must fortify his mandate in another general election.[3]

This tactic not only created occasional embarrassments for the Opposition – tabling amendments but not dividing on them – but also proved increasingly unpopular among younger Conservative backbenchers. Disquiet was expressed at meetings of the 1922 Committee and the Chairman, Edward du Cann, conveyed the feelings of the rank and file to the leader.[4] The tactic was abandoned, especially after the prospect of a June election had passed, and the Opposition proved willing to force divisions, on occasion being joined by other parties, or to join other parties in the lobby.

The combination of opposition parties against the Government was sufficient to deny the Government a majority in the division lobbies. In the course of less than two months – from 19 June to 30 July, when the House rose – it suffered a total of seventeen defeats.[5] The principal casualties were the Finance Bill (five defeats, including on the rate of income tax) and the Trade Union and Labour Relations Bill (seven defeats). The Government also ran into difficulties in the House of Lords, where it suffered fifteen defeats (Table 11.1). In the Commons, all bar two of the defeats on the Trade Union and Labour Relations Bill were on motions to disagree with Lords amendments to the Bill. As Table 11.1 reveals, the Parliament was unusual in that the number of defeats in the Commons actually exceeded the number in the Lords.

The Government encountered opposition, however, not only from the other parties in the House of Commons but also from some of its own backbenchers. Despite its precarious political position, there were eight occasions when Labour MPs voted against it. Six of these involved twenty or more Labour members. The incidences of cross-voting by Labour backbenchers were embarrassing but not fatal: none of the six large-scale rebellions entailed voting with the Opposition. The eight occasions constituted less than 10 per cent of the 109 divisions held during the Parliament. (They also paled alongside the twenty-one

Table 11.1   Government defeats in Parliament, 1970–83

Parliament	*Number of defeats House of Commons*	*House of Lords*
1970–4	6	25
1974	17	15
1974–9	42	347
1979–83	1	45

Source: P. Norton, 'Behavioural Changes', in P. Norton (ed.), *Parliament in the 1980s* (Oxford: Basil Blackwell, 1985), p. 27.

divisions that witnessed rebellions by Tory backbenchers.) However, what the occasions of intra-party dissent lacked in breadth they made up for in terms of depth. No fewer than 132 Labour MPs cast one or more votes against the Labour Government.[6] Three of the votes were on motions related to the European Community. Eighteen Labour MPs voted against the renewal of the continuance order for the Northern Ireland (Emergency Provisions) Act, despite the pleas of the Northern Ireland Secretary, Merlyn Rees.

Such occasions were unhelpful for the Government, but they did not constitute the problems posed by the defeats forced on it by opposition parties. The frequency of the defeats rendered the Government's position largely untenable. After Parliament rose at the end of July, the expectation was that there would be an autumn election. On 18 September, Wilson announced that the election would take place on 10 October. The election saw the return of 319 Labour MPs, giving the Government an overall parliamentary majority of three. The majority was precarious and, in any event, short-lived. By-election losses, defections and the disappearance and then defection of Labour MP John Stonehouse resulted in April 1976 in the Government losing its overall majority.

The small and then non-existent majority rendered the Government vulnerable. It was vulnerable, after it slipped into its minority status, to opposition parties combining against it. It was also vulnerable throughout to dissent by its own backbenchers. What would appear to be intuitive assumptions about the Parliament are that most defeats are likely to have been imposed by opposition parties combining against a minority government and that any defeats imposed on it by Labour MPs cross-voting are likely to be the product of dissent by left-wing MPs. In fact, neither assumption is correct. Most of the defeats inflicted on the Government were the product of Labour backbenchers entering the opposition lobby (had they not done so, the Government would have survived) and, of these, only a small minority were attributable to left-wing Labour MPs voting against the Government.

In fact, during the Parliament, the Government's majority was under threat from three sources in the House of Commons, as follows.

Opposition parties

As we have seen, this was the principal threat during the short 1974 Parliament. It was also a threat in the 1974–9 Parliament, especially after the Government slipped into a minority in 1976. However, the scale of this threat should not be exaggerated. Although the Government was returned with an overall majority of three, its majority over the Conservatives was forty-two. There were thirteen Liberal, eleven Scottish National and three Plaid Cymru MPs, in addition to the twelve MPs from Northern Ireland. On many measures, the Government could count on the support of the Liberals and the nationalist MPs. The Ulster Unionist MPs were not noted for their assiduousness in attending parliamentary proceedings. The Government's majority was thus under threat only when opposition parties combined to vote against it and were able to ensure a full or virtually full turnout of their members.

For a particular period, from March 1977 to May 1978, the Government had the support of the Liberals in any vote of confidence – in return for support for various measures – but this had limited relevance to many of the votes that took place. The Liberals were keeping the Government in office but not necessarily supporting it in all the votes that took place in the House. Thus, the one period when one might assume that the Government was not under threat of defeat was one in which it was still vulnerable and did, in fact, suffer defeats at the hands of opposition parties (six defeats) as well as, more extensively, at the hands of its own backbenchers (nine defeats).

The expectation of defeat was generally greater than the reality. As Margaret Thatcher recalled, 'the press were inclined to exaggerate our chances of actually defeating a Government which, after all, still had a considerable margin of votes over the Conservatives'.[7] During the Parliament, no more than nineteen of the forty-two defeats suffered by the Government are attributable to opposition parties combining against it.[8] Even that figure is a maximum one. One defeat appears to have resulted from some confusion in the division lobbies and two others may have been a product of mismanagement and confusion. The Second Reading of the Reduction of Redundancy Rebates Bill was lost by one vote, in a division where the Prime Minister was absent without a pair.

Though Margaret Thatcher noted that 'our occasional victories did not seem to lead anywhere,'[9] some of the defeats were on important issues. The most significant and frequent were on finance and economics. In January 1978 an opposition amendment to devalue the Green Pound by 7.5 per cent was carried by 291 votes to 280. In May of the same year, an amendment to the Finance Bill, to reduce the basic rate of income tax from 34 per cent to 33 per cent, was carried (by 312 votes to 304) as was an amendment to raise the level at which the higher rate of income tax would apply (by 288 votes to 286). In July 1978, the draft Dock Labour Scheme was rejected by 301 votes to 291. In December 1978, an opposition amendment, opposing the Government's economic policy of sanctions against firms breaking the 5 per cent pay limit, was carried by 285 votes to 279 (and the amended motion then carried by 285 votes to 283). Opposition parties were also responsible for removing a clause from the Scotland Bill and another from the Wales Bill, though as we shall see it was dissent by Labour MPs that caused the most problems for the Government's devolution legislation. However, opposition parties scored their ultimate victory on 28 March 1979. Having previously failed in marshalling a majority to pass a vote of no confidence, on this occasion they were successful. The Government was defeated by one vote.

However, the biggest consistent impact of the official opposition lay more in its bark than its bite. There were plenty of backbenchers willing to make life difficult for ministers. They included acerbic debaters such as Norman Tebbit and George Gardiner, and groups of backbenchers were formed by John Peyton and Jasper More, with the approval of the whips, to co-ordinate tactics to harry ministers.[10] On one occasion, following claims that government whips had broken a pair, the Opposition refused to engage in pairing, thus causing chaos for Labour MPs. Though the Opposition may not be able frequently to defeat the Government, it was able to make life difficult; it took only a few opposition MPs to force government supporters to stay into the early hours in order to vote. 'Another long evening of three-line whips in the House' was a typical entry in the diary of one Cabinet minister.[11] There was always the possibility that Conservative MPs might return suddenly in some numbers and on occasion they did so. Although the Government was ultimately brought down by a vote of confidence, it was by that time basically worn out. However, it was not only opposition MPs who had worn it out. Some of its own supporters had contributed to the process.

The left wing of the parliamentary party

Left-wing Labour MPs were notable in the 1974–9 Parliament for being vocal and for their willingness to vote against a Labour Government. Their bark was more notable than their bite. They frequently embarrassed the Government but they rarely defeated it.

The Labour left constituted a clear factional element within the Parliamentary Labour Party (PLP). It was fairly well entrenched. It had strong roots outside the House, enabling left-wing members to be elected for safe seats, their position strengthening in the 1970s relative to MPs who were not identified with the left.[12] The faction took organisational form in the Tribune Group. The Group met once, sometimes twice, a week to debate issues of current concern, especially those coming before the House. Though not having a designated whip, the Group did co-ordinate the activities of its members.[13] The result was that, as in the 1966–70 Parliament, there was a strong positive correlation between voting against the Government on one issue and then voting against it on another.[14] This applied also in the short 1974 Parliament as well as in the 1974–9 Parliament. In the latter, Tribune Group MPs voted against the Government persistently and in substantial numbers. Of the sixty-nine votes in the Parliament in which forty or more Labour MPs voted against the Government, Tribune Group MPs constituted a majority in all but five of them. (The proportion ranged from 39 per cent to 87 per cent.) Of the eighty-six MPs who were members of the Group for all or part of the Parliament, *all* cast one or more votes against the Government, with a majority voting against on forty or more occasions.[15] (The figure includes ministers, as they were permitted to vote against the Government in the votes on European Community membership and the European Assembly Elections Bill.) Of the twenty-seven MPs who cast seventy or more dissenting votes, all were members of the Tribune Group.

The Tribune Group was thus a thorn in the Government's side. Members voted against the Government on a range of issues, albeit largely predictable in terms of their ideological stance. They opposed the Government's economic policy. They voted against it on immigration rules, defence, the civil list, renewal of the Prevention of Terrorism Act, pay beds in the National Health Service, as well as on direct elections to the European Parliament and devolution,[16] though in the last two cases they were joined by non-Group MPs. For Group members, the Government was moving more and more away from socialism and was increasingly indistinguishable from a Tory Government. The distancing of the Group from the bulk of Labour MPs reinforced what Pat Seyd has identified as the left's cultural orientation as 'outsiders'.[17]

As outsiders, they were often strident in their criticisms of government. However, it was largely to little effect. As Geoff Hodgson noted, 'the Tribune Group, schooled in the long tradition of parliamentary oratory, pressured the Government not with muscles but with words. With their narrow parliamentary outlook they stood amazed as the government paid no heed.'[18] They lacked muscle because they were usually on their own. They often voted against the Government but rarely did so with Conservative support. When Tribune Group MPs trooped into the lobby against the Government, the Opposition usually either abstained or voted with the Government. As a result, few of the defeats attributable to dissent by Labour MPs were caused by Tribune Group MPs.

Of the twenty-three defeats suffered by the Government as a result of Labour MPs entering the opposition lobby, only six can be attributed to Tribune Group MPs. Of these, the most high-profile defeat was on the Expenditure White Paper in March 1976, forcing the Government to seek a vote of confidence the following day. The defeat delighted the left. Tony Benn noted in his diary,

> the defeat last night has transformed the situation; it has ended the phoney peace and people see now that the Government is supported by the right-wing forces in society, that they can't carry the Labour Party in the way they have.[19]

For many Cabinet ministers, the rebels were no more than thugs, some of whom according to Jim Callaghan would not mind a Tory Government.[20]

The defeat was the most high-profile defeat achieved on the floor of the House. The other main impact of left-wing dissent occurred in Standing Committee, where the votes of one or two Labour MPs could be crucial.[21] During committee stage of the 1977 Finance Bill, two Labour Members – Jeff Rooker and Audrey Wise – tabled amendments which, with opposition support, were carried. The amendments raised the levels of income tax allowances and partially indexed them against inflation. The Government decided to accept the defeats, but – as one minister recalled – 'repercussions from the Finance Bill Committee defeat simmered on throughout the summer, with the Prime Minister becoming very angry'.[22] These defeats, coupled with the other defeats on the floor of the House, had an effect on public policy, but they were isolated successes, occurring against a backdrop of growing animosity within the PLP and frustration on the part of the left.

MPs drawn from different wings of the PLP

The left had the loudest bark, but the effective bites came from Labour MPs drawn from different wings of the Party combining with the Opposition to defeat the Government. The left and the Conservatives were not natural allies. It was easier for Labour MPs from different wings of the Party to enter the lobby on issues, such as devolution, that were not obviously definable in ideological terms. During the Parliament, they did so and to effect.

Of the twenty-three defeats inflicted by Labour dissidents, six as we have seen were the result of dissent by left-wing MPs. A further two can be attributed to dissent by right-wing MPs (on an attempt to lift the disqualification on councillors in Clay Cross, who had refused to implement provisions of the 1972 Housing Finance Act, and on the central provisions of the Dock Work Regulation Bill). The remaining defeats – the most significant in both quantitative and qualitative terms – were the product of MPs drawn from different parts of the PLP entering the lobby to vote against the Government.

During the Parliament, the PLP was split on a range of issues. However, the two most prominent and persistent were membership of the European Community and devolution. The divisions over European integration were deep and intense and they existed within the ranks of ministers as well as among backbenchers. So deep was the split that ministers were permitted to speak in favour of a 'no' vote in the 1975 referendum on continued membership of the EC (though not in the House – one who did so was dismissed) and given a free vote on the European Assembly Elections Bill in July 1977, even though the Government's advice was to support the Bill. (The Bill provided for direct elections to the European Parliament and stipulated the use of the regional list system. The House later rejected, on a free vote, the regional list method of election.) During the Parliament, there were no less than fifty-one divisions on EC and EC-related matters in which Labour MPs voted against the Government. There was a concentrated core of Tribune Group MPs who regularly voted against the Government but they were joined by others from different wings of the Party. However, their action had little effect on outcomes. The stance taken by the Government was normally supported by the Opposition, which itself was split on the issue. Hence, votes were not usually those involving the Government versus the Opposition, but rather a majority of Labour and Conservative MPs combining against a dissident minority of both parties.

Devolution was a different matter. Though both parties were split, the official opposition line was to oppose the Government and there were more dissidents on the Labour benches than on the opposition benches. The Government proceeded with legislation despite opposition from its own backbenches. Its first bill providing for elected bodies in Scotland and Wales was abandoned when, in February 1977, twenty-two Labour MPs voted with the Opposition against the guillotine motion for the Bill. The motion was lost by 312 votes to 283. The Government then introduced separate bills for Scotland and Wales. The Government suffered defeats on both. Of these, the most significant were those providing for a threshold in referendums. The Government had not planned to have referendums in Scotland and Wales, but because of dissent within its ranks had agreed to hold them. During the passage of both bills, amendments were carried providing for a 40 per cent threshold of all voters voting 'yes' in referendums in order for devolution to be implemented. Committee stage of both bills was taken on the floor of the House. The threshold requirement was agreed in committee on the Scotland Bill by 166 votes to 151; an attempt by the Government to overturn the defeat at Report stage was defeated. An amendment to the Wales Bill, incorporating the same provision, was carried by a sizeable margin: 280 votes to 208. The Government suffered no fewer than thirteen defeats to its devolution legislation as a result of Labour MPs voting against it; a further two defeats, as already noted, occurred because of opposition parties combining against the Government. The most dramatic consequence derived from the Government accepting the case for referendums and the imposition of a threshold requirement. When voters in Wales voted 'no', and the proportion voting 'yes' in Scotland failed to meet the 40 per cent threshold, the Government tabled the requisite orders to repeal the Acts. As a consequence of what had happened in Parliament, the Government failed to implement its central constitutional measure. The failure of the referendums also set in train the events leading to the Government losing the vote of no confidence on 28 March 1979.

For the Government, it was thus a gruelling Parliament. The defeats it suffered constituted the tip of an iceberg as far as dissent by its own backbenchers was concerned. The number of divisions witnessing dissenting votes by Labour backbenchers grew in each succeeding session, from 14.5 per cent in 1974–5 to a staggering – and unprecedented – 45 per cent in the final 1978–9 session. In other words, by the end of the Parliament, almost one in every two divisions involved Labour MPs voting against the Government. The Parliament experienced the greatest level of intra-party dissent in post-war history. The Government thus faced a threat from opposition parties and from its own backbenchers. In the circumstances, survival was the principal goal.

Nor was the Government under threat solely from the House of Commons. As Table 11.1 reveals, it was defeated even more times in the House of Lords. As the table shows, the Government lost 347 votes in the Lords during the course of the Parliament. Few bills escaped amendment by the Upper House. The problem for the Government, though, was not simply the fact that it lacked a majority in the Lords. (There had been a preponderance of Tory peers since the time of Pitt the Younger.) What created problems was the fact that it had a tiny and then non-existent majority in the Commons. It could thus not be certain that it could muster a majority to reverse a defeat in the Lords. Of the defeats it suffered in the Commons, seven were on motions to disagree with Lords' amendments. Furthermore, even if the Government could muster a majority, there was the danger the Lords would insist on their amendments. Even if ultimately the Upper House gave way, it was for the Government a time-consuming process. The business managers were thus prone to press for compromise rather than confrontation. As Tony Benn recognised, there were certain measures – such as his 1975 Industry Bill – which some senior ministers were not unduly concerned whether they reached the statute book or not.[23] They were thus not going to get into a fight with the Lords. Though on occasion the use of the Parliament Act was discussed as a way of ensuring a measure got on to the statute book, it was never employed.

The House of Lords contributed to the Government's problems with its devolution legislation – four of the Government's defeats in the Commons were on motions to overturn Lords' amendments to the Scotland and Wales Bills – as well as to the troubled passage of the Aircraft and Shipbuilding Industries Bill. The Bill, designed to take the industries into public ownership, had not survived the short 1974 Parliament, had been reintroduced in the 1975–6 session, spent fifty-eight days in Standing Committee, and then been delayed because a Conservative backbencher, Robin Maxwell-Hyslop, had claimed that it was a hybrid bill. Attempts by the Government to overturn the Speaker's ruling, involving allegations of cheating in the division lobbies (a 'paired' Labour MP voting to give the Government a majority of one), led to Michael Heseltine famously swinging the mace, in protest, in the chamber. When the Bill went to the Lords, the House voted by 190 votes to 90 to remove ship repairing from its provisions. It was not the only bill during the Parliament that, courtesy of members of both Houses, gave the Government's business managers headaches.

Survival

It was thus a troubled Parliament but its most remarkable feature was its longevity. The survival of the Government into a fifth session may be ascribed to three variables.

First, there was the relative rarity of opposition parties combining to defeat the Government. On a range of issues, the Liberals and nationalist MPs had more in common with Labour than with the Conservatives. It was this, more than anything else, that ensured that the Government was able to carry all but forty-two of approximately 1,500 votes held during the course of the five-session Parliament. Furthermore, opposition parties were not always enthusiastic about the prospect of an early election. Though the Conservatives were at times riding high in the opinion polls – in early 1977 the Party in one poll enjoyed a lead of more than 16 per cent – the electoral fortunes of other parties were not necessarily so rosy. For nationalist MPs, an early election would not necessarily have been to their electoral advantage. The same applied to the Liberals. In 1977, when co-operation with the Government was being discussed, David Steel received the results of findings from party officials of whether the Party was prepared for an election: 'Their conclusion was that though the Party was not anxious for an election we were marginally more ready than in February 1974.'[24] Though Liberal MPs agreed to vote against the Government if the Party did not achieve the concessions it wanted, the backdrop was one that, in electoral terms, was not necessarily favourable. During the period of the

Lib–Lab Pact, Liberal support in the polls slipped, from 11.5 per cent in April 1977 to 8 per cent by the end of the year.[25]

Second, there was the successful operation of the whips and the Government's business managers. The effectiveness of the whips lies not in their disciplinary powers (they have very few) but rather in their power of persuasion and their organisational skills. The Government chief whips in the Parliament, Bob Mellish and Michael Cocks, were highly effective, assisted by a deputy, Walter Harrison, generally acknowledged by Labour MPs as being an outstanding occupant of that office. During the Parliament, the whips plied their skills with vigour. As one government whip, Betty Boothroyd, recalled: 'we were the first to arrive and the last to leave'.[26] The whips made sure they knew where all their MPs were and, as necessary, kept them in the House for important votes or brought them back from wherever they were – Shirley Williams was called back from China after a seventeen-hour flight getting there.

> That Whip's Office, without the help of any mobile phones, pagers etc., simply because these things had not been invented, knew the whereabouts of every one of the 300-odd Labour MPs instantly. And if they did not they could damn well soon find them.[27]

If MPs showed signs of wavering, the whips adapted their skills accordingly. Cocks and Harrison, according to a fellow whip, were skilled at playing the 'good cop, bad cop' routine, being able to play either role effectively.[28] They could, as occasion demanded, be forceful: 'I once saw hardman Harrison grab hold of Eric Heffer by his lapels on the Commons Terrace and threaten to throw him over the wall into the Thames if he didn't get into the Chamber and effin' vote.'[29]

The whips were helped by the Leader of the House, Michael Foot, who proved a skilled negotiator, as well as by the culture that prevailed in the Government. There was a recognition from the top down that Parliament was an important institution. Wilson, like his successor, took the House seriously. Wilson 'resisted almost every attempt to pay overseas visits while the House of Commons was sitting'.[30] He spent time in the House. So too did his ministers. They were needed for votes, so they spent time being visible in the House. It was not unusual, recalled one backbencher, to see ministers in the tea room at 2 or 3 a.m.[31] It was not just the whips who stayed in touch with backbench opinion. So too did Downing Street. Wilson held a Friday morning meeting with the Chief Whip and Leader of the House, and others, to discuss House of Commons matters.[32] Bernard Donoughue, the Prime Minister's Senior Policy Adviser, would usually go over from Number 10 two evenings a week to spend time in the tea room and bars to hear what members' concerns were.[33] It was thus possible for the PM and ministers to anticipate reaction and to meet worried backbenchers.

The whips were also helped by the fact that channels of communication were institutionalised, as in previous periods of government, through a Liaison

Committee, composed of backbenchers and ministers (including the Chief Whip and Leader of the House), to act as a conduit between the Government and backbenchers. The Committee also had the task of ensuring the effective functioning of backbench subject groups. The groups, previously many in number but failing to attract much of an attendance, were reorganised in the 1976–7 session.[34] The changes did not necessarily have all the effects hoped of them: the expansion of the number of backbenchers on the Liaison Committee to make it more representative still left it dominated by centre–right MPs; by 1977 no backbench member of the Tribune Group served on it. The subject groups remained less influential than their Conservative counterparts. Nonetheless, some members, especially chairmen of the groups, believed that the groups had some influence on policy;[35] one backbencher believes that, given the imperatives of the situation, ministers were more willing to listen, with the Foreign and Commonwealth Affairs Group being especially active.[36] Backbench regional groups, set up to liaise with regional party organisations, were also active. The effect of this institutionalisation was that there was an infrastructure that could absorb criticism and ensure views reached whips and ministers before being made public.

Third, there were negotiations with opposition parties. The most visible, but not the only, effect was the Lib–Lab Pact. This lasted for just over a year and ensured that the Government stayed in office.[37] In return for a government commitment to consult and to pursue certain measures, such as devolution and the European Assembly Elections Bill, the Liberals 'would work with the Government in pursuit of economic recovery'. This meant support from the Liberals in key votes. It was negotiated in order to save the Government in a confidence vote in 1976 and, as such, it succeeded. However, it was of limited utility. The Liberals were not averse to voting against the Government on a range of issues and they got relatively little from the Pact. It was also not popular with all Liberal activists or with all members of the PLP. In many ways, a more effective relationship, though not amounting to a pact, was achieved with another opposition party, the Ulster Unionists. The Unionists, led by James Molyneaux, were effective negotiators and Callaghan and Foot established good relations with Molyneaux.[38] As a consequence, the Unionists achieved the House of Commons (Redistribution of Seats) Bill, providing that the number of parliamentary seats for Northern Ireland, then set at twelve, should be 'not greater than eighteen or less than sixteen'. The Ulster Unionists got more out of negotiations than arguably the Liberals. The Government achieved its aim of staying in office.

The Government thus survived well into a fifth session of Parliament. It was only brought down by the combination of the outcome of the devolution referendums – triggering the tabling of a motion of no confidence – and the serious illness of a Labour MP, Dr Alfred Broughton. The whips had variously brought in sick and injured MPs for crucial votes – the MPs staying in ambulances in New Palace Yard to be nodded through by the whips – and on occasion Dr Broughton, who was seriously ill, was brought in against the advice of his doctor.

Though other sick MPs were brought in for the confidence vote, on this occasion Broughton's doctor said that if he were brought in for the vote he would go public. After reflecting on the matter, Callaghan made the decision that Broughton should not be brought in.[39] The Government lost by one vote. Alfred Broughton died a few days later.

Consequences

The consequences of what happened during the 1974–9 Parliament were significant for the institution itself. The most important and lasting consequence was structural.

For Parliament, the period from 1974 to 1979 was both the best of times and the worst of times. It was the best of times in that Parliament was able to affect the outcomes of public policy. It was a constraint on government. Such was its impact that one academic study concluded that it was developing the capacity to be a transformative legislature, able to mould and shape measures of public policy.[40] It was the worst of times in that the House of Commons limited the Government only on a sporadic basis and it was but one of many influences on the Government – and a reactive one at that. The Government achieved passage of most of the measures it wanted. Wilson was able to draw attention to the fact that, in terms of legislative output and parliamentary activity, the 1974–5 session was busier than the busiest sessions of the reforming 1945–50 Parliament.[41] The Government was influenced by many bodies, including the International Monetary Fund, some of which were more important than Parliament in the *making* of public policy. Though the Government might anticipate parliamentary reaction, MPs were not involved in the genesis and formulation of measures of public policy. There were no formal mechanisms through which MPs could be involved. The party backbench groups offered some means of specialisation and there were some select committees in the House, but there was no comprehensive means by which the House could have some consistent and targeted involvement in the policy process.

During the Parliament MPs thus exhibited some political strength (the essentially negative power to say 'no' to the Government) with a growing sense of frustration. This frustration found various outlets. In 1976, for example, Edward du Cann, the Chairman of the Public Accounts Committee, drew attention to the fact that the House lacked 'adequate machinery for scrutinising expenditure plans before being called on to vote the money involved'.[42] Other criticisms of the incapacity of the House to scrutinise and challenge the Government effectively were voiced by MPs and commentators.[43] The Government acknowledged the case for a review of practice and procedure – an acknowledgement embodied in the Queen's Speech in 1975 – and, following a debate in February, the House in June 1976 appointed a Procedure Committee 'to consider the practice and procedure of the House in relation to public business and to make recommendations for the more effective performance of its functions'.

The Procedure Committee, comprising some significant parliamentary figures,[44] held sixty-eight meetings before reporting in July 1978. The Committee's report argued that

> the balance of advantage between Parliament and Government in the day to day working of the Constitution is now weighted in favour of Government to a degree which arouses widespread anxiety and is inimical to the proper working of our parliamentary democracy.[45]

The Committee believed that 'a new balance must be struck' and made recommendations for reform of the legislative process as well as for replacing the piecemeal system of select committees with 'a system of new, independent, select committees, each charged with the examination of all aspects of expenditure, administration and policy in a field of administration within the responsibilities of a single government department or two or more related departments'.[46] Between them, the committees would cover all government departments.

Pressure built up in the House for the Committee's report to be debated. Michael Foot, as Leader of the House, resisted the demands: he believed in the centrality of the chamber as the debating arena of the nation. (He argued that draining away the energies of MPs in committees would 'destroy the distinctive qualities of the British House of Commons'.) His opposition to change was shared by members of the Cabinet. However, the pressure from backbenchers was too great and Foot conceded a debate. In the debate, in February 1979, he resisted demands for a vote on the Committee's recommendations. Again, pressure from MPs on both sides was such that he conceded the case for a vote. As *The Economist* recorded, 'MPs were in no mood to be fobbed off. Support for the proposals and demands for a vote came from all sides of the House.'[47] Before a vote could be arranged, the Government fell. In the new Parliament, the reform-minded Leader of the House, Norman St John-Stevas, moved quickly to put motions before the House. In June 1979, the House – by 248 votes to 12 – agreed to the establishment of a series of departmental select committees.

The committees that are now a central and indispensable part of the parliamentary landscape thus have their origins in the 1974–9 Parliament. Members' frustrations, and the recognition that, through their votes, they had some political leverage, led to the most important parliamentary reform of the past fifty years.

There was also a consequence in terms of behaviour and attitudes. Underpinning the structural reforms was a change of attitude, deriving from the behavioural change of the 1970s. MPs in the 1970s proved willing to defeat governments in the division lobbies. This willingness was demonstrated first under the Heath Government of 1970–4: the Government suffered six defeats when Tory MPs entered a whipped opposition lobby.[48] The defeats demonstrated that governments could lose votes in the House without losing office. The Heath Government acted in line with past practice. This was important for what happened under the Labour Government. On the one hand, it showed government backbenchers that they could defeat the Government on particular issues without the defeat having any wider, constitutional implications. On the other, it allowed the Government to accept defeat and move on. The Wilson–Callaghan Government acted in line with precedent in reacting to defeats. If defeated on a vote of confidence, it followed convention and sought a dissolution (the alternative was simply to resign). When defeated on a major issue (as on the Expenditure White Paper in 1976), it could resign or (the favoured alternative) seek a vote of confidence from the House. On all other defeats, it had only to decide whether to accept the defeat or seek, in effect, to reverse it at a later stage.[49] It could thus continue in office despite a string of defeats. For backbenchers, they could continue to impose defeats.

Recognition of what they could achieve through such behaviour led to a change of attitude on the part of MPs, or rather some MPs. In the words of Sam Beer, they discarded their previous deferential attitude in favour of a more participatory attitude: they wanted to be more involved in the making of public policy.[50] They therefore favoured select committees and were willing to press government in a way they had not previously been prepared to do. In subsequent Parliaments, MPs had less effect, largely because of the parliamentary arithmetic: a large overall majority can absorb small levels of backbench dissent more effectively than a small one. Even so, dissent was not without effect: there were various defeats in standing committees during the 1980s and the Thatcher Government lost the second reading of the Shops Bill in 1986 when seventy-two Tory MPs voted with the Opposition: it was the first time in the twentieth century that a government with a working majority had lost a bill at second reading. Dissension also remained a feature of Labour's ranks in the 1980s, though in the 1990s it was overshadowed by the publicity attracted by Conservative dissent: the split over European integration under a Conservative Government (1992–7) with a small and at times non-existent majority attracted media attention. The fact that Labour MPs were split on a wider range of issues than Conservative MPs largely passed unnoticed.[51]

Labour MPs in the wake of victory in the 1997 general election were largely united in supporting the Government.[52] The contrast with the 1974–9 Parliament is stark. The Government in 1997 enjoyed a large parliamentary majority and for most of the Parliament it was riding high in the opinion polls: it appeared to be delivering what was expected of it. There were not significant external pressures on backbench MPs leading them to question what the Government was doing. This may have been facilitated by the high turnover in the 1997 election: one-third of MPs were new. However, for the Parliament returned in 2001, the contrast with 1974–9 is less stark. The Government saw its support dip, there was widespread popular disquiet over several policies, and backbench dissent became a significant feature of the Parliament. Its policy on Iraq led to the largest rebellion suffered by any government in modern British history on a major issue of policy. By the middle of the Parliament, it was witnessing a situation not dissimilar to the Wilson–Callaghan Government of

1974–9 in terms of the willingness of most of its backbenchers to refuse to support the Government on one or more occasions. The Government's overall majority has proved able to absorb the dissent, but there appears to have been behavioural and attitudinal changes that mirror those of the 1970s. There has also been growing backbench frustration at the failure to be able to scrutinise and influence the Government. Demands for reforms of practice and procedures have been as marked as in the 1970s.

There are, though, two significant differences that have rendered the Blair Government vulnerable. The first has been the attitude of the leadership. Though some ministers have been good at negotiating with backbenchers, Tony Blair has not followed Wilson and Callaghan in taking Parliament seriously.[53] He has met groups of backbenchers (with greater frequency than did Wilson or Callaghan) but there is not the same attention to, or the same attendance in, Parliament as exhibited by Wilson or Callaghan. Harold Wilson once made a point of attending a debate to listen to a junior minister make his first speech at the despatch box. There is little likelihood of Tony Blair ever contemplating such an action. He is, in essence, detached from the process.

The second has been the work of the whips. Here the problem has been one of emulation when it has not been necessary. In the 1997 Parliament, the whips were largely viewed as ineffective.[54] Despite the Government's large overall majority, the whips treated many votes as requiring a large attendance of members. The approach was somewhat mechanistic and took compliance as a given. Chief Whip Nick Brown exhibited 'an air of quiet menace'[55] when such a stance was not necessary to achieve the desired outcome. Unlike in 1974–9, backbenchers could not see why they should be required to turn out in such numbers. The means of communication between back- and frontbenches were not as extensive or as effective as in the 1970s.

The combined effect of apparent indifference on the part of the leadership and stringent expectations on the part of the whips created the conditions for disquiet and dissent. The difficulty for the Government comes not from the 'usual suspects' – the Campaign Group of left-wing MPs – but from members of all parts of the Party combining against it. That was the case in 1974–9 and it remains the case. The Wilson–Callaghan Government could not avoid attracting opposition from different parts of the PLP, but it had in place mechanisms for reducing its extent. The Blair Government lacks the attitude and infrastructure necessary to achieve the same.

Notes

1   Mezey, M., *Comparative Legislatures* (Duke University Press, Durham, NC, 1979); Norton, P., 'Parliament and Policy in Britain: The House of Commons as a Policy Influencer', in Norton, P. (ed.), *Legislatures* (Oxford University Press, Oxford, 1990), pp. 177–80.
2   Wilson, H., *Final Term: The Labour Government 1974–76* (Weidenfeld and Nicolson/Michael Joseph, London, 1979), pp. 13–14.
3   David Wood, *The Times*, 9 May 1974.

4　*The Times*, 10 May 1974; 14 June 1974; Norton, P., *Dissension in the House of Commons 1974–1979* (Clarendon Press, Oxford, 1980), p. 450.

5　Norton, *Dissension in the House of Commons 1974–1979*, p. 491.

6　Norton, P., 'Intra-Party Dissent in the House of Commons: The Parliament of 1974', *The Parliamentarian*, LVIII(4), October 1977, pp. 240–5.

7　Thatcher, M., *The Path to Power* (HarperCollins, London, 1995), p. 312.

8　Norton, *Dissension in the House of Commons 1974–1979*, pp. 491–3.

9　Thatcher, *The Path to Power*, p. 312.

10　Tebbit, N., *Upwardly Mobile* (Futura, London, 1989), p. 182.

11　Castle, B., *The Castle Diaries 1974–76* (Weidenfeld and Nicolson, London, 1980), p. 466.

12　Berrington, H., 'The Labour Left in Parliament: Maintenance, Erosion and Renewal', in Kavanagh, D. (ed.), *The Politics of the Labour Party* (George Allen and Unwin, London, 1982), pp. 83–4.

13　See Norton, *Dissension in the House of Commons 1974–1979*, pp. 433–4.

14　Piper, J.R., 'Backbench Rebellion, Party Government and Consensus Politics: The Case of the Parliamentary Labour Party 1966–70', *Parliamentary Affairs*, 27, 1974, pp. 384–96.

15　Norton, *Dissension in the House of Commons 1974–1979*, p. 434.

16　Ibid., Table 3, p. 432.

17　Seyd, P., *The Rise and Fall of the Labour Left* (Macmillan, London, 1987), p. 15.

18　Hodgson, G., *Labour at the Crossroads* (Martin Robertson, Oxford, 1981), p. 114.

19　Benn, T., *Against the Tide: Diaries 1973–76* (Arrow Books, London, 1989), pp. 529–30.

20　Benn, *Against the Tide*, p. 30. See also Castle, *The Castle Diaries 1974–76*, pp. 680–3.

21　From 1974 to 1978, the Government suffered a total of sixty-four defeats in standing committees as a result of Labour MPs cross-voting. Schwarz, J., 'Exploring a New Role in Policy Making: The British House of Commons in the 1970s', *American Political Science Review*, 74, 1980, pp. 23–37. We do not have data showing how many of these were attributable to cross-voting by Tribune Group MPs.

22　Barnett, J., *Inside the Treasury, 1974–79* (Andre Deutsch, London, 1982), p. 120.

23　Benn, *Against the Tide*, p . 372.

24　Steel, D., *A House Divided* (Weidenfeld and Nicolson, London, 1980), p. 35.

25　Gallup Poll; Recorded in *The Political Companion*, 27, Summer 1978, p. 80.

26　Boothroyd, B., *The Autobiography* (Century, London, 2001), p. 99.

27　Ashton, J., *Red Rose Blues* (Macmillan, London, 2000), p. 182.

28　Ted Graham (Lord Graham of Edmonton) to author, 2003.

29　Ashton, *Red Rose Blues*, p. 180.

30　Haines, J., *Glimmers of Twilight* (Politico's, London, 2003), p. xiv.

31　Former Labour MP to author, 2003.

32　Callaghan, J., *Time and Chance* (Fontana, London, 1988), p. 300; Lord Donoughue to author, 2003.

33　Lord Donoughue to author, 2003.

34　Norton, P., 'The Organization of Parliamentary Parties', in Walkland, S.A. (ed.), *The House of Commons in the Twentieth Century* (Clarendon Press, Oxford, 1979), pp. 24–5, 44–7.

35　Norton, 'The Organization of Parliamentary Parties', p. 45.

36　Labour member of the 1974–9 Parliament to author, 2003.

37　See Michie, A. and Hoggart, S., *The Pact* (Quartet, London, 1978); Butler, D., *Coalitions in British Politics* (Macmillan, London, 1978), ch. 5; Steel, *A House Divided*.

38　See Callaghan, *Time and Chance*, pp. 454–5.

39　Former Labour whip to author, 2003.

40　Schwarz, 'Exploring a New Role in Policy Making: the British House of Commons in the 1970s', pp. 23–37.

41　Wilson, *The Final Term*, p. 122.

42 *The Times*, 22 October 1976.
43 Norton, P., *The Commons in Perspective* (Martin Robertson, Oxford, 1981), p. 207.
44 The members included Kenneth Baker, Alan Beith, George Cunningham, Norman Lamont, David Marquand, John Peyton, Enoch Powell, Giles Radice, David Renton and Nicholas Ridley.
45 First Report from the Select Committee on Procedure, Session 1977–8, vol. 1. HC 588-I, para. 1.5, p. viii.
46 First Report from the Select Committee on Procedure, para. 5.21, p. liv.
47 *The Economist*, 24 February 1979, pp. 23–4, cited in Norton, *The Commons in Perspective*, p. 231.
48 Norton, P., *Conservative Dissidents* (Temple Smith, London, 1978).
49 Norton, P., 'Government Defeats in the House of Commons: Myth and Reality', *Public Law*, 1978, pp. 360–78.
50 Beer, S.H., *Britain against Itself* (Faber and Faber, London, 1982), p. 190.
51 Cowley, P. and Norton, P., with Stuart, M. and Bailey, M., *Blair's Bastards: Discontent within the Parliamentary Labour Party*, Research Papers in Legislative Studies 1/96 (Hull University Centre for Legislative Studies, 1996).
52 Cowley, P., *Revolts and Rebellions* (Politico's, London, 2002).
53 See Norton, P., 'Governing Alone', *Parliamentary Affairs*, 56(4), September 2003.
54 Cowley, *Revolts and Rebellions*, p. 152.
55 'Profile: Nick Brown', BBC News On-Line, 8 November 1998, cited in Norton, P., 'Parliament', in Seldon, A. (ed.), *The Blair Effect* (Little, Brown, London, 2001), p. 53.

12 Central and local government

Kevin Theakston and Ed Gouge

Under both Labour and Conservative Governments, the 1960s and the early 1970s had seen major reforms and reorganisation of central and local government, affecting the civil service, the pattern of Whitehall ministries, the organisation and functions of local authorities, and local councils' management structures. However, the reform impetus slackened and was lost under the 1974–9 Labour Governments. In Whitehall, Labour had to its credit the establishment of the Number 10 Policy Unit advising the Prime Minister and the introduction of ministerial political advisers, but its record in other respects (e.g. on the freedom of information issue) was disappointing and served only to fuel criticism and pressures for reform. Central and local government co-existed without severe conflicts in these years, but – against a background of economic crisis – the issues of local government spending and of central controls over local finance and local policies began to surface, and the first steps were taken towards greater control by Whitehall. After 1979 the institutions and personnel of central and local government were on the receiving end of much more radical, determined and intrusive reforming policies and actions than anything the 1974–9 Labour Governments envisaged or attempted.

Labour and Whitehall

The theme of civil service sabotage and obstruction of socialist ministers had been voiced on the Labour left before Labour took office in 1974. 'Whitehall: The Other Opposition' was the suggestive title of a *New Statesman* article in March 1974, arguing that the Government would face an uphill struggle to avoid being baulked and its policies emasculated by the civil service: 'a great deal of blood will have to be spilt in Whitehall'. In opposition, Marcia Williams had written of Labour's 'defeats' in the 'battle against the civil service' 1964–70, and Barbara Castle had published an influential article ('Mandarin Power') about her experiences in the 1960s, in which she had painted a picture of the negative power of the civil service and of embattled ministers locked in combat with a hostile bureaucracy. Richard Crossman's diaries also fuelled the 'central conspiracy theory' view of the civil service machine.[1]

In a book published soon after Labour's defeat in 1979, purporting to explain *What Went Wrong*, Michael Meacher indicted the process of government itself, condemning Whitehall's 'abuse of power' and arguing that the civil service 'subverts the effect of the democratic vote'. The Labour Party NEC Machinery of Government Study Group, chaired by the left-wing MP Eric Heffer and meeting 1976–8, claimed that civil service power eroded ministerial account-ability and called for the creation of ministerial 'political offices' (or *cabinets*) and for greater ministerial control over top civil service appointments, with ministers able to remove or transfer senior officials in their departments. (If this recom-mendation had been acted upon, it is likely that Labour rather than Mrs Thatcher would have been accused of politicising the higher civil service.) The civil service had an 'inbuilt anti-socialist bias', insisted members of the Study Group, and its supposed impartiality was 'a constitutional myth which acts to the positive detriment of a Labour government'.[2]

Brian Sedgemore, Tony Benn's PPS, launched a vitriolic and widely publi-cised attack on Whitehall and on officials in an alternative first chapter of the 1977 Expenditure Committee report on the civil service, backed by all except one of the Labour MPs on that parliamentary committee. On this view the civil service was a threat to democracy, politically biased, frustrated radical ministers, and was 'stuffed with reactionaries ruthlessly pursuing their own reactionary policies'. Tony Benn, who wrote in his diary of 'the terrifying power of officials', believed that Sedgemore's critique was 'absolutely right'.[3]

At the Department of Industry and then at Energy, Benn effectively shut himself off from his officials and operated independently with his special advisers. Some of his officials were unhappy about his policies and supported Number 10 against their own minister. But Benn's experience suggests that when a Labour Prime Minister and Cabinet are clear about what they want, they do not find the civil service blocking their way, though as in that case, a departmental minister out of step with his political colleagues may choose to complain of civil service obstruction. If Benn and his policies had had the confidence and backing of the Prime Minister and Labour Cabinet, the story would have been different.

Some ministers on the Labour right subsequently testified to the power of the Whitehall machine. The abrasive David Owen recalled clashes with some staff in the Foreign Office who 'seemed to want to carry on conducting foreign policy on the lines that they thought right, irrespective of what ministers wanted'. Joel Barnett, on the basis of his time as Chief Secretary to the Treasury, bluntly stated that ' "the system" can defeat ministers'. Shirley Williams described the civil service as 'a beautifully designed and effective braking mechanism', producing 'a hundred well-argued answers against initiative and change'. But she (correctly) insisted that it was wrong to describe the civil service as a collec-tivity as being either pro-Conservative or pro-socialist; each department had its own ethos and outlook.

There was an impressive group of Whitehall 'top brass' in post in this period, including John Hunt (Cabinet Secretary), Frank Cooper (Defence), Patrick

Nairne (DHSS), Ian Bancroft (DoE then CSD), Douglas Wass (Treasury) and Leo Pliatzky (Treasury). Wilson's relations with officials, 1974–6, were good, though his close aide Marcia Williams (Lady Falkender) continued to suspect civil service 'plots'. For his part, Callaghan valued the 'wait a minute' function of the civil service. He had initially been wary of the Foreign Office diplomats in 1974 but soon established excellent working relations. As PM, he strongly supported the traditional model of a neutral and un-politicised career civil service (believing in the 1990s that it had become more politicised under the Conservatives). His Number 10 aides felt that the Education Department's response to Callaghan's 'Great Debate' Ruskin speech revealed Whitehall at its complacent, self-satisfied and unimaginative worst. In this vein, Denis Healey shrewdly criticised Whitehall's 'obsession with procedure rather than policy', its poor record at handling change, and the system's 'tendency to produce a soggy compromise'. His view was that it was the 'sheer intractability of the process of government' that was the problem rather than 'bureaucratic sabotage or political prejudice' on the part of the civil service.

With an election looming, the feeling that the Government was a lame duck was detectable in some parts of Whitehall from 1978 onwards (to the concern of both Benn and, apparently, Callaghan).[4] The civil service certainly found the experience of the late 1970s, and particularly Labour's lack of a firm majority, debilitating and frustrating. During the 'Winter of Discontent', key officials were cautious in the face of union power, opposed to the use of troops and to declaring a state of emergency – as were most ministers. The 1979 election had the positive result from Whitehall's point of view of producing a government with a clear mandate and firm policies. But, overall, the power of a conservative civil service machine is not a convincing explanation for the failure of the Wilson and Callaghan administrations to meet their objectives.

The 1974–9 Labour Governments extended and institutionalised the practice of ministers bringing advisers from outside the civil service into their departments. The total number of these special or political advisers working in Whitehall was around twenty-five to thirty, spread around departments mainly in ones or twos (though four or five worked in the DHSS and half a dozen in the Number 10 Policy Unit). This was, on balance, a successful innovation in government, providing extra eyes, ears and arms for hard-pressed ministers. Special advisers were able to supplement and complement the work of officials by variously: helping to keep ministers in touch with the Party (including Transport House, NEC subcommittees and the unions) and with relevant pressure groups; by providing alternative ideas on policy options to those presented by the department; by playing a 'mine-detector' role on politically sensitive issues; by 'progress chasing' on decisions; by helping to handle the media (and here there was nothing like the post-1997 controversies about 'spin-doctors'); and by briefing ministers on Cabinet agenda items outside their departmental fields of responsibility. Whereas some advisers contributed impressive subject expertise (e.g. Brian Abel-Smith at the DHSS), others were more general political aides and party linkmen (e.g. Jack Straw at the same department). Though some were marginalised and ineffective, and there were clashes and tensions in some departments (e.g. with Benn and his clique of advisers), senior officials generally came to welcome the contribution that special advisers made and, indeed, persuaded some ministers of the advantages of appointing them. There were too few special advisers to supplant the mass of career bureaucrats and they had no executive powers or place in the administrative chain of command implementing decisions. They also failed to develop an effective interdepartmental net to parallel that of the civil service. But if they were not a 'counter civil service', neither were they a 'minor cosmetic'.

The Treasury is often a hate-object and scapegoat in Labour circles, and 1974–9 was no exception. Its critics were not just on the Labour left, however, for Number 10 advisers like Bernard Donoughue and Joe Haines were mistrustful of its power and motives, and Callaghan displayed a mixture of respect for and suspicion of the Treasury. But on key economic policy issues, the 1974–9 Labour Governments took their own decisions rather than rubber-stamping the Treasury's. There are accusations that the Treasury tried to 'bounce' ministers into accepting a statutory incomes policy in 1975, but this pressure was resisted by Number 10 advisers and the Chancellor, Denis Healey, eventually abandoned his own officials' proposals, resulting in Labour's pay policy being a voluntary rather than statutory one. During the 1976 IMF loan crisis, there were claims that some Treasury officials were secretly briefing the US Government and the IMF in order to increase pressure on the Government for large spending cuts. It was also suggested that public sector borrowing figures were inflated to create a crisis atmosphere and panic ministers into cutting spending (though Healey does not blame the Treasury for this – outside forecasters did not have a better record than the Treasury). In fact the Treasury was divided: there were a minority of 'hawks' who backed the IMF line and wanted savage cuts, but other officials opposed cuts or came round finally to accept them but not on the scale the IMF wanted (the course the Cabinet adopted). It is worth noting that the introduction of cash limits in 1976, which led to massive under-spending against targets (at times on a scale matching the Cabinet's planned cuts), received strong political support from Labour's Treasury ministers and actually faced some opposition from within the Treasury itself.

As Prime Minister after 1976, Callaghan showed the Treasury no deference. His Policy Unit, a more assertive Cabinet Office headed by Sir John Hunt and the PM's top-secret 'Economic Seminar' all challenged its power and helped the PM to tighten his political grip on the key economic discussions and decisions. There was no monolithic 'Treasury line' constraining Labour ministers – there was at official level a spectrum of opinion about the management of the economy, from Keynesians through to monetarists. The Treasury was of course influential between 1974 and 1979, but it was not a decisive voice.

In contrast to the technocratic and reforming attitudes of the 1960s, which had inspired the appointment of the Fulton Committee on the Civil Service and led the then Labour Government to accept its main recommendations in 1968, Labour ministers in the 1970s appeared for the most part to be firm supporters of the Whitehall status quo. Attitudes at the top towards Whitehall reform during the 1974–9 Governments were very different from in 1964–70. Wilson in 1974 had none of the modernising zeal of 1964. His approach to the machinery of government had become much more low key, and he dismembered the giant Department of Trade and Industry largely for reasons of Cabinet management and political balancing between Labour's factions. Although he carved out a separate Department of Transport from the Department of the Environment, Callaghan, too, shared the caution and scepticism prevailing in the mid-1970s among senior politicians of both main parties and among senior officials as regards the likely benefits of structural redesign in central government.

It had been Callaghan (then Chancellor of the Exchequer) who had actually formally recommended to Wilson back in November 1965 the appointment of a committee to carry out 'a wide ranging inquiry' into the civil service, saying that some 'pretty radical' measures might be necessary. He later (in 1993) said that he supported 'the broad thrust' of the Fulton report and claimed that he would have liked 'to have seen more done' about civil service reform during 1976–9 but that he was constrained by the lack of a majority and the pressure of other urgent issues. However, his biographer, Kenneth Morgan, argues that as Prime Minister, 'Callaghan felt that the civil service worked well and efficiently and was a model for other nations. There was no need to tamper with it. ... [He] felt that the civil service should be left alone.' He vetoed the idea of an inquiry into the civil service when Labour's election manifesto was being put together in April 1979.[5]

Progress on the Fulton reforms of the civil service had petered out or been halted by about the end of 1972, under Heath. Labour's 'Fultonites' – Norman Hunt (Lord Crowther-Hunt), Robert Sheldon and John Garrett – continued to evangelise on behalf of the totemic report, Garrett and Sheldon putting forward (in a 1973 Fabian Society pamphlet) radical proposals for a Prime Minister's Department, 'programme budgeting' and 'departmental agencies' (similar to the Next Steps agencies introduced in the 1990s). But the Labour Government was not really interested in and had no stomach for another round of administrative reform. Little headway was made in developing institutions and techniques to improve management efficiency and policy analysis in government. Heath's Programme Analysis and Review (PAR) technique of 'management by objectives' lingered on under Labour but had no real bite (it was abolished by Mrs Thatcher in 1979, whose Efficiency Unit headed by Derek Rayner from Marks & Spencer spearheaded a radical management shake-up). The role of the Heath-created Central Policy Review Staff (CPRS) was also more narrowly defined under Labour – Wilson regarded it with some suspicion in 1974 as a 'Tory Trojan horse' while Benn attacked it as a tool of a conspiratorial bureaucracy.

When in 1976–7 the House of Commons Expenditure Committee reviewed progress since Fulton in civil service recruitment, training, organisation and management, the Government's response was notably cautious and defensive, promising action only on minor recommendations.[6] The post-Fulton reforming impulse was now nearly spent, and the Expenditure Committee's inquiry seemed very like an inquest or even a wake. Whether the Civil Service Department (CSD), created in 1968 to run the civil service, was a success or whether responsibility for Whitehall efficiency and staff control should be transferred back to the Treasury was an issue strongly debated at this time. MPs on the Expenditure Committee favoured the latter, strengthening the Treasury and making the CSD into more of a personnel department. The Government was non-committal in its official response, but behind the scenes Bernard Donoughue, head of the PM's Policy Unit, was critical of the 'elephantine' and 'imperfect' CSD, which seemed more concerned to protect rather than energise 'cosseted bureaucrats', and wondered whether it should be abolished (as Mrs Thatcher was to do in 1981). Callaghan was apparently also mulling over splitting the Treasury to make a Ministry of Finance and a Bureau of the Budget – which would absorb the CSD – though Denis Healey's opposition scotched these tentative plans. (Had Labour won the 1979 election, Callaghan may have returned to that issue.)[7]

The Government's unwillingness to contemplate major reform of the Whitehall machine and of the mandarinate was also seen in the case of the Foreign Office and the diplomatic service. The CPRS's Review of Overseas Representation (ROR) exercise (1976–7) canvassed radical surgery and called into question the continued survival of the diplomatic service, which it criticised for its elitist social tone and proposed should be merged into the home civil service. The Foreign Office fought back, and the think tank's recommendations about the BBC's external services and the British Council also helped to ensure a devastating Establishment counter-attack, severely damaging the CPRS's reputation. It was not surprising that the Callaghan Government ditched the ROR's main recommendations. Foreign Secretary David Owen had his own ideas about the need to weed out 'duds' and promote younger able staff, and the Government simply brought forward proposals for more interchange with the rest of Whitehall, modest staff economies and further reviews of detailed subjects. Labour was not going to 'take on' the Foreign Office.

The mid- and late 1970s were in fact a crisis period for the civil service. Its size, its power, its (in)efficiency and its perceived 'privileges' (particularly inflation-proofed pensions) all came in for critical scrutiny from politicians and the press. The civil service had stood at 694,000 at the start of 1974, growing to a post-war peak of 746,000 by 1977. The CSD mounted a 'cost of central government review' and the long-term growth of bureaucracy was checked, numbers falling to 733,000 by January 1979. (Mrs Thatcher then went on to make swingeing cuts in the 1980s.) With its 'Wider Issues Review' the CSD tried to introduce a more modern approach to personnel management (a key report, 'Civil Servants and Change', being published in 1975), but this fell victim to the economy drive, cash limits, staff cuts, poor (and deteriorating) labour relations and growing public hostility. The 'Priestley' civil service pay system (dating from the 1950s and based on outside comparisons) seemed less affordable in the harsher economic climate and with government more concerned to limit public spending. Pay research was suspended in 1976 (it was restored two years later but abolished by the Thatcher Government in 1980). The Treasury's cash limits set the parameters for pay bargaining and settlements. Civil service union militancy increased and half a million civil servants went on strike in 1979 to press for a 26 per cent pay claim, defeating the Government's civil service pay policy. The scene was set for further confrontations and cutbacks in the 1980s – and Mrs Thatcher was to be much more aggressive towards the civil service than Labour had been.

Freedom of information and open government reform was another area where the Labour Governments of 1974–9 disappointed would-be Whitehall reformers. Criticism of unnecessary secrecy in government had been mounting since the 1960s. The 1964–70 Labour Governments had introduced a thirty-year rule (previously it had been fifty years) for access to public records. Heath had set up the Franks Committee to review the operation of the draconian and 'catch-all' 1911 Official Secrets Act, which had recommended in 1972 that criminal sanctions should apply to narrower and defined categories of information, but the Conservative Government had taken no further action.

Labour's October 1974 manifesto included a commitment to 'replace the Official Secrets Act by a measure to put the burden on the public authorities to justify withholding information'. Most Labour ministers, however – with Tony Benn a very public and radical exception – were as unenthusiastic or hostile to this as their civil servants, seeing only potential embarrassment and inconvenience in making more information available to the public. Denis Healey and the Treasury took a more liberal view to the extent of being willing to rely on the civil service discipline code rather than the criminal law to protect against the disclosure of economic information. But an early signal was given by the Government's unsuccessful legal battle in 1975, arguing the need for Cabinet confidentiality, in an attempt to ban publication of the Crossman diaries.

Roy Jenkins, who chaired the Cabinet committee on open government set up by Wilson, ruled out a US-style Freedom of Information Act as 'costly, cumbersome and legalistic'. The 1975 Queen's Speech promised that proposals would be prepared, but little had been done when Callaghan succeeded Wilson in April 1976. Unsympathetic to Secrets Act reform, Callaghan was stung by the *New Society*/child benefit scheme leak in June 1976 and decided that he wanted more effective protection of government information. He now chaired the Cabinet committee on this issue. Another leaked memo revealed his view that disclosing any information about the Cabinet committee system 'would be more likely to whet appetites than to satisfy them'. His Home Secretary Merlyn Rees talked, menacingly, of replacing the 'blunderbuss' of Section 2 of the 1911 Act with an 'Armalite rifle'; he dismissively told a Labour backbench critic that probably only two or three people in his constituency were concerned about the open government issue. Proposals unveiled in a White Paper in July 1978 were widely criticised as inadequate and still too restrictive.[8]

A policy of more voluntary disclosure of background factual and analytical information used in policy making was introduced in an attempt to appease and head off critics. This took effect in the 1977 'Croham Directive', which – ironically – only became public knowledge after it was leaked to the press. But the results were limited: the flow of documents from departments was uneven and in some parts of Whitehall the exercise simply became part of the normal public relations machine. Put under pressure by the Labour Party NEC (which prepared its own draft freedom of information bill, approved by the Party Conference in October 1978), by other outside campaigners, and by Liberal MP Clement Freud's private member's FoI bill (January 1979), the Government published in its last days a consultative Green Paper. Playing for time, this talked about the desirability of an evolutionary approach, suggested a possible code of practice on open government, and rejected a statutory right of access to information.[9] However, the Labour left insisted on including a pledge to introduce freedom of information legislation in the Party's 1979 manifesto – Labour's defeat thus perhaps saving Callaghan further opprobrium on this issue. The events of 1974–9 showed the extent of insider resistance to secrecy reform and at the same time fuelled outside critics' and left-wing demands for change. The complexity of the issues involved, the Government's precarious parliamentary position, and the lack of agreement on the details of secrets law reform among its advocates all hindered action. But the Government did not come well out of the story, Labour ministers being criticised as elitist and reactionary even by aides like Bernard Donoughue.

Labour and local government

Anthony Crosland was appointed as Secretary of State for the Environment in 1974, to the brief that he had held in opposition, and, when Callaghan made him Foreign Secretary in 1976, he was replaced by Peter Shore, who remained until the end of the Government. Two key local government issues remained important during their periods in office. The first was that the Labour cities were unhappy with the reorganisation of local government areas and responsibilities which had just been carried out by the Conservatives and so looked to the Government to give them more powers. The second was concern among householders and businesses who were facing sharp rises in 1974 in the rate, the local property tax, that they paid to local authorities. The issue of local government spending soon became more problematic as the economic crisis worsened and the Treasury sought controls as an essential part of the overall limitation of public expenditure. This led to questions of the reform of local government finance and the extent of central control of spending. In addition, ministers had manifesto commitments in policy areas that they shared with local government, in housing, education, land and the inner cities.

Labour entered office in the middle of a major reorganisation of local government which it had opposed when in opposition. The pattern of local authorities had not significantly changed since the reforms of the 1880s and 1890s and the argument had developed in academic and civil service thinking that modern local government had to be larger to be efficient, and to integrate urban and rural areas to catch up with new social and economic relationships. In the old system county borough councils covered the main cities and ran the whole range of services. Many had a strong tradition of innovation and urban improvement and Labour was relatively strong here, though the Conservatives had a stronger suburban vote here than they do today and could take control in good years in cities such as Leeds, Manchester and Newcastle. Elsewhere there was a two-tier system with county councils controlling major services and a patchwork of authorities, some even smaller than 2,000 in population, with more limited functions.[10] London had already been reformed in 1963 in line with the new principles to create a Greater London Council, fairly large London Boroughs and a special purpose Inner London Education Authority.

The previous Labour Government, supported by the Redcliffe-Maud report,[11] had pursued the idea of unitary authorities of some 250,000 in population, based on the major cities. The disappearance of the rural counties and districts was very unpopular with Conservatives and their new Secretary of State for the Environment, Peter Walker, moved quickly to adopt a different pattern. Metropolitan counties were created for the conurbations but were made relatively weak to preserve the power of Conservative-controlled suburban districts in the tier below them. The county boroughs now became second-tier authorities within a pattern of county councils that acquired the major education, social service, planning and transport functions. Rural areas and smaller towns were merged into second-tier authorities below the counties. Similar reorganisations were carried out in Scotland and Wales.

After nearly a hundred years of stability in local government structure, the Local Government Act, 1972, which was meant to set the pattern for decades ahead, was instead the first of a series of reorganisations which have even now not stabilised. Labour councillors in the cities were hostile to a new pattern that saw them disappear into Conservative-dominated counties or lose powers to the new metropolitan counties, even though the latter were likely to be Labour controlled. Labour had opposed the reorganisation in Parliament for creating a wasteful two-tier system but the frontbench felt that the system could not be unravelled when they came to office and so Crosland committed them to maintaining the reforms after the election, though the Act might be amended or individual boundaries changed. The new councillors had been elected in 1973 and the new authorities were to come into being on 1 April 1974 after a major effort in reorganising staff and services and transferring records. Labour councillors kept up their pressure, however, and by 1978 Shore, while avoiding a full reorganisation, was proposing a process of 'organic change' by which central government would approve the transfer of some responsibility for services from the counties to the larger districts on a case-by-case basis. The general election came before anything could happen, but paradoxically it was the Conservatives who began to argue that the two-tier system was wasteful and abolished the metropolitan counties in the second Thatcher Government and the Welsh and Scottish top-tier authorities and some of the non-metropolitan counties under Major. The chaotic reforms of the early 1990s have produced a pattern that is still unstable with a mixture of two-tier counties and unitaries (Berkshire was abolished because it was reviewed earlier in the process when it would have survived under criteria used at the end).[12] The Labour Party and, to some extent, Labour ministers remain sympathetic to the idea of large unitary authorities and have suggested that this may be the consequence of elected regional authorities.

Since the war many commentators on local government had bemoaned its loss of power to central government as the latter provided more of the funding and became more involved in housing, education, planning and other policies.[13] In practice, the relationship remained subtle with considerable room for manoeuvre by local authorities. The rate support grant, which provided 90 per cent of central government funding, could be spent as local authorities wanted and, although central government had to give permission to borrow for major capital projects, these could also be financed out of revenue or from capital receipts. Most central government policies entailed persuasion rather than direct control.

The new Labour Government faced a local authority system that was changing. There were fewer local authorities as a result of reorganisation, making them large by European standards. They were also more interventionist. The Mallaby, Maud and Bains reports in the previous decade had all emphasised the importance of better trained staff and an officer and committee structure which would allow authorities to look broadly at problems in the community rather than concentrate narrowly on the provision of services.[14] Larger authorities could afford to employ staff in new policy areas and all except one county and ten districts in England appointed a chief executive to oversee the new processes. The Institute for Local Government Studies (INLOGOV) at the University of Birmingham provided an important mechanism for disseminating the new ideas. The new authorities were more expensive. New policies, the costs of reorganisation and high levels of inflation meant that rate increases of up to 50 per cent were expected in the spring of 1974.

When Crosland took over as Secretary of State the level of rate support grant had already been fixed by the previous Government. As part of this the Conservatives had added in a relief payment to cope with the cost of reorganisation. This provided little help to the largest cities where changes in boundaries were more limited, and only 7 pence in the pound in London where there was no change, but up to 40 pence in the pound in other areas. Crosland took a decision to provide a standard level of relief across the country to benefit poorer urban areas despite pressure from Labour MPs who felt that the existing help should be maintained because it benefited suburban areas and medium-sized towns where there were many more marginal constituencies. In this and other key decisions Crosland saw the redistributive effects of policies as more critical than the need to develop middle-class support. He noted, himself, about the decision, 'good and socialist policies not electorally popular'.[15]

In the first year Crosland took two further decisions to try to sort out the problems of local government finance. One of the limitations for local authorities is that, in contrast to many other countries, they have only had the rates as a means to raise revenue locally and this had always been an unpopular tax. Crosland set up the Layfield Committee to consider the whole subject and after a long period of hearing evidence it reported in 1976.[16] Layfield concluded that the problem was a lack of clear accountability for local authority spending. One alternative was for central government to take responsibility, provide all the funding, determine what each local authority should spend and become involved in the complicated process of setting standards of service. The other alternative was to ensure local accountability and provide local authorities with a wider financial base by means of a local income tax. By the time Layfield reported the decision was for Peter Shore and he rapidly rejected the idea of a local income tax even though the Labour Party's own review, chaired by John Cartwright, had supported this option.[17] Instead, civil servants soon picked up some of the centralisation discussion in Layfield and promoted a unitary grant system that depended on an assessment of what each authority should spend. The system was in place for the control of rate levels that the Thatcher Government was to carry out and the responsibility for local government spending remains as confused now as it did in the 1970s.

Crosland's other decision was to create a channel of communication with the local authorities. The Conservative round of expenditure cuts for 1973–4 had been criticised as chaotic by the local authorities and the Conference of Permanent Secretaries had discussed the need for a sounding board with local authority representatives. Crosland took up the suggestion and set up the Consultative Council on Local Government Finance that consisted of the Treasury and other relevant government departments and the local authority associations. The Treasury was now making it quite clear that it believed that local government spending was rising disproportionately within total public spending and that it was diverting resources that could go into exports and industrial investment. It is possible that the Consultative Council was seen by the DoE as a device to prevent the more direct controls over local authorities that the Treasury favoured.[18] The Consultative Council was meeting nine times a year by 1976 and was generally well received by the local authorities, though they felt that they were being informed of what was happening rather than being genuinely consulted or able to give any input into the process of public expenditure review.

The first rate support grant settlement that Crosland controlled, for 1975–6, saw a considerable increase in government support from £3,431 million to £5,430 million, covering 66.5 per cent instead of 60.5 per cent of relevant expenditure.[19] This was needed to meet expectations from Labour councillors and the public for improvements in services under the new government and to limit rate rises. Thereafter the developing financial crisis and the Government's economic policies required a reduction in local authority expenditure. Even before Crosland's well-known 'the party's over' speech in May 1975, Gordon Oakes, the parliamentary Under-Secretary, and John Silkin, the Planning and Local Government Minister, had made similar speeches about the need to limit rate rises and not to assume that the Government would underwrite them.[20]

Local authorities broadly co-operated and by 1977 Shore was praising them for keeping rate rises in check.[21] This was no doubt made easier by the change in control to Conservative by many local authorities in the elections of 1976 and 1977 as the Government became unpopular. By 1978 all the local authority associations were Conservative controlled and in any case would support expenditure limitations. Even among Labour authorities, though unhappiness about the Government's policies existed among councillors and local parties, the leadership had not yet begun to move to the left and was kept in line by key figures such as Sir Lou Sherman at the London Boroughs Association.

Issues of local authority organisation and finance absorbed ministers but they were equally concerned with key policy commitments which local authorities would need to implement. Crosland had wanted the Chancellorship in 1974 but saw no prospect of receiving it while Wilson remained Prime Minister. Nevertheless, he was fully conversant with the DoE brief, having held it for the last five years, and came to enjoy dealing with strategic decisions in a large ministry. Labour's manifesto for February 1974 contained some key commitments with implications for local policy. Labour was pledged to repeal the Conservative's Housing Finance Act which had had the effect of forcing councils to increase council house rents. Labour councillors across the country had delayed implementation and those in Clay Cross in Derbyshire had refused to implement it at all and became heroes of the Labour movement. The Government District Auditors had the power to surcharge all these councillors to pay back any money lost as a result of their decisions and this could lead to bankruptcy and disqualification from office. Labour had also promised more housebuilding in all sectors, and a rent freeze in the private housing sector was one of Wilson's main points during the campaign. Comprehensive, nursery and 16–18 education were all in the manifesto. The 1974 Labour Government, like all previous ones, was committed to land reform. The 1997 Labour Government was the first not to include this in its programme. Labour had inherited from radical liberalism the argument that increases in the value of land result from development and economic activity by the whole community but the benefit in increases in land prices accrued solely to landowners as an 'unearned increment'. The property speculation of the early 1970s had made the issue more salient. Finally, there was a vague promise in the manifesto to improving services in the inner cities.

These manifesto commitments were ones that Crosland himself had advocated in *Socialism Now* which was published soon after Labour came into office.[22] This update of *The Future of Socialism* showed his continuing commitment to social democracy and the role of the state in promoting equality. Although the existence of a capitalist economy was accepted as necessary for economic growth, *Socialism Now* accepted two social democratic principles important to local policy which remain uncertain with New Labour. The first was that the power of landlords was not in the interests of the community, so that private rented housing should be controlled by the state and where possible taken over by local authorities, and that control of land by the public sector was necessary for the effective planning of land use. The second was that local authorities would continue to play as big a role as ever in the direct provision of services. Although experiments were carried out in the way that public provision worked, there was no suggestion between 1974 and 1979 that the private sector should play a bigger role in any of these areas.

Within a week of taking office Crosland had frozen rents in the public and private housing sectors. The Housing Rents and Subsidies Act, 1975, gave power over rents back to local authorities and security of tenure was extended to tenants in furnished, private rented housing. Crosland perceived that, despite these short-term decisions, the existing system of housing finance was inequitable because subsidies benefited home owners and better-off council tenants rather than many poorer tenants in public and private housing. He therefore set up a wide-ranging review of housing finance to question the system but with little success. Labour saw council tenants as its natural constituency and in need of protection, particularly with the Social Contract operating. The Shore period saw only one significant change in housing policy and this was a relaxation of the sale of houses to tenants in new towns following pressure from the Conservatives who were constantly promoting the issue in Parliament.[23] Crosland had also to decide what to do about the councillors who had refused to implement the Conservative legislation on council house rents. At the 1973 Party Conference Ted Short, without consulting the frontbench, had committed the Party to removing their disqualification from office.[24] After considerable discussion, the Cabinet decided to honour the promise and Crosland reluctantly passed the necessary legislation, in contrast to later Labour frontbench views on an amnesty to those charged during the miners' strike and councillors who defied rate capping legislation in the 1980s.

Policies in other areas equally ran into problems. Wilson and Crosland were both strongly in support of land reform.[25] John Silkin, whose father had introduced legislation on this topic in the 1945 Government, saw the Community Land Act through Parliament against fierce Conservative opposition. Local authorities were to acquire land under the Act which could then be developed but most of the financial gain from selling land with planning permission was to go to central government. Reductions in public spending meant there were few resources for acquisition, the increasing number of Conservative authorities were reluctant to use it, and civil servants showed little enthusiasm, almost wrecking the policy with the negative circular of November 1976.[26] In the end it became mainly a superior form of compulsory acquisition for Labour authorities trying to stimulate growth in declining industrial areas rather than a means of gaining the profits that could be made in areas of rapid development. Crosland turned from housing to review transport policy in 1976 and again showed his ability to consider the redistributive effects of existing policy. He shocked DoE officials by questioning the benefits of a motorway programme which served business people (and tongue in cheek suggested that bumpy surfaces resulting from a cutback in motorway maintenance would ensure that drivers did not go to sleep) and also the commuter rail subsidy which helped middle-class suburban and rural residents. The Green Paper instead argued that poorer people used buses and coaches and these should have priority in funding. A lack of resources again limited a change in policy and the Transport Act, 1978, made few changes, though, in any case, Bill Rodgers as the Transport Minister in the later part of the Government showed less sympathy with these priorities.

Peter Shore's main contribution was to develop a new inner city policy. Crosland had seen the whole system of urban aid as chaotic but was preoccupied with too many other urgent issues. An increase in unemployment in previously prosperous areas such as London, Birmingham and Manchester, some electoral success by the racist National Front amongst working-class white people, and his own experience as an MP for an East London constituency led Shore to question existing priorities. Subsidy had gone to traditional areas of higher unemployment such as the North East and South Wales and also to social projects in areas of high black immigration under the assumption that this was a transitional problem of integration which public subsidy could lessen. There now appeared to be a serious problem of the collapse of manufacturing in all big cities. The Inner Urban Areas Act, 1978, allowed local authorities to help declining industrial areas and central government provided new subsidies to the inner city areas with the most problems. Policy failed to consider the more radical alternatives which were either to accept the decentralisation of economic activity from the inner cities and plan for it by a new programme of new towns that could achieve social democratic objectives, or to adopt the more left-wing solution of attempting to control and direct private investment to revive the inner cities and poorer regions.[27] The Conservatives were to adopt a third radical alternative of subsidising and decontrolling the private sector to encourage it to develop inner areas with consequences that Crosland would have been dismayed by.

The period of 1974–9 was one in which central and local government were jointly concerned with key policy areas and co-existed within these without severe conflict. Separate spheres of 'high' and 'low' politics may have existed before 1939,[28] but after 1945 governments were very much concerned with housing and education and, to a significant degree, with other local services as well.[29] In other ways the central–local government relationship was changing. Central government in Britain in 1974, unlike in many continental countries where civil servants have operated 'field services' at the local level, had limited understanding of the details of local services. The experience of the working parties of the Consultative Council and the reorganisation of central grants led service sector groups in central government to make estimates of what different levels of service should cost. New mechanisms introduced between 1972 and 1978, Housing Investment Programme Statements, Transport Policy and Programmes, land use Structure Plans and the central–local Inner City Partnerships, became means by which local government had to provide more detailed statements which increased the knowledge base at the centre. They could then be used for control. Bill Rodgers cut back transport grants to Labour South Yorkshire because of its low-fares policy and to Conservative Oxfordshire because it did not subsidise buses enough.[30] In both cases the local authority had the resources and confidence to ignore central government but the first steps had been taken along the road to rate capping by the Thatcher Governments and the Best Value regime with service standard levels under the Blair Governments. Nevertheless, despite their common involvement with local authorities in areas of policy, Crosland and Shore still respected the existence of separate worlds of local and central government. Local authorities were encouraged into policies, they made their own individual decisions over spending within the centre's framework, there was no attempt to decide the public–private balance and there was no attempt to interfere in the internal operations of local authorities to change the traditional committee system.

Notes

1 See in general for this section: Theakston, K., *The Labour Party and Whitehall* (Routledge, London, 1992).
2 'Reform of the Civil Service', NEC Statements to Annual Conference (Labour Party, London, October 1978); RE 775/September 1976 (Labour Party Archives).
3 Benn, T., *Conflicts of Interest: Diaries 1977–80* (Arrow Books, London, 1990), pp. 157, 215.
4 Benn, *Conflicts of Interest*, pp. 290, 304.
5 Callaghan to Wilson, 1 November 1965, PRO PREM 13/1357; Treasury and Civil Service Committee, *The Role of the Civil Service: Interim Report*, vol. II, Minutes of Evidence (HC 390-II, 1992–3), questions 592–4; Morgan, K.O., *Callaghan: A Life* (Oxford University Press, Oxford, 1997), pp. 509–10; Benn, *Conflicts of Interest*, p. 486.
6 Expenditure Committee, The Civil Service (HC 535, 1976–7); The Civil Service: Government Observations on the Eleventh Report from the Expenditure Committee, Session 1976–77, Cmnd 7117 (HMSO, London, 1978).
7 Donoughue, B., *Prime Minister: The Conduct of Policy under Harold Wilson and James Callaghan* (Cape, London, 1987), p. 27; Donoughue, B., *The Heat of the Kitchen: An Autobiography* (Politico's, London, 2003), pp. 246–7; Hennessy, P., *Whitehall* (Secker and Warburg, London, 1989), pp. 265–6.
8 House of Commons Debates, 22 November 1976, cols 1878–81; 19 July 1978, cols 546–7; *Reform of Section 2 of the Official Secrets Act 1911*, Cmnd 7285 (HMSO, London, 1978).
9 *Open Government*, Cmnd 7520 (HMSO, London, 1979).
10 Richards, P.G., *The Reformed Local Government System* (Allen and Unwin, London, 4th edition, 1980), p. 34.
11 Report of the Royal Commission on Local Government in England, 1966–9, Cmnd 4040 (HMSO, London, 1969).
12 Davis, H., 'Reviewing the Review', *Local Government Studies*, 23(3), 1997, p. 13.
13 Gyford, J., *Local Politics in Britain* (Croom Helm, London, 1976), p. 13, lists authors with this view though he himself sees the relationship as more subtle.
14 Report of the Maud Committee, *The Management of Local Government* (HMSO, London, 1967); Report of the Mallaby Committee, *The Staffing of Local Government* (HMSO, London, 1967); Report of the Bains Committee, *The New Local Authorities: Management and Structure* (HMSO, London, 1972).
15 Crosland, S., *Tony Crosland* (Coronet, London, 1983), p. 266.
16 Report of the Committee into Local Government Finance, Cmnd 6453 (HMSO, London, 1977).
17 *The Times*, 11 January 1975.

18 Taylor, J.A., 'The Consultative Committee on Local Government Finance: A Critical Analysis of Its Origins and Development', *Local Government Studies*, 5(3), 1979, p. 13.
19 *The Times*, 16 January 1975.
20 *The Times*, 5 and 6 February 1975.
21 *The Times*, 29 October 1977.
22 Crosland, C.A.R., 'Socialism Now', in Leonard, D. (ed.), *Socialism Now, and Other Essays* (Cape, London, 1975).
23 *The Times*, 23 May 1978.
24 Castle, B., *The Castle Diaries 1974–76* (Weidenfeld and Nicolson, London, 1980), p. 64.
25 Wilson, H., *Final Term: The Labour Government 1974–76* (Weidenfeld and Nicolson, London, 1979), p. 45.
26 Ash, M., 'Is There a Land Problem?', *Town and Country Planning*, 46(5), 1978, p. 251.
27 Lawless, P., *Urban Deprivation and Government Initiative* (Faber and Faber, London, 1979), pp. 224–6.
28 Bulpitt, J., *Territory and Power in the United Kingdom* (Manchester University Press, Manchester, 1983).
29 Young, K. and Rao, N., *Local Government since 1945* (Blackwell, Oxford, 1997).
30 Skelcher, C., 'Transportation', in Ranson, S., Jones, G. and Walsh, K. (eds), *Between Centre and Locality: The Politics of Public Policy* (Allen and Unwin, London, 1985), pp. 159–60.

13 Devolution

Dilys M. Hill

Introduction

For Harold Wilson:

> Devolution is a boring word, a boring and soporific subject so far as legisla-
> tion is concerned, but potentially a most powerful means of achieving one of
> the highest aims of democracy, bringing the process of decision-making as
> close as possible to the people affected by it.[1]

For John Smith, Minister of State, Privy Council Office, in James Callaghan's
Government:

> We are pioneering something fresh and new. ... We see devolution as some-
> thing positive – a creative evolution of our constitution that will decentralise
> powers, increase local democratic accountability, and give the people of
> Scotland and Wales a much more important say in their own affairs.[2]

The devolution project of the Wilson and Callaghan Governments of 1974–9
raises two important points of Labour doctrine. The first arises from the nature
of the state and of the constitution that legitimises it. The key factor here is
Labour's ability to control and change the political institutions of the state to
enable it to govern. From this perspective the place of the countries and nations
of the United Kingdom is a central constitutional question. A further constitutional issue arises from this: in a political system based on majoritarian rule and
parliamentary sovereignty, what is the place of referendums in guiding the direction of change? The second element of Labour doctrine has been the socialist
tradition that, in Aneurin Bevan's words of 1946, devolution was 'not Socialism
[but] escapism'.[3] The main aim of socialism was economic and social justice for
all, regardless of place, and determined by national policy and standard setting.
But these doctrinal points were unresolved and, in the end, the pursuit of devolution brought down the Callaghan Government.

To explore these issues, this chapter considers five areas. These are: Labour
and devolution before 1974; the Royal Commission on the Constitution (the

Kilbrandon Commission); political realities facing the Labour Government; the impact of constitutional factors; the collapse of the devolution bills in 1979 and the end of the Labour Government.

Labour and devolution before 1974

Historically, Keir Hardie, Ramsay MacDonald and Tom Johnston ((Labour) Secretary of State for Scotland during the Second World War) had all supported the principle of Home Rule for Scotland. But when Labour came to power in 1945, it viewed devolution as a distraction from the Party's true aims of governing in the name of universal economic and social justice. To this end, centralisation was preferable to devolution. In the 1970s' debates these views were still being expressed. In the two-day adjournment debate on devolution of February 1975 Welsh MP Neil Kinnock and Scottish MP Tam Dalyell defended the socialist position. Tam Dalyell asserted: 'I must say to the electors of West Lothian … that I would rather be a defeated Socialist candidate than a victorious national candidate.'[4] Neil Kinnock said that the aims of the class he represented 'can best be achieved in a single nation and in a single economic unit'. Nor was devolution the best way to achieve greater participation and reduce feelings of alienation.[5] In the same debate John Morris, Secretary of State for Wales, justified devolution on the grounds that there was a need to bring the process of decision making closer to the ordinary people who were affected by it.[6]

Pragmatically, the Labour Government's view in the mid-1960s, when nationalist strength was increasing, was that this was a protest vote which would subside as quickly as it had grown. Economic setbacks had raised the threat of the nationalist parties,[7] as had Britain's decline as a world power which had reduced attachment to the idea of the United Kingdom as a whole. In Scotland the view gained ground that 'Whitehall decision-making should be replaced by Scottish control of Scotland's economy'.[8] In July 1966 Gwynfor Evans won the Camarthen by-election to become the first Plaid Cymru MP at Westminster and in November 1967 Winifred Ewing won the Hamilton by-election for the SNP with 46 per cent of the vote.[9] Nationalists were replacing the Conservatives (and Liberals) as the focus for anti-Labour feeling. But the Government believed that its fortunes would recover given that, while nationalist success in local elections in 1967 and 1968 grew dramatically, support fell back at the 1970 general election.[10]

Early in 1968 the Labour, Conservative and Liberal Parties all responded to the Hamilton shock. On 30 March 1968, at the Scottish Labour Party Conference attended by Harold Wilson, a motion from the Glasgow Hillhead constituency calling for a Scottish Parliament was defeated. This was a victory for the old guard of the Scottish Labour Party under Secretary of State William Ross. But, as was noted at the time, the young turk Donald Dewar, elected to Parliament in 1966, believed in much greater devolution within the United Kingdom.[11] In May 1968 the Conservative leader Edward Heath, at the

Scottish Conservative Conference in Perth, proposed a Scottish Assembly (which might be elected or selected); he went on to establish a Constitutional Committee under former Conservative leader Sir Alec Douglas-Home.[12] The Liberal Party, for its part, favoured a unicameral parliament in Scotland elected on the single transferable vote. It proposed a federal assembly for Britain elected by proportional representation; there would be no separate all-England Parliament but a system of provincial assemblies.[13]

The Secretary of State for Scotland William Ross – 'the hammer of the Nats' – remained strongly opposed, and persuaded Harold Wilson, and the majority in Cabinet, to his view. James Callaghan, MP for Cardiff South East, was also opposed at this stage, though the Welsh Council of Labour favoured an elected Welsh Council.[14] Crossman, initially critical of Labour's local government reform proposals for Wales, became a supporter of strong regional devolution for Wales and Scotland.[15] Although Prime Minister Harold Wilson took the nationalist threat seriously, he stated that there were no plans for separate parliaments for Scotland and Wales.[16] The Cabinet view was a victory for those who wanted to do nothing in anticipation that the nationalist vote would fall as the economy improved.

To meet the charge that London was insensitive to the plight of the periphery, it was decided to appoint a Royal Commission (a favourite device of governments faced with thorny problems), with whom the whole subject could be safely left until after the next general election.[17] The decision to establish the Royal Commission was taken in the autumn of 1968, its members appointed in April 1969 – but it did not report until 1973, three years after Labour lost power.

In the case of Scotland, the arrangements for handling Scottish business had become unsatisfactory.[18] Attempts before 1974 to enhance the role of the Scottish Grand Committee did not meet the demands for a proper political forum for Scotland. The Select Committee on Scottish Affairs, set up in February 1968, had limited powers to examine economic development and land-use planning, but was not reappointed by a Conservative administration in 1971. And the growth in Scottish Office functions, while giving greater power to the Secretary of State and to civil servants, did not enhance democratic accountability. But it remained the case that it was not independence or separatism which drew support to the SNP, but rather its role as a successful pressure group – the Party that 'speaks for Scotland'. In addition, oil came to reinforce support for the SNP rather than causing it. Oil had played no part in the Hamilton by-election campaign of 1967, or in the 1970 general election; it was not until the October 1973 North Edinburgh by-election campaign that the SNP asserted, as Tam Dalyell reports it, 'It's oor oil!'[19]

A further reinforcement of the SNP position came from UK entry into the EEC. On the one hand, membership offered hope to the claims of small countries for a separate voice; on the other, Scotland's place on the UK periphery would become even more marginal as the economic advantages of the South East overshadowed Scotland's position, a claim favoured by Jim Sillars, the

Labour MP who broke away from the Party to found the Scottish Labour Party (and subsequently to join the SNP).[20]

The position in Wales was complicated by Labour's thinking on local government reform. In 1966 Secretary of State Cledwyn Hughes proposed an elected Welsh Regional Council, responsible for secondary legislation and in effect a 'national' upper tier of local government. But while Richard Crossman supported this, both William Ross, as Scottish Secretary, and James Callaghan, as a Welsh MP, opposed it, fearing it would arouse further demands in both Scotland and Wales. The result was that the proposal for a Welsh Regional Council emerged from the Cabinet as a nominated body with only advisory powers.[21] And when in January 1968 Cledwyn Hughes was replaced as Welsh Secretary by anti-devolutionist George Thomas, the battle with the Welsh Council of Labour was engaged. As early as 1964 this body had been advocating an assembly for Wales. George Thomas's own position, however, underwent a sea change: in the name of the Labour Opposition he moved an amendment to the 1972 Local Government Bill calling for an elected Welsh Council. At local and national levels, however, the Labour Party remained divided.

The Kilbrandon Commission[22]

James Callaghan, as Home Secretary in Wilson's Government, established the Royal Commission on the Constitution in April 1969. But neither Wilson nor Callaghan accepted the offers of Lord Wheatley (Scotland) and Lord Redcliffe-Maud (England and Wales) to cease work on their own local government Royal Commissions. Its appointment was seen as an excuse for inaction. It was designed, in William Ross's words, to kill devolution.[23] Neither the Prime Minister nor the Home Secretary showed much interest in the Commission's work, 'both finding it boring and irrelevant to the real problems facing the Government',[24] and believing that they could rely on Lord Crowther to produce an uncontentious solution which would defuse the nationalist challenge. Nor was the example of Northern Ireland seen as a possible model. The antagonism between the two communities had erupted into open violence in 1968 and led to the suspension of devolved government. In addition, the Parliament of Northern Ireland was not established to meet a nationalist or separatist threat but on the contrary to maintain the position of those who wished to remain as members of the United Kingdom.[25]

The Kilbrandon Commission defined devolution as 'the delegation of central government powers without the relinquishment of sovereignty'.[26] While the political and economic unity of the United Kingdom should be preserved, a uniform system of government over its component parts was unnecessary. Separatism would not provide good government and there was little demand for federalism. Only responsibility for prescribed matters should be devolved, leaving the Westminster Parliament sovereign. The UK Government would also have the power to veto devolved legislation considered unacceptable. Once the assemblies were in place, the number of MPs for Scotland and Wales should be reduced and the offices of the two Secretaries of State abolished.

The Commission's majority report proposed elected assemblies in Scotland and Wales, elected by a plurality voting system using the single transferable vote.[27] Both Scotland and Wales should have legislative assemblies. Each would have its own budget, tax-raising powers, and responsibility for a wide range of functions and services. In England, however, it suggested only nominated regional bodies with tenuous powers.[28] The dissenting minority report of Lord Crowther-Hunt[29] and Professor Alan Peacock proposed that Scotland, Wales and five large regions in England should be treated equally.[30] The assemblies would all have roughly the same powers, including the right to raise tax by a sales tax or a surcharge on income tax. The majority report, while understanding the political problem, provided only very limited constitutional reasons for change. The minority report did recognise the need for constitutional principles but, in the words of Drucker and Brown, 'was utterly devoid of political sense', since England neither wanted a regional tier nor were there strong sentiments attached to them.[31]

Reaction to the publication of the Kilbrandon report in 1973 was muted, and there was no immediate debate at Westminister. Labour anxiety had diminished with results of the 1970 General Election and, on the Conservative side, the proposals of Lord Home's Committee were discretely shelved. In the autumn of 1973 the Labour Party rejected a separate parliament for Scotland with executive and legislative powers, and internal party discussions stressed that the right of the Scots to its full number of MPs at Westminster would be undermined by a legislative Assembly in Edinburgh.[32] The Kilbrandon Commission's proposals for an elected Assembly met with a mixed reception inside the Scottish Labour Party between those who backed rejection on the grounds that it would be the first step on the slippery slope to independence and those who thought it would draw the teeth of separatists among the SNP.[33] The Scottish Trade Unions Congress had changed its mind while the Commission was sitting, from opposition to support for legislative devolution. The Scottish Council of the Labour Party believed that the best interests of Scotland would be served by a process of extending administrative and legislative devolution within the overall framework of the UK parliament. But the position changed radically when, at the Govan by-election of November 1973, the SNP's Margo MacDonald dramatically overcame a Labour majority of 16,000 to win the seat by 571 votes. Though it reverted to Labour at the February 1974 General Election, the SNP gained six seats on that occasion (four from Conservatives and two from Labour); for Harold Wilson these gains confirmed polls which showed nationalist sentiment on the increase in Scotland.

Tam Dalyell believed that while the Commission had put the issue on ice and was thus a reasonable method of finding responses to problems which avoided the Government taking precipitate action, he finally concluded that the Scotland and Wales Bill was 'hastily cobbled together in order to meet the electoral threat posed by the Scottish National Party'.[34] In 1974 the Scottish

Executive Committee of the party voted against an elected assembly by six votes to five. Under pressure from London, a special conference was held in September 1974. Following 'arm-twisting' by the devolutionists, with the assistance of the trade union block vote offered to the Government as part of the Social Contract, the decision of the Scottish Executive was reversed.[35] In Wales the Welsh Labour Party, again under pressure from London, supported an elected assembly with executive, not legislative, powers. In essence, the Labour Party's commitment to devolution was made from the centre and forced on the periphery.[36]

Political realities facing the Labour Government

By 1974 the Government was facing severe economic problems. This, and the Government's small majority, meant that a further general election could not long be delayed. Barbara Castle argues that Harold Wilson 'was firmly convinced that a radical devolution of power to Scotland, and to a lesser degree to Wales, was the only way to head off the Nationalists'.[37] Roy Jenkins was opposed to the idea, while Tony Crosland was for procrastinating. William Ross, whose opposition had been overruled, was by 1974 committed to making devolution work. Commentators have suggested that when Lord Crowther-Hunt, brought in as constitutional adviser, took responsibility for outlining proposals, there were already five groups of civil servants within the Privy Council Office working on a devolution project which bore a strong resemblance to the Kilbrandon majority report. Lord Crowther-Hunt persuaded the civil servants to consider the minority report as well, 'but it was too late to make much difference'.[38] Barbara Castle records that 'officials clearly don't like the idea of devolution at all and have come out for legislative devolution as being, though dangerous, less so than the sweeping ideas on executive devolution that Norman Hunt had pressed'.[39] Although for the eight months after February 1975 politicians had held the cards and made the decisions, it was the civil service who made the running thereafter.[40]

The major Cabinet debate on devolution took place at Chequers on 16 June 1975.[41] A group within the Cabinet (including Roy Jenkins, Tony Crosland, Denis Healey, Shirley Williams, Eric Varley, Tony Benn and Lord Elwyn-Jones) appeared determined to deny the assemblies significant industrial and economic powers. Wilson, in typical mode, stayed neutral.[42] By that stage Denis Healey, Roy Jenkins and others believed that the Common Market referendum in Scotland showed that the nationalists were, in Barbara Castle's reportage, a busted flush.[43] In that same meeting Tony Benn argued that decentralisation was the strongest argument for devolution, and the Cabinet had a clear election commitment which it must honour.[44] Though against relinquishing central government's economic powers, Benn was committed to the principle of devolution, a position he had held since 1968. The momentum for devolution continued, particularly with the Government's small majority and its need to placate the minority parties.

In the October 1974 general election the SNP won eleven seats, up from seven in February. Although the Conservatives won sixteen seats in Scotland in October, the SNP's total vote was well ahead of that of the Conservatives, and this, together with its local election gains, made it clear that it was the second party in Scottish politics.

At the February 1974 general election neither the Conservatives nor Labour made positive references to devolution, though the Labour Party's manifestos in Wales and Scotland included the commitment. And the Queen's Speech of March 1974 merely stated that discussions in Scotland would be initiated and proposals published. That same day, however, Wilson's speech to the House – goaded by interruptions from Winifred Ewing – promised 'of course we shall publish a White Paper and a Bill'. In June the Labour Government published the hastily drafted discussion document *Devolution within the United Kingdom: Some Alternatives for Discussion.*[45] This listed the seven 'A' to 'G' suggestions for devolution recommended by the Kilbrandon Commission. Scheme A of the White Paper, which followed the Kilbrandon majority report (though without legislative powers for Wales), formed the basis of the Government's subsequent proposals. In September 1974 the White Paper *Democracy and Devolution: Proposals for Scotland and Wales* (Cmnd 5732) was produced, and Labour's October 1974 manifesto pledged the creation of elected assemblies in Scotland and Wales.

Labour responded to the SNP's October 1974 election gains with a Queen's Speech which promised directly elected assemblies, though the Government rejected Kilbrandon's recommendation of proportional representation, and Wilson records that the Government was not planning to get legislation through Parliament in the new session.[46] Edward Short, as Lord President of the Council and Leader of the House of Commons, his Minister of State Gerry Fowler (later replaced by Lord Crowther-Hunt), and aided by the Constitution Unit in the Privy Council Office, were given responsibility for devolution planning. [47]

The first debate following the September White Paper was held in February 1975. In that debate Edward Short said that the Government was committed to preserving the unity of the United Kingdom, to a new relationship between Scotland, Wales, the English regions and the central government. The heart of the matter was, as Prime Minister Wilson had emphasised, a desire for greater participation and moving decisions closer to where people lived.[48] But the White Papers were not published until November 1975: *Our Changing Democracy: Devolution to Scotland and Wales* (Cmnd 6348); August 1976: *Devolution to Scotland and Wales, Supplementary Statement* (Cmnd 6585), and the Consultative Document of December 1976: *Devolution: The English Dimension.*

Following Harold Wilson's retirement, James Callaghan became Prime Minister in March 1976, and it was he who introduced the Scotland and Wales Bill in December 1976. The Bill was given thirty days for debate and, as was the convention for constitutional bills, the Committee stage was taken on the floor of the House. Callaghan moved the Second Reading of the Bill on 13 December, and undertook to consider the calls for a referendum on the issue. He spoke of the need to bring government in Scotland and Wales closer to the people and to lessen the sense of alienation. The Conservatives opposed the legislation, declaring that the Bill was a confused solution to decentralisation problems which could be better met through administrative devolution and, in Scotland, the provision of another chamber of Parliament.

In the debate on the Second Reading of 13–16 December 1976 a number of Labour MPs, including Eric Heffer, James Sillars and Denis Canavan, advanced the 'socialist not nationalist' argument. To head off rebellion within Labour's ranks, Michael Foot, under Callaghan the President of the Council and Leader of the House of Commons, introduced proposals for a referendum.

Vigorous debate across party lines concerned the powers to be devolved to the (around 150-member) Scottish Assembly and the (around 80-member) Welsh Assembly, including tax and economic powers. The Government would retain major responsibilities for industry and investment in order to preserve the economic unity of the United Kingdom. Much veto, reserve and consent power remained in the hands of Westminster. Callaghan stated that the Government would lay down guidelines governing the use of the industrial investment powers of the Scottish and Welsh Development Agencies. The Government also dropped the power of the Scottish Assembly to levy a surcharge on the rates, and proposed that the two assemblies would be financed through a block grant from the centre. In Scotland, a 'Westminster' model provided for a Cabinet – the Scottish Executive – consisting of a Chief Executive and other members, appointed by the Secretary of State on the advice of the Assembly and the Chief Executive. In Wales, the Welsh Assembly would be organised into a number of subject committees whose chairmen would form the Assembly's Executive Committee under the chairmanship of a Chief Executive.

There were also strong objections to the provisions in the Scotland and Wales Bill which gave the Secretary of State for Scotland powers to judge when devolved legislation clashed with Westminster – giving him what some called a 'colonial governor' role. Subsequently, the Government changed the provisions, removing jurisdiction of the *vires* of Assembly laws from the Secretaries of State, and locating it in the Judicial Committee of the Privy Council. The Secretary of State could now only interfere if it was thought the Assembly's actions would affect a non-devolved matter.

Though the Second Reading was passed by a substantial majority, there were signs of future difficulties for the Government when ten Labour members voted against the Government and a further twenty-nine abstained. Debate in Committee became protracted, with many amendments tabled by opponents on all sides. In response the Government proposed a timetable ('guillotine') motion and the debate took place on 22 February 1977. The Government lost the guillotine motion by 312 votes to 283, with twenty-two Labour MPs (many representing north of England constituencies) voting against and twenty-one abstaining. The Bill was dropped for the rest of the parliamentary session. The Scottish and Welsh nationalists became opponents of the Government's other policies, and the proposed bill on industrial democracy was not introduced.

Following the loss of the guillotine motion and the fall of the Bill, James Callaghan reaffirmed the Government's commitment to the principle of devolution and offered all-party talks. But the nationalists were unappeased. On 17 March 1977 the SNP, in the debate on the public expenditure cuts which were the price of the IMF loan, insisted on dividing the House at the end of an adjournment debate. The following day Margaret Thatcher, as Leader of the Opposition, put down a no confidence motion. The Government won that debate on 23 March. In the face of the crisis, the Government reached an agreement with the Liberals – the Lib–Lab Pact – enabling the Government to continue. The Liberals were anxious that the Devolution Bill should be resubmitted to the Commons, and Michael Foot and James Callaghan undertook to offer both Houses a free vote on whether Assembly members should be elected by proportional representation (the Lords voted in favour, the Commons against; the proposal was lost).

The legislation was reintroduced at the beginning of the new parliamentary session in November 1977 as two separate bills for Scotland and Wales, and, with the support of the Liberal Party, guillotined from the first day – an unprecedented move for a constitutional bill. Labour MP George Cunningham, with the support of Labour and Conservative members, had proposed that if the referendums contained in the bills resulted in less than 40 per cent of the total electorate supporting devolution, then the referendums would be lost – and with them the legislation. Erstwhile Labour opponents to the legislation, including Robin Cook and Neil Kinnock, supported the bills in order to be able to campaign against their implementation at the subsequent referendums. With the Cunningham amendment included, both the Scotland and Wales bills passed in July 1978, twenty months after the introduction of the original Bill.

In the referendums, the 'Yes' majority in Scotland supporting devolution represented only 32.9 per cent of the electorate and so did not fulfil the 40 per cent requirement. In Wales, 20.2 per cent of the votes cast supported devolution, 11.8 per cent of the electorate. Devolution was lost.

The impact of constitutional matters

The long debates that begin today mark a great constitutional change.[49]

Prime Minister Callaghan, opening the Second Reading debate, asserted that a new settlement between the nations would mark a move away from the existing highly centralised state and provide a more democratic government. An enduring constitutional framework would reconcile Scottish and Welsh demands for control over their own affairs with the continued unity of the United Kingdom and would afford that recognition of the identity of the component parts of the United Kingdom which had become so essential.[50] Sir Harold Wilson, speaking from the backbenches, described devolution as 'the most fundamental constitutional development in this century'.[51]

Callaghan also stressed that 'constitutions should not be lightly tampered with, but neither should they be rigid and inflexible'.[52] Relations between the different countries of the United Kingdom would be modified. The Government would not reject Scottish legislation where it judged it *ultra vires* but would refer it to the Judicial Committee of the Privy Council, whose ruling would be paramount. The Westminster Government could reject any bill which it regarded as contrary to the United Kingdom's international obligations, since those remained the responsibility of the central government. But the Government did reject Kilbrandon's recommendation for separate civil services for Scotland and Wales, in favour of a continued unified service.

Critics of the devolution legislation, including Leader of the Opposition Margaret Thatcher, foresaw inevitable constitutional conflict following from the division of powers between the different jurisdictions. The Liberals castigated the Scotland and Wales Bill's lack of discernible fundamental principles. The Liberals wanted legislation to be based on federal principles, called for proportional representation to be considered and highlighted the overrepresentation of Scottish and Welsh MPs at Westminster. For Unionist MPs from Ulster, by contrast, the Bill undermined the integrity of the United Kingdom. In response to the critics, John Morris, the Secretary of State for Wales, claimed that there was nothing in the Bill which sought to divide the United Kingdom or which derogated from the sovereignty of Parliament.[53] But, as was to occur again in the late 1990s, the Labour Government was prepared to introduce what were asymmetric schemes of devolution which did not treat all parts of the United Kingdom equally.

The spectre of conflict remained. In the case of Scotland, as Bogdanor observed, the Act, unlike the 1920 Government of Ireland Act, laid down transferred rather than reserved powers, and did so in an extremely detailed way. The result could be increased uncertainty about the powers of the Scottish Assembly and produce disputes between Edinburgh and London.[54]

In the case of England, critics argued that the Government's discussion document on the English regions, *The English Dimension*, was disingenuous if not misleading. The document held that not a great deal would change in the government of the United Kingdom in that the supremacy of Westminster would defend English interests, but that schemes for devolution to the English regions were impracticable. That is, the problems which had been played down by the Government when applied to Scotland and Wales were exaggerated in relation to England, arguably to prevent such disruptive innovations.[55]

The devolution debates of the 1970s are also remarkable for what came to be known after its instigator Tam Dalyell, Labour MP for West Lothian, as the West Lothian question. This raised the issue of whether or not Scottish MPs at Westminster should have the right to vote on English policy matters which, in Scotland, were devolved – a right which was not reciprocated for English MPs on Scottish devolved policies. The issue remains unresolved, arising in the devolution debates of the late 1990s and in relation to the Government's proposals for health care in England in 2003.[56]

On the constitutional question of a referendum, the debate went back to 1975. In November 1975, following the EEC referendum, the Welsh Labour MPs Neil Kinnock, Donald Anderson, Leo Abse and Fred Evans signed an Early Day Motion calling for a referendum – essentially in the hope that this would bury devolution. Edward Short, Leader of the House of Commons, declared that such a referendum would be 'inappropriate'. In the 1976 Second Reading debate Harold Wilson reminded MPs that the proposals for a referendum on the Common Market had been denounced as unconstitutional. But though he was not against a devolution referendum, he speculated that 'what we defended then has now become more widely accepted and is in danger of becoming too widely accepted'.[57] The SNP saw the EEC referendum as an historic constitutional divide which marked for the English an abdication of sovereignty and for Scotland a reawakening of a future role as a small North European country.[58]

Both Conservatives and Labour were divided on the issue. Some saw it as a way of dealing with separatism, some as the only way to approach constitutional change, while yet others saw it as a challenge to parliamentary sovereignty. And those MPs who did support a referendum differed over the timing (before or after the Scotland and Wales Bill became law), the questions it put, and whether it should be open to all countries of the United Kingdom or only Scotland and Wales.

On the final day of the Second Reading debate John Smith, Minister of State in the Privy Council Office, announced that the Government had accepted the principle that referendums should be held in Scotland and Wales before the schemes could be put into effect.[59] Then, as in the late 1990s, this did not really resolve the issue as to whether referendums were intended to be advisory or mandatory, to override Parliament or to endorse its position. Nor were the desiderata for introducing referendums resolved. In the summer of 2003 there was political disagreement over the need for a referendum to endorse the forthcoming EU constitution, with the Conservatives calling for a referendum and the Labour Government resisting the demands. The legacy from the 1970s and the 1990s is thus that there is no general legislation covering the holding of referendums; a separate Act is required for each specific case.

Michael Foot, Lord President of the Council and Leader of the House of Commons, wound up the Second Reading debate by stressing that the Government's motive in bringing forward the Scotland and Wales Bill was to maintain UK unity and the supremacy of the House of Commons. He rejected federalism since it would fundamentally alter the constitution and give the final word to a supreme court or written constitution.[60] These high motives, however, came to nothing as the legislation failed.

The collapse of devolution legislation and the fall of the Government

The referendums were held on 1 March 1979. Because the parties could not agree, there were no party political broadcasts, and no official information leaflet. The referendum in Wales was defeated by four to one (11.8 per cent voted 'yes', 46.5 per cent 'No' and 41.7 per cent did not vote). There was a slim majority in favour in Scotland (32.5 per cent 'Yes', 30.4 per cent 'No' and 37.1 per cent did not vote), but it did not meet the 40 per cent figure and the proposal was lost. In Scotland, the result was in part due to the declining fortunes of the SNP: this was confirmed in the subsequent 1979 general election when the Party lost nine of its eleven seats and surrendered its second place in Scotland to the Conservatives.

The failure in the referendums meant the demise of the legislation, and brought down the Government. Michael Foot suggested that the Government could survive if he were to lay a Repeal Order before Parliament but invite the House to reject it, on the grounds that this would leave the Scottish Act on the statute book in accordance with the wishes of those who had voted. It would not come into force until a second order, known as a Commencement Order, was laid, and this should be postponed until after a general election. James Callaghan rejected this suggestion, having himself used an order and inviting the House to reject it when, as Home Secretary, he was concerned with constituency boundary changes ten years earlier. Though he had won the vote, he had been heavily criticised and felt that Michael Foot would suffer the same charge of unconstitutional behaviour. And there was no guarantee that the Government would be able to muster the necessary votes.[61] Instead, Callaghan announced that, since a majority of those in Scotland had been in favour, there should be talks between the parties, including the minority parties, on how devolution might be carried forward. The calls for talks were rejected, serving only to precipitate the SNP's bringing forward of a no confidence motion.

Defeat in the referendums could not have come at a worse time for the Government, following the strike-bound 'Winter of Discontent' and with only seven months of Labour's period of office to run. In fact the two discontents fed on each other: public dislike of the Government after the January 1979 strikes contributed to the poor result in the Scottish referendum and defeat in Wales. The SNP set down a motion of censure for the Government's failure to secure devolution. Mrs Thatcher as Leader of the Opposition followed it with her own motion, confident that the Conservatives could win a general election. The vote took place on 29 March.

The Government lost the motion by one vote – the first time since 1924 that a government had lost a confidence vote – and Callaghan called the general election for 3 May 1979. The referendums had become a plebiscite on Labour's governing performance. In June 1979, following the Conservative victory in the general election, the House of Commons, under the Conservative Government's direction, repealed the Scotland Act.

Conclusion

As Healey put it: 'our attempt to provide devolution for Scotland and Wales proved a disastrous failure, like so many other attempts to reform the British

Constitution before it'.[62] That failure was embedded in the divisions within the Labour Party itself, the long process of deliberation, and in the frailties of the Government's majorities in the 1970s. The long-drawn-out battles over devolution, however, had had the advantage of distracting parliamentary attention from a preoccupation with the state of the economy, enabling the Government to retain support of the minority parties and providing valuable breathing space.[63]

The Wilson and Callaghan administrations were agreed on the fundamentals of the devolution problem. Both faced the difficulties of resisting the nationalist threat while holding the Labour Party together. Wilson saw growing nationalism as undermining Labour's electoral dominance in Scotland and Wales. Callaghan, from opposing a Welsh Council as offering hostages to fortune, became a supporter of devolution as a way of preserving the unity of the United Kingdom. Where the two premiers differed was in their handling of the situation. Wilson, always sensitive to political pressures, used delaying tactics, primarily through the Kilbrandon Commission, very effectively. Callaghan's tiny and fragile parliamentary majority, especially after the Lib–Lab Pact, gave him much less room for manoeuvre. He had to accommodate these constraints, yielding to pressures for separate bills after the defeat of the Scotland and Wales Bill, and to the demands for referendums on terms which were potentially – and as it proved – highly damaging.

The issue would not die. Labour's internal party debates became increasingly concerned with decentralisation. In 1982 the Labour Party reaffirmed the commitment to devolution for Scotland (which appeared in the Party's 1983 general election manifesto). The Campaign for a Scottish Assembly (a cross-party organisation formed after the failure of the 1979 referendums) was a low-key affair until, after the 1987 general election, it launched the report *A Claim of Right for Scotland*, in July 1988, followed by the establishment of the Scottish Constitutional Convention in 1989.

The Labour Party's policy reviews of the late 1980s, particularly under John Smith's guidance, moved to a Scottish Assembly with legislative powers and with the ability to make (relatively marginal) variations in tax rates in Scotland. The Party's decision-making bodies became, according to Geekie and Levy, dominated by devolutionists despite the disquiet among English Labour MPs, particularly from the north of England, that they would be severely disadvantaged by Scottish devolution.[64] By this time Labour politicians felt comfortable with the idea of a referendum, despite its constitutional implications, and appeared to agree to the idea of a 'Scottish mandate'. The Blair Government of 1997, while committed to the devolution inheritance of John Smith, was determined that the mistakes of the 1970s would not be repeated and that legislation would not go ahead until referendums had been held. Blair himself appeared not to pursue the policy from personal conviction but as a debt of honour to John Smith, an 'interesting experiment in New Labour coalition politics' and a means of curtailing the SNP.[65]

The legacy of the devolution issues which so damaged the Wilson and Callaghan Governments of 1974–9 was to make the unthinkable possible. The decentralisation debate may still be incomplete, and arouse political as well as academic argument, but without the Wilson and Callaghan eras it might not have emerged. Nor are the independence and separatist fears of those years entirely overcome. As always, however, gradualism remains the dominant mode. We have no formal agreement on when referendums may appropriately be held. Nor do we have a formal written constitution embracing the relations between the different countries and nations of the United Kingdom; perhaps the establishment of a new Department for Constitutional Affairs in June 2003 will prove to be a step on the road to that formalisation.

Notes

1 Wilson, H., *Final Term: The Labour Government 1974–76* (Weidenfeld and Nicolson/Michael Joseph, London, 1979), p. 36.

2 Smith, J., Minister of State, Privy Council Office, House of Commons *Debates*, vol. 922, 16 December 1976, col. 1753 (Debate on Second Reading, Scotland and Wales Bill). He so impressed James Callaghan with his work on the Devolution Bill that he was invited to join the Cabinet, as Secretary for Trade.

3 Bogdanor, V., *Devolution in the United Kingdom* (Oxford University Press, Oxford, 1999), p. 152.

4 House of Commons *Debates*, Fifth ser., vol. 885, Session 1974–5, 3 February 1975, col. 1048.

5 Ibid., cols 1031 and 1035.

6 Ibid., col. 1176.

7 Plaid Cymru was founded in 1925; the National Party of Scotland, the direct precursor of the Scottish National Party, in 1928.

8 Callaghan, J., *Time and Chance* (Collins, London, 1987), p. 504.

9 The mining seat of Hamilton was, as Tam Dalyell reminds us, not just any old Labour constituency. With its links to Keir Hardie and other pioneers it was an embodiment of the socialist heartland. Dalyell, T., *Devolution: The End of Britain?* (Cape, London, 1977), p. 76. At the general election a year before it had been Labour's second safest seat in Scotland. At the by-election three-sevenths of the huge Labour majority switched to the SNP, as did four-sevenths of those who had previously voted Conservative. 'By-elections: Labour safe nowhere?', *The Economist*, 225, 11 November 1967, p. 599.

10 The SNP lost its deposit in forty of the sixty-five seats it fought and while it won the Western Isles from Labour, Winifred Ewing lost Hamilton. In Wales, Plaid Cymru achieved its highest ever total of 175,000 votes but Gwynfor Evans lost Carmarthen, the Party's only seat.

11 'Scotland: Labour for 1707?', *The Economist*, 226, 30 March 1968, p. 21. Also in 1968 John P. Mackintosh, Labour MP for Berwick and East Lothian and Professor of Politics at the University of Edinburgh, published the Penguin Special *The Devolution of Power* which advocated nine elected regional councils in England and elected assemblies for Scotland and Wales.

12 In March 1970 the Douglas-Home Committee recommended a directly elected Scottish Convention, sitting in Scotland, to take over from Westminster the Second Reading, Committee and Report stages of Bills. Between 1970 and 1974 the Conservative Government did not go ahead with these plans, citing the need to consider the reports of the Wheatley Commission on local government reform in Scotland, and of the Kilbrandon Commission. But in May 1977 Francis Pym, opposition spokesman on devolution, announced that the Party's commitment to a directly

elected Scottish Assembly had become 'inoperative'. Forman, F.N., *Constitutional Change in the United Kingdom* (London, Routledge, 2002), p. 82.

13 'Scotland: Home rule all round', *The Economist*, 235, 4 April 1970, p. 26.

14 At the 6 November 1973 meeting of Welsh MPs, twenty-six of the twenty-seven made a commitment to devolution which then appeared in the Labour Party manifesto in Wales in February 1974, but not the national manifesto. The twenty-seventh MP, not present at the 6 November meeting, was the member for Cardiff South East, James Callaghan.

15 Crossman, R.H.S., *Diaries of a Cabinet Minister*, vol. 2 (Cape, London, 1976).

16 House of Commons *Debates*, Fifth ser., vol. 745, Session 1966–7, Written Answers, 20 April 1967, col. 151. Harold Wilson had appointed James Griffiths as the first Secretary of State for Wales in 1964, with a new Welsh Office in Cardiff and London. Cledwyn Hughes took over as Secretary of State in 1966. The Labour Government passed a Welsh Language Act in 1967.

17 'Reports and Surveys: The Report of the Royal Commission on the Constitution 1969–1973', *Political Quarterly*, 45, 1974, pp. 115–23. The author of this section of 'Reports and Surveys' was John P. Mackintosh.

18 Op. cit., p. 86; pp. 88–9. And cf. Myers, P., 'The Select Committee on Scottish Affairs', *Parliamentary Affairs*, 27, 1973–4, pp. 359–70.

19 Dalyell, *Devolution: The End of Britain?*, pp. 45–6.

20 Jim Sillars, elected for South Ayrshire in 1970, resigned to form the Scottish Labour Party in 1976. He lost his seat in the 1979 general election and disbanded his new party to join the SNP. He married Margo MacDonald and won the Govan seat in 1988, which she had won in 1973. He lost this seat in 1992.

21 Dalyell, *Devolution: The End of Britain?*, p. 142.

22 The Commission was set up in 1969. Its first Chairman was Lord Crowther, Chairman of *The Economist*; on his death in February 1972 he was succeeded by Lord Kilbrandon, a Scottish judge. Its terms of reference were: 'to examine the present functions of the central legislature and government in relation to the several countries, nations and regions of the United Kingdom; to consider, having regard to developments in local government organisation and in the administrative and other relations between the various parts of the United Kingdom and to the interests of the prosperity and good government of our people under the Crown, whether any changes are desirable in those functions or otherwise in present constitutional and economic relations; to consider, also, whether any changes are desirable in the constitutional and economic relations between the United Kingdom and the Isle of Man'.

23 Drucker, H.M. and Brown, G., *The Politics of Nationalism and Devolution* (Longman, London, 1980), p. 54.

24 Dalyell, *Devolution: The End of Britain?*, p. 90. Callaghan's Home Office advisers were convinced that the Commission would not recommend anything that went beyond the negative findings of the Speaker's Conference of 1920 (concerned mainly with Ireland) which recommended no change in the Scottish relationship.

25 Bogdanor, V., *Devolution* (Oxford University Press, Oxford, 1979), pp. 42–3.

26 Kilbrandon Commission, *Report*, vol. I, Cmnd 5460 (London, HMSO, 1973), para. 543.

27 Speaking in January 1976 Lord Kilbrandon confirmed that the reason behind this proposal was the fear expressed by many witnesses to the Royal Commission that a Scottish Assembly elected on the first-past-the-post system would be ruled indefinitely by a one-party Labour Government. Proctor, J.H., 'Party Interests and the Electoral System for the Projected Scottish Assembly', *Political Quarterly*, 48, 1977, p. 194.

28 Kilbrandon Commission, *Report*, vol. I, Cmnd 5460 (London, HMSO, 1973).

29 Following the Queen's Speech in March 1974, Harold Wilson appointed Lord Crowther-Hunt (an Oxford don and no relation to the Commission's first Chairman Lord Crowther) as constitutional adviser to the Government. After the

October election he became Minister of State in charge of higher education, and was later transferred to the Privy Council Office as minister on devolution questions.

30 Crowther-Hunt, N. and Peacock, A., *Memorandum of Dissent from the Royal Commission Report on the Constitution*, vol. II, Cmnd 5460-I (London. HMSO 1973).

31 Drucker and Brown, *The Politics of Nationalism and Devolution*, p. 64.

32 Dalyell, *Devolution: The End of Britain?*, p. 95.

33 Callaghan, J., *Time and Chance* (Collins, London, 1987), p. 505.

34 Dalyell, *Devolution: The End of Britain?*, p. 89; p. 43.

35 Bogdanor, *Devolution* (1979), p. 116. A detailed account of the machinations inside the Scottish Executive of the Labour Party, the National Executive, and the trade unions, is given in Dalyell, *Devolution: The End of Britain?*, pp. 99–104.

36 Drucker and Brown, *The Politics of Nationalism and Devolution*, p. 95.

37 Castle, B., *The Castle Diaries 1964–1976* (Macmillan, London, 1990), p. 442.

38 Drucker and Brown, *The Politics of Nationalism and Devolution*, p. 90.

39 Castle, *The Castle Diaries 1964–1976*, pp. 487–8, 645–6.

40 Drucker and Brown, *The Politics of Nationalism and Devolution*, pp. 87, 96, 100.

41 Bernard Donoughue, Senior Policy Adviser to the Prime Minister and Head of the new Downing Street Policy Unit between 1974 and 1979, thought the Cabinet Committee discussions on devolution occupied an enormous amount of time but were important 'as a device to resist the advance of Scottish and Welsh nationalism'. Donoughue, B., *Prime Minister: The Conduct of Policy under Harold Wilson and James Callaghan* (Cape, London, 1987), p. 59.

42 'Devolution: Keeping the Nats happy', *The Economist*, 254, 1975, pp. 20, 23.

43 Castle, *The Castle Diaries 1964–1976*, p. 616.

44 Benn, T., *Against the Tide: Diaries 1973–76* (Arrow, London, 1989), p. 402.

45 Though designated a White Paper it did not carry a command number.

46 Wilson, *Final Term: The Labour Government 1974–76*, p. 188.

47 As a member of the Kilbrandon Commission Lord Crowther-Hunt had backed its recommendation of proportional representation but, 'as a member of Her Majesty's Government', reversed his decision in the House of Lords.

48 House of Commons *Debates*, Fifth ser., vol. 885, Session 1974–5, 3 February 1975, cols 957–8.

49 House of Commons *Debates*, Fifth ser., vol. 922, Session 1976–7, 13 December 1976, col. 922.

50 Ibid., col. 976.

51 House of Commons *Debates*, vol. 922, 13 January 1976, col. 209.

52 Ibid., col. 992.

53 Ibid., col. 1575.

54 Bogdanor, V., 'The English Constitution and Devolution', *Political Quarterly*, 50, 1979, p. 46.

55 Gunn, L., 'Devolution: A Scottish View', *Political Quarterly*, 48, 1977, p. 139.

56 In July 2003, in the Commons debate on the Health and Social Care Bill, the Government's 166 majority fell to 35 over the proposals for foundation hospitals. Critics within and outside Labour argued that Scottish Labour MPs supported the Government's policy, which would affect only England and Wales (though no pilots were in fact proposed for Wales), while such hospitals would not be introduced in Scotland, where the Scottish Executive had rejected them. If the sixty-seven Scottish and Welsh MPs had abstained on this 'English' legislation the proposals would arguably have been lost.

57 House of Commons *Debates*, vol. 922, col. 1007.

58 George Reid (SNP, Clackmannan and East Stirlingshire), ibid., col. 1359.

59 Ibid., col. 1736.

60 Ibid., col. 1866.

61 Callaghan, *Time and Chance*, pp. 559–60.
62 Healey, D., *The Time of My Life* (Michael Joseph, London, 1989), p. 460.
63 Callaghan, *Time and Chance*, pp. 508, 509–10.
64 Geekie, J. and Levy, R., 'Devolution and the Tartanisation of the Labour Party', *Parliamentary Affairs*, 42, 1989, pp. 399–411.
65 Forman, *Constitutional Change in the United Kingdom*, p. 83.

14 Northern Ireland

Brendan O'Leary

I

The Callaghan Government was defeated on a motion of 'no confidence' in the House of Commons in May 1979, precipitating the general election that brought the Conservatives to power for eighteen years. This parliamentary humiliation was caused by two pivotal abstentions, that of Frank Maguire, an independent Irish nationalist MP, and that of Gerry Fitt, the then Leader of the Social Democratic and Labour Party of Northern Ireland. The latter explained and justified his abstention as direct retaliation for Roy Mason's conduct as Secretary of State for Northern Ireland. Within a year Fitt had resigned his leadership position, and John Hume, a more intelligent, dynamic and more nationalist figure, renewed the SDLP. After Maguire's death in 1981 his Fermanagh and West Tyrone seat was won by Bobby Sands, an IRA prisoner convicted of scheduled offences – then leading a hunger strike that would end his own life. Sands's triumph at the ballot box and his subsequent martyrdom were the decisive moments in the electoral breakthrough of contemporary Sinn Féin. These stories affirm a forgotten truth: the radicalisation of Irish nationalism in the 1980s was a by-product of the outgoing Labour Government, and not the exclusive responsibility of the Thatcher Cabinet. Many of the Irish in Great Britain and their sympathisers were also radicalised by the Irish policies of Callaghan's Government. By 1981 the National Executive Committee of the Labour Party had embraced a policy of seeking Irish unification (by consent), the same policy as the SDLP – a platform commitment that would not be dropped until Tony Blair became Leader of the Party.

II

The first Wilson Government (1964–70) had intervened in Northern Ireland, politically and militarily, to redress the worst of the institutional discrimination and policy legacy of fifty years of government by the Ulster Unionist Party.[1] In so doing, Harold Wilson had partly acted from conviction, and partly reflected the dispositions of his Liverpool constituents. He had also been animated by the fact that during 1964–6 (when he had had a parliamentary majority of three) the

Ulster Unionist MPs at Westminster had acted as a loyal platoon of the Conservatives. When Wilson's Government intervened in response to the civil rights movement, and the unionist backlash against it, Richard Crossman, its most subsequently distinguished diarist, made the following entry: 'we have now got into something which we can hardly mismanage'.[2] This statement now sounds as ironic as imaginable, but in 1969–70 there was a widespread hope that London would preside over substantive reform in the region. Wilson handed responsibility to James Callaghan as Home Secretary, and thereby revived his fading career – as he enjoyed his only unambiguous moment as a reformer. Callaghan would hold all four of the great offices of state, the Premiership, the Chancellorship, Foreign and Home Secretary, and have an unenviable record in all of them, but his brief flurry of constructive activities in Northern Ireland in 1969–70, especially in housing and policing policy, were the exceptions amongst his disappointing ministerial performances – even prompting a mildly self-congratulatory book on the subject.[3] Subsequent events collectively put paid to the optimism that had surrounded Callaghan's actions: the surprise return of the Conservatives to office in June 1970; Reginald Maudling's conduct as Home Secretary; the British Army's hardline conduct, especially in Belfast; the rise and aggression of the Provisional IRA; the independent aggression of loyalist paramilitaries; and the fateful and foolish decision to permit internment without trial in 1971.

The Army's shooting of unarmed civilians, protesting against internment on 30 January 1972, Bloody Sunday, paved the way for the suspension of the Stormont Parliament later that spring. Heath's Tories were forced to think, and rethink. Eventually, in late 1973, prompted by the goodwill of Willie Whitelaw, and one of Heath's rare acts of skilled statecraft, a power-sharing settlement was negotiated at the Civil Service College in Sunningdale.[4] Three major Northern Irish parties, the official UUP, the Alliance and the SDLP, under the watchful auspices of both the UK and Irish governments, endorsed power sharing in Belfast and a Council of Ireland to link the Dublin and Belfast Parliaments. Brian Faulkner of the UUP and Fitt of the SDLP led the Executive, established by the Sunningdale Agreement. It had been in office since 1 January 1974 when Heath called a general election for Westminster the following month, only to lose almost as surprisingly as Wilson had lost in 1970. In both 1970 and February 1974 the change of incumbent government at Westminster had adverse consequences for Northern Ireland. Whereas in 1970–2 the Conservatives fanned the flames of conflict through partisanship towards the unionists, especially by introducing internment and soft pedalling on loyalist violence, in 1974 Labour would undermine the Sunningdale settlement through abject spinelessness before the strike of the Ulster Workers' Council (UWC); and after October 1974 it would start to renew the repressive errors of the Tories, albeit with more finesse and hand-wringing regret.

The Wilson (1974–6) and the Callaghan (1976–9) premierships differed in style and underlying preferences, but much less in substantive decisions and non-decisions. As regards Northern Ireland both prime ministers acted as if they were in office but not in power, devoting little but frustrated attention to the region. Statements they made before and after their premierships showed they had formulated preferences substantively different from the status quo, but in office did nothing that significantly advanced these goals. Wilson would have preferred a united Ireland, and in November 1971 had put forward a fifteen-point programme to that effect when Labour was in opposition.[5] Point 2 included a creditable proposal to generate tripartite talks between Great Britain, Northern Ireland and Ireland, the formula that would eventually be adopted in the making of the Sunningdale Agreement in 1973, and more comprehensively and inclusively in the making of the Good Friday Agreement during 1995–8. In opposition Wilson rejected internment without trial, and would, to his credit, make good on that pledge when he returned to office. He went so far as to meet with IRA personnel in 1972 – though he managed to exclude this episode from the relevant section of his memoirs.[6] The Head of his Policy Unit, Bernard Donoughue, described Wilson as having had 'radical instincts' on the Irish question,[7] and he was permitted, along with Wilson's Press Secretary, Joe Haines, to develop dramatic policy options, including (a) an 'Algerian solution', i.e. withdrawal; and (b) imposed dominion status, i.e. independence with connections to the Crown. In May 1974 Wilson drafted his own 'Doomsday Scenario', though Donoughue describes his premier as being frightened by his own thinking, which sounds typical of the man.[8] Tony Benn's diary entry of 10 April 1974 records the following after a Cabinet meeting:

> it was agreed, again under the highest secrecy, that we would begin considering the implications of a total withdrawal. Of course, if that got out, it would precipitate bloodshed but we felt we simply had to do it. Roy [Jenkins] took that view. Jim [Callaghan] looked very doubtful but thought it needed to be done. Fred Peart, Peter Shore and Willie Ross are 100 per cent pro-Protestant. So the Cabinet would divide on Catholic–Protestant lines in the event of this happening.[9]

The sole significant public evidence that the Wilson Government was contemplating such radical options came, ironically in light of later developments, from Roy Mason, then Secretary of State for Defence. He made a speech on 24 April 1974 warning that pressure in Great Britain was mounting for a pullout of troops and to set a date for withdrawal. His ministry promptly issued a statement denying that there had been any change of policy. One wonders whether Mason simply made an error, flew a kite for Wilson, or whether he sabotaged the withdrawal option in the light of opinion within his ministry.[10] Benn's diary records the following for the Cabinet meeting of 25 April:

> the first item was a speech by Roy Mason yesterday in which he had hinted that British troops might be withdrawn. … Harold [Wilson] said that Ministers must consult with the FO, and in particular with the Northern Ireland Secretary before saying anything. Merlyn [Rees] told me he was

desperately worried ... it encouraged the idea that the British Labour Government was a soft sell. Harold said the speech was a breach of the Procedure for Ministers.[11]

This admonishment would appear to exclude the idea that Mason flew a kite for Wilson. These months aside, in which he made a rhetorical attack on the UWC's strikers as 'spongers', Wilson was to show no determination to pursue any radical, or indeed simply ambitious, agenda on Northern Ireland during the rest of his premiership – a Cabinet subcommittee did consider the withdrawal option but rejected it. From May 1974

> Wilson and his successor tried not to get too deeply involved in the Irish problem. Our policy became one of consolidation, trying to contain terrorism and just get through from year to year. The Irish situation regularly appeared on the agenda of the Cabinet Committee ... but it was mainly a question of reporting information ... and rarely was anything taken higher to Cabinet. ... [T]he Cabinet Committee ... never after 1974 actually discussed Northern Ireland *policy*: it only discussed law and order.[12]

Callaghan, by contrast with Wilson, entertained no radical options on Northern Ireland as Premier. His memoir *Time and Chance* conveys his world-weary resignation: 'at no time did I feel we were doing more than breasting the tide'.[13] He blamed the locals, albeit in polite language:

> it was frustrating to watch every initiative destroyed from within, and I can but repeat the opinion I expressed to my Cabinet colleagues eighteen years ago at the outset of the present troubles in January 1969: 'the cardinal aim of our policy must be to influence Northern Ireland to solve its own problems'.[14]

Out of office he had a change of heart, making a speech in July 1981 that proposed a timetabled period for a negotiated agreement before an ordered British withdrawal and the formation of an independent Northern Ireland.

The stylistic differences between the premiers were reflected in the personnel they chose to manage the region. The two Secretaries of State, Merlyn Rees (1974–6) and Roy Mason (1976–9), were remarkably different in personality and profile,[15] though both were on the right of the Party, and associated with Callaghan's patronage. An LSE alumnus, Rees had the shambolic gait of a badly dressed and over-promoted headmaster – he had been a teacher. His indecisiveness made it difficult to believe he had been an RAF officer during the Second World War. His Welsh name and roots belied a largely English persona – he had been the MP for Leeds South since 1963. His heavily lined face was 'lived in', worried and anxious – with his glasses constantly threatening to fall off his nose. He was a sincere man, thoughtful, capable of listening, but held by his civil servants to be incapable of decision making; and when he did decide, caution usually triumphed over his intellect. His memoirs are a copy-edited version of the man – garrulous, intermittently coherent, a collection of anecdotes and episodes, but with little eye for the main story. Nevertheless, they display occasional flashes of genuine insight, showing the intelligence and moral commitment that had brought him to political office.[16] He held, for example, the interesting view that Ireland stopped just outside of the Belfast region – which he saw as the only genuinely British part of the island; and he observed of his abusive and threatening correspondence that 'there was little to choose between the two sides except that more religious sectarianism was shown by the majority population and more anti-unionism by the minority'.[17] Ideologically, he was right-wing Labour, but with a touch of romanticism. He referred to trade unionist and non-conformist people as 'my kind of people'.[18] He was at home with trade unionists, and briefly entertained naïve beliefs that working-class loyalist Protestants could be won to non-sectarian socialism. He developed a detailed knowledge of the region, still evident many years after his exit from office, but remained burdened by the memory of his role – in my interviews he was very defensive about Labour's crisis decision making of 1974. One would have to be very tough, cynical and world-weary not to have liked Merlyn Rees, even if one disagreed with his politics. He could provoke irritation and exasperation, but active animosity towards him was difficult. 'Dithering' was the term of criticism most often applied in interviews with British and Irish officials that I conducted in the late 1980s and early 1990s. A contemporaneous newspaper description quoted one of his officials declaring, 'I don't mind Merlyn wrestling with his conscience for ages over every issue. What I mind is that the result always seems to be a draw.'[19]

Such evaluations did not apply to Roy Mason, whom friend or foe regarded as decisive. He too was right-wing Labour, a Yorkshireman, also with a military past. The former Secretary of State for Defence was the true political thug of the Callaghan administration – a description normally and wrongly applied to the brilliant, loquacious and effortlessly intelligent Denis Healy. Mason was educated, but did his best to hide it – in a manner once common in the class-conscious north of England. Whereas Rees agonised, Mason appeared barely to reflect, during or after his tenure in office. He spoke in clipped, blunt language, with none of Rees's verbosity or warmth. The MP for Barnsley was an embarrassing example of working-class royalism and authoritarianism. Hosting the Queen in Northern Ireland on the occasion of her Jubilee in 1977 was plainly the highlight of his life. That his evident pleasure in toe-curling deference to the Crown might be politically offensive to Irish nationalists, 'Greens' as he called them, either did not deter him or did not occur to him. 'He's probably the Protestants' favourite Secretary of State', said Roland Moyle, a Labour junior minister in the Northern Ireland Office (NIO).[20] Not until Peter Mandelson's appointment would so many unionists be so happy with a Secretary of State. Whereas Rees was mildly and tacitly unionist – he would later not support the passage of the Anglo-Irish Agreement of 1985 [21] – he was, however, genuinely interested in conflict resolution. While ultimately willing to follow the advice of counter-insurgents and those suggesting that civil liberties should be traded for order, he took no self-indulgent pleasure in his difficult brief for the Union. Rees, like Callaghan, was willing to contemplate 'radical' steps *after* he had left office: expressing his willingness to cede South Armagh to Ireland.[22] Mason, by contrast, revelled in the prefectoral nature of the Secretary of State's role, beholden to no local parliament. He was a unionist and a trade unionist, with the repertoire of imagination associated with both of these traditions. His civil servants thought of him as a viceroy, Irish nationalists as vice-Roy.

III

Between 1972 and 1985 successive UK Governments presented themselves as neutral arbiters of conflict in and over Northern Ireland.[23] It was not an unfamiliar self-designation. In retreat from empire, mandates and protectorates, UK Governments had claimed to be neutral arbiters of the rival claims of Hindus and Muslims in the Indian subcontinent, Arabs and Jews in Palestine, and Greek and Turkish Cypriots. This self-designation was usually accompanied by a functionally appropriate amnesia over the contribution of imperial governance to national, ethnic and communal conflicts. Northern Ireland was problematic, however, because it was not a colony that could be differentiated by the twin tests of salt-water *and* skin-colour differentiation from Great Britain. It was plainly the oldest colonial legacy, but it was not immediately clear to Westminster and Whitehall whether to treat it as an internal or external matter, British or colonial, or both. They decided in general on an internal treatment, especially in the NIO, which soon become unionist with a small 'u', and would seek to exclude the Foreign Office from its brief as much as possible. The border would not, it was said, be an issue. The elephant in the room would not be discussed with the British public. It was comforting for London to treat the conflict as fundamentally religious rather than as ethno-national or colonial. Such typification made the conflict the sole responsibility of the locals. Self-presentation as neutral arbiters had other attractions. It was in keeping with traditional British rhetoric on Irish matters. It offered a mode of crisis management less drastic than that entailed by imposing Irish unification, Northern Ireland's independence, a new partition, or joint sovereignty. Arbitration avoided the problematic option of treating Northern Ireland as unambiguously British. As all now know better, the notion of British, or British homogeneity, is itself ambiguous. If Northern Ireland was to be British did that mean it should be governed as England, Scotland or Wales – or as Northern Ireland? Was it not the case that the British, historically, were Protestants, unified by their opposition to the Catholic powers of Europe and the Catholics of these islands? Arbitration as neutrality between the Reformation and the Counter-Reformation offered UK Governments the chance to present themselves as tolerant, reasonable and post-religious, if not wholly secular. Arbitration also had international presentational advantages. It was acceptable – if not always ideal – to Irish Governments, and to the US State Department. It had the benefits of ambiguity – London could opt to see any Northern Ireland item as internal or as external, as judged most convenient. Labour had intervened with troops in 1969 because the Royal Ulster Constabulary (RUC) had been partisan – and was exhausted with riot control (or riot creation, depending upon one's perspective). But, it had also intervened because the Irish Government appeared likely to mobilise on the border, and because a further Protestant backlash was feared. The story of this intervention was rewritten, in part accurately, as being motivated to keep the warring factions apart.

Three fundamental premises comprised the arbitration orientation under the Wilson and Callaghan Cabinets: encouraging Protestants and Catholics to work together towards an agreed, largely internal political accommodation, while retaining the stance of the honest broker; reforming or modernising Northern Ireland along the lines of the post-war British consensus; and impartial security policies that eventually rested on the criminalisation of political violence.

Rees tried the first element with some determination, even though he and Wilson had wholly failed to stabilise the Sunningdale settlement, a failure treated separately below. After the destruction of the Sunningdale enterprise Rees paved the way for elections to a constitutional convention in 1975. They were designed to exclude the involvement of the Irish Government, and put the United Kingdom in the role of mediator rather than as the active director of a political initiative. Neutrality on the part of the Secretary of State consisted of refusing to enforce a reunification of Ireland (the anti-nationalist axiom), and refusing any restoration of a devolved government on the strongly majoritarian lines of the Stormont regime (the anti-unionist axiom). When the convention's unionist majority in its final report insisted on a majoritarian executive, and described the SDLP as fundamentally republican and incapable of being loyal members of a Belfast Government, Rees dissolved the body in March 1976 – leading to twenty-three years of direct rule from Westminster.

Mason, by contrast, pursued no significant power-sharing initiatives, directly or otherwise. He believed they heightened expectations and created instability. Benevolent direct rule on the second premise of arbitration policies constituted his understanding of his mission. He declared he was more worried by the region's economy than its political or security problems. Rees and Mason, like some of their Conservative predecessors and successors, saw one of their key tasks to be the institutionalisation of professionalised public services, cleansing the partisan, clientelist and supremacist conduct of local governments and state organisations prevalent under the Stormont Parliament. The police were detached from their role as the armed wing of the UUP. The appointments of magistrates and judges, public prosecutions and the franchise for local govern-ment and regional elections were put under Westminster's control. Fairer administration of education and health boards flowed from direct rule, it was thought. Human rights watchdogs, ombudsmen and anti-discrimination legisla-tion, under both the Tories and Labour, showed formal evidence of good intentions. Public expenditure and employment would no longer be overtly dictated by the political patronage imperatives of the UUP.

If professionalising public bureaucracies was regarded as evidence of Labour's determination to provide good instead of agreed government, its security policies were eventually intended to show ministers as firm governors. The Labour Government had been seen to respond to coercion. Nationalists judged, correctly, that Wilson and Rees had capitulated before the coercion of the Ulster Workers' Council strike. A determined loyalist minority, which eventually mobilised a majority of the majority community, was able to dictate outcomes to a cross-community majority within Northern Ireland – irrespective of the local Assembly's election returns, mandate or current preferences. Unionists also judged that the Government was negotiable before the assaults of republicans. Ceasefires and experiments in negotiations with the IRA were tried in 1975 – and fed loyalist fears of a sell-out. But while the constitutional convention was in progress Rees and his officials reconsidered security policy – reflecting the tendency for British policy makers to partition party political and security matters without deep appraisals of their mutual connections. These reconsiderations would be implemented under Mason.

They involved three themes: criminalisation, Ulsterisation and normalisation. In part, they stemmed from the Gardiner report, which had been commissioned to rid London of the embarrassment of internment without trial. Initiated in August 1971 internment had been overtly incompetent and partisan. The first loyalist was not interned until February 1973. While the policy operated between 1971 and 1975, 2,060 republicans were detained, by comparison with 109 loyalists.[24] Readers can appraise for themselves the bias in this policy from one piece of comparative data: whereas republicans were twenty times as likely as loyalists to be interned, they were responsible for just over twice as many deaths in this period.[25] Gardiner recommended the restoration of judicial processes, insisting that suspects should be dealt with through the courts, and, fatefully, that the 'special status' category for the targeted prisoners should be phased out. The Gardiner report softened the Diplock report of 1972, which had recommended the suspension of the right to a jury trial for certain indictable offences, new relaxed rules on the admissibility of evidence, and on the onus of proof, and enhanced powers for the security forces – the police and the army. These commendations had been duly incorporated in the Emergency Provisions Act (EPA) of 1973, which had retained the power of internment. While the EPA had been portrayed as a reform, because it was accompanied by the repeal of the hated Special Powers Act of the Stormont Parliament, it was widely and rightly diagnosed as containing many of the same threats to the fair administration of justice: up to one-half of the new Act was directly inspired by the older legislation.[26] Criminalisation, of course, depended for its success on two contentious predictions: that the United Kingdom would be able to present itself as relying on normal legal processes, and that the efforts to de-legitimise political violence as criminal violence would work within the constituent populations of republicans and loyalists. The first prospect was destroyed because the Government continued to depend on juryless single-judge Diplock courts, and to derogate from the European Convention on Human Rights on the grounds that there was an emergency – which contradicted the suppositions of 'normalisation'. In addition, the abandonment of internment led to an increased reliance on confessions, extracted by coercive and dubious questioning techniques.[27] This prompted the embarrassment of vigorous criticism by Amnesty International in 1978.[28] Mason was forced to permit an inquiry and the Bennett Committee proposed new controls on police conduct, which did lead to a decline in complaints after Mason had left office. The second prospect, winning legitimacy for the criminalisation of paramilitaries, had some limited effect within the loyalist working class; resistance within the republicans' constituency would wholly defeat it.

'Ulsterisation' involved the use of locally recruited police and military in the management of security – and sought a downsizing in the role and numbers of the British Army in the region. The policy had obvious public relations advantages for Whitehall. Between 1969 and 1975, 270 British soldiers were killed in the conflict, compared with 148 of the local security forces; between 1976 and 1984 the figures were 150 and 235 respectively.[29] The use of locals in security duties helped press briefings intended to fend off interpretations of the conflict as colonial. It was thought that the British Army's vanguard role made it easier for the IRA to argue that it was fighting a national war of liberation. Presentation of Ulsterisation was bolstered by the adoption of 'police primacy' as part of 'normalisation' in 1976. The police had doubled in size between 1969 and 1972. Mason oversaw another dramatic expansion: by 1982 the RUC comprised 7,700 regulars and 4,800 reservists. The ratio of police officers to residents in Northern Ireland's small population soon was over four times that in South-East England. This comparison rightly suggests that 'normalisation' was not with respect to some English norm. The police did develop greater responsibility for security, but this was accomplished by militarising the police. The flak-jacketed, heavily armed, armoured Land-Rover-borne RUC did not resemble English bobbies. Plastic-bullet-firing police were less lethal, and usually more circumspect, than soldiers using live ammunition, but they were still engaged in political repression. The RUC made little use of normal police methods of gathering intelligence, especially in Catholic-dominated areas, and used military snatch-operations rather than low-key modes of arrest. The army was fully present in a back-up role, but almost exclusively deployed in republican-dominated districts – thereby undermining both police primacy and efforts to portray impartiality in the administration of policing.

'Ulsterisation' and 'normalisation' were not confined to the RUC. In 1969 Callaghan as Home Secretary had overseen reports and measures intended both to disarm the RUC and to disband the B-Specials, the exclusively Protestant paramilitary auxiliary back-up to the RUC. The latter objective was formally achieved; the former was rapidly reversed, in part in response to IRA actions. By 1979 Mason, Callaghan's appointee as Secretary of State, had professionalised but militarised the RUC, and had overseen the expansion and extensive deployment of the Ulster Defence Regiment, the UDR, a locally recruited and deployed section of the British Army. The UDR had a highly partisan name, almost as offensive in nationalist ears as that of the RUC's; and they were seen as the new B-Specials. Within a decade of Labour's first intervention Mason was presiding over nearly 20,000 jobs in the RUC and UDR establishments, mostly staffed by working-class Protestants. Once again Catholics and nationalists were being policed, para-policed and soldiered by the local majority of Protestants and unionists. 'Ulsterisation' had predictably become unionist-ulsterisation; and it had other foreseeable consequences. The IRA (and the INLA) switched their focus of attack towards the most visible security personnel, i.e. the RUC and the UDR. The result was that the conflict was waged more directly between locals, imparting an apparently greater sectarian coloration to a mutually dirty war, making it even more difficult for unionist politicians to contemplate power sharing with their nationalist neighbours. The credibility of normalisation was further undermined by the Government's public deployment of the army's most feared specialist intelligence unit, the SAS, in Armagh; and the decision either to permit a dirty war opened by MI5, MI6, the SAS and specialist units of the RUC, or not to look closely into the actions and inactions of the said agencies.[30]

'Criminalisation' posed a serious threat to the IRA. The first response of its prisoners arrested and convicted under the new rationalised legal procedures was to go 'on the blanket', refusing to bear prison uniforms. This was followed by the 'dirty protests', smearing their prison walls with their own excrement – again in a determined rejection of the criminal designation. The 'H blocks', the recently designed high-security prison units, became locally, and then internationally, notorious, and plainly the site of incarceration of the politically motivated. 'Criminalisation', however, would not be decisively defeated by the IRA until after Labour had left office. In the struggle between the UK authorities and republican prisoners, culminating in ten dead hunger strikers in 1981, the prisoners would win *de facto* recognition of their special status while the Government would formally avoid the concession of political status.[31] But no one was fooled. The prisoners won at the ballot box. The outcome was Sands's and subsequently Sinn Féin's electoral breakthrough – Sinn Féin was able to widen the battlefields, and the IRA was able to shake off the criminal label within its own constituency and beyond. The long-run repercussions of Rees's and Mason's criminalisation policies were to build Sinn Féin a strong political constituency, one that threatened the SDLP's nationalist flanks, and would eventually re-send London's negotiators back towards an accommodation with the Government of Ireland. Ulsterisation, like criminalisation, bought short-run gains at the expense of long-run contradictions. Direct rule became overtly *British* rule through local Ulster unionist instruments. The image of the impartial arbitrator would be shredded as the UDR replaced the B-Specials; as the RUC became a rationalised, expanded and overwhelmingly Protestant force – its reform primarily confined to its detachment from the UUP; and as a steady stream of episodes and scandals persuaded nationalists of extensive collusion between the security forces, intelligence agencies and loyalist paramilitaries.

Above all, a social democratic government might have been expected to have strongly endeavoured to achieve significant reform in employment – in eradicating direct and indirect discrimination in employment; in encouraging the development of genuinely bi-national or non-sectarian trade unions; and in encouraging the confrontation of public prejudices and stereotypes. A Fair Employment Act was passed in 1976; the legal framework would prove naïve and ineffective, while the agency it established would lack sufficient powers to make a difference. Catholic male unemployment would remain over twice that of Protestants for the next two decades. Labour did nothing of importance with its trade union allies to build common ground within the working class. Its initial dalliance with the Northern Ireland Labour Party, which disappeared amidst the polarisation of the 1970s, had given its leaders concrete evidence that British Labour could not perform the types of cross-community mobilisation it had managed in Scotland. Thinly funded and anaemic efforts to promote good community relations, and to encourage integrated education on the part of Lord Melchett, a junior minister under Mason, symbolised good intentions. But they were comprehensively undermined by the failure to stabilise Sunningdale, or to deliver a positive outcome from the constitutional convention of 1975–6, and, of course, by the repercussions of Ulsterisation and criminalisation.

What of order, if not law and the rule of law? How might one evaluate Labour's governance of security? Within Northern Ireland the years 1972–6 were marked by the highest levels of political violence in the current phase of the conflict, as tracked by the key indicators of killings, injuries, explosions, shootings and armed robberies. Levels of violence on all these indicators in general fell sharply from 1977 onwards, thereafter reaching a generally steady state until the IRA and loyalist ceasefires of 1994–7. Should these data be deployed in defence of the Labour Government? It at least dampened levels of violence – including in Great Britain, where the horrors of the Guildford and Birmingham pub-bombings were to trigger the passage of the Prevention of Terrorism Act. But several caveats need to be entered into any such appraisal. The high death toll in the early years is best explained by three factors. The first is the decision of the Provisional IRA to engage in urban and rural guerrilla warfare and urban terrorism – producing large numbers of casualties amongst inexperienced police and army personnel, whereas its commercial bombings led to a large number of civilian deaths. The second was the loyalist backlash, first against civil rights demonstrations in the late 1960s, and then in the form of very high levels of sectarian assassinations against Catholics between 1971 and 1975. The third factor was the introduction of internment without trial in August 1971: initially targeted (but inaccurately) exclusively at the nationalist community the policy acted as a recruitment agency for the IRA.

The reductions in all major indicators of conflict from 1977 are related to these three factors. The IRA changed its strategy. Weakened by the ceasefire of 1975, on which more in a moment, it reorganised in small cells, or active service units. It settled down for a 'long war', abandoning its hopes of rapid victory. It switched its foci towards military and political targets – reducing its scale of commercial bombing, where the impacts had often adversely affected their own base of support. Second, loyalist paramilitaries reduced their assassinations of Catholics, in part because their fears of a British withdrawal had diminished. Moreover, over time they were more likely to be arrested than before, and their organisations became more factionalised, corrupt and directionless. Third, greater numbers and effectiveness on the part of the security forces dampened down levels of violence. Police primacy reduced the army's propensity to be more trigger-happy. The price was high: huge investments in security devices, surveillance systems, cordoned-off town centres, checkpoints, forts, observation posts and computerised civilian screening on a massive scale. Urban landscapes and housing were redesigned to be less friendly to the urban paramilitant. Emergency legislation that became permanent removed certain standard civil liberties and judicial safeguards (notoriously those accused and convicted of the Guildford and Birmingham pub-bombings were entirely innocent of the charges against them).

This brief appraisal suggests why purely on order criteria some are tempted to assess the Mason years positively – they turned the corner on the worst of the violence. This is a verdict especially held by many unionists. The Labour Cabinets certainly deserve credit for abandoning internment without trial. Conflict reduction is not, however, conflict resolution, neither is it proof of sensible conflict management. The reduction in violence was partly caused by perversities and actions for which governments were not responsible; and government actions created new perversities. Residential segregation increased extensively as people chose to live safely with 'their own': the early 1970s reduced radically the numbers of genuinely 'mixed areas'. The absence of a politically negotiated settlement encouraged a long war of attrition, a 'non-result', a continuous and bleeding stalemate – bringing up whole new cohorts of mutually distrustful citizens and politicians. The sealing off of the Protestant middle class and better-off working class both from the visible signs and the economic costs of the conflict reduced their incentives to engage in power sharing, let alone accept an Irish dimension. The institutionalised interests of large sections of the Protestant working class in security and security-related occupations made them more indifferent towards peace. A distinguished Cambridge economist, Professor Bob Rowthorn, would come to describe Northern Ireland as having a workhouse economy, in which the participants in an unproductive economy either engage in surveillance of one another or exchange non-marketed services. The growth of Sinn Féin and the radicalisation of the SDLP were by-products of the policies of Rees and Mason, and arguably both developments postponed the prospects of a cross-community settlement. The Government's manipulation of the IRA's ceasefire in 1975, while seen as tactically acute by counter-insurgents, had negative long-run costs. Merlyn Rees in his memoirs maintains that the Government's quasi-negotiations during the IRA's ceasefire were coherent, to create the conditions in which the Provisional IRA's military organisation might be weakened. The longer the ceasefire lasted, the more difficult it would be for them to start a campaign from scratch and in this period of peace I hoped political action would be given a chance.[32]

The rationale of his officials was certainly to distract and demobilise the IRA by discussing withdrawal but not negotiating it. And the IRA was weakened by the ceasefire, but that only ensured that after its reorganisation it would become wholly overtly hostile to ceasefires or truces without a British commitment to withdrawal, and would treat NIO officials as deceitful counter-insurgents. The summer that Labour lost office saw the INLA and the IRA succeed in their most spectacular killings to date: the INLA blew up Airey Neave in the House of Commons car park, while the IRA blew up Lord Louis Mountbatten, and killed eighteen British soldiers at Warrenpoint. The ceasefire experience of 1975 partly explains why the IRA broke its 1994 ceasefire; it suspected the Major Government of stringing it along in the way that Rees's officials had done two decades before. This culture of suspicion still drives the current IRA leadership's reluctance to complete the decommissioning of its weapons until the British Government has comprehensively and unambiguously delivered on all its public and legal obligations under the Good Friday Agreement. Lack of trust in New Labour amongst Irish republicans is not just the result of Peter Mandelson's dreadful performance as Secretary of State; it is rooted in entrenched memories of the IRA's manipulation at the hands of Rees's officials. The entrenchment of distrust was not confined to nationalist quarters. Unionists had seen the Labour Government as negotiable, and as willing to bend to coercion. Once Labour had lost its parliamentary majority at Westminster the UUP extracted concessions of an integrationist kind, notably an expansion in Northern Ireland's representation at Westminster, and could rely on its veto power on the floor of the Commons to inhibit any prospect of power sharing or an Irish dimension. The Labour Government, under both its premiers, therefore reduced the capacity of UK ministers to provide credible commitments to the locals, let alone the Irish Government. Being distrusted and disliked by both communities was seen by some as a badge of honour; a more sensible appraisal is that earning contempt and distrust all around earns no politicians worthy reputations, either at the time or later.

IV

The collapse of the Sunningdale experiment was the decisive event of the Labour Government of 1974; it haunted the rest of Labour's term of management; and it is the event by which Labour's ministers should be judged. That is why it is addressed at the end rather than the beginning of this chapter. Evaluation requires a rapid analytical narrative. The Sunningdale Agreement was both an agreement and an agreement about further possible agreements. It included immediate consent to the formation of a cross-community coalition government in Northern Ireland, comprising Faulkner's Official Unionists, Fitt's SDLP, and the Alliance Party, a unionist party in lower case 'u', which drew support from cultural Protestants and Catholics. An eleven-member executive was formed with six UUP, four SDLP and one Alliance ministers. In this respect the Agreement was a voluntary consociation. The three parties had between them won nearly 61 per cent of the first preference votes cast in the Northern Ireland Assembly elections held in the summer of 1973, and the UUP (though divided) and the SDLP were the largest parties in the unionist and nationalist blocs respectively. The Agreement also envisaged a Council of Ireland, at the SDLP's insistence, but with the support of the UK and Irish Governments. The Council harked back to unfulfilled elements of the Government of Ireland Act of 1920.[33] It was to consist of a council of ministers, seven from each of the two jurisdictions on the island, a secretariat, and a sixty-member consultative assembly (with thirty members from Dáil Éireann and thirty from the Northern Ireland Assembly). Decisions of the council of ministers were to be unanimous, thus providing veto powers to both sides – and indeed subsections of both delegations. The Council of Ireland was to be experimental, vested with minor consultative and research functions, but it was to have a 'harmonising' role, and the door was left open for it to become the embryonic institution of a reunified Ireland – though plainly only through mutual co-operation. Sunningdale also had an agenda too often forgotten today – including consideration of major reforms of the RUC, and a review of the policy of internment without trial. A commission was promised to examine the contentious issue of cross-border extradition of those suspected of terrorist offences. Faulkner and his colleagues hoped to win acceptance for power sharing and the Council of Ireland amongst unionists by emphasising the potential security benefits from co-operation with the Irish Government, the largely symbolic nature of the Council, the unionist veto over the Council's evolution, and the *de facto* recognition of Northern Ireland's current status contained in Article 5: 'the Irish Government fully accepted and solemnly declared that there could be no change in the status of Northern Ireland until a majority of the people of Northern Ireland desired a change in that status'.

The Agreement got off to an inauspicious start, even though many of its ministers were to prove effective holders of their portfolios. It was evident that it would be opposed by both sets of paramilitaries. On 4 January 1974, four days after the executive took office, the Ulster Unionist Council of the UUP voted to reject the Agreement. Three days later Faulkner resigned from the UUP, forming the Unionist Party of Northern Ireland (UPNI). He managed to bring over only seventeen of his initial supporters in the Assembly to his new party, leaving the three parties in the executive with the unambiguous support of forty-five of the seventy-eight Assembly members,[34] a majority, but now with only a majority of nationalists on its side. Within the Assembly many of the anti-Agreement unionists would behave boorishly and thuggishly, especially towards Faulkner's unionists. At the end of January a constitutional challenge to Ireland's signature to the Agreement was placed before Dublin's Supreme Court (*Boland* v. *An Taoiseach*). The Court would uphold the constitutionality of the Agreement; it was not in breach of Articles 2 and 3 of Ireland's constitution; but the Irish Government was obliged in the case to defend its position as *de facto* rather than *de jure* recognition of Northern Ireland's status as part of the United Kingdom. The Taoiseach, Liam Cosgrave, insisted in the Dáil on 13 March that 'Northern Ireland ... is within the United Kingdom and my Government accepts this as a fact.' Ireland's Attorney-General declared more emphatically that 'any person living in this island and knowing our history could not possibly construe the Sunningdale declaration as meaning that we did not lay claim over the six counties'.[35] These statements, while true, could not help Faulkner's unionists.

The Westminster general election of February 1974 displaced the Conservatives who had negotiated the Sunningdale settlement. In his first Cabinet post, Rees was therefore in charge of a settlement that Labour had not made. Worse, Westminster's backward electoral system, plurality rule in single-member districts, served to weaken the position of the power-sharing parties. They had benefited from proportional representation in multi-member districts in the Assembly elections, but they could not agree common pro-Agreement candidates in winner-takes-all contests. By contrast, all the anti-Agreement unionists mobilised behind the United Ulster Unionist Council (the UUUC) with an agreed candidate in each constituency. Their platform declared that 'Dublin is only a Sunningdale away.' They won eleven out of twelve of Northern Ireland's seats at Westminster. It bears emphasis, however, that this 92 per cent share of the available seats was won with just 51 per cent of the votes cast, in an election that had no mandated authority over either the Sunningdale Agreement or the jurisdiction of the Assembly. Obviously from then on Faulkner's UPNI would be in serious trouble. By the end of April the UUUC had held a conference that agreed the following platform: the abolition of the power-sharing executive and the Sunningdale Agreement; immediate new Assembly elections; and the return of security policy management to a new Assembly. This agenda was directly hostile to the Agreement just negotiated by the two sovereign governments, and to the majority of the Assembly elected in 1973.

Within three weeks, on 14 May, the Ulster Workers' Council (the UWC) called a general strike in support of the objectives of the UUUC. A shadowy confluence of trade unionists and loyalist paramilitaries it was not then – or later – a major body. It called the strike, even though many of the politicians within the UUUC had cold-shouldered the UWC, doubtful of its success and reluctant to embrace such overt militancy. On the first day of the strike it seemed those politicians had judged correctly: the overwhelming majority of workers went to their enterprises, offices and shops. The major loyalist paramilitary organisation, the UDA, then deployed its militants, marshalled by their leader Andy Tyrie. The UDA's orchestrated intimidation, witnessed by the author as a young man of 16, made the strike bite, extensively in eastern Northern Ireland, and then wherever Protestants were demographically dominant. Roads were blocked. Masked men, hooded men, men with sunglasses and parka jackets 'visited' factories, and blocked the exits to housing estates. Toughs and aspiring toughs in the tartan fashions of the time manned makeshift barricades. The UWC had critical support within the electricity power stations. What began as a largely unsupported strike soon became very effective. As it spread, Protestants supported it more. For many, especially for Catholics, it became a lockout, not a strike. The army did nothing about the intimidation. The police matched their indifference. General Sir Frank King later admitted:

> when the strike started I remember having a conference and deciding not to get mixed up in it ... we never had any aggro at all with the strikers. Dealing with intimidation was a police job. The fact that the RUC didn't do too much about it was no concern of ours. We were angry at the time but it wasn't our job. If Rees had ordered us to move against the barricades we would have said, 'with great respect, this is a job for the police. We will assist them if you wish, but it's not terrorism'.[36]

The head of the army did not regard organised thuggery by the UDA as terrorism, or not the type of terrorism to which he was mandated to respond. The Ministry of Defence and the army claimed that they could not run the power stations properly or comprehensively. Pessimistic scenarios flooded into Rees and Wilson – warning them of sewage in the streets, epidemics, food shortages and power-free hospitals. In Dublin and Monaghan loyalists planted bombs, the most devastating in the conflict to that date, killing twenty-five people in the Irish capital and seven in the border town. Many would subsequently believe the loyalists had had the assistance of British intelligence operatives – operating to 'encourage' the Irish Government to move on extradition, or pursuing some other agenda of their own.[37] Within the executive nationalists made compromises: the Council of Ireland would be postponed until after the next Assembly election. It did not stop the strike. The UK Government at last moved to control oil and petrol supplies and distribution; Wilson condemned the strikers as 'spongers' – which upset the relevant targets; but two weeks into the strike Faulkner resigned after Rees refused to open negotiations with the strikers. Rees then dissolved the executive and the Assembly.

How should we assess this event over a quarter of a century later? The most incisive journalist account of the time, by a brilliant reporter, Robert Fisk, is surprisingly irresolute in its conclusions, and wrong that the strike had broken the will of the British to stay. What the strike broke was the will of London Governments to have a significant Irish dimension in addressing the conflict, a will that would not be recovered until Margaret Thatcher and Garret FitzGerald negotiated the Anglo-Irish Agreement in 1985. *The Point of No Return: The Strike Which Broke the British in Ulster* is, correctly, highly critical of the NIO, the police and the army – the last, of course, as we have seen is condemned from its commanding officer's own words. Not all responsibility can be attributed to these agencies or their leading personnel, but they were responsible for allowing a strike to bite through intimidation. It was not their duty to have an opinion on the executive's future prospects; that was the job of their masters. Political communications from the NIO and Number 10 were very poor, but if there is no decisive message communications cannot help. Whether or to what extent the NIO's officials, the police's senior ranks or the army's top brass colluded with loyalists, or whether such collusion occurred at lower ranks, is something we may know more about later, but whatever we may learn in these respects, in the absence of vigorous political direction from the top the conduct of the security forces was less appropriately focused than it might have been. It was after all loyalist violence that escalated during early 1974; republican violence remained at much the same pitch. It is, of course, evident that popular unionist support for the Agreement had fallen dramatically before the executive collapsed, and that there would have been continuing difficulties between the UPNI and the SDLP within the executive over internment, police reform, extradition and the implementation of the Council of Ireland. But the fact remains that before the strike developed there was still a majority in the Assembly available to support the executive. Sunningdale need not have died in May 1974, even if it may have had an inevitable later rendezvous with a coroner.

It has to be said: Rees, as the local Secretary of State, Wilson, as Prime Minister, and to a lesser extent Mason, as the Secretary of State for Defence, were the key officials with political responsibility for what happened. Rees did not believe in Sunningdale. He thought it lost from very early on, well before the strike. Later, he would damn Sunningdale before his Cabinet colleagues as a piece of 'British suburban illusion, a sort of *Guardian* solution which was no solution'.[38] When a Labour politician casually attacks the *Guardian* cheap and desperate arguments are being mustered. Sunningdale was no illusion; it was the fruits of both the cities and the suburbs of Great Britain and both parts of Ireland. Rees was only not capable of credible commitment; he simply lacked conviction – and he would not have been the best in any crisis, to put it mildly. Later, he would claim in a television interview 'I didn't let them win. They were going to win anyway. It could not be done, that's the short answer. The police were on the brink of not carrying out their duties and the middle class were on the strikers' side.'[39] This is just unconvincing. The police initially were not given direction. The Protestant middle class were won to the strike; they did not start in its ranks. Rees was politically incapable of thinking about how to break the strike, a reactionary strike against three elected governments – he did not think of an early crackdown, instructing his senior military and police commanders to behave appropriately; neither did he think later of martial law, or of taking powers to order workers and managers to man the electricity stations; or, indeed, of letting the strikers live with what would have been the devastating and delegitimising consequences of full-scale power-cuts. In 1977 Roy Mason would prove far more resolute in response to a second loyalist strike orchestrated with Paisley's support; in 1986–7 Margaret Thatcher would resist even more widespread initial unionist antipathy to a British and Irish constitutional initiative. Decisive action by Rees and his colleagues might have made the lives of his successors easier. The loyalist strike leaders certainly expected a crackdown; they went into hiding in anticipation; theirs was an unexpected victory. Wilson too lacked the courage of his convictions – choosing not to withhold funds for Northern Ireland's loyalist-dominated shipyards in response to the strike (even though he contemplated the idea in private). The head of his Policy Unit would find the craven response of his Government and the sudden collapse of the executive perplexing, inexplicable and suspicious.[40] In 1974, as the minister responsible for defence and the army, Mason arguably did not prompt the senior military to prepare properly for manning power stations or get them to link strike breaking to breaking paramilitarism. None of the three men, or their biographers, have any compelling riposte to John Hume's comment in his memoirs,

> the establishment of power-sharing was a tribute to the political courage of the then Conservative government. … Unfortunately the Labour administration which succeeded it … showed no similar courage, and in May of that year, in what was one of the most squalid examples of government irresponsibility, it surrendered its policy in the face of a political strike organised by a paramilitary minority on the Unionist side.[41]

Thus far the Blair Government has proven much more robust in defence of the Good Friday Agreement than its predecessors were in defence of the Sunningdale Agreement. Blair's Government helped make the Good Friday Agreement, and whatever its subsequent deficiencies, occasional acts of cowardice and misjudgements, especially under Mandelson, it is most unlikely to earn the disrespect attached to the conduct of Northern Ireland policy and administration under Wilson, Callaghan, Rees and Mason.

Notes

1   For an account of the UUP's regime of control see O'Leary, B. and McGarry, J., *The Politics of Antagonism: Understanding Northern Ireland* (Athlone Press, London, 2nd edition, 1996), pp. 107–80.

2   Crossman, R.H.S., *The Diaries of a Cabinet Minister*, vol. III (Hamish Hamilton, London, 1977), p. 620.

3   Callaghan, J., *A House Divided* (Collins, London, 1973). Callaghan creditably initiated the construction of a new, non-discriminatory housing executive that materialised in 1971. He records Crossman as having told him that he would be dismissed in an autumn reshuffle in 1969, but was reprieved because of his management of Northern Ireland, Callaghan, J., *Time and Chance* (Collins, London, 1987), p. 272.

4   For a treatment of Sunningdale's differences with the Good Friday Agreement see Wolff, S., 'Context and Content: Sunningdale and Belfast Compared', in Wilford, R. (ed.), *Aspects of the Belfast Agreement* (Oxford University Press, Oxford, 2001), pp. 11–27.

5   Wilson, H., *Final Term: The Labour Government, 1974–76* (Weidenfeld and Nicolson/Michael Joseph, London, 1979), pp. 68–70; see especially the chapter 'John Bull's Other Island', pp. 66–80.

6   See note 3.

7   Donoughue, B., *Prime Minister: The Conduct of Policy under Harold Wilson and James Callaghan* (Cape, London, 1987), p. 128. Donoughue opens his narration on 'the problem' of 'Ireland' by saying that as a 'former professional historian' he knew it to

be 'insoluble'. Why professional historians, former or otherwise, might have such knowledge is not explained.

8 Ibid., p. 129.
9 Benn, T., *Against the Tide: Diaries 1973–76* (Arrow, London, 1989), pp. 137–8.
10 Rees describes himself as 'left wondering why the speech had been made', Rees, M., *Northern Ireland: A Personal Perspective* (Methuen, London, 1985), p. 61.
11 Benn, *Against the Tide*, p. 142.
12 Donoughue, *Prime Minister*, p. 132, emphasis in the original.
13 Callaghan, *Time and Chance*, p. 500.
14 Ibid., p. 500.
15 The former kindly agreed to be interviewed by the author (18 December 1990), and generously reviewed one of his co-edited books for the *LSE Magazine*. The latter refused all requests for interviews, the sole ex-Secretary of State to refuse the author such a request in the 1980s and 1990s.
16 Rees, *Northern Ireland: A Personal Perspective*.
17 Ibid., p. 317.
18 Ibid., p. 71.
19 Cited in McKittrick, D. and McVea, D., *Making Sense of the Troubles* (Penguin, London, 2001, revised edition), p. 106.
20 Interview 3 January 1991. Donoughue described him as seeming more 'Protestant' than the 'Prods', *Prime Minister*, p. 131.
21 In his memoir he declared that 'Grandiose Anglo/Irish solutions will not work', Rees, *Northern Ireland: A Personal Perspective*, p. 352. This too was defensive. The Anglo-Irish Agreement, which paved the way for the Good Friday Agreement, stemmed from the two sovereign governments taking action, precisely the path Rees and Mason closed off after 1974.
22 Rees, *Northern Ireland: A Personal Perspective*, p. 351.
23 What follows draws upon joint work with John McGarry, especially in *The Politics of Antagonism*, ch. 5, 'Deadlock, 1972–85: the limits to British arbitration'.
24 Hogan, G. and Walker, C., *Political Violence and the Law in Ireland* (Manchester University Press, Manchester, 1989), pp. 93–4.
25 Between 1971 and 1975 all republican paramilitaries were responsible for 806 deaths in and over Northern Ireland, whereas loyalists were responsible for 385. In 1974 and 1975 the death tolls caused by each set of paramilitaries were very close in number. The data and the simple calculation in the text are based on the definitive work of McKittrick, D., Kelters, S., Feeney, B. and Thornton, C., *Lost Lives: The Stories of the Men, Women and Children Who Died as a Result of the Northern Ireland Troubles* (Mainstream, Edinburgh, 3rd edition, 2001), p. 1496.
26 Hogan and Walker, *Political Violence and the Law in Ireland*, p. 197.
27 Taylor, P., *Beating the Terrorists?* (Penguin, Harmondsworth, 1980).
28 Report of an Amnesty International Mission to Northern Ireland 1977 (1978).
29 Calculated from McKittrick *et al.*, *Lost Lives*, Table 1.
30 For diverse materials on the dirty war, especially works dealing with British intelligence, informers and loyalist paramilitaries, see Bradley, A., *Requiem for a Spy: The Killing of Robert Nairac* Mercier, Cork, 1993); Bruce, S., *The Red Hand: Protestant Paramilitaries in Northern Ireland* (Oxford University Press, Oxford, 1992) and 'Terrorists and Politics: The Case of Northern Ireland's Loyalist Paramilitaries', *Terrorism and Political Violence*, 13(2), 2001, pp. 27–48; Dillon, M., *The Dirty War* (Hutchinson, London, 1990); Foot, P., *Who Framed Colin Wallace?* (Macmillan, London, 1989); Holroyd, F. with Burbridge, N., *War Without Honour* (Medium, Hull, 1989); Murray, R., *The SAS in Ireland* (Mercier, Cork, 1990); Taylor, P., *Stalker: The Search for the Truth* (Faber, London, 1987); Urban, M., *Big Boys' Rules: The Secret Struggle Against the IRA* (Faber, London, 1992); and Wright, P. with Greengrass, P., *Spycatcher* (Heinemann, Australia, 1987).

31 On the IRA and the hunger strikes see especially Beresford, D., *Ten Men Dead: The Story of the 1981 Irish Hunger Strike* (Grafton, London, 1987), *and* on republicans see, *inter alia*, Bishop, P. and Mallie, E., *The Provisional IRA* (Heinemann, London, 1987); O'Brien, B., *The Long War: The IRA and Sinn Féin from Armed Struggle to Peace Talks* (O'Brien, Dublin, 1995); Coogan, T.P., *The IRA* (Fontana, London, 1970, 1980, 1987); O'Malley, P., *Biting at the Grave: The Irish Hunger Strikes and the Politics of Despair* (Beacon, Boston, 1990), critically reviewed by the author in *Irish Political Studies* (1991); and Taylor, P., *Provos: The IRA and Sinn Féin* (Bloomsbury, London, 1997). On Sinn Féin see Brian Feeney's fine study, *Sinn Féin: A Hundred Turbulent Years* (O'Brien, Dublin, 2002).

32 Rees, *Northern Ireland: A Personal Perspective*, p. 224.

33 Mansergh, N., 'The Government of Ireland Act, 1920', in Barry, J.G. (ed.), *Historical Studies* (Blackstaff, Belfast, 1974).

34 The NILP's one Assembly member meant that the power-sharing parties had forty-five of the Assembly on their side, compared with thirty-three opposed unionists.

35 *Irish Times*, 22 April 1974, cited in O'Leary and McGarry, *The Politics of Antagonism*, p. 200.

36 Cited in McKittrick and McVea, *Making Sense of the Troubles*, pp. 103–4. Another general later rationalised matters differently: the 'Executive was doomed before the strike began. … I think it was a mercy Merlyn Rees was there. … He didn't make any decisions of any kind. If you'd had a decisive man who had arrested the strikers on the first day it would have created chaos', *Irish Times*, 15 May 1984, cited in Bew, P. and Patterson, H., *The British State and the Ulster Crisis: From Wilson to Thatcher* (Verso, London, 1985), p. 67, n. 118. One wonders whether the general believed chaos was not created as much by inaction.

37 The victims' accounts and campaigns for an inquiry are narrated in Mullan, D., *The Dublin and Monaghan Bombings: The Truth, the Question and the Victims' Stories* (Wolfhound, Dublin, 2000). An inquiry on the subject under the direction of Justice Barron is scheduled to report in September 2003; see also Bowyer Bell, J., *In Dubious Battle: The Dublin and Monaghan Bombings 1972–1974* (Poolbeg, Dublin, 1996).

38 Benn, *Against the Tide*, p. 526.

39 Cited in McKittrick and McVea, *Making Sense of the Troubles*, p. 106.

40 Interviews and conversations with Bernard Donoughue, including at Bishopsgate Investments and LSE, spring 1991; and see 'Ireland', in his *Prime Minister*.

41 Hume, J., *Personal Views: Politics, Peace and Reconciliation in Ireland* (Town House, Dublin, 1996).

15 The Labour Party

Eric Shaw

Conflict between left and right – between 'those who cling to the basic principles of the creed and favour speedy advance toward the party's goals, and those who are willing to trim the doctrine and to proceed at a slower, more cautious pace'[1] – has been a perennial feature of the Labour Party, like all social democratic parties. Usually running parallel with this is the tension between activists and leaders. As Peter Shore observed, 'it is in the nature of a democratic party of the Left that a majority of its most enthusiastic and active members will be anti-authoritarian, restless for change, distrustful of assertive leadership'.[2] The latter, their eyes fixed both on the immediate burdens of government and on winning the next election, seek maximum flexibility in policy and strategy; the former fear that in the process party ideals may be sacrificed. But not only was the scale and intensity of conflict unparalleled in the years 1974–9 but it assumed an entrenched and institutionalised form in the clash between the Party and the Government – which was to explode into a veritable civil war after 1979. Why did this occur? What was the pattern of Party–Government relations in the five turbulent years of the Wilson and Callaghan administrations?

In addressing these questions this chapter consists of the following sections: the first outlines the situation in the Party in the run-up to the election of February 1974. The second and third review the main policy flash-points of controversy between the Government and the extra-parliamentary party, over current policy and the framing of the manifesto for the next election. The fourth explores the clash between Labour's National Executive Committee (NEC), the body responsible for internal party management, and the Government over two highly sensitive internal party matters: parliamentary selection procedures and the challenge of Trotskyist entryism. The fifth hazards an explanation for why relations between the Party and the Government corroded so seriously and the final section comments on the lessons drawn by Tony Blair.

The run-up to February 1974

What were the powers and duties of the various institutions that composed the Labour Party in this period? Conference was the supreme authority, 'the parliament of the movement', responsible both for policy development and for internal management of the Party. The manifesto, the only policy document formally binding upon the Party, was based upon Labour's programme, which consisted of resolutions and NEC statements adopted by Conference by a two-thirds majority on a card vote. A joint meeting of the Parliamentary Committee (i.e. Cabinet or Shadow Cabinet) and the NEC – the so-called Clause V meeting named after the relevant section of the constitution – decided which items of the programme would be included in the manifesto. However, the Parliamentary Labour Party (PLP) had some latitude over the order and timing of the implementation of the manifesto. The NEC was entrusted with enforcing the constitution and rules of the Party and vested with the disciplinary powers necessary to discharge this task. For example, it had the power to ratify or refuse parliamentary candidatures, and to expel from the Party. Most actions taken by the NEC had to be ratified by the annual conference, 90 per cent of whose votes were, in this period, in the power of the affiliated trade unions. The Shadow Cabinet (or frontbench) was elected by the PLP in opposition but the Cabinet itself chosen by a Labour Prime Minister. The twenty-nine-member NEC was elected in a variety of ways, roughly a quarter by the Constituency Labour Parties (CLPs), eighteen were either solely or largely elected by the unions, and the Leader and Deputy Leader of the Party (elected by the PLP) were ex-officio members.

In short, constitutionally prescribed power was apportioned amongst a range of party bodies reflecting Labour's status as a pluralist party institutionalising the principles of the separation of powers and checks and balances. This meant that there was always a possibility of gridlock: of institutionalised conflict amongst its constituent bodies and policy impasse. In practice this had never occurred – until the 1970s – because party pluralism was countermanded by two structural conditions:

The autonomy of the PLP. In office Labour's acceptance of established practices and conventions relating to parliamentary politics and Cabinet government ensured a high measure of autonomy from the extra-parliamentary party. This meant that in practice, whilst Labour was in office, the Cabinet had effective control over the shaping of policy and could not be held to account by the wider Party. However, the NEC did retain responsibility for the management of internal party affairs: hence the overriding importance of the second condition.

Elite consensus and institutional interlock. From the 1930s to the 1960s the bulk of the most powerful unions was controlled by right-of-centre figures whose general political outlook corresponded closely to that of the parliamentary elite. The unions used their authority in all party institutions (Conference, the NEC and the PLP where a substantial number of trade-union-sponsored MPs were for the most part solid, right-of-centre loyalists) to bolster the authority of the leadership. On the great majority of issues, the leader and the frontbench could rely on guaranteed and firm majorities in both the NEC and at Conference. Elite consensus and the pattern of concurrent majorities in turn gave rise to institutional interlock, the welding together of the key institutional hierarchies and the placing of their powers at the disposal of the parliamentary leadership. Thus historically Labour's NEC contained a solid majority of centre–rightists ensuring that it was responsive to the wishes of the parliamentary leadership. It understood its role, whilst Labour was in office, as providing general political and organisational support for the Government. It performed a gate-keeping function – regulating the flow of inputs into the policy system – on behalf of the parliamentary leadership. Thus, during both the 1945–51 Labour Government and for much of the life of its successor from 1964 to 1970 the NEC defended the Government against internal party dissenters by deflecting and defusing their protests and demands as much as possible: it 'behaved with a devoted loyalty, publicly mute and privately circumspect in its criticisms'.[3] The effect was to offset to a substantial degree the constitutional pattern of checks and balances and give rise to a firm and cohesive leadership control system. However, from the mid-1960s onwards elite consensus and institutional interlock began to unravel. As a result the structural dynamics of party pluralism began to manifest themselves. The left-wing contingent on the NEC, traditionally a small minority, began to swell in size. This was in response first to a leftwards tilt in the constituency parties. But these only elected seven members so the pivotal change was the unprecedented shift of the unions to the left, notably the election of left-wingers to the leadership of the two largest unions, the Transport and General Workers' Union (TGWU) and the Amalgamated Union of Engineering Workers (AUEW – now, after a further merger, called Amicus), the redoubtable Jack Jones and Hugh Scanlon. This meant, first, that the votes at Conference of union affiliates were much more evenly divided between left and right than ever before, and, second, the securing by an increasing number of left-wingers of seats elected largely by the unions. This was a slow process because union voting decisions on the NEC were influenced by convention and internal union bargaining, but the effect was that, by 1974, the left obtained for the first time ever a majority, initially very narrow but in the following years steadily enlarged.

In the final year or so of the 1964–70 Wilson Government the role played by the NEC perceptibly evolved as it began to occupy a stance more independent of the Government and willing even to identify publicly with critics.[4] In opposition – with the standing of the parliamentary leadership undermined by electoral defeat and a widespread perception that the 1964–70 Government had made but modest progress in advancing party goals, and with the dominant centre–right majority seriously divided over British membership of the EEC (in the process of being negotiated by the Heath Government) – the left on the NEC began to assert themselves. They received a most valuable reinforcement as a result of the unusual political trajectory of Tony Benn.

Never in his earlier years associated with the left, Benn's rise within the Party had initially been as a protégé and close ally of Harold Wilson and by the late 1960s he was a senior minister. In opposition he veered strongly to the left, becoming highly critical of the record of the Government in which he had served with some distinction. Benn was a charismatic figure, an extraordinarily fluent and lucid speaker, who succeeded in attracting the enthusiastic allegiance of many within Labour's grass-roots and swiftly emerged as the chief standard bearer of the left. Barbara Castle reported being 'dazzled by his brilliance in analysing what was wrong with our society and his skill in promoting his ideas'. His capacity 'for putting mundane issues in philosophical context was unmatched, and it was what the rank and file hungered for. He could entrance audiences and lift his speeches to dazzling heights which impressed even non-socialists.'[5] He rapidly became the most influential figure on the NEC, elected Chairman of the NEC's Industrial Policy Subcommittee and (in 1975) of the most influential of its committees, the Home Policy Committee.

Advised by the economist and former Downing Street adviser, Stuart Holland, the Industrial Policy Subcommittee devised a radical, interventionist industrial strategy. Keynesianism, the pivotal element in Labour's social democratic creed, broke with neo-classical orthodoxy by postulating full employment and growth as the chief ends of economic policy, and by prescribing an active government role in the management of the economy. Demand management of the economy relied on fiscal and monetary policy to influence the pattern of choices made by business organisations and consumers in the market. As such it also represented a notable retreat from the socialist commitment to extensive public ownership and planning. The Industrial Policy Subcommittee (much influenced by Stuart Holland's book *The Socialist Challenge*) contended that because of the growth of a 'meso-economic' level of economic activity, characterised by the growing dominance of the world economy by multinational corporations, fiscal and monetary policy were no longer alone capable of effective regulation of the economy. The Subcommittee's report, included in the policy document *Labour's Programme 1973*, argued that the interests of large corporations 'cannot be expected to coincide with the interests of the national economy' whilst 'social reform of itself cannot bring about effective progress towards equality', since the roots of inequality lay in the system of production. To 'act *directly* at the level of the giant firm itself' the Party proposed two new instruments: a National Enterprise Board (NEB) and Planning Agreements which would considerably extend public ownership and planning of the economy. [6]

Labour's Programme 1973 was approved by Conference and – shorn of some of its most radical ideas – formed the basis of the 1974 manifesto. *Let us Work Together: Labour's Way Out of the Crisis* pledged Labour to introduce a 'powerful' NEB and a system of Planning Agreements. It also promised to take over 'profitable sections or individual firms in those industries where a public holding' was essential to enable the Government to meet its economic objectives and 'to plan the national economy in the national interest'.[7] The February 1974 manifesto was the most radical since that of 1945 – but those sections which most bore the imprint of left-wing NEC members (especially industrial policy) did not enjoy the support of the parliamentary leadership. The leaders acquiesced because they thought that Labour's prospects of winning the election were so slim. They were correct in that, compared with 1970 when it was evicted from office, the Party lost almost half-a-million votes but the massive electoral success of the Liberals returned Labour to power, by a quirk of the electoral system, first as a minority government and then, after the October 1974 election, with a minuscule majority.

Flash-points of controversy

Current policy

The parliamentary leadership found itself in a unique predicament – landed with a manifesto of which it did not wholly approve and with an NEC which it did not control. The left-led NEC construed its role in a way which departed markedly from that which the body had traditionally enacted whilst Labour was in office. It was to be the custodian of the manifesto and, more broadly, promoter of the will of the Party as articulated in Conference decisions. Its subcommittees and specialist working parties monitored the Government's performance, pinpointing the areas where ministers were falling short of manifesto commitments and where they were – as over the various instalments of public sector cuts and rising unemployment – adopting policies at odds with the Party's aims and values. As Peter Shore, a centrist minister who served in the Cabinet throughout the period, noted,

> contrary to the experience of all previous Labour Governments which had enjoyed the general support of the NEC and of its Head Office, the NEC became in these years a principal, if not the principal, source of criticism of the Labour Government.[8]

A collision was inevitable over industrial policy. Wilson believed that the dictates of party management left him no option but to appoint Benn as Industry Secretary, but he had not the slightest intention of implementing a policy that he regarded both as a wholly flawed and a serious threat to the Government's relations with the business community.[9] The White Paper drafted by Benn and his advisers was dismissed as 'wholly rubbish' by the Prime Minister who tartly commented: 'you can't have a marauding NEB going round the country grabbing firms'.[10] When it finally re-emerged in legislative form the industrial policy had been deprived of its teeth and was but a pale and shadowy version of the original conception. The NEC regularly protested against this emasculation but it received little support from the unions. Left-wing union leaders like Jones and Scanlon, though willing to affirm – in the formal casting of Conference votes – the *principles of* extended public ownership and planning, had not been involved in the policy's formulation and had little interest in or enthusiasm for it.[11] The lesson was clear: without backing from the unions, the NEC might bridle at the Government's actions but could do little to influence them.

The left's industrial policy was finally buried with Benn's departure from the Industry Department, a move Wilson always planned but only felt able to execute after the left's major reversal over the referendum for membership of the European Economic Community (or EEC as the European Union was then known). This issue occasioned the most spectacular breach between the Party and the Government. In opposition Labour had been bitterly divided over the terms for British membership negotiated by the Heath Government. There were fervent pro-marketeers, ardent opponents (mainly though not exclusively left wing) and straddling the middle ground a large group of pragmatists, amongst whom were to be found many senior frontbenchers including Wilson and Callaghan. They were on balance in favour of membership but, for reasons of political expediency, joined the anti-marketeers in opposing the Heathite terms. To hold the contending groups together the February 1974 manifesto contained a pledge to seek to 'renegotiate' the terms of entry and to hold a referendum (first suggested by Benn) on any bargain thereupon struck.

For Wilson the two prime objectives were to stay in the EEC and avert a split in the Party – no easy task. The agreement eventually renegotiated (in practice, there were few substantive changes) secured a Cabinet majority – though with a substantial dissenting minority. Less than half of Labour MPs backed the Government in the decisive Commons vote and, by eighteen votes to eleven, the NEC decisively rejected its terms and recommended a 'No' vote in the referendum. Furthermore, to signal the urgency with which it regarded the issue, it convened a special conference in April 1975. By a very large majority Conference endorsed the NEC's negative stance.

The open and highly public display of division over a major act of policy could easily have fractured Labour. It is, however, testimony to Wilson's skills as a party manager that it survived the trial with relatively minor after-shocks. 'He fudged and ducked and weaved' but he accomplished his twin objectives of keeping Britain in the EEC and holding the Party together.[12] His two main stratagems were to concede, on the one hand, a suspension of collective responsibility to allow the ministerial minority (including the formidable trio of Tony Benn, Michael Foot and Barbara Castle) to campaign against membership whilst, on the other, preventing the NEC from mobilising the party machine behind that campaign. The outcome of the referendum, a two-thirds majority backing continued membership, dealt a blow to the credibility of the left-led NEC. Wilson reshuffled his Cabinet with the major victim being Benn who was demoted from Industry to Energy.

Disagreement between the Government and the Party also raised the issue of the role and responsibilities of ministerial members of the NEC. Traditionally, the representation of ministers during periods of Labour Government had been seen as a useful mechanism to pull the executive into line with the Government – as long as these ministerial members were solid loyalists. But as became evident within months of Labour's return to office, over two high saliency foreign policy matters it also afforded the opportunity for dissenting ministers to intimate their disaffection with official policy. Chile was an extremely emotive issue for many in the Party since Pinochet's bloody American-backed coup against the democratically elected socialist President Salvador Allende in September 1973. The Heath Government had won a number of contracts for naval vessels and aircraft engines from the Pinochet Government. The Foreign Secretary, Jim Callaghan, and other right-wing ministers urged that the agreement be respected – to the outrage of many in the Party. At the NEC left-wing ministers including Michael Foot, then Employment Secretary, called upon the Government to review the decision.[13] Under pressure, Wilson agreed to cancel the sale (though one frigate had quietly slipped away) – a rare victory for the left and the NEC.

The problem arose again on South Africa a few months later, when three ministers, Tony Benn, Judith Hart and Joan Lestor, voted in favour of an NEC resolution criticising the Government over a joint British–South African naval exercise at the South African naval station of Simonstown. At Cabinet Wilson complained about 'a serious breach of collective Cabinet responsibility'. Ministerial members of the executive should recall that they were primarily ministers, 'totally and collectively responsible for everything done by the Government'. Callaghan declared that he was 'deeply shocked' by the conduct of the three dissenters, at which point Foot riposted that, if he had been present, he would probably have backed the Simonstown resolution.[14] Notwithstanding, Wilson despatched a blunt minute to the dissenting ministers warning them that their vote at the NEC had been 'clearly inconsistent with the principle of collective responsibility' and requiring them to give 'an unqualified assurance' that they would 'from now on comply with its requirements' on the NEC – or face the sack.[15]

As Minkin comments, 'it was never properly established to what extent the doctrine of collective responsibility stretched to the operation of the NEC'.[16] Benn drew a distinction between 'what the Government has done in the past, which in a sense we all have to defend because it was done with our consent, and what it is going to do next – where we all have a right to advise',[17] but this was a fine distinction. He agonised over how to respond to the ultimatum but eventually gave the necessary assurance. Both Wilson and Callaghan insisted upon the rigid application of collective responsibility but there was an element of the disingenuous here since it was common practice for Cabinet members to use calculated leaks and press briefings to flag *their* dissent, if they believed this would advance their careers and gain publicity. However, Benn (to their intense annoyance) contrived an astute balancing in future by conforming (just about) in form whilst in practice using strategic abstentions and absences to publicise his unhappiness with key government policies – thereby nurturing his popularity in the Party.

After 1975 the key issues that divided the Party and the Government were incomes policy and (especially) 'the cuts', that is the adoption of a deflationary, quasi-monetarist economic stance. On incomes policy the NEC backed (with reservations) the first two phases but then became more critical. Its opposition to the conduct of economic policy hardened after the IMF loan which pledged the Government to a slicing of public spending on top of major reductions already carried out. The executive – led by Barbara Castle, summarily sacked from the Cabinet by her old enemy, Jim Callaghan – urged rejection of the IMF loan with its onerous conditions (as did, initially, many ministers, including Foot and Tony Crosland as well as Benn). It also began to press for the Cabinet to adopt what came to be called 'the Alternative Economic Strategy', a neo-Keynesian approach entailing a more reflationary policy to curb rising unemployment, a reversal of the cuts, selective import restrictions and controls on capital outflows to repair the balance of payments deficit. There was no prospect of the Government heeding this advice which, both Number 10 and the Treasury felt, betrayed a complete failure to take the problem of inflation seriously, a blithe neglect of economic constraints and a Panglossian refusal to take seriously the need to cut public expenditure.[18] But it felt increasingly harassed by the Party's incessant disparagement at a time when it was desperately trying to restore the confidence of the financial markets and industry and to shore-up shrinking union support for pay restraint.

The 1976 Conference saw relations between the Party and the Government plummet to an all-time low. It was a stormy conference, with impassioned and sometimes virulent debates in which ministers were chastised in full view of the cameras. Unlike in the past, the NEC made no attempt to deploy the various managerial and procedural techniques at its disposal to deflect criticism from the floor of Conference: indeed 'the platform' often led the assault. As the Chancellor of the Exchequer, Denis Healey, dramatically turned back from Heathrow airport in response to a sterling crisis, the NEC urged delegates to approve a policy document pledging the next Labour Government to nationalise the banks and the insurance companies, in total defiance of government policy. Equally infuriating for the Government, Tony Benn, as Chairman of the NEC's Home Policy Committee, warmly commended *Labour's Programme for Britain 1976*, which was packed with proposals for extending public ownership, raising social spending, introducing industrial democracy and pressing ahead with constitutional reform: all schemes wholly unacceptable to the Government. 'Here we were running a government which was fast losing its majority,' David Lipsey, a senior Callaghan political aide, recalled, 'amidst a grave economic and political situation to be stabbed in the back month after month by those with no interest in winning the next election.'[19]

But, however vexing for the Cabinet, volleys from the executive usually fell to the ground with a dull thud. According to Geoff Bish, the Party's Research Secretary, the NEC was 'a mere pressure group, just one among many, sometimes gaining a minor policy concession but little of real substance in the way of changing the direction of Government policy'. The views of the NEC were rarely solicited in advance by the Government and no attempt was made to reach agreement on major proposed policy developments. 'In many cases, indeed, the NEC was at a disadvantage compared to other major interest groups, including the CBI, the City, the TUC and others.' The inconsequential status of the NEC in the eyes of ministers was reflected by their disinclination to attend the meetings of its subcommittees and study groups.[20] Although union power in this period has been considerably overstated,[21] it was undeniably substantial and modified government policy especially on industrial, pay and labour relations matters. That of the NEC was negligible.[22]

Framing the manifesto

If the Cabinet's hold over current policy was unshakeable, what of future policy? To what extent could the NEC act as the seedbed of fresh ideas and imaginative impulses: to use Richard Crossman's phrase, as the battering ram of change? The manifesto itself had (and still has) great political and symbolic importance within the Party. It is the only source of pledges which are widely considered within Labour's ranks to be binding on a Labour Government. Furthermore, it both encapsulates and symbolises the Party's collective and majoritarian approach to decision making – its belief that policy should be fashioned by the will of the movement.

Excluded from any involvement in government policy making, the NEC was determined to assert its constitutional prerogative to decide (along with the Cabinet) the contents of the manifesto. It sought to learn from the experience of the 1964–70 Government when 'efforts to transpose Conference policy into the Manifesto, as a way of binding the next Government, made little progress' against Prime Minister Harold Wilson's opposition and a 'bland, non-committal document was approved'.[23] For this reason a prime NEC objective in the period was the construction of 'a detailed, well-researched basis for our Manifesto, so that the latter would accurately reflect the views and priorities of the Party'.[24] As early as 1976 Conference endorsed a comprehensive statement of policy, *Labour's Programme for Britain 1976*, as 'the broad basis for the next Manifesto'.[25] This was supplemented by a range of policy documents developed by the NEC's subcommittees and working parties (which included Party-sympathetic experts) also approved by Conference. Aware that these contained many commitments unpalatable to the Government, with whom relations were by now very strained, the Party's Research Secretary Geoff Bish in February 1977 floated a proposal – accepted by the Prime Minister – for the setting up of a number of NEC–Cabinet Working Groups to try and narrow the gap between the two by a process of give and take.[26] Ministerial attendance, however, was so patchy that Callaghan sent a memo urging ministers to participate more fully in the work of the groups. But overstretched ministers remained reluctant to dedicate carefully husbanded psychic energy and precious time to what most saw as activities of little real import.[27] Notwithstanding, informal contacts did help smooth relations and the groups managed for the most part to narrow down differences. In December 1978 the Home Policy Committee of the NEC endorsed a document spelling out NEC proposals for the manifesto based on official party policy but taking account of the compromises reached by the groups. Between January and March 1979 a Manifesto Working Group comprised of members of the NEC and the Cabinet met regularly, using the NEC draft as a basis of discussion, and by March 1979 had managed to reach agreement over a series of texts, though substantial differences did remain. The aim was to arrive at a final compromise draft prior to the actual 'Clause V' meeting.[28]

But then the denouement. As the Research Secretary later recalled, 'the Prime Minister, at the last fence, decided to ignore the agreements. Instead he had prepared an entirely new "Number 10" draft for the manifesto.'[29] In truth, Callaghan had always been determined to keep the whole process firmly in his own hands.[30] Whilst the NEC wanted a manifesto containing precise commitments which would bind a future Labour Government, he wanted as free a hand as possible. 'The purpose of the Manifesto,' Callaghan insisted, 'is to appeal to the public and give the general direction of policy. The NEC wants detailed commitments and I shall resist this.'[31] As early as 1978 Tom McNally, his Senior Political Adviser, had worked on a preliminary Downing Street draft.[32] However, it was only quite late in the day that the Prime Minister finally concluded that there was absolutely no prospect of a satisfactory agreed outcome on the basis of the NEC draft, telling McNally, 'I think we'd better have a paper of our own ready for the meeting.' David Lipsey was instructed to produce the draft, with assistance from Bernard Donoughue's Policy Unit.[33]

The existence of the draft was only disclosed to the NEC on 29 March, the day after the Government was defeated in the House. With the election now imminent a drafting committee consisting of representatives of the NEC and Cabinet was hastily assembled. Callaghan, in his most avuncular manner, proposed that the Number 10 document be used as the basis for drafting since the NEC version contained too many – and too many unacceptable – pledges. Bish judged the Number 10 draft 'appalling. ... Not only did it ignore entire chapters of Party policy: it overturned and ignored many of the agreements which had been laboriously hammered out within the NEC–Cabinet Group.'[34] This was the climax of the whole process the NEC had been working towards for more than two years. A whole swathe of diligently developed policies were about to be cast aside. McNally expected 'blood on the carpet' with Benn proclaiming a major crisis and even calling the meeting to a halt. Instead, to his absolute astonishment, the NEC tamely agreed Callaghan's suggestion. 'It had taken two minutes,' McNally recalled, 'to sideline two years' work.'[35] At this, and the subsequent Clause V, meeting, NEC members sought to re-insert items from the NEC's draft into the Number 10 paper. In some cases an agreed formula (usually anodyne) was found but in others the Prime Minister was unyielding.[36] On all key issues his view prevailed (as was inevitable): there were to be no compulsory planning agreements, no commitments to further public ownership, no statutory access to open government and no abolition of the House of Lords, whilst pressure to reject nuclear weapons refurbishment (upon which a decision had already secretly been made) was swept aside.[37]

A member of the NEC's drafting team commented 'that's five years of policy-making down the drain'.[38] As the Research Secretary wearily concluded, 'despite all the planning over the previous two years, all the meetings, all the decisions, the NEC had been set up – to agree the very kind of Manifesto in the very circumstances it had always hoped to avoid'.[39] Callaghan's line had prevailed with less resistance than had been anticipated, but as Bish commented, it 'laid the basis for much of the bitterness and recrimination which was to follow'.[40]

The government of the Party

The selection of parliamentary candidates

Although the NEC lacked any effective instruments to impel a Labour Cabinet to implement manifesto policies or take note of Conference decisions it was responsible for the internal government of the Party, empowered to adjudicate and apply the rules, instigate rule change and enforce party discipline (though all subject to Conference ratification). Traditionally the NEC had used its powers to uphold the authority of the parliamentary leadership, defend its extra-parliamentary flank and quell dissent. By the mid-1970s it had redefined its responsibilities. It saw itself as the guardian of the views of the wider Party rather than as the guarantor of the prerogatives of the parliamentary leadership. This is demonstrated by its behaviour on two internal party matters of intensifying importance: pressure to alter the rules governing the re-adoption of sitting Labour MPs and the growth of Trotskyist-inspired infiltration of the constituencies.[41]

The autonomy of the PLP from the wider Party was one of the major props maintaining the ascendancy of the parliamentary leadership and one not easily shaken. However, if the independence of the PLP as a collective body appeared to be well secured it was wholly within the power of the wider Party to alter the relationship between a CLP and individual MPs, thereby rendering MPs more receptive to their constituency activists. In the past, MPs had enjoyed virtually freehold rights to their seats and any effort by left-wing constituency parties to prevent re-nomination on political grounds would be blocked by the NEC. But with the shift in the political balance on the NEC and in Conference, constitutional conventions were redefined. In 1973 what later came to be called the 'Mikardo Doctrine' was promulgated by the veteran left-winger Ian Mikardo. This stated that if a CLP chose to deselect its MP the NEC would only intervene on the grounds of procedural improprieties. There followed a small number of deselections of which the dismissal of Reg Prentice (MP for Newham North East and Cabinet member) was the most controversial. A large contingent of ministers and right-wing Labour MPs demanded intervention from the NEC to succour their beleaguered colleague but it refused and Prentice was deselected.[42]

Left and right drew completely different lessons from Prentice's fate. Whilst many MPs complained about the lack of adequate safeguards and pressed for the revocation of the Mikardo Doctrine, most activists drew the opposite conclusion: the procedure was too cumbersome, too time consuming and too vulnerable to exploitation by opponents of the Party. A growing number of CLPs, in a drive orchestrated by the Campaign for Labour Party Democracy (CLPD), urged a rule change stipulating that all MPs should be subject to procedures allowing for their incumbency to be challenged before each election – thereby inducing them to take more account of the views of their 'selectorates', the members of their General Committees. There followed an extended period of debate in an evenly divided executive in which alignments followed left–right lines. The PLP lobbied energetically against the proposal claiming that (what came to be called) mandatory reselection would, by undermining the security of MPs, damage their morale, discourage able people from seeking a parliamentary career, provoke 'unnecessary bickering' and incur damaging press publicity. Harold Wilson, as Prime Minister, and his successor, Jim Callaghan, both warned of the danger of full-timers from the extreme-left militant organisation being drafted into constituencies to oust sitting MPs.[43]

The NEC set up a working party drawn from all sections of party opinion, which eventually agreed on a compromise proposed by Mikardo (though some left-wing members dissented). This was a two-stage procedure under which, in each Parliament, CLPs with a sitting Labour member would initially vote upon whether to re-adopt the MP or carry out a new selection; formal selection procedures would only be activated if the latter course was agreed. The so-called 'Mikardo Compromise' was approved by the NEC, indicating a willingness on its part to accommodate on a matter upon which MPs felt very strongly. However, the more determined protagonists of mandatory reselection were not satisfied and no one had fully grasped the extent to which leadership control in the unions had lapsed. At the 1978 Party Conference the delegates of both the TGWU and (rejecting the advice of its leader, Hugh Scanlon) the AUEW rejected the Mikardo Compromise in favour of mandatory reselection, thereby guaranteeing it a majority. However, when he came to cast the union's vote a 'confused' Scanlon dropped it in the wrong box and, amidst uproar, the Party Chairman, Joan Lestor, refused calls for a re-vote and the motion was lost.[44] Thereby the matter was left in abeyance until after the general election.

If the NEC had enacted its traditional role – a shield of the parliamentary leadership – it could have deployed a range of techniques to delay, side-track and even suppress the demand for mandatory reselection. Instead, its open-minded response guaranteed that the demand would survive – and gather strength since momentum for change was sweeping the constituencies. Notwithstanding, between 1974 and 1979 the NEC operated less as an initiator of reform than as an arena of struggle. The interests and preferences of the parliamentary leadership had ceased to be the major factor determining how it performed its managerial function but it was as yet unwilling to act, in a forthright manner, as the voice of those in the constituencies demanding constitutional reform. This was to change after 1979.

Militant and entryism

The Militant Tendency had its origins in the Trotskyist Revolutionary Socialist League. In the 1960s the RSL decided to adopt an 'entryist' tactic: it set up an organisation, under the guise of supporters of its weekly *Militant*, aimed at expanding its influence, multiplying its cadres and disseminating its message by burrowing quietly within the Labour Party. The tactic was to 'dig roots' in constituency and branch parties many of which – an internal 1974 Militant document explained – were 'shells dominated by politically dead old men and women'.[45] Within three years of its establishment in 1967, Labour's new youth organisation, the Labour Party Young Socialists (LPYS), had fallen under Militant's control and it had gained useful footholds in a number of constituencies.

In 1975, the issue of 'Trotskyist infiltration' hit the headlines because of Militant's (wrongly) alleged role in masterminding the removal of Reg Prentice. In September, the NEC agreed to allow the National Agent, Reg Underhill, to prepare a report on Trotskyism in the Party. Entitled 'Entryist Activities' this was presented to the Organisation Committee in November. Underhill concluded that 'beyond any doubt whatever that there is a central organisation associated with Militant with its own membership and full-time organisers'. At the NEC the Cabinet minister Shirley Williams called for further investigation but this was rejected (by sixteen votes to twelve) by the NEC's left majority. Ian Mikardo dismissed Militant as 'more of a nuisance than a danger' whilst his left-wing colleague Eric Heffer (shortly to be appointed Chairman of the influential Organisation Subcommittee) suggested that Trotskyism could best be combated by political persuasion.[46] The matter remained dormant for a year and then flared up again. In the autumn of 1976, a leading Militant activist, Andy Bevan, was appointed as the Party's Youth Officer, by an NEC Subcommittee attended by two right-wing trade unionists and the General Secretary. There was immediate uproar, with the press denouncing the Party for choosing an extremist and the National Union of Labour Organisers up in arms. In his speech at the 1976 Conference Callaghan warned against 'a new factor creeping into the Party', political elements 'who seek to infiltrate our Party and to use it for their own ends'. But his demands that the NEC rescind Bevan's appointment and take firm action against Militant fell on stony ground. Instead it passed a resolution moved by Eric Heffer damning reports in the press of entryist activity as a 'calculated campaign' to instigate a 'frenzied witch-hunt' which was 'deliberately designed to damage the Party'.[47]

However, the following month the NEC set up a subcommittee to examine the Underhill documents, comprising Foot, Heffer, Tom Bradley and John Chalmers (the latter two both right-wingers) and the General Secretary, Ron Hayward.[48] But its report ignored the Prime Minister's repeated pleas. It expressed opposition to the use of discipline as a method of settling political arguments and argued that Militant's influence could best be countered by a membership drive, improved political education and a greater openness in the way the LPYS operated. On this issue the unstintingly loyal Michael Foot parted company with Callaghan, advising that pressure to engage in a 'witch-hunt' be firmly resisted. A proposal to publish the Underhill documents was rejected by thirteen votes to ten.[49]

It was now quite evident that a left-led NEC would not resort to sanctions to resist Militant's permeation of the Party. There were a variety of reasons given: Militant's members were just overenthusiastic but harmless youngsters who would, in time, see the error of their ways; Marxism had always been a legitimate strand within the Party; a 'witch-hunt' against the Tendency would rapidly spread to one against the left as a whole; the use of disciplinary action against those with minority views was wrong in principle, and the real enemies were on the right of the Party – 'there were no enemies on the left'. This was to prove a serious miscalculation by the mainstream left who were to suffer damage from their association with a body with dubious democratic credentials. But this was for the future. The immediate effect of the NEC's refusal to treat the problem angered the centre–right majority in the PLP and contributed materially to worsening relations between the Government and the Party. Militant used the respite profitably to expand its organisation, its full-time staff and its penetration of constituency parties. When action was taken, the Tendency was to prove a far harder nut to crack.

Conflict and cohesion in the Labour Party

Disagreement over policy, ideology and strategy is inevitable in large political parties containing members with very diverse political opinions and will always be compounded by clashing career aspirations, personal feuds and divergent institutional interests. So the real question is not *why* conflict occurs in political parties but how it can be regulated and parties held together. Cohesion, we suggest, is rooted in four institutional and normative conditions whose effects are maximised to the extent they are combined: institutionalised methods of conflict regulation, discipline, procedural consensus and ideological concensus. To what extent did they exist and function effectively in the period of the 1974–9 Labour Governments?

Conflict regulation

This involves utilising mechanisms for adjusting and accommodating divergent views in order to dampen conflict, thereby restraining its destabilising effects. Little effort was made to develop such mechanisms under Wilson's leadership. His response to criticism from the NEC was increasingly marked by exasperation and in the year preceding his retirement he rarely appeared at the NEC – and when he did so could be quite confrontational. Callaghan took the NEC more seriously than his predecessor and attended quite regularly.[50] He was a highly experienced, extremely astute political manager, emollient in style – though this was coupled with a steely determination. 'I was only too aware,' Callaghan recalled in his memoirs, 'of the need to keep Ministers and members of the NEC in tandem if possible. ... And I not only enjoined on ministers the need to consult, but established a machinery for regular consultation.'[51] The Head of his Political Office, Tom McNally, fulfilled 'an indispensable liaison role', keeping the Prime Minister informed about party developments and alerting him to problems likely to arise.[52] He instructed McNally to find as much common ground as possible whilst avoiding any major substantive concessions. It was agreed to hold quarterly meetings between the NEC and the Cabinet though these mainly acted as opportunities to let off steam: the NEC raised grievances about the Government whilst ministers justified their record. These meetings rarely succeeded in defusing disagreements or composing differences for the policy rift between the Government and the Party steadily widened and, as the attempt to reach an agreement over the election manifesto showed, sharply opposing positions on key issues could not easily be reconciled.

Number 10, one senior political adviser recalled, made determined attempts to conciliate the NEC but 'the willingness to meet half-way was not there: it wasn't what the game was about'.[53] What was the game about? As Callaghan's closest political advisers saw it, the NEC was being used by Benn as a spring-board for a left-wing takeover of the Party. Relentless assaults on the Government were designed to impugn and diminish it in the eyes of the rank and file and demolish confidence in the right–centre bloc which had always controlled the Party, whilst the loss of the next election – a matter of indifference – would facilitate a left-wing takeover of the Party.[54] For this reason neither Benn nor his cohort on the NEC – so the reasoning ran – were interested in compromise: hence the propensity to make 'impossibilistic demands' knowing that the Government could never accede to them, a failure which would then be used to belabour it.[55] It followed that steps to regulate and limit antagonism could be more than a stop-gap measure since a decisive battle between the two sides was inevitable.

Discipline and central control capability

Discipline is a form of cohesion characterised by regular membership conformity within a political party with the decisions of the leadership, and occurs where the leaders have at their disposal a central control capability sufficiently robust to induce recalcitrant members to comply. Though Labour's leadership possessed a reasonably effective control capability in the generation from the 1930s to the 1960s, this had ceased to be the case by 1974. Powers to interpret and enforce the rules and enforce decisions were the prerogative of the NEC which alone had access to the various managerial powers and techniques which could, for example, have succoured besieged MPs and blocked the drive for mandatory reselection. Deprived of them, the capacity of the leadership to subdue grass-roots rebellion was fatally damaged. Indeed, by the close of the 1970s, the integrated control system of earlier years had been replaced by an adversarial system in which the NEC displayed an unprecedented responsiveness to rank and file sentiment.

The Government did make efforts to try and build up its support on the NEC. Traditionally the bedrock of loyalist allegiance has been the trade union section of the NEC and this remained the case between 1974 and 1979. Lipsey was responsible for liaising with these members, working closely with John Golding MP, a trade union official and a highly adept political operator who acted as an informal Number 10 whip on the NEC.[56] In addition, the determination of the leaders of the two largest unions, Jones and Scanlon, to sustain the Government come what may, and their mounting antagonism to the left-led NEC, suggested that there was some prospect of turning back the left-wing tide.[57] But this did not occur, for a variety of reasons. Voting on the NEC by unions was influenced by a complex set of conventions and arrangements, Jones was reluctant to break with the left and the diffusion of power within the AUEW meant that it was not within Scanlon's power to direct how the union cast its vote. As a result efforts to alter the balance of forces on the NEC made no progress and any possibility of a reconstruction of a strong central control capability receded.

Procedural consensus

Procedural consensus refers to agreement over the ground-rules and norms which structure and regulate the way power is distributed and decisions are taken. To the extent that it exists, and the rules of the game therefore widely endorsed, then contending forces within a party are more likely to accept as binding and authoritative its outcomes. From the 1960s onwards the wide measure of procedural consensus that hitherto existed within Labour's ranks began to erode and attitudes to the nature of intra-party democracy, representation, accountability and the appropriate location of power and ultimate authority increasingly polarised. This process accelerated after 1974 and was manifested in intensifying disputes over parliamentary selection procedures and other constitutional questions. On the one hand, the left-led NEC pressed for greater party control over the formulation of future policy, a larger say in the preparation of current policy and, in general, much more respect for Conference decisions. Democracy entailed greater collective accountability of the PLP, and especially the frontbench, to Conference, 'the parliament of the movement', which was constitutionally vested with determining Labour's programme. It also prescribed greater individual accountability of MPs to their local parties, who chose them and ought to have a right to remove them. This argument resonated with an activist base increasingly composed of radical young, university-educated, white-collar workers who expected and demanded a greater say in policy making.

On the other hand, the right, the bulk of the PLP and the leadership became more and more sceptical about 'the Party's traditional views on mandates, Conference sovereignty and intra-party democracy'.[58] The PLP should be accountable to the electorate, not the Party's rank and file, and individual MPs have the right and responsibility to exercise their judgement and not be held responsible to their constituency parties. Proposals to enhance the power of activists would be positively undemocratic since these activists tended to be unrepresentative of ordinary party members and, even more so, of ordinary Labour voters. Above all, they stressed that the Government was elected by and should be answerable to Parliament and the voters, not to the Party. Callaghan, in a speech to the 1976 Annual Conference, drew a clear distinction between the roles of the Government and of the NEC. The latter 'are responsible for their statements and their resolutions. But the Government is accountable for its actions and that is the difference between us. We are accountable, in a parliamentary democracy, to Parliament.'[59] This collision between sharply divergent conceptions of democracy and representation greatly impeded efforts to reach a modus vivendi between the Government and the Party. Without some shared understanding over how and where decisions could authoritatively be made mechanisms designed to compose differences (such as the various joint Cabinet–NEC bodies) were unlikely to prove very effective.

Ideological consensus

Ideological consensus refers to the holding in common of some core values and objectives defining what a party is about and setting broadly the direction in which it should move. In the past a kernel of consensus had helped hold Labour together: differences over nationalisation and foreign and defence policy were balanced by a shared aspiration to construct a universalist and redistributive welfare state, full employment and greater equality, and by a broad feeling that all were part of a common endeavour to achieve social justice. During the years of the 1974–9 Labour administration this kernel began crumbling. On the one hand, confronted by stagflation – a bewildering combination of high inflation, rapidly rising unemployment and stagnation which had never before been anticipated – many in the Government lost confidence in the value and viability of Keynesian economics and the social democratic formula of high spending on social programmes financed by progressive taxation. Both Callaghan and Healey were influenced by the 'crowding out' thesis which held that public expenditure beyond a certain point discouraged investment, whilst high marginal rates of taxation destroyed incentives and weakened the supply side of the economy.[60] The decision in late 1976 to accept an IMF loan, with its attendant rigorous conditions, was 'a turning point in the philosophical basis of economic policy and in the thinking of the Treasury about economic management'. The consensus over full employment as the foremost objective of economic policy was 'shattered'.[61] The result of the IMF-prescribed squeeze – on top of earlier reductions in spending – was that Labour 'presided over the largest cuts in real public expenditure that have occurred in the last fifty years'.[62]

To the left this was wholly unjustified and economically counter-productive. It signalled the bankruptcy of revisionist social democracy. 'The dilemma for social democrats,' Benn contended, was that high public expenditure based on full employment, which could then redistribute wealth, was no longer an option. There was a harsh choice to be made between monetarism and the Labour Manifesto, and that meant investment and public accounting and industrial democracy.[63]

Benn's analysis, as summed up by Peter Shore, comprised

> three overriding and mutually reinforcing beliefs: first, that capitalism in Britain had broken down irretrievably and must be replaced by a new and predominantly publicly-owned economy; second that a right-wing, weak-willed Cabinet and PLP were no match for, and were in constant danger of capitulation before, the entrenched forces of financial power, the hostile press, a resistant civil service and the institutional pressures of NATO, the IMF and the European Commission; third, that the only hope for Labour was to win the total allegiance of that organised working class, the trade unions backed up by the open support of the NEC and the Left in the PLP and the Constituency Labour Parties.[64]

This analysis was broadly endorsed by the NEC left and by many constituency activists: as the right marched to the right, the left was marching in the opposing direction.

With the polarisation of left and right within the Party, in Benn's words, 'the centre had fallen away'.[65] As Healey put it – dismissing the left's alternative economic strategy as 'the siege economy' – 'to move half way towards each other from opposite sides of the Grand Canyon would be a disaster'.[66] Left and right had always differed over the pace of reform, priorities and, indeed, the final destination. But common support for state intervention and Keynesian economic management to maintain full employment and promote equality and social justice through expanding welfare programmes had formed a core of consensus. When the leadership (and much of the right) abandoned these cherished tenets of Croslandite social democracy, and with the left demanding the adoption of more radical economic strategies which went well beyond them, the common ground between the two vanished. 'The consensual ethos' was now 'in total abeyance'.[67] It was this, the disintegration of ideological consensus, that was the ultimate cause of the intractability of the conflict between left and right, Party and Government, from 1974 to 1979.

Conclusion: lessons for New Labour

Tony Blair and his advisers have been much exercised by the experience of Party–Government relations from 1974 to 1979. 'All Labour governments have been torn apart by internal divisions over one group of people saying betrayal,' Blair declared. 'The Labour Party must never again lose the competence or capacity to govern because of internal differences.' He added that 'in the 1970s, the PLP and the Labour Party lost touch with each other – that must never happen again'.[68] Immediately prior to Labour's 1997 election victory the NEC prepared a major programme of internal party reform, *Partnership into Power*, designed to place relations between the Government and the Party on a much more stable and harmonious footing. Labour had to 'reconcile the requirements of two aspects of democracy: the democracy of the country and the democracy of the political party in question'. The new institutional architecture put in place by these reforms sought to do so via a 'stakeholder' model of policy making where all constituent parts enjoyed 'shared involvement and ownership' of the Party.[69]

Two striking institutional differences in the pattern of Party–Government relations since 1997 compared with the earlier period are worth noting. First, much greater efforts are made to engage with and solicit the views of the constituency rank and file – partly reflecting the fact that they now hold 50 per cent of the Conference vote. The hostility, neglect and even derision which typified many ministerial attitudes to the activists from 1974 to 1979 have not been replicated. Second, and more fundamentally, the system of checks and balances, though it still survives, does so only in a much attenuated form. A series of organisational changes implemented since the late 1980s have had as their goal the elimination of the NEC as an alternative centre of power and policy formation. Thus it has been stripped of its policy capability by divesting it of its research and policy-making resources. By the same token it has been largely relieved of its policy-development rights by transferring them to other institutions more susceptible to control by the leadership. Under Labour's pluralistic constitution there were in effect two sovereign authorities, the NEC answerable to the Party Conference and the frontbench answerable to the PLP – a situation, in Michael Foot's metaphor, akin to the status accorded to the Pope and the Emperor in the Holy Roman Empire: 'Neither was usually required or willing to bow to the other; each retained the trappings of supreme Power.'[70] This has to a substantial degree ceased to be the case. Whilst the wider Party retains the trappings of power, the reality has now been centralised in the hands of the parliamentary leadership. The partnership which officially characterises the Party–Government relationship is essentially one in which the latter has formal consultative rights but in which, in practical terms, the Government dominates. The affiliated unions remain, as organisations in their own right, significant interlocutors but the institutions of the wider Party per se have forfeited much of their capacity to operate as a check and balance on the leadership.

The purpose and effect of these reforms has been, *inter alia*, to drain power from the CLPs as organised forums which could be used for the purpose of activist mobilisation. Activists have to a considerable degree been sidelined and their capacity in any meaningful way to countervail the parliamentary leadership largely confiscated. But this poses Labour – or 'New Labour' – with a dilemma. 'A political party,' Tom McNally observed,

> has to have the capacity for dissent, otherwise it becomes a recipient for messages passed from on-high, and an organisation simply for delivering

votes. If you remove from activists the right to have some input into policy-making you forfeit their motivation and commitment – and party activism will wither on the vine.[71]

This may well now be happening, as membership figures plunge. Certainly Labour's physiognomy has been profoundly reshaped by Blair. It is true that much of the initial spadework was carried out under the Kinnock leadership. The Leader's Office, for instance, had already swollen substantially in both size and influence whilst the NEC had abandoned earlier aspirations to joint custody of the Party. The waning and fragmentation of the left had proceeded afar before Blair leapt into the leader's saddle. Notwithstanding, the driving conviction of the new leader and his advisers that drastic surgery was essential coupled with Labour's complete demoralisation after the unexpected 1992 defeat provided Blair with unprecedented room for manoeuvre. This he exploited with great vigour and indefatigability to drive through sweeping reforms in the Party's internal structures. The organisation over which he presides is far more centralised and tightly – and diligently – run than ever before. A return to the conditions prevailing in the 1970s, or even in earlier post-war decades, is difficult to envisage. But it does not follow that 'the Blair settlement' will always endure. In an age of evermore brittle party loyalties, voter volatility and mass desertion of the electoral process, it can be predicted with some confidence that no pattern of power or organisational format, however apparently entrenched, will persevere for long.

Notes

1　Turner, J.E., 'The Labour Party: Riding the Two Horses', *International Studies Quarterly*, 25(3), 1981, p. 388.
2　Shore, P., *Leading the Left* (Weidenfeld and Nicolson, London, 1983), p. 191.
3　Ibid., pp. 293, 298.
4　Ibid.. p. 300.
5　Castle, B., *Fighting All the Way* (Macmillan, London, 1993), pp. 446, 504.
6　Labour Party NEC, *Labour's Programme 1973*, p. 13, emphasis in the original.
7　Craig, F.W.S., *British General Election Manifestos 1959–1987* (Dartmouth, Aldershot, 1990), p. 91.
8　Shore, *Leading the Left*, p. 120.
9　Pimlott, B., *Harold Wilson* (HarperCollins, London, 1992), p. 665.
10　Benn, T., *Against the Tide: Diaries 1973–76* (Arrow, London, 1989), p. 194. Entry 9 July 1974.
11　Scanlon's attitude to the radical industrial strategy 'varied from the evasive to the dismissive', Minkin, L., *The Contentious Alliance* (Edinburgh University Press, Edinburgh, 1991), p. 173.
12　Donoughue, B., *The Heat of the Kitchen: An Autobiography* (Politico's, London, 2003), p. 157.
13　Benn, *Against the Tide*, pp. 141, 146. Entries 24 April, 1 May 1974.
14　Ibid., pp. 251–2. Entry 31 October 1974.
15　Quoted in Shore, *Leading the Left*, p. 108.
16　Minkin, L., *The Labour Party Conference* (Manchester University Press, Manchester, 1978), p. 302.

17 Benn, *Against the Tide*, p. 272, at a joint meeting of the NEC and the Cabinet, 22 November 1974.

18 However, there was validity in the NEC's charge that the IMF-driven cuts were both unnecessary and damaging, Burk, K. and Cairncross, A., *'Goodbye, Great Britain': The 1976 IMF Crisis* (Yale University Press, New Haven, CT, 1992), p. 225. According to Morgan 'the cuts were much more savage than was justified', Morgan, K.O., *Callaghan: A Life* (Oxford University Press, Oxford, 1997), p. 552; Healey, D., *The Time of My Life* (Penguin, London, 1990), p. 402.

19 Interview with Lord Lipsey.

20 Bish, G., 'The Programme of Work' Home Policy Committee of the NEC RD: 6 June 1979.

21 Minkin, *The Contentious Alliance*, pp. 159–91.

22 Both Wilson and Callaghan sought to bypass the NEC and downgrade its status as much as possible by working through the tripartite TUC–Labour Party Liaison Committee and the various bilateral meetings between ministers and senior trade union leaders where much of the real discussion and bargaining took place.

23 Minkin, *The Labour Party Conference*, pp. 313, 327–8.

24 Bish, 'The Programme of Work'.

25 Bish, G., *Drafting the Manifesto: The Record and the Lessons*, Home Policy Committee of the NEC RD: 23 July 1979.

26 Ibid.

27 Interview with Lord Lipsey.

28 Bish, 'The Programme of Work'.

29 Bish, 'The Programme of Work' Home Policy Committee of the NEC RD: 29 February 1983.

30 Butler, D. and Kavanagh, D., *The British General Election of 1979* (Macmillan, London 1980), p. 52.

31 Benn, T., *Conflicts of Interest: Diaries 1977–80* (Arrow, London, 1990), p. 479.

32 Butler, D. and Kavanagh, D., *The British General Election of 1979*, p. 147.

33 Interviews with Lord McNally and Lord Lipsey.

34 Bish, *Drafting the Manifesto*.

35 Interview with Lord McNally.

36 Benn, *Conflicts of Interest*, p. 482.

37 Morgan, *Callaghan: A Life*, pp. 687–8, Butler and Kavanagh, *The British General Election of 1979*, pp. 147–50; Benn, *Conflicts of Interest*, pp. 481–7.

38 Benn, *Conflicts of Interest*, p. 488; Butler and Kavanagh, *The British General Election of 1979*, p. 150.

39 Bish, *Drafting the Manifesto*.

40 Bish, 'The Programme of Work'.

41 These issues are discussed in detail in Shaw, E., *Discipline and Discord in the Labour Party* (Manchester University Press, Manchester, 1988).

42 Shortly after he joined the Conservatives and was briefly a minister under Mrs Thatcher.

43 Cledwyn Hughes, Chairman of PLP, 'Note on Selection of Parliamentary Candidates', NEC, 24 March 1976. *The Times*, 25 March 1976.

44 *Labour Party Conference Report* (Labour Party, London, 1978), p. 281.

45 Quoted in Crick, M., *The March of Militant* (Faber and Faber, London, 1986), p. 69.

46 NEC Minutes, 26 November 1975.

47 NEC Minutes, 15 December 1976.

48 NEC Minutes, 26 January 1977.

49 NEC Minutes, 25 May 1977; Benn, *Conflicts of Interest*, pp. 150–1. Entry 25 May 1977.

50 Though he often found NEC meetings 'complete purgatory'. Interview with Lord Lipsey.

51 Callaghan, J., *Time and Chance* (Collins, London, 1987), p. 459.

52 Morgan, *Callaghan: A Life*, p. 496; Callaghan, *Time and Chance*, p. 406.

53 Interview with Lord Lipsey. See also Donoughue, *The Heat of the Kitchen*, p. 127.

54 In 1976 Bernard Donoughue and Tom McNally, Heads respectively of the Number 10 Policy Unit and Political Office, made a joint request to Callaghan to fire Benn. The Prime Minister demurred: 'never put a man on the backbenches when he has the ability to do more damage than where he is'. Interview with Lord McNally.

55 Interviews with Lord Lipsey 15 May 2003 and Lord McNally 31 July 2003. As a result of this strategy, Lipsey believed, Benn was prepared to remain in the Cabinet notwithstanding 'the humiliations heaped on him'. During one heated Cabinet exchange in 1977 a 'red-faced' Callaghan charged Benn with 'working against us. ... You are leading a faction against us.' Benn, *Conflicts of Interest*, p. 205. Entry 29 July 1977, pp. 458–9. According to a Senior Party Researcher in a position to observe the behaviour of the NEC throughout the period there was little evidence to substantiate the belief held in Number 10 that the left actually wanted Labour to lose the 1979 election to undermine the right. Interview with Andy Thompson.

56 Interview with Lord Lipsey.

57 At one meeting Jones told ministers 'we'll do anything, anything we can' to help the Government, whilst Scanlon insisted on 'more loyalty' from the Party. Interview with Phil Wyatt, former Labour Party official.

58 Minkin, *The Labour Party Conference*, p. 11.

59 Shore, *Leading the Left*, p. 124.

60 Callaghan, quoted in Jackson, P., 'Public Expenditure', in Artis, M. and Cobham, D. (eds), *Labour's Economic Policies, 1974–79* (Manchester University Press, Manchester, 1991), p. 74. Crosland, social democracy's leading theorist, noted that 'some of those who thought of themselves as Gaitskellites had moved so far to the right that they disappeared from view', Crosland, S., *Tony Crosland* (Cape, London, 1982), p. 222. See Kevin Hickson's chapter in this volume.

61 Burk and Cairncross, *'Goodbye, Great Britain'*, p. 129.

62 Jackson, 'Public Expenditure', p. 73. Indeed, 'the cuts that took place in public expenditure under the Labour Government have no parallel in any other period in the post-war years'. Burk and Cairncross, *'Goodbye, Great Britain'*, p. 190.

63 Benn, *Conflicts of Interest*, p. 43.

64 Shore (*Leading the Left*), p. 106.

65 Ibid., p. 43.

66 Ibid., p. 38. Cabinet–NEC meeting held on 16 February 1977.

67 Morgan, *Callaghan*, p. 515.

68 Quoted in Davies, L., *Through the Looking Glass* (Verso, London, 2001), pp. 122, 99.

69 Labour Party National Executive Committee, *Partnership in Power* (Labour Party, London, 1997).

70 Foot, M., *Another Heart and Other Pulses* (Collins, London, 1984), pp. 160–1.

71 Interview with Lord McNally.

Part IV

Perspectives

16 The 1974–9 Governments and 'New' Labour

Steven Fielding

When they search for 'New' Labour's antecedents, few journalistic commentators look back further than the 1980s. For most consider Tony Blair a pale echo of Margaret Thatcher: that, after all, is how Blair wanted to be seen, at least during his first years as leader. Many academic analysts similarly look on Blair's enthusiastic acceptance of the market as the consummation of a 'catch-up' process that began with Neil Kinnock's attempt to improve the Party's electability after 1983.[1] This emphasis, however, exaggerates the extent to which 'Thatcherism' – as opposed to more profound, historically embedded, economic and ideological dynamics – dictated Labour's course. The nearly two decades of Conservative rule that followed 1979 obviously affected the Party in numerous ways. However, as some recognise, key policies associated with the Thatcher years (and so 'New' Labour) can trace their source to the 1974–9 Governments led by Harold Wilson and (after March 1976) James Callaghan.[2]

'New' Labour's roots in fact originate in many of the assumptions that underpinned post-war revisionism, especially as articulated by Hugh Gaitskell and Anthony Crosland.[3] For 'New' Labour is but the latest expression of a well-established, indeed usually dominant, ideological tendency within the Party leadership. This believed that the promotion of equality was Labour's most important aim; that this could be achieved through a reformed (but efficient) capitalism; and on that basis the Party could win support from voters mobilised as members of a national 'community' rather than of a particular class. The Party's 'modernisation', ostensibly initiated by Kinnock and continued by Blair, was therefore in reality the resumption of a venerable process, of which the Wilson–Callaghan years formed part. If interrupted by Labour's move left during the early 1980s, prior to that moment of (at least electoral) madness, the leadership tried to accommodate itself to the first expressions of those 'realities' Blair would later so ostentatiously embrace. The response of the 1970s leadership was, it is true, partial and hesitant – and was vigorously rejected by others in the Party – but if many of its policies differed from those adopted by Blair, their general aim was nonetheless the same. For the 1974–9 Governments were but one more example of the leadership's revision of means in light of changing circumstances, but adherence to constant ends, a bitterly contentious process that lies at the very heart of Labour history.

The 'Winter of Discontent'

In presenting the 1974–9 Governments as a staging post on what would become the road to 'New' Labour there is at least one basic problem: they are the most vilified of the post-war period. Not unusually for Labour administrations they were heavily criticised from the left, although party activists' accusations of betrayal were especially vociferous. More exceptionally, many of their leading members went on to attack the Governments' record. It is nevertheless the grim popular memory of the Wilson–Callaghan years that is truly without equal. This mainly comprised images of rubbish piling up in the streets and corpses turned back at cemetery gates due to a public sector strike wave – ostentatiously dubbed the 'Winter of Discontent' – that broke out in early 1979. While this memory was not without substance its partisan construction needs to be noted. For events were gleefully distorted by Conservative politicians and their many camp followers in the media. They exaggerated how bad things were under Labour to make Britain's supposedly miraculous (and itself inflated) economic recovery under Thatcher appear all the more remarkable.[4] As late as 1997 John Major's Party was still disinterring half-remembered footage of strikers huddled round braziers, which, they alleged, defined Labour's supine relationship with the unions and its consequent inability to manage the economy. Voters were encouraged to believe that what happened in the 1970s would be repeated should Labour ever again win office. This was a seriously tendentious view.

To do them anything like justice, the Wilson–Callaghan Governments need to be set against the appalling context in which they operated. The Party came to power at the end of a post-war 'golden age' of sustained economic growth and full employment. Thanks to the mismanagement of Edward Heath's Conservative administration the British economy was already experiencing severe problems – massive industrial discontent, rising inflation and declining production – although every industrial nation was hit hard when in 1973 the oil price quadrupled. To drag the country back from this brink Labour's leaders looked to the trade unions for help. At the time the unions exerted an unprecedented peacetime influence while their historic link to the Party meant at least some of their leaders were willing to co-operate with a Labour Government. Partnership at this time then looked viable and, more to the point, necessary: Heath had tried to coerce the unions and did not get far. The miners effectively ended his time in Downing Street when the Conservatives lost the February 1974 election, which Heath had called to mobilise support for his rejection of their wage demands. Wilson entered office as a result, but with 200,000 fewer votes than Heath – and without a Commons majority. Even after being re-elected in October Labour's position was not much improved: its majority of three seats (which due to by-election defeats disappeared in early 1976) left the Government in a precarious position. Politically and economically hemmed in, Wilson and Callaghan did not do such a bad job, all things considered. By winning the co-operation of the unions (principally by further strengthening their legal position in the workplace) the Government reined in wage militancy, reduced inflation and encouraged the return of economic growth. Those few weeks that formed the 'Winter of Discontent' were then atypical: despite what Labour's detractors claimed, rotting rubbish and cancelled burials did not define the Party's period in office.

Rather than debate the merits of the public's received view of the Wilson–Callaghan years, Blair and his cohorts calculated they should accept it and then disassociate themselves from those policies voters thought led to the 'Winter of Discontent'. In 1994 the most important thing was to win the next election, not defend what even its friends accepted was a flawed government. Thus, in claiming 'New' Labour to be literally a new party, Blair affected to disparage an 'Old' Labour that comprised not only the Bennite left but also the Wilson–Callaghan leadership, the former for their extremism and the latter for its reliance on state intervention and subordination to the unions. To add insult to injury, Blair chose to express his admiration for Thatcher. He assured the people 'New' Labour would never go back to what they supposed were the bad old days of the 1970s because it accepted Thatcher's transformation of industrial relations law, which – along with mass unemployment and the decline of heavy industry – had seriously weakened the unions. Blair claimed his Party now had a relationship with the unions very much like the one it enjoyed with business, one characterised by 'fairness not favours'. This audacious tactic had the desired effect: it neutralised the Conservatives' favoured line of attack, much to their bemusement, and encouraged hitherto resistant white-collar voters to identify with Labour.

There was, however, an ambiguity to 'New' Labour. If Blair said his was a new party he and others also claimed it marked a restoration of Labour's original essence.[5] 'New' Labour speakers liked to appropriate conveniently dead and distant figures from the Party's past such as Keir Hardie, R.H. Tawney and Clement Attlee to support this latter point. In contrast, so far as Wilson and Callaghan were concerned there was only equivocation. In *The Blair Revolution* (1996) Peter Mandelson and Roger Liddle made a strong case for believing Labour under Blair had been transformed.[6] For them the Wilson–Callaghan years were an unhappy time: by placing too great a reliance on the unions, ministers backed their demands even when they harmed economic efficiency. Labour's close relationship with the unions also meant the Governments remained tied to 'old assumptions about virtues of public spending and the operation of the public sector' just as many voters were becoming alienated from collectivism. Even so, the authors did not deny the Governments had some merit: they had after all reduced inflation without the divisive social consequences later unleashed by Thatcher in pursuit of the same end. Mandelson and Liddle additionally referred to ministers and advisers they termed 'social democratic radicals'. They were said to have been 'brimming with new ideas' but too often 'foundered on the rock of Labour's unwillingness to offend entrenched interests within the party', a rock of intransigence formed by the 'old Labour right and members of the traditional left'. Thus, while they belittled the Party's recent past for electoral reasons, even Blair's keenest partisans imagined that the seeds of the 'New' were present in the 'Old'.

Callaghan's 1976 Conference speech

Blair's 1995 Mais Lecture attracted attention at the time because he used it to underscore 'New' Labour's embrace of macro-economic stability and rejection of Keynesian demand management.[7] He endorsed the by-then conventional view that the Keynesian pursuit of full employment had created ever increasing levels of inflation that undermined Britain's international competitiveness. Most journalists took the lecture to be further evidence of Blair's break with 'Old' Labour so few noted that he traced the key element in this revered macro-economic stability – the primacy of the pursuit of low inflation – back to the Wilson–Callaghan years. For Blair claimed it was a Labour – not Conservative – Cabinet that, when faced by what he described as the 'most crucial decision in all our post-war economic crises', first prioritised reducing inflation over maintaining full employment. It is certainly true that in 1976 Prime Minister Callaghan could have withdrawn from the global economy by raising protective trade barriers behind which the state would have assumed the dominant position. Many on the left urged such a course. Instead, he pursued policies, principally the pursuit of low inflation, designed to improve the country's international competitiveness.

Wilson's Chancellor Denis Healey had in fact anticipated this change of direction in April 1975 when he rejected demand management as an appropriate response to the international slump. It is, however, worth recalling how Callaghan presented his Government's strategic priorities when addressing Labour's annual conference in September 1976. In the Blackpool Winter Gardens he bluntly informed apparently dumbstruck delegates:

> The cosy world we were told would go on for ever, where full employment would be guaranteed by a stroke of the Chancellor's pen, cutting taxes, deficit spending, that cosy world is gone …
>
> When we reject unemployment as an economic instrument – as we do – and when we reject also superficial remedies, as socialists must, then we must ask ourselves unflinchingly what is the cause of high unemployment. Quite simply and unequivocally, it is caused by paying ourselves more than the value of what we produce …
>
> We used to think that you could spend your way out of a recession, and increase employment by cutting taxes and boosting Government spending. I tell you in all candour that option no longer exists, and that in so far as it ever did exist, it only worked on each occasion since the war by injecting a bigger dose of inflation into the economy, followed by a higher level of unemployment as the next step. Higher inflation followed by higher unemployment. We have just escaped from the highest rate of inflation this country has known; we have not yet escaped from the consequences: high unemployment …

Now we must get back to fundamentals. First, overcoming unemployment now unambiguously depends on our labour costs being at least comparable with those of our major competitors. Second, we can only become competitive by having the right kind of investment at the right kind of level, and by significantly improving the productivity of both labour and capital.[8]

Blair's interpretation of Callaghan's policy, that it laid the foundations for Thatcher's approach to economic management, was plausible and echoed the work of some contemporary historians. As Martin Holmes put it in 1985, the Prime Minister's speech 'effectively broke the mould of post-war economic policy-making', marking as it did a 'watershed in attitudes to the expectations and effectiveness of government stimulus to the economy'. It was, Holmes concluded, the Callaghan Government that facilitated a 'change of intellectual direction' that preceded Thatcher's assumption of office.[9]

Yet, in his 1987 memoirs Callaghan distanced himself from this interpretation. He was uncomfortable being associated with the adoption of priorities that in Thatcher's hands resulted in a massive increase in unemployment and poverty. Callaghan instead claimed his speech had been a response to the dire position in which Britain found itself during 1976: inflation, unemployment and government spending had all reached post-war peaks. It was, he wrote, not a principled refutation of demand management for all time but addressed the short-term need to curb wage rises and to cut government spending severely. Ten years later Kenneth Morgan, Callaghan's official biographer and a Labour 'traditionalist' with his own misgivings about 'New' Labour, underscored this explanation by also stressing the political context in which the speech was delivered. The new Prime Minister, Morgan argued, had to persuade a disillusioned party and weary electorate to take unpleasant medicine and, for dramatic effect, overstated his case.[10]

All historians should be sensitive to context and it would be wrong to adopt a teleological view of Callaghan's speech: the Prime Minister's words did, however, have a very definitive ring to them. Yet, whatever Callaghan's attitude to monetary policy in 1976, he was very much a leading light of those Mandelson and Liddle referred to as the 'old Labour right'. While no man of the left, Callaghan was emotionally committed to what hackneyed Labour speakers used to call 'this great Movement of ours'. As one ministerial colleague put it at the time: 'those dreary committee rooms, the bad tea, the duplicating machines that get ink everywhere, the old ladies writing notices with exasperating slowness. Jim *likes* all that.'[11] As Prime Minister he was committed to improving economic efficiency, but through a state-sponsored industrial strategy in which ministers encouraged workers and employers to establish planning agreements. Accepting that technological transformation would only accelerate in the 1980s, and that it was imperative for Britain to keep up with the pace of change, Callaghan believed government should still intervene to protect jobs. Thus, he firmly disavowed Thatcher's proposed return to laissez-faire as unnecessary, claiming it would usher in 'a cruder, a more unjust, a more selfish society'.[12] As the Cabinet minister who led the opposition to Wilson's 1969 attempt to reform industrial relations through *In Place of Strife* he was moreover firmly committed to maintaining the Party's union link. A trade union official – albeit for the Inland Revenue Staff Federation – before elected an MP, Callaghan imagined he could and should do business with unions he saw as intrinsic to the 'Movement'.

Even so, Callaghan – like all Labour leaders before him – was aware that if his Government was to achieve anything it needed Britain's essentially market economy to compete with its main rivals. Productivity needed to improve, wages should be kept down so profits could rise and investment increase: that would then pay for improvements in the welfare state which, in themselves, could help reduce inequality. This basic dependence on capitalist success was something most union leaders accepted. Indeed, as left analysts complained, Wilson and Callaghan persuaded the much maligned union 'barons' not to advance 'socialism' but to draw the teeth from their members' militant demands, enabling ministers to restore an embattled capitalism to the semblance of health.[13] If true, it is, however, unlikely that, because they accepted the temporary need to cut government spending and temper wage rises, the Labour Cabinet and its union allies wanted to lay the foundations for a return to full-blooded free market capitalism. It was to prevent such an outcome they agreed to the measures they did.

Coming to terms with change

If it is unclear how far Callaghan stumbled rather than strode towards policies usually associated with 'New' Labour, some in the Party more deliberately adjusted their stance. As intimated by Mandelson and Liddle, these 'social democratic radicals' – or neo-revisionists – did their best to come to terms with the ending of the 'golden age'. The international slump hit revisionists especially hard because Crosland had based his influential reworking of Labour's historic purpose on what, during the 1950s, looked to be the plausible assumption that capitalism had reached a new stage, one defined by ineluctable growth.[14] He consequently argued that raising the tax revenues necessary to fund an expanding welfare state – for him the main means of promoting equality – would be fairly painless. For an expanding economy meant government income would rise in step: therefore tax rates need not be increased and, in some cases, even reduced.

The recession finally disabused revisionists that equality could be achieved without tears. The end of the post-war boom meant the welfare state would have to be financed by increasing relative levels of income tax – especially on those affluent white-collar and manual workers whose votes Labour desperately required. This situation was exacerbated when unemployment rose, meaning government put even more pressure on those in work. Thus, reducing inequality became evermore politically perilous as few taxpaying voters were keen to underwrite the creation of a fairer society from which they would not directly benefit.

Persuading himself the recession was a temporary blip, Crosland refused to update his earlier arguments while Roy Jenkins responded to the downturn by quitting the Cabinet and becoming President of the European Economic Community. Nonetheless, by the time Crosland died in 1977 the revisionist perspective was being revised by a younger generation of Labour MPs. To them the journey to an egalitarian society had undoubtedly reached a political and economic impasse. If the pursuit of equality had always involved the restriction of personal freedom, some now believed the trade-off between fairness and liberty was especially problematic. According to John Mackintosh, the leading neo-revisionist of this time, whose untimely demise was a severe blow to its development, equality 'may have gone far enough' and it was probably time to 'reassert' the 'freedom of the individual'.[15] Thus, while generally believing their aim should remain the reduction of inequality, neo-revisionists stressed this could only be achieved if government lifted some of its restrictions on the market. They also advocated, with increasing enthusiasm, the decentralisation of government so individuals could be more directly represented in decision making. In other words, to help the Party better achieve its agreed ends, they wanted it to recast the form (and in some cases the content) of how the state had addressed welfare provision and economic management after 1945.

Such iconoclasm was not restricted to social democratic radicals. If he was on the 'old right' Callaghan nonetheless proposed a number of reforms to collectivism. He famously focused attention on the importance of raising educational 'standards', especially in relation to the basic skills of literacy and numeracy. Prior to his 1976 'Great Debate' Labour had been preoccupied with the need to promote comprehensives, not because they would help pupils improve academically, but in the hope they would build a more egalitarian society. Under Callaghan's auspices education ministers also issued a Green Paper that stressed the need for all pupils to gain a 'basic understanding of the economy and activities … which are necessary for the creation of … wealth'.[16]

Callaghan also wanted to increase the accountability of public services to those whose interests they were designed to serve. While opposing council house sales he wanted tenants to be able to maintain and improve their homes as they saw fit and even won the applause of delegates at Labour's 1978 Conference when stating that council tenants were 'not just there for the convenience of town hall officials'.[17] Labour consequently entered the 1979 campaign with its leader advocating a tenants' charter as well as a parents' charter, the latter designed to give individuals more influence over their children's education. Indeed, in the foreword to the Party's manifesto Callaghan declared Labour was 'deeply concerned to enlarge people's freedom' in general and wanted to 'tilt the balance of power back to the individual' and away from bureaucrats.[18]

Callaghan knew this emphasis on 'freedom' was controversial within the Party. As his Special Policy Adviser Bernard Donoughue conceded, the Prime Minister was going against the 'producer socialism' of many Labour members, many of whom were public employees. Unfortunately, their desire to protect the position of public sector workers often appeared to be at the expense of those millions who relied on (and paid for) collective provision. Anticipating Blair's 'invest and reform' strategy, which emerged prior to the 2001 general election, Callaghan wanted the public services to operate more in the interests of those who used them, rather than in favour of those employed to run them.[19] Even so, while sometimes frustrated by the public services' lack of responsiveness the Prime Minister remained committed to their established character. If he imposed spending cuts on public spending during his tenure, Callaghan was not motivated by any principled desire to reduce the size of the welfare state.

Callaghan formed a pact with the Liberals during 1977–8 although, unlike Blair's later venture into co-operation, this initiative was motivated purely by the desire to ensure the Government's survival. In return for their support in the Commons Liberal MPs attended consultative meetings with ministers – although they exerted no formal influence. They nonetheless persuaded the Prime Minister to introduce a bill proposing the introduction of proportional representation to European Parliament elections. As an insufficient number of Labour MPs supported this measure it failed to see the light of day – until 1999. Similarly, to discourage Scottish and Welsh nationalist MPs from voting against him, Callaghan introduced legislation to devolve power to Edinburgh and Cardiff. While getting as far as holding referendums in the spring of 1979, this scheme failed due to lack of sufficient popular support. It remained 'unfinished business' until 1997.

The Labour leadership was not alone among West European social democratic parties to respond to the end of the 'golden age' by abandoning Keynesianism and questioning its reliance on an ever expanding state.[20] The Party was, however, the first to confront its implications head-on. Labour did not find itself in the vanguard of this international process of adaptation through choice but because the termination of guaranteed growth hit the British economy – and so Labour – much sooner and very much harder. Possibly because of this earlier and more dramatic need to come to terms, the response of the Party and union activists was even more violent than that evident in other centre–left parties. Many in the wider Party had after all hoped the Government elected in 1974 would take important strides towards further forms of collectivism – instead its leaders appeared to sound the retreat from state intervention. While Prime Minister, Callaghan just about managed to keep the Party together, but after the 'Winter of Discontent' and bereft of office he was powerless to prevent a decisive leftward shift that rejected each and every accommodation his Government had made with the ending of the 'golden age'. Thinking their Party had taken permanent leave of its senses, prominent neo-revisionists established the Social Democratic Party in 1981. It took the appalling defeat of 1983 conducted under a manifesto dictated by the Bennite left to start the move back to ground tentatively established during the Wilson–Callaghan years. In the end, however, mainly due to its failure to win back power in 1987 and 1992, the Labour leadership went much further than the likes of Callaghan ever anticipated.

Conclusion

If most commentators and academics believe that without 'Thatcherism', 'New' Labour would not have been possible, it could be equally argued that it would not have been necessary either. For, in the search for its antecedents it is too easy to give the impression that 'New' Labour was the inevitable outcome of historically determined events. Any historian worth their salt should shudder at such a suggestion: nothing is fated to happen, not even 'New' Labour.

Had Callaghan responded differently to events during the autumn of 1978 it is possible 'New' Labour would never have happened – because it would not have been required. In the late summer Labour's electoral position, which had once looked grim, appeared retrievable: the Party led the Conservatives in some opinion polls. The economy also seemed to be heading slowly in the right direction while most unions remained willing to keep wage demands within certain limits. At this moment there was fevered speculation the Prime Minister would call an election. Thinking the signs too tentative and that the best Labour might achieve was another period as a minority government Callaghan decided to battle on. If this decision still looks at least understandable, less excusable was his determination to fix the Government's fortunes to holding wage increases at 5 per cent. This was something he thought necessary if inflation was to be kept below 10 per cent, a target he saw as vital to the Party's re-election chances. Few considered this feasible, especially as private employers were unwilling to back the Government's line. Watching Ford grant its workers a 17 per cent increase was too much for low-paid public sector employees. They went on strike in the hope Callaghan would abandon his 5 per cent obsession. The resulting 'Winter of Discontent' turned the tide decisively against the Government (by undermining its claim that partnership with the unions was possible), laid the foundations for Thatcher's victory in May 1979 and inaugurated eighteen years of uninterrupted Conservative rule.

Had Callaghan won an election in 1978 – a big 'if' it should be conceded – he may not have felt it so necessary to uphold the 5 per cent norm and so probably could have avoided the public sector strikes. With the authority of continued prime ministerial office he would also have found it easier – but still difficult – to stall Labour's shift leftwards and hold on to all his Party's neo-revisionists. In such circumstances it is not inconceivable a Labour Government would have followed Callaghan's pragmatic instincts and the more clear-headed neo-revisionist perspective. During the 1979 election campaign he had after all floated the idea of reducing income tax, something Healey had already done on five occasions, although Callaghan made it clear this would have to be matched by increasing indirect taxes. Unlike Thatcher's more strident proposals, these cuts would moreover be targeted at those on modest incomes – and would not be financed through a reduction in public spending.[21] It is also not inconceivable that a re-elected Labour administration may have introduced a limited privatisation programme – the Government had already sold off shares in British Petroleum – and fostered other changes the British in their parochial way describe as 'Thatcherite'. Labour would not, however, have burdened the country with the gratuitously divisive consequences of Conservative rule. For Callaghan in the 1970s just like Blair at the start of the new millennium believed there was no contradiction in Labour trying to build an efficient economy *and* a fairer society.

Notes

1 For the best example of this view, see Hay, C., *The Political Economy of New Labour* (Manchester University Press, Manchester, 1996).
2 See, for instance, Coates, D., 'Labour Governments: Old Constraints and New Parameters', *New Left Review*, 291, 1996; Holmes, M., *The Labour Government, 1974–79* (Macmillan, London, 1985); and Ludlam, S., 'The Making of New Labour', in Ludlam, S. and Smith, M.J. (eds), *New Labour in Government* (Palgrave, London, 2001).
3 For a more detailed elaboration of this perspective, see Fielding, S., *The Labour Party: Continuity and Change in the Making of 'New' Labour* (Palgrave, London, 2003).
4 For more on the distorted image of the 1970s, see Tiratsoo, N., ' "Never had it so bad"?: Britain in the 1970s', in Tiratsoo, N. (ed.), *From Blitz to Blair: A New History of Britain since 1939* (Weidenfeld, London, 1997).
5 Fielding, S., 'New Labour and its Past', in Tanner, D., Thane, P. and Tiratsoo, N. (eds), *A Centenary History of the Labour Party* (Cambridge University Press, Cambridge, 2000).
6 Mandelson, P. and Liddle, R., *The Blair Revolution: Can New Labour Deliver?* (Faber and Faber, London, 1996), pp. 11–12, 25 and 195.
7 Blair, T., *New Britain: My Vision of a Young Country* (Fourth Estate, London, 1996), pp. 79–80.
8 Labour Party, *Report of the Seventy-fifth Annual Conference of the Labour Party* (Labour Party, London, 1976), pp. 188–9.
9 Holmes, *The Labour Government, 1974–79*, pp. 163, 179–82.
10 Callaghan, J., *Time and Chance* (Collins, London, 1987), pp. 425–7; Morgan, K.O., *Callaghan: A Life* (Oxford University Press, Oxford, 1997), pp. 536–7.
11 *Sunday Times*, 4 April 1976.
12 Labour Party, *Report of the Seventy-seventh Annual Conference of the Labour Party* (Labour Party, London, 1978), p. 233.
13 Coates, D., *Labour in Power? A Study of the Labour Government, 1974–1979* (Longman, London, 1980).
14 Crosland, C.A.R., *The Future of Socialism* (Cape, London, 1956).
15 Marquand, D. (ed.), *John P. Mackintosh on Parliament and Social Democracy* (Longman, London, 1982), pp. 84–6, 182–9; Mackintosh, J.P., 'Has Social Democracy Failed in Britain?', *Political Quarterly*, 49(3), 1979, pp. 266–7.
16 Fielding, S., *The Labour Governments, 1964–70*, vol. 1, *Labour and Cultural Change* (Manchester University Press, Manchester, 2004), pp. 86–90; Ellison, N., *Egalitarian Thought and Labour Politics* (Routledge, London, 1994), p. 47; Morgan, *Callaghan*, pp. 502–3, 540–1.
17 Labour Party, *Seventy-seventh Conference*, p. 240.
18 Labour Party, *The Labour Way is the Better Way* (Labour Party, London, 1979), p. 4.
19 Donoughue, B., *Prime Minister: The Conduct of Policy under Harold Wilson and James Callaghan* (Cape, London, 1987), pp. 111–13, 167–8; Fielding, S., 'Building Trojan Horses? "New" Labour's "Invest and Reform" Strategy', Paper delivered at the 2003 annual meeting of the American Political Science Association.

20 For this wider context see Callaghan, J., *The Retreat of Social Democracy* (Manchester University Press, Manchester, 2000).

21 *Financial Times* and *Western Mail*, 20 April 1979; *Scotsman*, 21 April 1979.

17 The industrial strategy

Stuart Holland

None of what follows is the whole picture. Ideas, institutions and interests range wider and deeper than individuals alone. But some leading figures played key roles in throwing away Labour's industrial strategy in the 1970s and, with it, the chance to avoid decades of de-industrialisation. Roy Jenkins denounced the National Executive Committee's (NEC's) Green Paper on the National Enterprise Board (NEB) as 'outdated nationalisation dogma', despite its scope and design being identical to the state holding he had himself earlier advocated.[1] Tony Crosland condemned the approach despite its extending his own case for competitive public enterprise. Harold Wilson stripped real power for the strategy out of the Industry Act. Tony Benn dogmatised it, and recklessly linked it to the 1975 referendum on Europe. Denis Healey then brutalised the chance to implement it. It is conventional wisdom to blame the unions for Labour's failure in the 1970s. It would be more appropriate to blame its leaders.[2]

Harold Wilson

As the Party's leader and future Prime Minister, Harold Wilson clearly should have been a central player. Before the publication of the Green Paper on the NEB, Judith Hart and I, by mutual agreement, decided to try to alert him to the fact that a major commitment by the NEC and the 1973 Party Conference was likely to be made to the NEB and planning agreements and asked for a meeting. Neither of us succeeded. When the NEC therefore published its Green Paper, Harold was uninformed and unprepared. He appears to have read the press reports – nearly all of which declared that Labour would 'nationalise the top twenty-five firms' – and presumed to try to 'veto' the Green Paper. Yet at a press conference some ten days after, he asked journalists whether they had actually read the Green Paper and advised them to do so because it was 'not as bad' as they had assumed. Clearly he had not read it when he 'vetoed' it.

When the draft Industry Bill later went to Cabinet, Harold carried the case for two key measures which gelded the industrial strategy. The first was that, unlike its Italian IRI model, the NEB should only take a shareholding in companies with the consent of their management. The second was that, unlike their French counterparts, planning agreements should be voluntary rather than bargained in return for public grants or purchasing. This was a worst case scenario. It would mean that instead of reinforcing and promoting industrial success, as in the original statement of the case for new public enterprise and planning agreements, the companies most likely to agree to either would be those which were in difficulty.

Harold also should have known better. I had first briefed him on the fact that French planners had moved from NEDC-style Modernisation Commissions or sector talk-shops to direct negotiation with leading firms in 1966.[3] Both then and the following year, when he brought me into the Political Office in No. 10, I made the case that planning-by-agreement with leading firms was how to re-launch The National Plan, which had collapsed with the deflationary package of July 1966, and that we could legitimate the shift on the same grounds as the French had just done, i.e. knowing whether the Government got value for public money granted to big business by knowing what it planned to do with it. I also argued that we should make medium-term planning flexible, including macro outcomes from changed performance by leading firms, and adapt medium-term targets on a rolling annual basis. He declared himself impressed, but did not follow through. This was among several reasons for my decision to resign from his Political Office in 1968 despite the fact that he offered to make me head of what would have been the first Strategy Unit in No. 10. It may have been an error. Had I continued the advocacy of planning agreements and a state-holding company on his behalf after 1970 (if Labour had then lost the election) the outcome in terms of implementing the industrial strategy might have been different. Or maybe it was not. Not needing Harold's approval at least meant that some of the real arguments were in the public domain.

Harold also bowdlerised the Social Contract. This was conceived and agreed as a voluntary commitment by the trade unions to wage restraint in return for commitment by the Government to the social aims of Labour's Programme 1973, allowing for joint renegotiation in the event that circumstances changed. It also allowed that skill differentials could be rewarded provided they were covered by productivity gains.[4] Harold simply used it as re-branding of a fixed rate incomes policy which meant that skilled workers saw no personal gain from productivity increases. It stayed that way through to the 'Winter of Discontent', when public sector workers after years of declining real wages ignored injunctions from their leadership, and struck. In the 1979 general election swathes of skilled workers then voted for Margaret Thatcher.

Tony Benn

Tony Benn was the politician most identified with the industrial strategy, but dogmatised it to the point of making it unrecognisable to some of its key advocates. Through 1973, and after, Tony kept talking publicly about the need for 'compulsory planning agreements with the top 100 companies'. At one of many meetings at his home with Party and union researchers, and union leaders, I remonstrated that 'compulsory agreements' were a contradiction in terms. You could oblige a company to enter negotiation with a view to an agreement if it wanted public grants or contracts, but not compel it to agree. The outcome would be a trade-off. In return for public money the companies would lengthen investment horizons, increase R&D in Britain, locate more in the regions, etc., i.e. the same objectives as for the NEB. If they would not, then no public money and no agreement. Also, that his talking of compulsory agreements with the top 100 companies projected the whole strategy as Gosplan and central command planning. When he then asked how many agreements I had in mind I replied that, after they introduced their equivalent in 1966, the French Ministry of Finance and Economy averaged one such agreement a month but with half their top officials engaged on them and more initial experience on direct bargaining of outcomes with companies. Granted that we would need to get the programme up and running, it would be a great success if we averaged six or seven a year of a kind which would change the investment, innovation and trade performance of key players in key sectors.[5] Tony appeared to accept this at face value, but in practice continued to make speech after speech advocating 'compulsory planning agreements with the top 100 companies', making the whole programme look dogmatic rather than pragmatic, old rather than new, and civil servants running industry rather than government bargaining outcomes with it.

He then compounded this with a fatal strategic error. At a meeting at his home after the October 1973 Party Conference, he suddenly claimed that we now had to admit that the industrial strategy was incompatible with British membership of the Common Market. I answered: 'Tony, you can't be serious. We modelled the NEB and planning agreements on Italian, French and Belgian experience.' He countered by saying: 'but public ownership is ruled out by the Rome Treaty'. When I replied that there was no such reference in the entire Treaty, he then volunteered the non sequitur that 'it may be alright for the French to say one thing and do another, but the British people will not stand for it. We must have a referendum on Europe.'

He wanted to move on, but I asked him whether he had heard of Léon Gambetta. He said he knew that streets and squares were named after him in France. I then asked if he knew why, which he did not. I told him that Gambetta became a national hero after escaping from the Paris Commune in 1871 in a hot air balloon and then worked ceaselessly around the country for years to unite the parties opposed to the Commune 'butcher' Thiers. 'So,' said Tony, 'how is this relevant?' I replied that he won an election on this basis, but then astonished his supporters by unilaterally declaring that he wanted a referendum on reform of the Senate. I pointed out that his friends warned him that if he called and lost a referendum he could lose the government, which he did. I likewise warned Tony that if he claimed in a referendum that the industrial strategy was incompatible with membership of the Common Market and then lost it, he also could lose the political base for the industrial strategy.

The warning, of course, was prescient. Within days of the outcome of the June 1975 referendum on the EEC, Wilson dismissed Tony as Industry Secretary, offered him the Department of Energy, and appointed Eric Varley and Gerald Kaufman to the Department of Industry. As Geoff Hodgson put it: 'after June 1975 it was all retreat for the Left'.[6]

None of the above exchanges appear in Tony's published diaries for 1973–6 from which, as one who knew commented, I had been airbrushed out as if I were Trotsky.[7] It was the last time for years that I had an in-depth political exchange with him. We appeared together on political platforms and I publicly defended and supported his right to run for Deputy Leader of the Party, both on principle and because I still hoped to turn him on Europe. I invited him for this reason to the conference of the 'Out of Crisis' network in Paris in 1983, whose programme then became the basis of the next two European manifestos of all the EC parties in the Socialist International. In political terms it wrote Labour's industrial and regional strategy, and the Social Contract, Europe wide.[8] But he did not come, writing that he was sure I would understand. I did. Since 1973 I had disagreed with Tony on Europe itself, on linking a referendum on Europe to the industrial strategy, his misrepresentation of the strategy, and his endorsement of import controls and a siege economy.

Fred Catherwood

Before this Tony made a tactical blunder which cost him the best candidate to run the NEB in the manner in which it was conceived and designed. Sir Fred Catherwood had been a member of the Industrial Policy Committee through 1972 and 1973. Following one of its key meetings he had asked me whether Tony had thought who might actually head the NEB. I said he never had mentioned it, but asked whether he was interested. He said he was, and volunteered that he also very much supported the case that trade unions should be able to take part in negotiating planning agreements.[9] He already had gone public in arguing that only a major wave of new public investment promoted through the NEB could prevent the de-industrialisation of the British economy. He had the experience of running one of the country's major construction companies, Laing, and had been Head of the National Economic Development Office which had run the sectoral NEDCs, which he agreed lacked any leverage on actual company performance.

Fred rang me when Harold appointed Tony as Secretary of State and I set up a meeting. The evening it took place, he rang me back to say that he was sorry but he could not accept the job. When I asked why he said that it was clear that Tony had a completely different view of the NEB and planning agreements from that which had been agreed by the Industrial Policy Committee, that he kept going on about compulsory planning agreements with the top 100 companies and workers' control. I remonstrated that he would be running the NEB and as its Chairman Designate could have a powerful influence on how planning agreements were drafted in the Industry Bill, and that I was a member of the Institute of Workers' Control but did not mean more by this than that workers should be invited, if they chose to take part in the negotiation of planning agreements with management and the Government on which several of them still were sceptical.

'No,' Fred replied, 'I'm sorry Stuart, but Tony is the Secretary of State and wants something entirely different. I just can't accept the job on his terms.' Tony's mishandling of Catherwood was a gift to Harold, who shortly thereafter announced that Sir Don Ryder was Chairman Designate of the NEB. Ryder knew nothing of, and cared nothing for, the case for it or for planning agreements, as he made plain at a meeting shortly thereafter with Judith Hart, Margaret Beckett and myself. He clearly had been remitted to 'stop Benn' and thereby comprehensively blocked any leverage by Tony on how the NEB would be run.

Denis Healey

When Labour came into government Denis Healey faced an unprecedented crisis not of Labour's making: the September 1973 quadrupling of oil prices by OPEC and the recession caused by most governments cutting domestic spending to reduce non-oil imports. At the October Labour Party Conference in 1974 both Judith Hart and Tony Benn told me that Denis wanted to speak with me and Francis Cripps, then Tony's economic adviser. When I met him he said that he was trying to find a way of reconciling the industrial strategy with the post-OPEC situation and would I draft something for him? I said that I would, provided that he would allow me to advocate it, with him present, before his top Treasury team. I stressed that he need not commit himself until the outcome of such a meeting. He agreed.

I then wrote a paper for Denis arguing how we could invest and innovate our way out of the recession, from which we anyway would gain as a North Sea oil producer, and do so by planning agreements in a manner which translated public grants and public purchasing into a broad wave of innovation-led investment.[10] I also argued the case that while leading firms with falling sales were bound to increase prices to preserve profit margins, an investment-led recovery would give them sufficient revenue to sustain profitability while moderating price increases. This, in fact, was the model which was implemented in the mid-1970s as a reaction to the 'oil shock' by Japan. Francis Cripps meanwhile wrote a paper for Denis advocating import and capital controls.

Denis totally disregarded his commitment to a meeting with Treasury officials and went to the next meeting of the Party's NEC and said: 'I have consulted your gurus. One wants import controls and the other does not. When you have made up your minds what you are doing, let me know.' He then prepared a series of the first monetarist budgets since before the war. It was not enough. The markets wanted more. The result was his notorious flight to the IMF in 1976 at which he agreed a major public expenditure cuts package and the abandonment of any full employment policy. It later transpired that the Treasury had understated tax receipts by some £4 billion which were the equivalent of the main cuts package initially demanded by the IMF.

Had the meeting with Denis and his senior Treasury officials taken place it was possible that the case for investing and innovating out of recession could have been won, not least since by then it was becoming clear that Japan was successfully pursuing its similar strategy by planning agreements with leading firms, encouraging and funding the accelerated translation of R&D into a broad wave of new investment. Also, for a decade, I knew and had been able to carry senior Treasury officials on key arguments. Frank Figgueres had known and supported me in inter-departmental committees since I had drafted the rationale for regional policy of the National Plan early in 1965, and stressed the importance of working through firms rather than offering general regional grants and incentives.[11]

Denis's opportunism almost certainly cost him the leadership of the Labour Party. Had he as Chancellor made an effort to use planning agreements to invest and innovate out of recession, and compensate firms for price restraint with sustained demand rather than tax rebates, his chances in the PLP election after Jim Callaghan's resignation could have been very real.[12] If he had pulled off a recovery through planning agreements with leading firms – as the Japanese did – he would have been able to work with rather than against the trade unions to do so. By mocking Labour's Programme, espousing monetarism, and blaming the unions for what at the time was a world economic crisis, he alienated them and much of the PLP. He also thereby legitimated Margaret Thatcher's claim that public spending drained rather than sustained the economy, and that there was no alternative but to cut, cut and cut again at public spending and the fabric of a welfare economy.[13]

Notes

1　I had drafted them both on the same basis. See further Jenkins, R., 'The Needs of the Regions', in *What Matters Now* (Collins/Fontana, London, 1972) and The Labour Party, 'The National Enterprise Board', Opposition Green Paper, London, April 1973.

2　I have recently covered the rationale for Labour's economic strategy and the role of Roy Jenkins and Tony Crosland in 'Ownership, Planning and Markets', in Plant, R., Beech, M. and Hickson, K. (eds), *The Struggle for Labour's Soul: Analysing Labour's Political Thought* (Routledge, London, 2004).

3　Holland, S., 'French Incomes and Prices Policy', Cabinet Office, 2 December 1966.

4　See further Holland, S., *The Socialist Challenge* (Quartet Books, London, 1975).

5　Changing trade performance by both more import substitution and also tackling transfer pricing, as the French were doing through their version of planning agreements or *Contrats de programme*.

6　Hodgson, G., *Labour at the Crossroads* (Martin Robertson, Oxford, 1981), p. 102.

7　After this was pointed out to Tony by Meghnad Desai, I surfaced in the third volume of his diaries where he kindly wrote that I would be a good Foreign Secretary. And, as many have commented, Tony is a kind man. But on key issues we disagreed, and in a retrospective on the period such as this volume it may be hard, but in order, to say so.

8　Holland, S., (ed) *Out of Crisis: A Project for European Recovery* (Spokesman, Nottingham, 1983).

9　Such worker 'empowerment' has since become a by-word for how the Japanese achieved their post-Fordist model of flexible production, for which see virtually any recent issue of the *Journal of Management Studies*. Such literature nonetheless rightly stresses the degree to which worker involvement can also lead to co-option – the same issue as caused several trade union leaders to be sceptical in the 1970s about involvement in negotiating planning agreements.

10 Ferranti, later in fact aided by the NEB, but then passed back to the private sector, was a classic case in point. As I had earlier argued on the Industrial Policy Committee of the NEC, for every 100 patents it registered, it could afford to translate only half a dozen into actual innovation. It was not alone. Britain had pioneered jet aircraft, television, video and major technical breakthroughs without the kind of support which, in Japan through industrial policy, and in the United States through defence spending, ensured their dominance in global markets. France through public ownership and planning agreements still is a modern industrial economy. Britain is not.

11 Frank also could have gained from advice. He was responsible for the £4 billion underestimate of tax revenues, which led Denis later to claim with scant disregard for ministerial responsibility that he had been 'misled' about the need for cuts.

12 In overreaction to aggregate data on falling profitability, Denis granted general tax relief on stock appreciation. With other allowances, this reduced effective taxation of industry from a nominal 52 per cent to 4 per cent. The top twenty-five companies after these concessions paid tax of some £40 million on profits of £4 billion. Small wonder therefore that there was too little revenue available to increase public sector pay. If effective taxation had been at 52 per cent, this would have given more than £2 billion from these companies alone, which was double the total resources allocated for the NEB. An imaginative budget would have taxed companies on what they actually earned but would have needed information on transfer pricing, as the French planners realised, to know what real profits were.

13 See further Holland, S., 'From Bustskellism to Howeleyism', *Guardian*, 16 June 1980.

18 Was Britain dying?

Kenneth O. Morgan

The Wilson–Callaghan era of 1974–9 is etched gloomily in the public memory – sleaze under Wilson, strikes under Callaghan. Much was made of this perception by Mrs Thatcher later on, drawing a contrast between her own liberation of Britain from the shackles of post-war socialism and the cultural despair of the Winter of Discontent: 'Do you remember the Labour Britain of 1979? It was a Britain in which union leaders held their members and our country to ransom ... the sick man of Europe.'[1] It was the obvious role of the Tories to keep these folk memories warm. Perceptions of the Wilson years were largely of a failure of style – the paranoid mood of the Kitchen Cabinet, the humiliation of the Lloyd George-style final honours list of 1976 on the famous lavender-blue notepaper, of which volumes of reminiscence by Joe Haines and Bernard Donoughue as late as 2003 faithfully reminded the public. Perceptions of the Callaghan years were rather of failures of policy – a Labour Government swamped by trade union militants on the loose; anti-cancer drugs left on the Hull dockside uncollected; union leaders like Moss Evans or Alan Fisher oblivious to any dangers from inflation; hospital wards and primary schools closed down by public sector stoppages; refuse bins overflowing; the classic image of the Liverpool grave-diggers in David Basnett's union refusing even to bury the dead. The literature of the late 1970s is apocalyptic, written in terms of 'collapse' or 'eclipse', a land as 'ungovernable as Chile' conducting the last rites of Attlee's social democratic post-war consensus. Americans were especially prominent in this kind of historical pathology. Isaac Kramnick's book of 1979 captures the mood vividly – *Is Britain Dying?*

This gloomy view of the 1974–9 Labour Governments continued to flourish in the 1980s and the 1990s, not only amongst Thatcherite Conservatives but equally within a reviving Labour Party. Neil Kinnock and John Smith urged the comrades to embark on a fresh start, a new sense of discipline and unity without sacrificing the values of democratic socialism on which the Party was founded. New Labour under Tony Blair's leadership from 1994 went further still in lamenting the Party's past. Its strategists drew a stark comparison between the dark days of Old Labour in the 1970s and the bright promise of New Labour under its youthful leader. Philip Gould saw the Wilson–Callaghan era as crucial evidence of 'the failure to modernise' in 'the century Labour lost'.[2] Peter

Mandelson's jointly authored work *The Blair Revolution* (1996) attacked the era of the Social Contract which saw 'every wage claim and every strike as justified. ... In the eyes of the public the Labour Government appeared a helpless bystander.'[3] If the formation of the SDP in 1981 proved to be an ultimately abortive challenge to the Old Labour past, its ethic lived on, not least in the New Labour leadership of 1994–7. Blair's battle to ditch Clause 4 was a crusade to rid Labour of this symbolic incubus of destructive socialism. The commentators and historians tended to follow this line, especially in welcoming the Blair Government from 1997. A rare exception was the Oxford Australian historian Ross McKibbin, in 1991. His article 'Homage to Wilson and Callaghan' acclaimed the commitment of the Labour Governments of the 1970s to greater social and racial equality, public expenditure and commitment to the public services.[4] They had, after all, little or no parliamentary majority (they were defeated fifty-nine times in 1974–9). Yet they rescued the country from the miners' strike, the three-day week and 30 per cent inflation. The contrast with the divisiveness of Thatcherism was underlined. But such favourable analyses were rare.

But gradually, perhaps inevitably, interpretation of the Labour 1970s has begun to modify. Lengthy biographies of Harold Wilson and Jim Callaghan, predictably no doubt, spread a more positive view, as to a degree does Edward Pearce's of Denis Healey (2002). Ben Pimlott's and Philip Ziegler's lives of Wilson (1992, 1993) focused much more on the Government of 1964–70 but did pay proper tribute to the Premier's political skills especially in negotiating the referendum on the European Common Market without splitting the Party. My own biography of Callaghan (1997) was kindly received although journalist reviewers focused with predictable emphasis on the Winter of Discontent and episodes of prime ministerial depression in the last months of 1979, with Callaghan sadly telling Ken Stowe 'I let the country down.'[5] My attempt to highlight the far lengthier period of economic and social advance from the IMF crisis in December 1976 to the late autumn of 1978 (when many people thought Callaghan would go to the country to cash in on his popularity) met with far less attention, as did chapters on foreign and defence policy. Other writers have noted the high calibre of the members of the Government: administrations that boasted Healey, Jenkins, Crosland, Dell, Lever, Shore or Shirley Williams in this period did not lack intellectual power. Callaghan's own array of advisers in the Policy Unit – Bernard Donoughue's team of dons like Andrew Graham and Richard Smethurst, and the brilliant young economist Gavyn Davies – were amongst the 'best and the brightest' of their generation. The 'Think Tank' had figures like Ken Berrill and Tessa Blackstone; economic advisers included Douglas Wass, Bryan Hopkin and Leo Pliatzky. Even in the Second World War the country had scarcely more distinguished people at the helm. Again, with Callaghan's Press Office under the low-key but reliable management of Tom McCaffrey, the British Government in 1976–9 was largely spin-free. There were few PR disasters, other perhaps than Peter Jay, the Premier's son-in-law, going to the Washington embassy.

Apart from these personal matters, historians such as Jim Tomlinson have pointed to the growing economic success of the later 1970s. Douglas Jay wrote of it as 'one of the few examples of any Western government ... reducing both inflationary pressures and unemployment at the same time'.[6] The pound's value went up month by month, yet exports improved; foreign currency reserves accumulated, down to November 1978. Gloomy contemporary perceptions in the press were at variance with the economic realities. It is also generally acknowledged that, following the IMF crisis, the judgements of the Treasury on public sector borrowing proved to be far too gloomy. With North Sea oil coming on stream, Britain's economic prospects in the Callaghan years were relatively buoyant. The apocalyptic prophets of doom around 1979–81 seem harder to justify today. Even the strike days lost were exaggerated: 98 per cent of manufacturing establishments had no strikes at all. Many Blairites now recognise that the stark contrast between moribund Old Labour then and modernising New Labour now has been overdone.

My own view is that, with reservations, a more positive view should be taken of the achievement of the Labour Governments of 1974–9. The two should, however, be distinguished since they were very different. The last Wilson ministry of 1974–6 was a time of survival and self-doubt under an ailing and dispirited Premier, surprised to win in February 1974. The Callaghan years saw governmental trust and collective responsibility revived; they are an episode in their own right, not a mere interlude as many accounts seem to imply. The last Wilson administration was a troubled one, with inflation soaring to alarming levels until Jack Jones's flat-rate pay restraint initiative of June 1975. Even so, they were an improvement on the corporate collapse and mass strikes of the Heath years. Harold Wilson's skilful confirmation of British membership of Europe – aided by Callaghan's canny diplomacy which was 'negotiating for success', and by the powerful diplomatic backing of the German Chancellor, Helmut Schmidt – was perhaps his major contribution to British history.

Callaghan, a cautious man four years older than Wilson who had never expected to enter No. 10 at all, proved to be a remarkably effective leader for most of the time, praised as such by Healey and Benn alike. The economy progressed in the wake of the skilful handling of the IMF crisis, while Michael Foot kept lines of communication with the unions open. In economics, unreconstructed Keynesianism came to an end. A vigorous regional policy brought new life to Wales and Scotland. Callaghan's Ruskin speech of October 1976 was a powerful stimulus to national debate on educational standards in the maintained schools, which foreshadowed Tony Blair's famous mantra two decades later.[7] There were major reforms in welfare policy, notably the state earnings-related pensions scheme (SERPS), an achievement identified with Barbara Castle whom Callaghan had sacked from the Cabinet, and the establishment of the first effective Race Relations Board. Devolution first emerged as a legislative priority. It failed in the Welsh and Scottish referendums of March 1979 (it was the switch of Scottish Nationalist votes, not Tory or Liberal opposition, that later brought the Government prematurely down in the Commons), and Callaghan himself was not enthusiastic, but it was a powerful portent of constitutional change. To a degree also, the Labour Government re-established itself as the party of the nuclear family, and of law and order, with PC Jim, once spokesman for the Police Federation, depicted in cartoons as a Dixon of Dock Green character urging us all to 'mind how you go'.

Above all, it was a constructive period in foreign policy, quieter than the later Blair years, but with more obvious achievement and certainly no risky adventure like an invasion of Iraq. Wilson and Callaghan played their full part in negotiating the Helsinki CSCE Treaty on European security in 1975 which closed this phase of the Cold War. Callaghan was quietly effective in protecting the nascent democratic revolution in Portugal against American pressure; in defending the Falklands against Argentine threats and without war; in helping Jimmy Carter negotiate the Camp David settlement between Israel and Egypt; in working towards strategic arms limitations with the Russians; and even in the international conference at Guadeloupe in January 1979, eternally overshadowed by memories of the sun-tanned Prime Minister coming home and saying something perilously similar to 'Crisis, what Crisis?' Steve Richards recently wrote that Old Labour was thought of as anti-American and weak on defence.[8] That accusation could never be brought against Callaghan who revived, for good or ill, the British nuclear deterrent, and who really acted as the honest broker between the Americans and Europe that Blair later sought to be. Callaghan's shrewd diplomatic style enabled him to serve as a bridge between two world leaders who broadly disliked each other – his fellow Baptist ex-sailor President Carter, and the German Chancellor, Helmut Schmidt, an intellectual Hamburg socialist who admired Callaghan as an authentic leader of working-class social democracy.[9] Callaghan basked for a time amidst some acclaim both as an international statesman and a pilot who had weathered the IMF storms at home. There was also the bonus of a successful royal jubilee in 1977, highly congenial to an old naval patriot from Portsmouth whose father had served on the royal yacht. His Cardiff constituents noted that Wales kept winning rugby's triple crown. Cledwyn Hughes hoped that Jim would not become too swollen-headed with all this success.[10] Maybe, indeed, that is where the leader found nemesis after hubris in the end. Certainly his bizarre rendition of a music-hall song at the September 1978 TUC Conference smacked of overconfidence.

There is much to be said for these Governments and, to a degree, their leaders. And yet, the 'declinist' interpretation of these years is not without substance. The Cabinets were effective, even successful. The Labour movement was not. The Party had been in numerical and ideological decline since the mid-1960s; it was becoming barren in ideas and lapsing into factional warfare symbolised by the divisive if charismatic figure of Tony Benn. It was unduly dependent on special interest groups such as public sector unions and council house tenants. No document of genuine intellectual renewal came from Labour in these years: Tony Crosland's *Socialism Now* (1974) was in some measure an elegy on the failure of the ethos of planning and economic growth in the 1960s. The unions were undoubtedly provoked by Callaghan's later misjudgements, notably the commitment to a 5 per cent pay norm which 'just popped out' in a radio interview, but they were also out of control.[11] The loss of Jack Jones through retirement was a colossal blow and, with his possible successor, Harry Urwin, also close to retirement, the advent of Moss Evans to head the massive Transport and General Workers' Union was a political and industrial disaster. There were many positive features about the 1974–9 period. The country was generally competently run, with far greater commitment to social equality or public compassion than was shown either in the Thatcher revolution of the 1980s, or the Blairite managerialism of post-1997. But fundamentally a Labour Government must connect with its political and industrial base. The decay of that base, the fundamental tensions within Keir Hardie's old Labour alliance at a time of global capitalist crisis, left the Government bereft. As a result, the efforts to rehabilitate the Wilson–Callaghan years, let alone pay them homage, can never be more than a partial success.

Notes

1 Speech to 1985 Conservative Party Conference at Blackpool.
2 Gould, P., *The Unfinished Revolution: How the Modernisers Saved the Labour Party* (Little, Brown, London, 1999), p. 36.
3 Mandelson, P. and Liddle, R., *The Blair Revolution: Can New Labour Deliver?* (Faber and Faber, London, 1996), p. 25.
4 McKibbin, R., 'Homage to Wilson and Callaghan', *London Review of Books*, 24 October 1991.
5 Morgan, K.O., *Callaghan: A Life* (Oxford University Press, Oxford, 1997), p. 633.
6 Jay, D., *Sterling: A Plea for Moderation* (Sidgwick and Jackson, London, 1985), p. 162.
7 *Guardian Educational Supplement*, 16 October 2001.
8 *Independent on Sunday*, 1 June 2003.
9 Interview with Helmut Schmidt, 30 November 1994.
10 Cledwyn Hughes, Diary, 2 March 1978 (Lord Cledwyn papers, National Library of Wales, Aberystwyth).
11 Morgan, *Callaghan: A Life*, p. 583.

19 Forgetting history

How New Labour sees Old Labour

Peter Riddell

Whenever Tony Blair talks about previous Labour administrations, he invariably refers to the Attlee Government of 1945–51, and almost never to the Wilson and Callaghan Governments of 1974–9. This is deliberate. For the Blairites, the Labour Governments of the second half of the 1960s and 1970s were failures, not least because they did not succeed in being re-elected for two full terms. The Attlee Government is now so far in the past – beyond the memories of most voters – that it can safely be praised without risk, as the creator of the National Health Service and 'coming closest to building a new Jerusalem'.[1]

But the Blairites have adopted a ground zero approach to the recent past: less the end of history than forget history. Hence, the central importance of the New versus Old Labour distinction. As Tony Blair said at the Royal Festival Hall victory party on the morning of 2 May 1997: 'we have been elected as New Labour, we will govern as New Labour'.

Creation of New Labour

Yet the creation of New Labour was the end of a long process. Tony Blair had also moved a long way himself. When the Callaghan Government fell in spring 1979, he had been a Labour member for just three and a half years. Blair's views were similar to many of those on what became known as the soft-left. They were critical of the caution and pragmatism of the old Labour right. But they also disliked the confrontational absolutism of the hard or Bennite left. Few people then thought the Party would have to change fundamentally to regain power. The Thatcher Government was seen as a temporary phenomenon, doomed to fail as its economic policies led to unacceptably high levels of unemployment. The Bennite left saw the answer in organisational changes that would prevent another 'betrayal' and would guarantee 'socialism'.

The Labour right was divided. The majority, like Denis Healey, believed that the Bennite upsurge would recede in time. The minority who split away to form the SDP in 1981 believed that such a revival was impossible without establishing a one-member–one-vote party without the trade union block vote. Yet, in policy terms, three of the Gang of Four did not reject the broad economic approach of the Callaghan and Wilson years. For them, while the organisational enemy was the Bennite left, the ideological enemy was Thatcherism. Only David Owen appreciated, mainly after 1983, that Margaret Thatcher, and not the SDP, had broken the ideological mould.

An insight into Blair's thinking at the time is provided by a lecture he gave in Australia in August 1982, shortly after he had fought and lost the Beaconsfield by-election. In the lecture, discussed in John Rentoul's biography, Blair criticised the SDP for 'having isolated themselves from organised labour, a fatal mistake for any radical party'.[2]

The key event in the birth of New Labour was not the loss of office in 1979, but the landslide defeat of 1983. It was only then that Blair and his future allies slowly began to realise how much Labour would have to change. First came the defeat of the hard-left (begun with the expulsion of Militant under Michael Foot) and the long trauma of the miners' strike. But Labour was still unelectable in 1987. The subsequent policy reviews shed many unpopular policies. Blair played a key role as Employment Spokesman from 1989 until 1992 in forcing Labour, and reluctant trade unions, to come to terms with the Thatcher Government's employment legislation, which he had so strongly condemned only a few years earlier. But that was not enough and the fourth election defeat in 1992 showed how Labour was still exposed on tax and spending.

American lessons

New Labour was, first, a campaigning strategy, before it was a programme for government. The Blairite approach of triangulation – defined against both the traditional or Old Labour Party and the Conservatives – was consciously copied from the United States, and Bill Clinton's victory in November 1992. Philip Gould first brought the good news from Little Rock to Walworth Road. After spending the last few weeks of the campaign in the Clinton 'war room', he wrote a long document summarising the main lessons.

> Above all Labour needed a fresh start: 'a changed Labour Party is the basis of a new relationship of trust with the British electorate.' And this change must be open: 'Labour has not changed until it announces it has changed.' This was exactly what the Democrats had done when they called themselves the 'New Democrats'.[3]

Gould's document went down like a 'lead balloon' with the party leadership under John Smith, the epitome of the old Labour right. They did not regard the 1974–9 period as a failure since they were so prominent in government then. Yet the Gould analysis was taken on board by Blair, Gordon Brown and Peter Mandelson. For them, the Wilson and Callaghan years were a period of failure and to be regretted. But the key linkage was from electoral failure to policy change. Because Labour had lost in 1979, and then the three subsequent elections, there was a need to change policy, and to reinvent the Party.

Past policies, the close links with the unions and the high- spending/taxation image, were associated with repeated electoral failure, and that is why they had to be dropped.

After Blair was elected Labour leader in July 1994, he followed the Gould strategy. That is why the rewriting of Clause 4, on the party's objectives, was so important. Where Gaitskell had failed, Blair succeeded – lending weight to his claim that Labour had proved that it was now a new party, so it could now be trusted again in government.

To create a new party involved a rejection of the past, and, in particular, of the Wilson and Callaghan years. No matter that the Labour Government had faced, partly aggravated and then, at least temporarily, overcome serious economic problems. It still managed, for example, to introduce child benefit and important legislation on equality and health and safety. Blair had sympathy with Callaghan's predicament: a small, then non-existent, parliamentary majority; an increasingly strident rank and file with left-wing-led unions; and, finally, the wave of public sector strikes over the winter of 1978–9. But Blair still saw the 1974–9 period as years of failure and disappointment. If for the Bennites the Callaghan Government was defined by the International Monetary Fund loan of autumn 1976 and the resulting 'cuts' in public spending (in reality, very small); for the Blairites, the key moment was the 'Winter of Discontent'. The two events were connected. Kathleen Burk and Alec Cairncross argue that, despite the adoption of monetary targets and tight borrowing limits, the commitment was not permanent: 'there was little change of heart in the Labour Party'.[4] So the key for Blair and his allies was to persuade voters that Labour could be economically competent and not in thrall to the unions.

To reinforce the new image, New Labour, as it was always called by Blair, made commitments intended to reassure voters. Gordon Brown promised to stick to existing Conservative public spending plans and not to raise the basic or higher rates of income tax. This was in marked contrast to the big spending commitments promised in Labour's February 1974 manifesto and to Denis Healey's famous, though often misreported, comment in October 1973 about 'howls of anguish from the 80,000 people who are rich enough to pay over 75 per cent on the last slice of their income'. (In 1997, the top rate of tax was 40 per cent.) Tony Blair and Gordon Brown were much more concerned with keeping the 80,000 happy and nurturing them. Corporatism, socialism (Blair preferred social-ism), redistribution and equality were out as Blair sought – and largely succeeded in both the 1997 and 2001 elections – in broadening Labour's support in middle-class Middle England, as well as eliminating the Tories in Scotland and Wales. It was a formidable electoral achievement.

Tony Blair has always been keen to claim that his New Labour approach is shared by other centre–left parties around the world – as shown in the annual meetings held under the Third Way/Progressive Governance label. On the Blair view, all centre–left parties had to come to terms with the international economic pressures produced both by globalisation and by the changed expectations and attitudes of the electorate. A common centre–left approach was at least partly true during the Clinton years, up to the end of 2000, not least in the sense noted above that the creation of New Labour was consciously and recognisably based on the success of the New Democrats in the United States in the 1990s. Other centre–left parties took a similar ideological route, notably in Australia (especially under Paul Keating) and New Zealand, and also to some extent in the Netherlands and, more ambiguously, Sweden and Italy. The main exception was the French socialists who specifically rejected the Anglo-American embrace of globalisation by Clinton and Blair. The French left still talked the language of socialism, particularly in defending the European social model. Yet under both François Mitterrand as President and Lionel Jospin as Prime Minister the French left did come round to accepting a more competitive market structure and a tight monetary and fiscal framework. The German Social Democrats were out of office in the 1980s and 1990s for nearly as long as Labour in Britain, and their eventual electoral success under Gerhard Schroeder in September 1998 was more to do with the unpopularity of Helmut Kohl than the result of a reinvention of the SPD. While Schroeder copied some of the style and rhetoric of Blair – and a joint policy document entitled the Third Way/Neue Mitte was produced in late spring 1999 – the SPD remained a largely unreformed and divided party. Schroeder was in some ways more of a Harold Wilson type of leader manoeuvring between factions.

A leader apart

But how different has New Labour been in practice? Tony Blair is not alone in having chosen Labour rather than been born into the Party, as he often says. The same could be said of Attlee, Gaitskell and Wilson. Yet all three had deep roots within the Labour movement by the time they became leader. As anyone who has been in the conference hall listening to leaders' speeches over the years knows, Blair is respected, but not liked, as some of his predecessors were. For all his success, he has never been part of the Party. This is unlike Gordon Brown who has often disguised a pro-capitalist and pro-markets message in Old Labour language. Blair's main concern has been with the public as a whole rather than just with party activists.

Revealingly, Blair was much closer to Roy Jenkins than to James Callaghan, to the historian and advocate of the progressive centre rather than the pillar of the old Labour right. Blair has much preferred the company of leading industrialists to that of leading trade unionists, whom he has largely despised as weak and reactionary. This lack of sympathy has been reciprocated, as the Blair Government has repeatedly refused to repeal the Tories' industrial relations legislation – though it has extended the employment rights of individual workers in some areas such as parental leave. Blair would never have that sense of personal disillusionment with the trade unions which Callaghan felt after the 'Winter of Discontent' since he has never had any illusions about them in the first place.

Blair has been a leader apart in another sense. His easy victory in July 1994 in winning the party leadership was, in part, a *coup d'état*, a takeover by a small group committed to changing the whole direction of the Party. Most of his allies were from the soft-left, Kinnockite camp. By 2003, the Blair Cabinet included three members of Kinnock's Private Office – Charles Clarke, Patricia Hewitt and John Reid. Many others in Blair's inner circle have either been personal friends, like Charlie Falconer, and/or do not have deep roots within the Labour Party, including some former SDP activists. By contrast, no one ever doubted that Wilson and Callaghan's inner circle came from the Labour movement.

The old Labour right has backed him because they broadly agreed with his views on the economy, defence and Europe. But the right have been suspicious of Blair's big tent approach – his unconsummated flirtation with Paddy Ashdown of the Liberal Democrats during his first term. Of course, the Callaghan Government had to agree a deal with David Steel and the Liberals in 1977. But this was an arrangement of convenience merely to stay in office, not part of an attempt to create a new progressive centre. Blair's repeated disavowal of party tribalism has made him suspect to Labour tribalists on both the hard-left and the traditional right, and left him more isolated when he has run into trouble, as over the Iraq War in 2003.

Yet, in practice, for all the far-reaching constitutional legislation (on devolution, local mayors, the Human Rights Act, freedom of information and regulation of party funding and elections), Blair has been at most a half-hearted pluralist. His heart has never really been in constitutional reform and he has been willing to bow to Labour tribalists over both the abandonment of the Jenkins Commission's proposals on partial electoral reform for the Commons and in rejecting a largely or wholly elected House of Lords (where the Blairites have been split).

A strong centre

Blair's style of governing has also been very different from Wilson and Callaghan's, let alone Attlee's. It is a mistake to see this just in terms of an obsession with media management and presentation, spin as it has become known. But spin was not invented in 1997. Wilson was just as obsessed with the details of placing stories and influencing journalists. Of course, the approach has changed from when what mattered were just a few top television executives and a dozen lobby correspondents. The world of twenty-four-hour news has required different techniques of instant rebuttal.

The real difference is less appreciated. The Blair Government was, from the top downwards, the least experienced Labour administration since Ramsay MacDonald's first Government in 1924. The four top offices of state were held by politicians who had never before been ministers and three (Blair, Brown and Jack Straw) had not even been MPs during the Callaghan years – though Straw had been a special adviser to both Barbara Castle and Peter Shore. So, for all the euphoria of May 1997, the incoming Blair team did not know how to operate the levers of power. Because Blair had never worked his way up the ministerial ladder, and was unfamiliar with the ways of Whitehall, he preferred to work, as in opposition, with close advisers and with Gordon Brown. The inexperience of many ministers, and their largely unjustified suspicion of the civil service, also led many of them to prefer working with special advisers whom they knew well. This also led to a focus on presentation, on endlessly repackaged new initiatives, especially when public spending was tightly constrained.

The charge of presidentialism is an oversimplification, but is not entirely wrong. Blair's style was presidential in the sense that he was depicted as somehow above the rest of the Cabinet, apart from Brown. The myth of presidentialism and centralised media management outran the reality. Blair often complained of the frustrations and limitations of his position. However, the scale of the Downing Street operation was greatly expanded, both in the number of policy advisers (where Blair enlarged the Policy Unit created by Wilson in 1974 and retained by Thatcher and Major) and in the media and press operation. Blair did not create a Prime Minister's Department as such, but the expanded Number 10 and its associated units amounted to one in everything but name. This extension of 'prime ministerialism' worried some of the earlier generation of Labour ministers, who, while admiring Blair's boldness, were worried that he might be overreaching himself.

One senior civil servant who closely observed Blair during his first few years in 10 Downing Street has privately commented that, at heart,

> Blair would rather have liked to be a President, above the battles of Congress, and with a direct ability to be a major figure on the world scene. In that sense, however subliminally, or even partly intentionally, Blair and his political team in 10 Downing Street have copied the American television series 'the West Wing'. ... Blair saw Clinton perform as President and believed he could do better.[5]

On this view, Blair envied Clinton's position to set the agenda, the 'bullypulpit' of the White House, if not his problems. Moreover, Blair increasingly enjoyed handling foreign affairs, where he could operate more on his own and outside Brown's shadow. The foreign policy side of 10 Downing Street was strengthened considerably after the 2001 election with the creation of two senior posts, one in charge of European policy and the other effectively a national security adviser. So policy over, say, Iraq in 2002–3 was run from Downing Street, not the Foreign Office. Yet in many ways Blair's relations with Clinton, Bush, Schroeder and Chirac were not that different from Callaghan's with Carter, Schmidt and Giscard d'Estaing. The increased focus on links between heads of government started in the late 1970s when the annual G7, later G8, summits began.

Blair shared power with Brown and, like all Prime Ministers, had to work through departmental ministers to implement desired policies. He might command, but he could not deliver. At first, he regarded the weekly Cabinet meetings almost as a formality, some lasting less than an hour. When criticised on this point, Blair referred, with apparent horror, to being told about the nine, often very long, full meetings of the Callaghan Cabinet needed to agree the IMF package in 1976. That would never happen under him. In his early weeks, the Cabinet was not formally involved, and had not yet even met, before the momentous decision to make the Bank of England formally responsible for setting interest rates.

Yet, in his second term, Blair did involve the full Cabinet more, if not to take decisions, then as a form of political insurance, binding other ministers in. The Cabinet was informed weekly about developments on Iraq in 2002–3, and dissenting ministers, like Robin Cook, first raised their doubts at these meetings. So his resignation on 17 March 2003, on the eve of war, was no surprise. Similarly, the full Cabinet had a say in the decision not to join the euro in May/June 2003, even though this position had previously been agreed by Blair and Brown.

Social democratic tradition

For all the emphasis of newness, modernity and difference, the Blair Government remained recognisably in the social democratic tradition. There were clear links of objective and policy, if not of style, with the past. Blair and Brown might be more frank about embracing the global economy and encouraging enterprise. But their aim was still to broaden opportunity and to improve state-financed public services – even if these services might be provided by a wider range of non-profit, voluntary and even private sector groups. Brown introduced several measures to help those worst off, particularly the poorly paid, such as introducing a national minimum wage and an extensive system of tax credits, in effect means-tested benefits. This amounted to redistribution by stealth.

The key was public spending and taxation. Even in the early years of restraint, there were still loopholes and exceptions. There was the one-off levy on the utilities to fund the welfare-to-work programme and then various other tax-raising measures, dubbed by the Tories as 'stealth taxes'. Because of this initial fiscal squeeze, and the buoyancy of the economy, Brown was able to raise spending substantially from 2000 onwards. He benefited from much more favourable economic circumstances than any previous Labour Chancellor of the Exchequer. One of the most striking contrasts with the late 1970s was the absence of a currency or fiscal crisis, as well as Brown's generally cautious approach, at least up to 2002.

Labour was evasive in the 2001 election about whether taxes would have to be raised. The promise not to raise the basic and higher rates of income tax, and to broaden the VAT base, was repeated. But in the 2002 budget Brown announced a big increase in taxes by raising National Insurance contributions for both employers and employees. This was within the letter of the election pledge, if not its spirit, since the effect was the same for most people as raising income tax – though unlike the past there was no attempt to tax the rich. But the increase was justified, and largely accepted, because the extra money was specifically allocated to the NHS.

So if the Blair Government is different in its language and governing style from the Wilson and Callaghan Governments of the late 1970s, notably in its relations with the unions, many of its policies showed continuities with the past. Blair's natural home was more in the centre than any of his predecessors, but his Government's policies still tilted towards the progressive left.

Notes

1   Blair, T., Fabian Society Lecture, 'Progress and Justice in the 21st Century', Old Vic Theatre, London, 17 June 2003.
2   Rentoul, J., *Tony Blair: Prime Minister* (Little, Brown, London, 2001), pp. 69–70.
3   Gould, P., *The Unfinished Revolution: How the Modernisers Saved the Labour Party* (Little, Brown, London, 1999), pp. 175–6.
4   Burk, K. and Cairncross, A., *'Goodbye, Great Britain': The 1976 IMF Crisis* (Yale University Press, New Haven, CT, 1992), pp. 227–8.
5   Riddell, P., *Hug Them Close: Blair, Clinton, Bush and the 'Special Relationship'* (Politico's/Methuen, London, 2003), p. 9.

20 The worst of governments

Robert Skidelsky

Not much can be salvaged from the Wilson–Callaghan years of 1974–9 except lessons.[1] They were among the low points of British Government in the twentieth century, perhaps the lowest point. At no time since before the First World War was there such a feeling that Britain had become ungovernable, and that a change of regime – a change in the way of governing, and not just a change of government – was required. This change came about through the election of Margaret Thatcher, who inaugurated eighteen years of Thatcherism. But the previously congealed mould of politics was also broken by the emergence of the SDP which promised, for a time, to replace the Labour Party. Today's Blair Government is the stepchild of both Margaret Thatcher and David Owen. A new style of governing has become entrenched and, barring a political or economic earthquake, is likely to endure.

The interesting question is why the years 1974–9 were so awful. Two trivial explanations can be dismissed. The first attributes the failure of the Wilson–Callaghan Governments to their lack of a working majority in Parliament. But this simply limited the damage Labour could do. Had the Labour Government been given the majority to carry out the programme on which it was elected, it would have collapsed. As it was, Wilson and the right-wing leaders were able to use the electoral stalemate to wriggle out of manifesto commitments which would have turned Britain into an East European state. But they could not devise a constructive agenda of their own.

It is also true that the Governments of 1974–9 faced a much more difficult international situation than Wilson's first Labour Government had done in 1964–70, following the quadrupling of the oil price in 1973–4. But other developed countries recovered from this shock without the prolonged inflation and industrial disorder which occurred in Britain.

The failure of the Governments of 1974–9 cannot be explained, that is, by reference to the events which took place in those years alone. We need to bring into the frame the expectations and disappointments of 1964–70. The 1964–70 Labour Government was by no means barren of achievement, though this was mainly in the field of social reform: Roy Jenkins at the Home Office, Tony Crosland at Education. On the central issue of economic management, it failed abysmally. Wilson had come to power in 1964 on a promise to rejuvenate the

British economy through a combination of Keynesian expansionism and socialist planning, including the planning of incomes. The belief was that a planned expansion of output would cause enough economic growth to avoid inflation and balance of payments problems. Increased output would pay for a much expanded level of social services without an electorally damaging increase in taxation. In the upshot 'planning for growth' produced an even lower rate of growth than the Conservatives had managed in their 'thirteen wasted years'. All the Government's economic policies broke down one by one, leaving as their legacy a bloated public sector, higher taxes, rising inflation and rising unemployment. The Government's one economic success was the twin budget and balance of payment surplus, achieved by Roy Jenkins as Chancellor in 1969–70. But this came too late to save it from the electoral wrath caused by its previous failures.

The right in the Labour Party learnt no lessons at all from the economic failures of 1964–70. All the learning was done by the left, and it was their assessment of what had gone wrong in 1964–70 which created the programmes on which Labour fought the February 1974 election. The main lesson the left learnt was that British capitalism was in terminal decline and that the British economy could not prosper unless it was comprehensively socialised. The left's main guru in the early 1970s was the economist Stuart Holland, and he was largely responsible for foisting on the Party an industrial programme, enthusiastically espoused by Tony Benn, which would have led to the decapitation of the private sector and a 'fundamental and irreversible shift in the balance of power and wealth in favour of the working people'.[2] This was the language of classical socialism, and it was backed by detailed proposals – for extensive further nationalisation, for acquiring majority state shares in the main private companies, for 'planning agreements' with other businesses, and Britain's withdrawal from the EEC – designed to convert words into deeds. Under the famous 'Social Contract' trade unions promised 'wage restraint' in return for large doses of socialism and increments of trade union power. This was tantamount to drawing up a death warrant for British capitalism.

In opposition from 1970 to 1974, the right in the Labour Party could only fight a rearguard action against this drive to disaster. In office, Wilson had to spend his first year and a half (helped in this by his wafer-thin majority and the device of a referendum on Europe) ensuring that the left programme remained words only. Meanwhile, government spending spiralled out of control and the unions were bought off by conceding their wage demands.

The disappointing results of Labour's political hegemony from 1964 to 1979 have given rise to two types of explanation. The first story emphasises personalities. It revolves especially round the myth of the 'lost leader'. This was given authoritative expression in Philip Williams's biography of Hugh Gaitskell, and has recently been revived by Giles Radice.[3] It may be called the Gaitskellite story of what went wrong. At its heart is Gaitskell's tragic death in 1963, leaving the succession to the tricky, unprincipled Harold Wilson. Gaitskell, not Wilson, would have been Prime Minister in 1964. He would have devalued in 1964, rather than clung to the defence of sterling for three years. This would have set in motion a virtuous circle of growth-led social reform. Labour would have won the 1970 general election consolidating its position as the 'natural' governing party.[4]

Instead, Wilson botched it. Wilson in due course gave way to Callaghan. Callaghan was better than Wilson, but he too must carry a heavy burden of responsibility, going back to 1969, and culminating in the 'Winter of Discontent', for failing to stand up to trade union power. Giles Radice has recently added to this alternative history. At its heart lies the failure of the leading Gaitskellites – Crosland, Healey and Jenkins – to come into their rightful leadership inheritance, due partly to Gaitskell's death, but also to the intensive political rivalry between them. Specifically, the failure of Crosland and Healey to support Jenkins for the leadership (as well as Jenkins's lack of ruthlessness) allowed a discredited Wilson to hang on in the 1970s, which opened the door for Benn and the left.

There is something in this. But if the argument is that the Gaitskellites would or could have turned the Labour Party into a Blairite party before Blair, it seems to be plain wrong. Brian Brivati shows that Gaitskell and the Gaitskellites were much more rooted in their times than later legend has it.[5] As he makes clear, the debates between right and left in the Labour Party in Gaitskell's day took place within a commonly accepted framework of economic planning, Keynesian demand management, a mixed economy, and an aggressive quest for equality through redistributive taxation. The so-called 'revisionists' still believed in nationalisation, though they relegated it to one means among many for securing control over the economy. Brivati also shows that Gaitskell was not averse to doing 'dirty work' with the trade union barons to realise his goals. Trade union power – in the Party and country – was a fact of life for Labour leaders in the pre-Thatcher era, which is why Gaitskell never challenged it. This is a part of the Gaitskell legacy which Gaitskellites prefer to forget.

An alternative explanation, drawing on these facts, has been suggested by Edmund Dell, a Labour Cabinet minister in the 1970s. According to Dell, it was the set of ideas and alliances which Labour carried into government in both the 1960s and 1970s which made it unfit to govern. The 'revisionists' were democratic socialists, not social democrats. Dell points out that Tony Crosland never revised his views from the point at which he left them in his classic *The Future of Socialism* in 1956. He remained an unreconstructed Keynesian planner. In 1969, he opposed Wilson's belated effort, in *In Place of Strife*, to curb trade union power, and in 1976 he led the opposition to the IMF loan needed to avert a British default on its borrowing from the United States. His answer to inflation was incomes policy, but he never understood that incomes policy was bound to fail, given the fragmented structure and confrontational attitudes of British trade unionism.

This second analysis, in terms of the failure of ideas, is much more substantial. The socialist commitment, enshrined in Clause 4 of the Party's constitution, was a problem for the pre-Blairite Labour Party, not because its leaders ever intended to socialise the whole economy, but because it frightened businesses, gave the left a ready rallying point, and stifled thought within the Party about how best to make a free enterprise system work. There was what would now be called a country-specific risk attached to Labour rule, stemming from the socialist commitment and the Party's close relationship with, but lack of control over, the trade unions. The effect of this 'double whammy' was markedly strengthened when sterling was made convertible, by the Conservatives against Labour opposition, in 1959. None of the varieties of revisionism on offer in the 1950s or 1960s addressed this central problem – neither Crosland's attempt to build equality on the profits of business, nor Wilson's promotion of socialist planning as the instrument of economic growth. Specifically, the failure of revisionist policies to secure economic growth in the 1960s left the door wide open for the left in the 1970s. Blair was therefore quite right to insist that the elimination of the old Clause 4 was the precondition not so much of Labour's electability as of its fitness to govern.

But the story of Labour's failure between 1974 and 1979 is only half-told. What this explanation ignores is that Edward Heath's Conservative Government of 1970 to 1974 failed just as badly as its successor. If it was the wrong ideas which were producing the crisis of governability, they were clearly not confined to the Labour Party. They were the product of a style of economic management common to both parties. It was the Conservatives under Margaret Thatcher who first realised this, which is why they, and not Labour or the SDP, broke the mould of the so-called post-war settlement.

At the heart of the British style was a full employment commitment dating back to 1944, backed, from 1961 onwards, by incomes policy to prevent unions pushing wages ahead of productivity at full employment. There were two things wrong with this. Full employment was absurdly interpreted to mean 2 per cent unemployment or less. (Keynes himself would have been content with between 3 and 5 per cent.) There was some talk in the late 1950s of running the economy with a 'greater margin of spare capacity', but this turned out to mean 2.5 per cent! The result was the inexorable build-up of inflationary pressure. The attempt to contain this pressure by incomes policy left out of account not just that part of the pressure was due to excess demand but that there was no way of making an incomes policy work, given the structure of the British labour market. It was in essence the attempt to maintain overfull employment by means of budget deficits coupled with the inability to make incomes policy work, except for very short periods, which led to the crisis of governability – as well as a crisis of business profitability – in the 1970s. With the failure of Heath's Industrial Relations Act and statutory pay policy of 1972, the only resource seemingly left to government was the appeasement of trade union leaders in the hope of securing their voluntary agreement to prevent their members from putting in inflationary wage claims – a promise on which they could never deliver.

Thatcher's break with the post-war settlement was to abandon this style of economic management. The full employment commitment, hitherto considered sacrosanct, and accompanying incomes policy were simultaneously dropped. Economic management was targeted on the single task of controlling inflation;

industrial policy was switched to breaking the trade union stranglehold on wages and creating a more flexible labour market. The level of unemployment became an outcome of other policies, not a target to be aimed for directly.

One way of describing the Thatcher revolution is in terms of an excess of modesty about what governments could and could not do in a free society, as a reassertion of the tradition of strong, but limited, government. Underlying the failed system of political economy was the doctrine of statism, which in retrospect looks like an extraordinary overconfidence in the competence, capacity and benevolence of governments. This was most strongly evidenced on the intellectual left of politics, but it also pervaded the last years of the Macmillan Government. Market failure was deemed to be pervasive; government failure was almost never discussed. The gentlemen in Whitehall really did know best.

The year Harold Wilson came to power in 1974 was the year Mao Tse-tung died. What a world we have left since then! But the overconfidence in the power of central direction is not quite dead. Traces are still to be found in Gordon Brown's over-complicated tax policies, and in Blair's centralising attempts to improve performance in education and the National Health Service. Some of these policies are a necessary corrective to the market simplicities of the Thatcher years. The danger is of a slow drift back to the mindset of the Wilson–Callaghan years – the assumption of governmental responsibility for outcomes which, under conditions of freedom, are best left to market and voluntary effort, and whose frustration is a standing temptation to extend the range of control. It is not a big danger, but permanent vigilance is required to guard against it.

Notes

1   The main events of the Wilson–Callaghan Governments of 1974–9 are sufficiently well known – the appalling drift of Wilson's first year when pay settlements and government spending spiralled out of control, the voluntary pay policy agreed with the TUC in July 1975, the sterling crisis of 1976 leading to the negotiation of the IMF loan in December and the final 'Winter of Discontent' of 1978–9, which ushered in eighteen years of Conservative rule.
2   For Holland's ideas see his *The Socialist Challenge* (Quartet Books, London, 1975). The quoted phrase is from *Labour's Programme 1973*.
3   Williams, P., *Hugh Gaitskell: A Political Biography* (Jonathan Cape, London, 1979); Radice, G., *Friends and Rivals: Crosland, Jenkins and Healey* (Little, Brown, London, 2002).
4   The idea that Labour had become Britain's 'natural' governing party was popular among political scientists at the time: see especially Butler, D. and Stokes, D., *Political Change in Britain* (St Martin's Press, New York, 1971).
5   Brivati, B., *Hugh Gaitskell* (Richard Cohen, London, 1996).

Conclusion
Reading and misreading Old Labour

Dennis Kavanagh

The emergence of New Labour has been the latest stage in the Party's continuing struggle to come to terms with changes in the social and economic structure and in British and global capitalism. In that sense there is nothing new about it. What is new is the dedication and the success with which party modernisers have rewritten and broken with the Party's past.

It is not unusual for party reformers to draw a line over the past. For example, following the Party's comprehensive defeat in the 1945 general election, Conservatives like R.A. Butler and Macmillan succeeded in persuading many voters that the 'new' Conservatism had moved on and now accepted policies of welfare and full employment. In opposition again, following the Heath Government's defeat in the 1974 election, Mrs Thatcher and Sir Keith Joseph began to shift the Conservative Party in a radically different direction. Over time they portrayed the Heath record as a wrong turning, particularly on economic policy.

After the Labour Government lost the 1979 general election, the left wing mounted the most comprehensive critique of the leadership and offered a new direction: they sought to break with Old Labour (which it identified with the right wing) although the term was not yet in use. But from the late 1980s, following a third successive general election defeat, a new group of modernisers were determined to overthrow what they regarded as the electorally disastrous excesses of the left. They targeted much of the left, but also some of the right as Old Labour. Significantly, by 1997 the modernisers had managed to construct a negative history of Labour in the 1970s and early 1980s, an amalgam of policies, personalities, institutions and values. They decided that to win approval for New Labour they had to dismiss much of the Party's recent past as outdated and unelectable, to bury much of the old before they could create the new.

The modernisers were helped in their task by constant warnings to voters, from the Conservatives and their tabloid supporters, not to risk going back to double-digit inflation, trade union power, strikes, and a Britain teetering on the verge of bankruptcy and ungovernability. This, they claimed, was the Labour Britain in 1979 from which Thatcher rescued us. The modernisers were also helped in their task by the flood of memoirs and diaries that were published by members of the Wilson and Callaghan Governments in the 1970s. The composite picture drawn by Messrs Barnett, Benn, Castle, Crossman, Dell, Donoughue, Jenkins and Rodgers *et al.* was deeply damaging. Yet the earlier Wilson Government was not much better. According to the Party's foremost historian: 'the Wilson years have served as a paradigm of economic failure, social indirection and political paralysis'.[1]

This chapter argues that the modernisers' negative portrait of Old Labour derives from a selective and abbreviated period, that is, the late 1970s and early 1980s; many significant changes in policy and party structure, indeed the foundations of New Labour, were achieved under Neil Kinnock. Tony Blair *et al.* built on these changes but claimed more openly that Labour had changed, that it was new. There is room for both structure and agency in explaining the rise of New Labour. Changes in social structure (e.g. the decline of the working class), the decline of manufacturing and globalisation of capital markets meant that parties of the left had to rethink their role. But the political choices and skills of Blair and Brown were also important.

Critique

The critique of Old Labour by Blair and his allies centred on a number of themes:

1   The damaging electoral and policy consequences of the role of *the trade unions* in the Party. Labour had to distance itself from the unions.
2   The *electoral limitations* of a class (i.e. working-class) orientation at a time when the working class were a steadily declining minority. The Party needed to appeal across all social classes.
3   The *party structure* had hardly been updated since its adoption in 1918 when Labour was hardly envisaged as a party of government and when the PLP was at best a co-equal player with the extra-parliamentary Conference and NEC.
4   The neo-Marxist phrasing of *Clause 4* (with its commitment to the common ownership of the means of production, distribution and exchange) and the rhetoric of economic planning were no longer appropriate in changed economic circumstances. The Party needed to be more positive about the role of the market and of business. The Party was also associated with a top-down and 'one size fits all' approach to providing public services; this increased the possibility of producer capture of the services and limited the scope for flexibility and responsiveness to consumers.
5   A dominant strand in the Party's ethos – its traditions and beliefs – was a suspicion among the grass-roots of bold *personal leadership*, reinforcing the structural constraints on the leader.[2]
6   The above features contributed to *immobilism* in thinking about policy or strategy. Policies were declared 'unthinkable' because of the hold of traditional nostrums and vested interests in the Party.

To a remarkable degree each of the above has been abandoned or qualified under New Labour. But it is worth restating that many previous leaders, notably Hugh Gaitskell, expressed concern over some of these features. The so-called revisionists in the 1950s were in some respects the precursors of Blair *et al.* They claimed that Labour had to adapt to changes to the social structure, particularly the spread of embourgeoisement, and to a capitalism that had become more socially responsible and economically more efficient than state ownership.

Coming to terms with these trends required the Party to change policies, electoral strategy and party structure. Something was done on the first two. But as long as Labour won general elections (it was in office for eleven of fifteen years after 1964, albeit usually by narrow majorities) potential modernisers kept their powder dry.

New Labour has been variously described as a 'coup' (and not only by left-wing critics), an evolution from the Wilson–Callaghan Governments, a marketing strategy to win elections, a completion of the revisionist agenda of the 1950s, or as a process of catching up with the impact of Thatcher.[3] In reality, it involves elements of all the above. The result has been a remarkable reinvention of the Party from the top, a feature that flies in the face of the Party's history, which suggests that Labour leaders have markedly fewer political resources when in opposition than in government.

Trade unions

Historically, the unions were a praetorian guard, protecting the parliamentary leaders against left-wing insurgents in the PLP and the constituencies. In return, the leadership was expected to respect the views of the unions in matters of industrial relations and wage bargaining. This understanding was reinforced by the abandonment, under union pressure, of the Labour Government's proposals for reforming industrial relations (*In Place of Strife*) in 1969. Labour's so-called Social Contract with the unions became the cornerstone of the Labour Government's anti-inflation policy in 1974. Its breakdown in 1979 was a symptom of Old Labour's crisis as a party of competent government. One trouble with trying to develop corporatist-type policies in Britain was that union leaders lacked the authority to commit their members to make deals with any government, particularly at a time when power was seeping to the shop floor. The 'Winter of Discontent' destroyed the Social Contract, was the prelude to an electoral disaster for Labour, exposed the unions to a radical Conservative Government, and signalled the end of the role of the unions as partners of government. There have been no more incomes policies or Social Contracts since 1979.

Labour modernisers, even while acknowledging the financial generosity of the unions, criticised the connection, because:

1   Labour's claim to be national was vitiated by the unions' dominant position in the Party, casting over 90 per cent of the votes on policy resolutions at the

annual conference, voting for a majority of the NEC members and spon-
soring a third of Labour MPs.

2 The unions were unpopular and many members did not vote Labour
   anyway. Even when party leaders criticised strikes, they still suffered electorally because of their association with the unions.

3 Sensitivity to the unions ruled out debate and action on important issues,
   including, for example, the closed shop, pre-strike ballots, restrictive practices, flexible pay bargaining and the introduction of new technology.

4 Unions – and by extension the Party – were identified more with the
   producers than with the consumers. This was notably the case in the more
   unionised public sector.

The electorate

More than any other factor electoral failure undermined Old Labour. Most of
the working class and trade unionists, the Party's core constituency, were
declining in number and failing to support it. Over the four general elections
between 1979 and 1992, including a high level of unemployment in 1983 and an
economic recession in 1992, Labour trailed the Conservatives by an average of
10 per cent of the vote. Regardless of whether it moved sharply to the political
left in 1983 or back to the middle ground in 1992, Labour still did badly.

But this decline did not begin in 1979. Since 1951 Labour's share of the vote
had fallen at every general election, except for 1966. The Party had long been
losing touch with its working-class support on such key issues as the power of the
trade unions, public ownership and social welfare.[4] The working class were also
becoming more divided between the skilled and the unskilled. On income tax,
welfare and council house sales the former were becoming more aspirational and
losing sympathy with the Party's policies. Moreover, social change meant that
demography was moving against Labour.

More unsettling perhaps were the findings about the voters' values. Although
Thatcherite values, according to the opinion polls, were not widely accepted
among the electorate in the 1980s, this was no consolation to Labour. In a
private 1992 memo Philip Gould referred, *inter alia*, to the voters'

• diminishing affinity with Labour, as the electorate was becoming more
   upmarket and more aspirational;
• more open statement of self-interest, to explain their votes;
• perception of the price of voting Labour, in terms of higher tax and interest
   rates;
• mistrust of Labour, encompassing fear of strife, fear of unions and fear of
   change;
• doubts about the Party's leadership and economic management.

Labour was now identified with society's losers – the unemployed, sick and poor
– rather than the succeeders. Voters who wanted to own their own homes,

improve their living standards and gain a better education for their children looked to the Conservative Party as the vehicle for meeting their aspirations for greater choice and opportunity.[5] Labour was associated with levelling down and holding back. Meeting the aspirations of such target voters required more than changes in policies; it called for a fundamental makeover of the Party. Labour had to take account of what voters liked and disliked about it, rather than seeking better ways of promoting unpopular policies.

The Party had fought good campaigns in 1987 and 1992 but lost, because of the severe weaknesses on policy and image. It was no longer a question of improving campaign techniques but of fundamentally changing policies and images. But advocates of a marketing approach faced problems with Labour's structure (see below) and the views of many of the activists. After Labour's third successive general election defeat in 1959, Dick Crossman had said: 'those who assert that the sole object ... should be to regain office seem to me to misconceive not merely the nature of British socialism, but the working of British democracy'. The Party should, apparently, wait for the electorate to 'catch up' with it. Over twenty years later one could still hear such views in the Party.

The modernisers claimed that the electoral majority was now with the middle class and the prosperous working class. Relying on the have-nots was no longer enough and if the Party wanted to help the former then it had to gain the support of the middle class. With each election defeat, however, the choice between adherence to socialist principles (often coupled with opposition-mindedness) and the search for electoral success became starker and moved in favour of the latter. The sharper hunger for victory entailed a greater willingness to accept the role of opinion polling, public relations, a catchall electoral strategy and the courting of the press and business.

Party structure

When Labour's federal party structure was drawn up in 1918, there was only a handful of Labour MPs in the House of Commons, they had a chairman rather than a leader, and the Party was beholden to the unions for resources. The parliamentary leaders paid lip service to the ideas of internal democracy, collective decision making and their accountability to the mass party. What might happen in the event of a Labour Government clashing with Conference or the NEC was left open. The dominance of the trade unions, use of the block vote at Conference, and guaranteed representation of women but not other 'minorities', reflected conditions at the time. By the end of the century, however, these last conditions no longer prevailed.

The system endured for two reasons. One was the self-restraint of key actors, which meant that clashes were avoided; the second was that Labour was so often in opposition. Hence the questions about the compatibility of the sovereignty of Conference with the authority of the parliamentary leaders, or with the British constitution, were not raised until Hugh Gaitskell defied Conference over its defeat of his defence policy in 1961.

Yet it had many disadvantages:

1   Decision making was slow as the various bodies deliberated, reported upwards, and Conference met only every twelve months. Increasingly, however, Labour leaders needed speed and flexibility, not just for making policy decisions but also for campaigns and coping with twenty-four-hour media.

2   Divisions and bitter personal attacks at Conference made for riveting TV spectacles and press headlines, particularly when the leader was under siege, as so often in the 1970s and 1980s. But they were a huge embarrassment and an obstacle to the Party's attempts to present itself as a credible and united party of government. Tony Benn in the 1980s was able to use his support in the extra-parliamentary institutions to mount regular and well-publicised challenges to the parliamentary leadership. At this time it was as if there were two Labour parties.

3   Conference decision making was a democratic sham. The unions' block vote was often cast following scant or no consultation with members. Mandates were often opaque, because resolutions at trade union conferences had been passed months beforehand. The Conference agenda was manipulated through a complex system of compositing and remitting resolutions. There was also a form of vote buying as constituency parties and unions had some discretion over how many members they wished to affiliate.[6]

4   The block vote meant that power in the Conference was effectively in the hands of the five largest unions, which between them had a majority of the votes.

Party leaders tolerated this system because, as long as they had the major unions on their side, they could carry Conference. From the late 1960s, however, the old ways of managing Conference broke down. Some unions moved to the left and the Party leaders increasingly challenged the unions on the sensitive issues of industrial relations and wage bargaining.

In his classic *British Political Parties*, Robert McKenzie had shocked Labour politicians and commentators by claiming that the Party was 'a living lie'.[7] He showed that Labour leaders, while contrasting the Party's internal democracy with the elitist Conservative Party, exercised the same autonomy in government as their Tory counterparts. In opposition, they usually acquiesced in embarrassing Conference resolutions but in government regularly ignored them. Harold Wilson dismissed Conference resolutions that repudiated his Government's policies with the retort: 'the job of a Labour government is to govern'. The leader's authority was dramatically demonstrated in 1979, when James Callaghan vetoed the left's efforts to include party policies in the election manifesto.

But after 1979 the left exacted their revenge. They sought to close the gap between a literal reading of the Party constitution and the practices that had evolved. The election of the Party leader was extended from the hands of MPs alone to the extra-parliamentary membership, which further increased the power of the activists by introducing the mandatory reselection of Labour MPs, and came close to giving the NEC the dominant role in deciding the contents of the election manifesto. All this was done in the name of democracy. But without tackling any of the above shortcomings (particularly the failure to ballot union and local party members), the reforms were more about empowering the activists (and the left), rather than increasing the representativeness of the party institutions. On all the available evidence the activists were quite unrepresentative of Labour voters (a steadily reducing number). The policies of unilateral defence, greater public ownership, opposing council house sales and extending trade union rights meant that the Labour Party increasingly alienated its own supporters.

Not surprisingly, the party structure, and the ethos that it represented, was a prime target for the modernisers.

Leadership

The Party's constitution and its ethos did not preclude the possibility of bold leadership but they did make it difficult. The constraints, reflected in the annual elections of the leader, and of the Shadow Cabinet by MPs, authority of Conference (dominated by the unions) over policy, and appointment of key party officials by the NEC all provided a sharp contrast to the powers available to the Conservative leader. Ramsay MacDonald's 'treachery' in 1931 only reinforced the culture of distrust of the leader and the self-righteousness of spokesmen for the rank and file. In themselves the procedures were not damaging but they could become so when the Party was divided between factions. Leaders fudged policies and ensured that appointments to Cabinet were balanced between left and right. The leader had to operate under these constraints and Gaitskell in 1959, Wilson in 1969 and Callaghan in 1978, for example, all paid a heavy price for not carrying trade unions with them on key policy initiatives.

The modernisers therefore argued for more central control of policy and political strategy and support for the leader. They claimed that these were crucial if urgently needed policy changes were to be made and a clear message communicated to the media and voters. New Labour regarded Callaghan's decision to hold nine Cabinet meetings in 1976 to win acceptance of the IMF terms for a loan as evidence of weak leadership, rather than skill at keeping the Party together. In the past, leaders had managed to get their way on procedures and policies, but only at the cost of great demands on their time and energy and political capital.[8] The Party's structure and ethos made for an unheroic style of leadership, whereas successful modern campaigning required 'strong' leadership, à la Thatcher.

State and markets

New Labour was firmly convinced that reversing the Party's reputation for economic incompetence was vital to regaining the trust of voters. The record of the Wilson–Callaghan Governments associated Labour with high levels of taxation, inflation and interest rates and a minimal improvement in living standards. Increases in welfare spending in the early stages of the 1964 and the 1974 Governments had been followed by sterling crises, spending cuts and pressures on living standards. In 1949 and 1967 Labour had devalued the pound and in 1976 resorted to help from the IMF. Joel Barnett, a Treasury minister in the 1974–9 Governments, reflected how his colleagues spent money with no thought of where it was coming from.[9] Subsidies were often granted to firms in response to union pressures, short-term electoral calculations, or constituency interests of ministers. In nationalised industries, the combination of government subsidies and incomes policies increased the leverage of the trade unions. Gaining the confidence of the financial markets was a perennial problem. Neil Kinnock and John Smith had supported British membership of the ERM in 1990, in spite of its deflationary tendencies, on the grounds that it would reassure the market about Labour's commitment to price stability and its 'fitness to govern'.

These views interacted with fresh thinking about welfare. Modernisers wanted the system to provide claimants with incentives to get off and find work. In a slow-growing economy flat-rate universal benefits were inevitably modest or worse and did not help those genuinely in need.

New Labour argued that the Party would have to turn over a new leaf in approaching the economy. Globalisation, and the ease with which capital and production could move across national boundaries, particularly in an open economy like Britain's, limited the power of national governments. The need to encourage economic competitiveness and maintain the confidence of the markets meant that the priority for any government had to be low inflation and macro-economic stability.

Immobilism

A number of policies, for example a reduction in marginal rates of income tax, more selectivity in welfare, or a legal framework for industrial relations, or even the introduction of one-member–one-vote inside the Party, were off the agenda. This was largely because 'Conference (or the trade unions) won't wear it.' Of course, the Labour ministers did manage to make some reforms in spite of internal party opposition, but often it was done by stealth. Policy making was internalised, responding more to the views of party activists and union conferences than to ordinary Labour voters, and operated as a powerful veto.

Reforms

New Labour has managed to change many of the above features of Old Labour and most would have been unthinkable in the Wilson–Callaghan years. For example, the role of the trade unions in the Party has been substantially reduced. The share of union votes at the Party Conference fell to 49 per cent; the block vote ended and one-member–one-vote introduced; its share of the electoral college to elect the leader was cut from 40 per cent to 33 per cent and cast in proportion to how individual members had voted; and union sponsorship of parliamentary candidates ended. The bulk of the Conservative legislation on industrial relations remained. Most of this preceded Blair; the 1992 party manifesto, for example, had promised 'there will be no return to the trade union legislation of the 1970s'.

On public ownership, the repeal of Clause 4 in 1995 was of more symbolic than substantive importance. After the policy review (1987–9) the Party had already effectively abandoned monolithic public ownership. Blair's new clause (welcoming 'a dynamic economy', 'the enterprise of the market' and 'a thriving private sector') was designed to dramatise Labour's change; it also demonstrated firm leadership and removed a weapon from Conservative critics as well as from left-wing advocates of more public ownership. Blair's Government accepted the Conservatives' privatisation measures and has made great use of the Private Finance Initiative to finance and undertake major projects. On the public services, in spite of considerable opposition from the unions and Labour MPs, the Government has accepted the new forms of service delivery introduced by the Conservatives, including privatisation and contracting out, extended the range of user charges and means testing, and increased the involvement of the private sector. Some of the changes, including the acceptance of Thatcher's council house sales, privatisation of the utilities and trade union reforms, date back to 1987 and 1992. The shift is incremental from Kinnock to Blair.

On economic policy, Gordon Brown acknowledged the constraints imposed by globalisation, the voters' resistance to higher taxes and the need to reassure the markets. A key passage in the Party's 1997 election manifesto stated: 'we accept the global economy as a reality and reject isolationism'. He accepted the Conservative Government's tight spending limits for the first two years of government and ruled out any increase in marginal rates of income tax. An important step was handing over interest rate decisions to the Monetary Policy Committee of the Bank of England. New Labour boasts about its financial prudence and its macro-economic stability have been aimed not only at the Major Government, but at previous Labour Governments as well.

On election strategy, the Party explicitly appealed to a new range of target and non-Labour voters, largely those who had become disillusioned with the Conservatives. Such voters were concerned about Labour's reputation for a weak stand on law and order, high taxation and trade union power. Blair and Brown were therefore determined to provide reassurance. Surveys and focus groups were conducted on a greater scale and more openly than ever before. The choice of 'soft' Tory voters as target voters meant that it was their views rather than those of activists and of decisions of union and party conferences that were used in framing electoral strategy; the objective was to capture non-Labour voters. In its quest for more votes the Party was more of a preference-accommodating than a preference-shaping party.[10] A frustrated Neil Kinnock accused those who denied the point of such survey evidence as being dismissive of voters and regarding 'electoralism' as a bacillus. Contra

Crossman, Philip Gould, Blair's pollster, asserted: 'New Labour should be obsessed with winning. Winning has to be the central aim of politics, because only with power can genuine politics start.'[11]

The strategy succeeded. By the time of the 1997 election there were significant improvements in the image of the Party on questions about unity, economic competence, trust, leadership and having a clear sense of direction.

On party structure, substantial changes were achieved or set in train under Kinnock. One-member–one-vote was introduced under Smith, and Blair has used ballots of members for the draft manifestos for the 1997 and 2001 general elections, in part to outflank activists. A less adversarial format of policy making has been introduced via the policy commissions where the initiative lies with shadow ministers (until 1997) and ministers, not the NEC. The role of Conference in making policy has been downgraded, and there has been a definite tilt in influence to the Joint Policy Committee, the last chaired by the Party leader and its members drawn evenly from the Cabinet and NEC. The traditional checks and balances within the Party have been weakened, and the role of the PLP and the Party leader enhanced.

Complaints about or praise for assertive leadership did not start with Tony Blair. Neil Kinnock certainly provided strong leadership. He established such bodies as the Campaign Strategy Committee and the Shadow Communications Agency, and made them accountable to him, as a way of bypassing the NEC. He also established a powerful leader's office, something that Tony Blair expanded. Before the 1992 general election left-wing MPs were complaining of Kinnock's 'Stalinism' and autocratic and unaccountable decisions. Blair took initiatives to show that he was independent of his Party, even presenting the 1997 election manifesto as his personal contract with the voters. So far, with the possible exception of electoral reform for Westminster, it is difficult to point to the Party imposing a veto on the leadership. New Labour accepted the outgoing Conservative Government's rigorous spending limits in 1997, has made a wide range of welfare benefits subject to means testing, and is planning to introduce top-up fees in higher education and foundation hospitals in the NHS.

Discussion

New Labour was not the inevitable successor to Old Labour. As noted, the immediate beneficiary of the 1979 election defeat was the left. The widespread sense of the Labour Government's failure discredited the parliamentary leadership. Some critics on the left who had long claimed that Labour was an obstacle to the realisation of socialism in Britain felt vindicated. The Party, they claimed, was imprisoned in the capitalist state, constrained by membership of NATO, the EEC and the IMF, and too deferential to the parliamentary culture and institutions that helped the opponents (particularly capital) of radical change. It was merely reformist, making marginal and ameliorative changes while leaving the structure of capitalism intact.[12] The left warned of the failure of Keynesian demand management, as multinational corporations and international finance were able to escape the control of national governments. They recommended an alternative economic strategy of exchange and import controls, withdrawal from the EC, a big reduction in defence spending, economic planning, government controls over business and finance, and economic redistribution through welfare and the tax system. This was the left's answer to:

1   Labour's electoral decline, particularly among the working class – a socialist programme would mobilise more votes, and educate voters into an understanding of their 'real' interests; and
2   the decline of manufacturing.

Also on the left, the Campaign for Labour Party Democracy (CLPD) claimed that it was vindicated by the Government's record and defeat in the 1979 general election. The 1974 Labour Government had failed to listen to Conference and ignored the wishes of the NEC in writing the 1979 manifesto. The CLPD campaigned for greater power for the extra-parliamentary institutions, thereby ensuring that a Labour Government gave effect to party policies. In the short term it had some success in reforming the Party but not in making it more electable.

Blair *et al.* were not the only architects of the modernising project. Neil Kinnock did more than anybody to begin the process and make significant changes in policy and party structure. He is the key link between the old and the new. But neither he nor John Smith would have embraced the term New Labour. Many on the centre–right of the Party, like Healey or Hattersley, had spent too long in the Party to be credible modernisers. Although aware of the Party's shortcomings they thought that as long as the electoral pendulum continued to swing and that they and people like themselves had the top jobs, the status quo was tolerable. What Blair added was further constitutional changes, the pledge not to return to tax and spend, the media charm offensive and a voter-friendly personality particularly to middle England.

There were other midwives, intentional or not, of New Labour. They include those senior Labour politicians like Roy Jenkins, David Owen, Shirley Williams and Bill Rodgers, who left in 1981 to form the Social Democratic Party. Influential commentators, like the former Labour MPs David Marquand and Brian Walden, as well as political journalists like Peter Jenkins and Hugo Young, gave up on the likelihood of achieving social democratic policies through the Labour Party. The politicians' exit weakened the centre–right in the Party, placed those who remained under suspicion, and helped the left to claim their prize. By creating some of the conditions for the disaster in the 1983 general election – and the resultant sense of shock in the Party – one can argue that the SDP prepared the way for New Labour.[13]

Another architect is clearly Thatcher. Aided by the tabloid press she and ministers like Norman Tebbit portrayed Labour as extreme, dangerous, incompetent, in thrall to the far left and the trade unions, and incapable of defending the country against external threats. Thatcher also removed or weakened

significant barriers to voting Labour for some, by privatising many of the utilities, lower rates of income tax, and generally weakening union power. Her
Governments did much to break with the post-war consensus and Keynesian
policies of demand management. A result of the Thatcher years was a smaller,
hollowed-out state, although one that still retained great powers over what
remained of the public sector. Any successor government would find fewer
instruments to intervene directly in the economy than had been available in the
1970s. There were no longer incomes policies, regional industrial policies, an
NEDC, exchange controls or substantial government controls over the utilities.
There were also limits on the state in the form of more integration in the EC
and from global institutions and forces.

These structural factors relate to a broader pattern of constraints on Old
Labour and incentives for the New. They include demographic change in the
electorate (see above), the shift to a post-Fordist economy, and the growing power
of international financial markets. As with Thatcher, there has been a strain of
the leader as 'hero' in some of the writing on New Labour (see Gould). But like
Thatcher there was a strong echo of 'there is no alternative' in the speeches of
Blair and Brown, particularly on economic policy and election strategy.

Such lessons were reinforced by the successes and failures of centre–left
parties abroad. In France, President Mitterrand abandoned his efforts to introduce socialism in one country. More market-oriented economic policies were
being introduced by the late 1980s in states with centre–left governments.
More positively, Blair and Brown learnt from the United States where Bill
Clinton ran as a 'new' Democrat and captured the Presidency in 1992. The
Democrats had won only one of the previous six presidential elections. Clinton
played down the policies which fed the tax and spend reputation of 'old'
Democrats, targeted 'mainstream' voters who had left the Party, promised tax
cuts for the poor and the hard-pressed middle class, as well as welfare reform
and tough policies on crime.

Conclusion

One has to avoid the pitfalls of homogenising Old Labour and New Labour.
According to Shaw, the two concepts are stereotypes, or

> simplified and value-loaded mental images designed to project a particular
> view of reality and like most stereotypes they were misleading, squeezing
> and distorting complex reality by neatly parcelling up people into crude
> categories which did little justice to the diversity of views within the Party.[14]

Indeed, one can point to some New Labour policies and themes that date back
to 1983, the 1970s and even earlier. In 1983 the party manifesto promised
constitutional reforms, a minimum wage, a freedom of information act, and a
ban on foxhunting, all of which were delivered after 1997. James Callaghan
raised concerns in 1976 over law and order and school standards and also made

a parliamentary alliance with the Liberals. He and his Chancellor Denis Healey realised that the changed international economic conditions and the growing power of the trade unions had reduced the relevance of Keynesian social democracy. This was dramatically underscored in the 1976 budget and the spending cuts in the same year, even during a recession, and Callaghan's famous conference speech announcing the end of Keynesianism. The degree of economic planning and state ownership achieved under Wilson and Callaghan was more rhetorical than actual. Only one planning agreement was made after 1974 and the state rescues of British Leyland, the docks, aerospace and ship-building were because they all faced imminent bankruptcy. There is a long history of Labour Governments working hard to gain the co-operation of business, as the left have complained.

The damaging claim that the Wilson–Callaghan Governments were in thrall to the unions has to be set against the fact that the union leaders provided crucial support for the pay restraint between 1975 and 1978 and acquiesced in the spending cuts in 1976. The 'Winter of Discontent' and the breakdown of incomes policies illustrated less the power of trade union leaders than their actual weakness in the face of discontented members and the rising power of shop stewards. The picture is therefore more complex than caricatures of Old Labour would have us believe.

Old Labour ministers would look enviously at the Blair Government. Since 1950 all Labour Governments have struggled to manage a weak economy and cope with an unfavourable economic legacy on taking office, particularly in 1974. Except for 1966–70, they also operated without a working parliamentary majority. In contrast, Blair's Government inherited an economy with falling levels of unemployment and inflation and has enjoyed landslide majorities. The Government in 1997 came into a different world from the 1970s: the issues of rampant inflation, powerful trade unions, overmanned nationalised industries and incomes policies were no longer part of the political agenda.

Some New Labour changes would have been expected as a party responds to changing circumstances. What has been new about Labour under Blair has been the reputation it has earned for economic competence (in the 1997 election it was level pegging with the Conservatives on this in the polls) and constitutional reform, and for its emphasis on law and order and educational standards, and top-up fees in universities. It remains to be seen, however, how permanent the changes will be; some commentators have seen Gordon Brown's boost to public spending and tax rises as a return to Old Labour.

But even if the Wilson–Callaghan Governments had enjoyed a larger majority or had decisively won re-election in, say, October 1978, it is still difficult to believe that there would have been many signs of New Labour. Given the mood of the unions and the constituency activists and the influence that the party structure and culture gave them, it is inconceivable that Labour ministers would have embarked on the Thatcher agenda of privatisation, income tax cuts and union reforms that New Labour came to terms with. The Wilson–Callaghan Governments were the last of Old Labour not the beginning of the New.

Notes

1 Morgan, K.O., 'The Labour Party Record in Office', *Contemporary Record*, 3(4), 1990.
2 See Drucker, H., *Doctrine and Ethos in the Labour Party* (Allen and Unwin, London, 1979).
3 See the chapters by Ludlam, S., Kenny, M. and Smith, M., in Ludlam, S. and Smith, M. (eds), *New Labour in Government* (Palgrave, London, 2001).
4 Crewe, I., 'Labour and the Electorate', in Kavanagh, D. (ed.), *The Politics of the Labour Party* (Allen and Unwin, London, 1982).
5 Radice, G., *Southern Discomfort* (Fabian Society, London, 1992).
6 Minkin, L., *The Labour Party Conference, Trade Unions and the Labour Party* (Penguin, London, 1978).
7 McKenzie, R.T., *British Political Parties* (Heinemann, London, 1964). Also see Kavanagh, D., 'Power in the Parties: R.T. McKenzie and After', *West European Politics*, 21(1), 1998.
8 Kinnock, N., 'Reforming the Labour Party', *Contemporary Record*, 8(3), 1994.
9 Barnett, J., *Inside the Treasury, 1974–79* (Andre Deutsch, London, 1982).
10 Hay, C., *The Political Economy of New Labour* (Manchester University Press, Manchester, 1999).
11 Gould, P., *The Unfinished Revolution: How the Modernisers Saved the Labour Party* (Little, Brown, London, 1999).
12 See Miliband, R., *Parliamentary Socialism* (Merlin, London, 1972).
13 For a different view, see Crewe, I. and King, A., *The SDP: The Birth, Life and Death of the Social Democratic Party* (Oxford University Press, Oxford, 1995).
14 Shaw, E., *The Labour Party since 1945* (Blackwell, London, 1996), pp. 217–18. Also see Fielding, S., *The Labour Party: Continuity and Change in the Making of 'New' Labour* (Palgrave, London, 2003).

Select bibliography

Artis, M. and Cobham, D. (eds), *Labour's Economic Policies, 1974–79* (Manchester, Manchester University Press, 1991).

Barnett, J., *Inside the Treasury 1974–79* (Andre Deutsch, London, 1982).

Benn, T., *Against the Tide: Diaries 1973–76* (Arrow, London, 1989).

Benn, T., *Conflicts of Interest: Diaries 1977–80* (Arrow, London, 1990).

Bogdanor, V., *Devolution in the United Kingdom* (Oxford University Press, Oxford, 1999).

Bosanquet, N. and Townsend, P. (eds), *Labour and Equality: A Fabian Study of Labour in Power, 1974–79* (Fabian Society, London, 1980).

Britton, A., *Macroeconomic Policy in Britain 1974–1987* (Cambridge University Press, Cambridge, 1991).

Burk, K. and Cairncross, A., *'Goodbye, Great Britain': The 1976 IMF Crisis* (Yale University Press, New Haven, CT, 1992).

Butler, D. and Kavanagh, D., *The British General Election of February 1974* (Macmillan, London, 1974).

Butler, D. and Kavanagh, D., *The British General Election of October 1974* (Macmillan, London, 1975).

Butler, D. and Kavanagh, D., *The British General Election of 1979* (Macmillan, London, 1980).

Butler, D. and Kitzinger, U., *The 1975 Referendum* (Macmillan, Basingstoke, 1976).

Callaghan, J., *Time and Chance* (Collins, London, 1987).

Carver, M., *Tightrope Walking: British Defence Policy since 1945* (Hutchinson, London, 1992).

Castle, B., *The Castle Diaries, 1974–76* (Weidenfeld and Nicolson, London, 1980).

Castle, B., *Fighting All the Way* (Macmillan, London, 1993).

Coates, D., *Labour in Power? A Study of the Labour Government 1974–1979?* (Longman, London, 1980).

Coates, K. (ed.), *What Went Wrong: Explaining the Fall of the Labour Government* (Spokesman, Nottingham, 1979).

Crosland, C.A.R., *The Future of Socialism* (Schocken, New York, 2nd edition, 1963).

Crosland, S., *Tony Crosland* (Cape, London, 1982).

Dalyell, T., *Devolution: The End of Britain?* (Cape, London, 1977).

Dell, E., *A Hard Pounding: Politics and Economic Crisis 1974–76* (Oxford University Press, Oxford, 1991).

Dell, E., *The Chancellors* (HarperCollins, London, 1996).

Dell, E., *A Strange and Eventful History: Democratic Socialism in Britain* (HarperCollins, London, 2000).

Donoughue, B., *Prime Minister: The Conduct of Policy under Harold Wilson and James Callaghan* (Cape, London, 1988).

Donoughue, B., *The Heat of the Kitchen: An Autobiography* (Politico's, London, 2003).

Fielding, S., *The Labour Party: Continuity and Change in the Making of 'New' Labour* (Palgrave, London, 2003).

George, S., *The Awkward Partner* (Oxford University Press, Oxford, 1990).

Glennerster, H., *British Social Policy since 1945* (Blackwell, Oxford, 1995).

Gould, P., *The Unfinished Revolution: How the Modernisers Saved the Labour Party* (Little, Brown, London, 1999).

Haines, J., *Glimmers of Twilight* (Politico's, London, 2003).

Harmon, M., *The 1976 UK–IMF Crisis* (Macmillan, London, 1996).

Hatfield, M., *The House the Left Built: Inside Labour Policy-making 1970–75* (Gollancz, London, 1978).

Hattersley, R., *Who Goes Home?* (Little, Brown, London, 1995).

Hay, C., *The Political Economy of New Labour* (Manchester University Press, Manchester, 1999).

Healey, D., *The Time of My Life* (Michael Joseph, London, 1989).

Hennessy, P., *Prime Minister: The Office and Its Holders since 1945* (Allen Lane, London, 2001).

Hickson, K., '1976 IMF Crisis and British Politics', (IB Tauris, 2004).

Hodgson, G., *Labour at the Crossroads* (Martin Robertson, Oxford, 1981).

Holland, S., *The Socialist Challenge* (Quartet, London, 1975).

Holmes, M., *The Labour Government of 1974–79* (Macmillan, London, 1985).

Jefferys, K., *Anthony Crosland: A New Biography* (Cohen, London, 1999).

Jefferys, K. (ed.), *Labour Leaders* (I.B. Tauris, London, 1999).

Jefferys, K. (ed.), *Labour Forces* (I.B. Tauris, London, 2002).

Jenkins, R., *A Life at the Centre* (Macmillan, London, 1991).

Jones, J., *Union Man: The Autobiography of Jack Jones* (Collins, London, 1986).

Kavanagh, D. and Seldon, A., *The Powers behind the Prime Minister* (HarperCollins, London, 1999).

Keegan, W. and Pennant-Rea, R., *Who Runs the Economy?* (Temple Smith, London, 1979).

Leonard, D. (ed.), *Socialism Now and Other Essays* (Cape, London, 1975).

Lowe, Rodney, *The Welfare State in Britain since 1945* (Macmillan, London, 1993).

Lowe, Roy, *Education in the Post-war Years* (Routledge, London, 1988).

Lowe, Roy, *Schooling and Social Change, 1964–1990* (Routledge, London, 1997).

Ludlam, S. and Smith, M. (eds), *New Labour in Government* (Palgrave, London, 2001).

Mandelson, P. and Liddle, R., *The Blair Revolution: Can New Labour Deliver?* (Faber and Faber, London, 1996).

McKibbin, R., 'Homage to Wilson and Callaghan', *London Review of Books*, 24 October 1991.

Morgan, K.O., *Labour People* (Oxford University Press, Oxford, 1992).

Morgan, K.O., *Callaghan: A Life* (Oxford University Press, Oxford, 1997).

Norton, P., *Dissension in the House of Commons 1974–1979* (Clarendon Press, Oxford, 1980).

Owen, D., *Time to Declare* (Michael Joseph, London, 1991).

Pearce, E., *Denis Healey* (Little, Brown, London, 2002).

Pimlott, B., *Harold Wilson* (HarperCollins, London, 1992).

Pliatzky, L., *Getting and Spending: Public Expenditure, Employment and Inflation* (Blackwell, Oxford, 1982).

Rodgers, W., *Fourth among Equals* (Politico's, London, 2000).

Shaw, E., *The Labour Party since 1945* (Blackwell, Oxford, 1996).

Shore, P., *Leading the Left* (Weidenfeld and Nicolson, London, 1983).

Taylor, R., *The Fifth Estate: Britain's Unions in the Modern World* (Pan, London, 1978).

Taylor, R., *The Trade Union Question in British Politics: Government and the Unions since 1945* (Blackwell, Oxford, 1993).

Taylor, R., *The TUC: From the General Strike to New Unionism* (Palgrave, London, 2000).

Theakston, K., *The Labour Party and Whitehall* (Routledge, London, 1992).

Whitehead, P., *The Writing on the Wall* (Michael Joseph, London, 1985).

Whitehead, P., 'The Labour Governments 1974–79', in Hennessy, P. and Seldon, A. (eds), *Ruling Performance: British Governments from Attlee to Thatcher* (Blackwell, Oxford, 1987).

Wickham-Jones, M., *Economic Strategy and the Labour Party: Politics and Policy-making, 1970–1983* (Macmillan, London, 1996).

Wilson, H., *Final Term: The Labour Government 1974–76* (Weidenfeld and Nicolson/Michael Joseph, London, 1979).

Young, J.W., *Britain and European Unity, 1945–99* (Macmillan, Basingstoke, 2nd edition, 2000).

Young, K. and Rao, N., *Local Government since 1945* (Blackwell, Oxford, 1997).

Ziegler, P., *Wilson: The Authorised Life* (London, 1993).

Index